Transforming Higher Education Through Universal Design for Learning

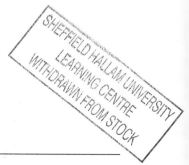

Providing insight into the background, theory and practical applications of Universal Design for Learning (UDL), *Transforming Higher Education Through Universal Design for Learning: An International Perspective* examines and shares best practice in UDL implementation worldwide to provide strategies for strengthening student accessibility, engagement and learning outcomes through the development of flexible learning environments.

Drawing upon insightful, research-based contributions from educators and student service specialists in Australia, Belgium, Brazil, Canada, Ireland, Israel, Norway, South Africa, Spain, the UK and all across the USA, this book:

- considers diversity in the form of disability, minority ethnic groups, gender identities, first generation university students and varying socio-economic backgrounds;
- brings together key thinkers and actors in the field of UDL and expertly maps its practices to the higher educational domain;
- explores the multiple means of representation, expression and engagement that combine to create a successful UDL framework.

Each chapter not only provides a different perspective of how UDL has helped meet the needs of all students to ensure that education is accessible, culturally responsive and socially just, but also considers how this can then be implemented into higher education environments the world over. This book is a crucial read for those who want to make a positive difference in higher education provision and outcomes.

Seán Bracken is a Principal Fellow of the Higher Education Academy in the UK. He is a Principal Lecturer and a Learning and Teaching Coordinator at the University of Worcester, where his research and practice incorporates Universal Design for Learning and inclusion in all sectors of education. For the past 30 years, Seán has worked internationally as a teacher, teacher educator, lecturer and educational project manager. He is passionate about enhancing learning opportunities and outcomes for all students.

Katie Novak is an internationally renowned ⟨ ⟩ ising leader in education as an Assistant Superinter⟨ ⟩ a graduate instructor. Katie designs and pres⟨ ⟩ internationally, focusing on implementation ⟨ ⟩ universally designed leadership to increase ac⟨ ⟩ regardless of variability.

Transforming Higher Education Through Universal Design for Learning

An International Perspective

Edited by Seán Bracken and Katie Novak

Routledge
Taylor & Francis Group

LONDON AND NEW YORK

First published 2019
by Routledge
2 Park Square, Milton Park, Abingdon, Oxon, OX14 4RN

and by Routledge
711 Third Avenue, New York, NY 10017

Routledge is an imprint of the Taylor & Francis Group, an informa business

British Library Cataloguing-in-Publication Data
A catalogue record for this book is available from the British Library

Library of Congress Cataloging-in-Publication Data
A catalog record for this book has been requested

ISBN: 978-0-8153-5472-7 (hbk)
ISBN: 978-0-8153-5473-4 (pbk)
ISBN: 978-1-351-13207-7 (ebk)

Typeset in Galliard
by Apex CoVantage, LLC

MIX
Paper from
responsible sources
FSC
www.fsc.org FSC® C013056

Printed and bound in Great Britain by
TJ International Ltd, Padstow, Cornwall

Contents

About the contributors

Ashiya Abdool Satar is a lecturer in the Department of Communication Science at the University of South Africa (Unisa) where she teaches undergraduate and post-graduate students, a position she has held since 2013. Ashiya has a BA degree with majors in Industrial Psychology and Communication Science, and also has a degree in Organizational Communication, both earned at Unisa. She has presented papers internationally, on themes including digital literacy, Islamic and gender identities, and the role of media. Her interests lie in organizational communication research, media studies, UDL and Open Distance and e-Learning (ODeL) in the Higher Education sector. Ashiya is a current PhD student.

Kate Anderson is a Senior Lecturer in Disability and Inclusion at Deakin University, and a Fellow at the Centre for Research in Assessment and Digital Learning (CRADLE). She is driven by a passion for inclusive and equitable learning across the lifespan. Her research interests focus around information access and capacity building: for instance, how people who use Augmentative and Alternative Communication (ACC) learn about and use this technology in their home and learning environments. Kate incorporates disability, diversity and accessible design in her learning, teaching and research of higher education.

Ornit Avidan-Ziv is an Israeli occupational therapist and a licensed service accessibility expert who has 15 years of experience working with people with cognitive disabilities. Her extensive clinical experience started with community work with people with chronic mental health challenges and she was the manager of community-based residential facilities for this population. In the past 8 years she was the director of individual programing at Agudat Ami, which serves people with intellectual disabilities, and developed a unique cognitively accessible gym for this population. Ms. Avidan-Ziv is one of the leading experts on cognitive accessibility and since 2012 has served as the manager of the Israeli Institute on Cognitive Accessibility of Agudat Ami and Ono Academic College.

Liz Berquist is the Coordinator of Professional Learning for the Baltimore County Public School District (BCPS) in the US, where she designs and delivers professional learning for district leaders serving over 113,000 students. Liz spent eight years as a faculty member at Towson University in Maryland. At TU, Liz worked with pre-service and in-service educators and taught a variety of undergraduate and graduate courses. Liz was also responsible for the design administration of a multi-year Universal Design for Learning Professional Development Network (UDL PDN). Her research is focused on Universal Design for Learning, conceptual change, faculty professional development, and enhancing university-school partnerships in professional development schools. Since 2010, Liz has been a member of the CAST faculty cadre and has an international profile of CPD supporting school districts and institutes of higher education. Dr. Berquist is a facilitator for the Harvard Graduate School of Education Summer Programs at the UDL Institute.

Jodie Black is a Canadian educator who has worked in post-secondary accessibility services and curriculum development for 9 years. Her passion is working collaboratively to create quality, accessible learning experiences for all learners at the college level. She holds a B.A. from Dalhousie University, a B.Ed from the University of New Brunswick, and will complete her M.Ed from the University of New Brunswick in August 2017. Currently, she is a Teaching and Learning Specialist at Fleming College in Peterborough Ontario.

Petra Brown is a Teaching Scholar in the Faculty of Arts and Education at Deakin University in Australia. Petra has completed research on UDL and its application to support students transitioning to higher education. Petra has also applied the UDL framework to coach casual (non-tenured) academic staff to enhance teaching, learning and assessment strategies.

Brian Butler works in the Disability Support Service at University College Cork in Ireland. Brian is also a Fellow of the Center for the Integration of Research, Teaching and Learning (CIRTL) and uses this expertise to coach on the online professional development program for staff at UCC. He is passionate about the application of UDL in the HE context and recognizes its potential to maximize student learning.

Eleanor (Ellie) Castine is a Ph.D. candidate in Counseling Psychology in the Wheelock College of Education and Human Development at Boston University in the US. As part of a National Science Foundation Intern grant, she conducted collaborative research with CAST, Inc. Her research demonstrates her deep interest in, and dedication to, the intersection of developmental science, psychology, and education, with the overarching goal of promoting racial equity and social justice. More specifically, her research interests include career development among youth and adolescents, especially those from marginalized backgrounds. Ellie is also interested in how students learn more broadly about social categories, such as race, and in turn, the development of effective interventions to promote persistence of underrepresented groups in science learning and STEM careers.

Elizabete Cristina Costa-Renders is currently professor at the Municipal University of São Caetano do Sul (USCS) in the State of São Paulo in Brazil. She is responsible for the Postgraduate School of Education and she also leads on the ACESSI (Acessibilidade Escolar e Sociedade Inclusiva/School Accessibility and Inclusive Society) research group. This group's main aspects for research include; human rights in education, inclusion paradigms, and enabling accessibility in its multiple dimensions through Universal Design for Learning and using narrative research to share learning experiences and insights. Elizabeth has contributed to the formation of legislation and policy for inclusive education within São Paulo and beyond.

Kimberly Coy is an Assistant Professor in the Kremen School of Education and Human Development at the California State University, Fresno. Dr. Coy concentrates on supporting future teachers in their quest to create inclusive educational settings. Kimberly believes that Professors and Instructors in Higher Education need to proactively model UDL in all educational domains including digital and online learning spaces.

Mary Dracup is leader of the Inclusive Education Project at Deakin University, which aims to make inclusive education routine practice at the university. She has used UDL as a framework for higher education curriculum design and evaluation, and led an evaluation of a range of inclusive curricula to identify not only what works to improve outcomes for students in disadvantaged groups, but also systemic barriers and enablers to inclusive practices in higher education.

Frederic Fovet is Associate Professor at the School of Education and Technology, Royal Roads University in Canada. He is an academic, researcher, consultant, and UDL & Inclusion specialist. Over the period of his doctorate, Frederic held the position of Director of the Office for Students with Disabilities at McGill University. In this role he initiated a sustainable campus-wide move towards UDL implementation. Frederic provides UDL consultancy in both the K-12 and post-secondary fields. He was instigator, and Program Chair, of the two first Pan-Canadian conferences on UDL.

Ruth Fraser is currently working at Douglas College in Vancouver, BC in Canada as the Associate Director of Student Affairs and Services. Ruth has a Master's Degree in Education and has some 15 years' experience in higher education where her primary focus has been to advance accessibility in higher education by changing how we think about, and serve, students with disabilities. Her experience includes policy development, service-delivery model design, and UDL implementation in college and university settings.

Ann Heelan is the Executive Director of AHEAD (Association of Higher Education Access and Disability) a national organization in Ireland that works to shape a future where students with disabilities can succeed in education and work. The organization is based on values of human rights, independence, engagement and universal design for learning. She began her career as a teacher and has worked in second level, further and higher education. Throughout her career, Ann has worked tirelessly to assist students with disabilities overcome barriers to accessing Higher Education. She has also championed access to internship and getting employment for persons with disabilities.

Danielle Hitch is Senior Lecturer in Occupational Therapy at Deakin University. Danielle has worked on several projects around the use of universal design in higher education, and the development of online resources and case studies for teaching staff. Her work is informed by the belief that universal design for learning provides a rigorous and robust framework to support the participation of all students in higher education.

Richard M. Jackson is Associate Professor of Education at Boston College in the US. He is also a Senior Research Scientist with CAST. In 1999 Richard introduced the UDL framework to Boston College through his affiliation with CAST. He has directed the Teaching Practices Partnership for the National Center on Accessing the General Curriculum (1999–2004). He has also acted as the lead for the infusion of the UDL framework into Boston College's teacher preparation programs (2004). He is the Principal Investigator for Boston College's Program to Prepare Leaders in UDL at the Postdoctoral Level (2009–2015). Richard is recognized as a thought leader for Boston College's UDL Initiative (2012- present).

Sam Catherine Johnston is a researcher at CAST. Sam's primary research focus is on social learning processes and the use of online and blended learning to support peer-to-peer knowledge transfer. Sam is co-principal investigator for two National Science Foundation research studies in the US. With support of the Gates Foundation, Sam also recently led the development of UDL On Campus (udloncampus.cast.org)—a collection of online resources to aid postsecondary educators in implementing UDL. Sam holds a BA from McGill University and a master's and doctorate in education from Harvard.

Kjetil Andreas Knarlag is the founder and head of Universell, which is the national Norwegian coordinating organization for Inclusion, Universal Design and Accessibility in Higher Education. Kjetil has an educational background in pedagogy, policymaking, universal design and project management. He has twenty years of experience in the field of inclusion and has used this experience to disseminate UDL information and strategies throughout the HE sector. He has led a number of national and international projects, including an Erasmus+ Strategic Partnership (these are inter-European strategic partnerships for HE funded by the European Union). This substantial project entitled *UDLL – Universal Design for Learning: License to Learn*, focused on how Universal Design can be applied to enhance experiences and outcomes for students with disabilities. He co-authored the UDL Best Practice Guidelines for universal design for teaching and learning, which was an outcome of the project.

Scott D. Lapinski is a PhD candidate at Boston College's Lynch School of Education in the USA. He is currently supporting graduate students with disabilities at Brandeis University, a research-based university in Massachusetts. Scott has formerly acted as a research associate at CAST, and he is acknowledged for his application of the UDL framework to inform course development and to strengthen support provided by academic student services.

Geoff Layer is recognized as a leading contributor to inclusive educational policy and practice throughout the UK. In August of 2011 Geoff was appointed as the Vice Chancellor of the University of Wolverhampton. Previously, he was Deputy Vice Chancellor (Academic) at the University of Bradford and also worked at Sheffield Hallam University as a Lecturer in Law. Between 2000 and 2006 he was the Director of Action on Access, an agency established to advise on the national Widening Participation Strategy. He has been a consultant to Universities UK, Higher Education Quality Council and many universities in Widening Participation and Learning and Teaching Strategies. Geoff is a Principal Fellow of the Higher Education Academy and was awarded the OBE for services to Higher Education in 2003.

Neta Linder-Katz is an occupational therapist with unique experience in the area of child development. She is the project manager of the Inter-faculty Center for Academic Equality and Inclusion at Ono Academic College and as such is leading an organization-wide UDL implementation project. In addition, Ms. Linder-Katz is a lecturer at Ono Academic College in Israel and has an extensive background in clinical training especially in the area of occupational therapy.

Susie Macfarlane is a Senior Lecturer managing a Learning Design and Interactive Media team at Deakin University, Australia. Susie is passionate about promoting student diversity and agency in university teaching and assessment through inclusive, participatory and emergent approaches to staff capability building and organizational change. Her research explores the intersections between higher education teaching and assessment, inclusive practice, technology and networks. Susie has published over 20 articles and book chapters and is undertaking a PhD at Deakin University's Centre for Research in Assessment and Digital Learning.

Terry Maguire is Director of the National Forum for the Enhancement of Teaching and Learning in Higher Education in Ireland. She spent 14 years working in higher education in Scotland where she pioneered flexible and blended approaches to teaching and learning. After returning to Ireland, she worked with the further education and training sector before completing her PhD at the University of Limerick. In 2006, Terry was appointed as the Head of Lifelong Learning in the Institute of Technology Tallaght, Dublin. In 2013, she was selected as the inaugural Director of Ireland's National Forum and worked to establish the Forum as a critical contributor to the enhancement of higher education in Ireland. Terry has a particular interest in the professional development of those who teach and adult mathematics education more generally. She is an educator and senior manager who is committed to transforming lives through teaching and learning.

Marian McCarthy is the Director of the Centre for the Integration of Research, Teaching and Learning (CIRTL) at University College Cork (UCC) in Ireland. She is also a board member of the Association for Higher Education Access and Disability (AHEAD). Marian designs and leads accredited courses for staff professional development, enhancement and teaching in higher education.

Eric Moore currently works as a UDL Specialist at the University of Tennessee in the US, where he earned his PhD in Inclusive Education. Eric began his career working with students with support needs as a teacher's aide in high school and went on to earn his B.S. in English Education. Subsequently, his educational career involved teaching in high schools in the US and in international schools in Indonesia and Korea. Eric's experiences with student variability has informed his research passion and commitment to inclusive curriculum design.

Abigail Moriarty joined De Montfort University, Leicester over ten years ago from a National Health Service academic and professional background. In January 2016, she was appointed as the University's Director for Learning and Teaching. Subsequently, she collaboratively led a whole institution approach to Universal Design for Learning. This played a significant part in DMU being awarded Gold for its Teaching Excellence Framework submission (the TEF is a national benchmarking process for rating teaching and learning in HE institutions throughout the UK). Abigail has presented at several conferences on UDL and its pedagogical implications.

Jane Neapolitan has more than 30 years' experience as teacher and administrator in higher education. She currently serves as Assistant Provost, Office of Academic Innovation, at Towson University (Maryland, USA). In this role she supports faculty as leaders in teaching, scholarship, and service. The Office of Academic Innovation is part of a national trend toward innovation in higher education that improves outcomes for students and faculty by using an intentional approach to curriculum and teaching. Dr. Neapolitan develops partnerships that result in opportunities for people from all backgrounds to strengthen learning outcomes through redesigning courses using the principles of Universal Design for Learning. She has led campuswide faculty professional development efforts, including universal design for learning, scholarship of teaching and learning, and blended and online learning. She has also served as the Director of Distance Education.

Geraldine O'Neill is a Principal Fellow of the Higher Education Academy in the UK and is an Associate Professor and educational developer in University College Dublin in Ireland. Geraldine has led, supported and evaluated many institutional teaching, learning and assessment projects in UCD and beyond. She was recently seconded to the National Forum for the Enhancement of Teaching and Learning in Ireland where she coordinated a national project (Enhancement Theme) on 'Assessment OF, FOR and AS Learning'. This project developed a sector-wide review of assessment practices and policies in HE. A key aspect of this national project was the shift towards empowering students in assessment processes. Her research focus in the last 15 years has been on professional development, curriculum design and assessment. Most recently, she has begun to incorporate principles and practices from UDL to inform whole organizational change management.

Elinor Jeanette Olaussen is advisor at Universell, which is the Norwegian national coordinator organization for inclusion, universal design and accessibility in Higher Education. Olaussen has background from organizational psychology, pedagogy, coaching and organizational management. She began her career accommodating for students with disabilities, and for the last five years, she has worked to develop and share sustainable systems for individual adaptation and universal design among disability officers, academic staff and management working in universities and university colleges all across Norway. She participates in the coordinator team in the first Erasmus+ project about universal design for learning in Europe, and has co-authored a Best Practice Guideline for universal design for teaching and learning in higher education.

Kavita Rao is an associate professor in the Department of Special Education of the College of Education at the University of Hawai'i at Mānoa. Her research focuses on assistive and instructional technologies, Universal Design for Learning, online learning for non-traditional students, and technology-related educational strategies for English language learners and culturally and linguistically diverse students. Kavita has worked with pre-service teacher candidates and in-service teachers in Hawaii, Guam, American Samoa, Commonwealth of the Marianas Islands, Palau, Republic of the Marshall Islands, and the Federated States of Micronesia and developed curriculum resources, multimedia materials, and online programs and for Pacific educators.

David Rose has been on the faculty of the Harvard Graduate School of Education (HGSE) for over 30 years. Rose is a developmental neuropsychologist and educator whose primary focus is on the development of new technologies for learning. In 1984, Rose cofounded CAST, a not-for-profit research and development organization whose mission is to improve education for all learners through innovative uses of modern multimedia technology and contemporary research in the cognitive neurosciences. That work has grown into the field called Universal Design for Learning which now influences educational policy and practice throughout the United States and internationally.

Phil Scarffe has worked in the HE sector for the last 17 years, the last 4 of which have been as Head of Student Welfare at De Montfort University. He co-founded the UMHAN (University Mental Health Advisors Network) charity. He also designed and acted as program director for the 'Disability Enhancement Programme' (DEP, a strategic program aimed at taking a whole university approach to disability). Phil has made a significant contribution to the Department for Education's national HE guidance 'Inclusive Teaching and Learning in Higher Education as a route to Excellence' which was published in 2017.

Rebeca Soler Costa is Assistant Professor in the Faculty of Education, in the Department of Didactics and School Organization at the University of Zaragoza in Spain. Rebeca has published several research works about the analysis of the language of Pedagogy from a pragmatic-discursive and critic perspective, the power relationships in the didactic communication and in the political discourse in educative innovations and educative Acts. She has participated in international and national scientific conferences, developing teaching and research in her training perspective, participating as well in different postdoctoral research in foreign and Spanish universities. Her consolidated research lines are: discourse analysis in the didactic interaction, critical discourse analysis in education, the school organization for inclusive educative, and the use of Virtual Learning Environments as powerful didactic tools that convey the use of the new language of Pedagogy.

Tom Thibodeau is an Assistant Provost at the New England Institute of Technology in the US. He has been involved in online education since 1996 and has seen, first hand, the impact that positive planning and design can have on student engagement, especially when these are designed to meet the needs of all learners. Thibodeau has a BS degree in Secondary English Education and a MA degree in Broadcasting. He has worked as a videographer and editor in almost 2,000 programs and taught video production and teaching with technology for 27 years.

Janet Watson is the Research Project Officer of the Inclusive Curriculum and Capacity Building project at Deakin University, Australia. As part of this project, she has helped develop an active and well-regarded WordPress site within the university, which provides support, resources and tips for higher education teachers seeking to use universal design for learning skilfully.

Shira Yalon-Chamovitz is an occupational therapist and a licensed service accessibility expert. She was the founder and head of the Occupational Therapy program at Ono Academic College in Israel and was recently appointed the Dean of Students and the Head of the Inter-faculty Center for Academic Equality and Inclusion at Ono Academic College. In addition, she is an active advocate for the rights of people with cognitive disabilities. She served as an advisor to the Israeli Commissioner on Equal Rights for People with Disabilities in the Ministry of Justice, and is the Head of the Israeli Institute on Cognitive Accessibility of Agudat Ami and Ono Academic College. Dr. Yalon-Chamovitz's main research arenas are cognitive accessibility and practical intelligence and she developed a unique model of practice in these areas. She has published papers as well as book chapters based on her extensive research and advocacy experience and delivered numerous talks in Israel and around the world in these areas.

Foreword

One of the most delightful (and instructive) ironies of modern physics is that the most dramatic advances in our understanding of what really happens when a tiny teacup warms on the kitchen stove came only when physicists began to explore what really happens in parts of our universe that are unimaginably vast and far away. Similarly, Darwin's key advances in biology came not from closer and closer inspection of the fauna he knew, but from an opportune trip to parts of the world far away and rarely travelled.

The history of science is full of such advances, where explorations into new domains reveal that what had been thought of as "regular" and universal is recognized as unique and insular. What emerges from wider exploration is a science that is more robust, more broadly applicable, more generative, more accurate, more universal. What is left behind is a science that is unknowingly parochial, narrow, specialized, rigid, and often incorrect.

What this book admirably makes clear is that Universal Design for Learning (UDL), as presently conceived and practiced, is too parochial. The local ecology that once nourished UDL has too long dominated its perceptions, its strategies, and its values (those three principles again!). What this book also makes clear is that the future of UDL, even in the USA, lies in open-minded explorations of other cultures where inequalities in learning opportunities exist, and where they are being addressed in novel ways that stem from, and reflect, the different ecologies from which they emerged. Fortunately, this book does not merely highlight the present limits of UDL. Instead, it brings together wonderfully diverse and original reports from two kinds of explorations that will ultimately be critical for the future universality, and legitimacy, of UDL.

The first such exploration is evident in how the book initially addresses the ecology of higher education. While there have already been significant publications about the challenges and innovations in higher education, the vast majority of the early work in UDL has focused on children – a minority population in any culture. But what we know from developmental neuroscience is that adults aren't just older children, nor even are they older children with brains that have more stuff in them. Instead, adults have brains that are qualitatively different from children's.

The incredibly late maturation of prefrontal cortex (for example), is one of the most distinctive features that distinguishes humans from all of the other very smart mammals. When prefrontal cortex finally begins to mature (largely in adolescence and afterwards), it changes the whole ecology of the learning brain – there are new kinds of neurons not seen anywhere else, more extensive connections between old and new parts of the brain, and a new "heterarchy" in the way the brain is organized and functions.

Given this diversity, it would be quite remarkable if adults learned in the same ways as children do, or if the same kinds of teaching would be optimal for both. As a result, this book's extensive focus on older learners represents a necessary advance for UDL if only because it escapes the boundaries imposed by studying primarily children and extrapolating from them. It shouldn't surprise us, however, if in doing so we may also learn more about what is distinctive and critical in applying UDL principles to children (as well as elders, and many other sub- populations) in much the same way that studying far away galaxies taught us much about our own.

The second kind of critical exploration in this book is not obvious in the title, but in the diversity of its authors and their biographies. Up to now, most books about UDL have been written by researchers and practitioners from the USA and North America. While much has been learned from that relatively narrow slice of the world's cultures, the next stage in the development of UDL will clearly require explorations that are much more expansive, diverse, and inclusive. In this book, the foundations for those advances show up not just in the biographies of the authors but in their analyses of the diverse values, resources, policies, strategies, technologies, and innovations within which education and development must succeed and thrive in their own cultures. Understanding the rich variety that exists in local cultures and ecologies is a critical next step in learning what UDL needs to address, and where it needs to find its solutions. What is most important about this book is that it recognizes the critical value of exploring other cultures and histories not just to apply UDL more broadly, but to imagine (and plan) the future of UDL itself. While other educators have charted, and touted, the benefits of bringing UDL to other cultures, this book recognizes that the benefits are reciprocal: only by studying the values, strategies, challenges, technologies, and innovative practices of other cultures and ecologies are we likely to construct a future UDL that is flexible and supple enough to work everywhere, and for everyone.

I like the honor and irony of writing a foreword for a book that is about moving forward, about taking UDL beyond its strong but parochial origins into a future where it must, and will, be more robust, more broadly applicable, more generative, more accurate, more universal. Kudos to Dr. Novak and Dr. Bracken for providing the imaginative and thoughtful leadership that the journey will require, and for gathering together such a stellar set of navigator/authors (many of whom have already been my teachers and colleagues) to accompany them. This book provides a vehicle, much like Einstein's imaginary trolley and Darwin's seaworthy Beagle, that allows us to begin a journey of discovery that is both universal and local. Along that journey we are likely to come to understand what the "universal" in "universal design for learning" really means.

Dr. David Rose
CAST's Co-Founder and Chief
Education Officer, Emeritus

Introduction

Universal Design for Learning: a global framework for realizing inclusive practice in higher education

Katie Novak and Seán Bracken

The University of Al-Karueein, in the city of Fes, Morocco is believed to be the longest serving degree-awarding university in the world. It was founded in 859 by a woman named Fatima al-Fihri (Arbaoui, 2012). Historically however, universities throughout the world have not acted as beacons of welcome for females, nor for others whose "differences" may have set them apart from traditionally normed male privilege. As a result, possibilities for gaining access to university were generally very highly restrictive. Given the competitive nature of admission to Western higher education institutions (HEIs), students who were fortunate enough to enroll were expected to assimilate to wider educational cultures established to serve and perpetuate systems of educational empowerment for the most elite members of society.

For centuries, HEIs continued to replicate this status quo, and whether unwittingly or purposefully, erected barriers that blocked participation from individuals or groups who differed from those traditional students who excelled with predictable, inflexible, "one-size-fits-all" curriculum and instruction.

Almost half a century ago, around 10% of college age students worldwide studied in HEIs for two years or more (Marginson, 2016). At that time, the HEI pathways were still primarily reserved for elites who took limited measures to address social, economic and educational inequalities worldwide. More recently, social and educational policies have begun to shift. As a result, by 2013, the percentage of students enrolled in HEIs had increased to 32.9%, with all high-income countries and most middle-income countries tending toward or exceeding the 50% mark (Marginson, 2016). Increasingly, barriers of exclusivity in HEIs are seen as unsustainable impediments to wider social and economic progression.

This increased participation and inclusion in higher education has come about primarily from the interplay between two significant and dynamic factors that have increasingly reshaped the nature of current HEIs. First, in many parts of the world, HEIs are currently experiencing a profound phase of increased democratization (Stefani & Blessinger, 2017). There is a general consensus that society benefits when the talents and experiences of diverse learner cohorts are better reflected in all aspects of the HEI experience. However, researchers recognize that moves toward generalized student diversification through widening participation initiatives are not of themselves sufficient to address systemic educational inequalities, especially in terms of strengthening equity of educational outcomes for all students (Hughes, 2015; Krutkowski, 2017).

Once students from diverse backgrounds pass through the portals of our HEIs and gain access to learning spaces and curricula, there is no guarantee that such journeys will be completed satisfactorily. Consequently, the nature of students' learning experiences, their retention in studies and their resulting learning outcomes have become an increasingly more important lens to understand the capacity of HEIs to foster both diversity and inclusion (Holmegaard, Madsen, Ulriksen & 2017).

The second major impetus leading to educational change within HEIs pertains to the seismic epistemological shifts in the ways that knowledge is being generated and shared among individuals, academic communities and their locales. As Professor Sally Brown (2018; personal correspondence) has remarked:

> Students nowadays have so many sources of information beyond the classroom that they are becoming co-constructors of knowledge. In reflecting on these recent dynamic developments in Higher Education, I've drawn on some of the ideas shared by E. L. Boyer (2016) who talks about the scholarship of integration as being the means by which people bring together ideas and concepts from a range of different sources in new and creative ways. It's within these exciting shifting spaces, using a diversity of new and traditional tools, that students integrate learning from many sources to create their understandings of content.

To optimize student learning, educators need to take advantage of the affordances inherent in enabling technologies to reconceptualize how all students, but especially those who may traditionally have been marginalized, can engage effectively with quality learning experiences in HEIs. New learning dynamics can be created empowering students to work with one another. These dynamics also offer potential for educators to work in a more collaborative manner with students, thereby opening up uncharted avenues for enabling and evidencing learning.

As HEI populations become increasingly diverse, policy makers, educators and student support service personnel all need to have a sharpened awareness about the types of learning environments and the modes of learning experiences that are likely to strengthen students' learning experiences. A critical consideration in this process entails determining how assessments can evolve to best enable students to represent their learning, within inclusive learning environments. Further, as the sector moves toward personalizing the educational experiences for diverse learners, it is important to have more informed understandings about the nature of students' lived social and cultural identities, because such awareness can help inform and shape the nature of learning, teaching and assessment within HEIs (Tumuheki, Zeelen, & Openjuru, 2016).

Because of the critical nature of this work, HEIs would benefit from being able to draw upon a research-based framework that provides a blueprint for better facilitating access, engagement and outcomes for all learners. Only when our HEIs are universally designed to meet the learning requirements of all learners, will student graduates realize their true learning potentials in the wider worlds of social well being, creativity and employment.

To some extent, the changing nature of HEI recruitment and learning environments has been impacted by wider global policy initiatives that are helping to reorient the HE landscape. For example, in June 2015, the Federal Senate of Brazil approved a new law establishing a legal framework for people with disabilities (Agencia Brasil, 2015). For the first time, under the guidance of the "Lei de Inclusão da Pessoa com Deficiência," it will be illegal to discriminate against people with disabilities. Significantly for HEIs, the legislation also stipulates that 10% of all places in higher education should be reserved for persons with disabilities. Previous legislation in Brazil had also identified that a proportion of places available in HEIs should be reserved for those from ethnic minority and indigenous groups.

Additionally, in the United States of America, the Higher Education Opportunities Act 2008 identified a specific role for Universal Design for Learning (UDL) to inform inclusive educational practice. Subsequently in December 2015, the US Congress passed the Every Student Succeeds Act (ESSA), which endorsed Universal Design for Learning (UDL) as best practice for all students. This legislation continues to have a profound impact on learning and teaching policy and practice at all levels of educational experience in the United States.

Similarly, over the past decade in the United Kingdom, the government has sought to increase and widen participation to include more students from groups that have traditionally been underrepresented in higher education, while simultaneously encouraging HEIs to maintain or further strengthen student retention. In January 2017, the UK's Department for Education (DfE) published a report entitled "Inclusive Teaching and Learning in Higher Education as Route to Excellence" (DfE, 2017). The report was specifically developed to inform strategic leadership within the HEI sector in the design and implementation of inclusive educational practices through the reconceptualization of curricula, pedagogy and assessment processes. Throughout the report, the role of Universal Design was explicitly identified as a suggested conceptual framework for facilitating organizational change.

A commitment to facilitating a more just approach to lifelong learning was also agreed at the World Education Forum held in Incheon, Republic of Korea in 2015, where 120 participating Education Ministers and heads of delegations agreed to promote a framework for consensus and action which identified that the role of education was pivotal in promoting overall societal inclusion as well as being:

> Crucial in promoting democracy and human rights and enhancing global citizenship, tolerance and civic engagement as well as sustainable development. Education facilitates intercultural dialogue and fosters respect for cultural, religious and linguistic diversity, which are vital for achieving social cohesion and justice.
>
> (UNESCO et al., 2015)

Globally, these policy changes provide an additional impetus for change in HEIs with the aim of making them more diverse and inclusive. Additionally, there is a desire among HEIs across the world, to ensure that all learners, regardless of variability, have the capacity to realize their full potential. If we expect the wider society that HEIs serve to benefit from the potential contributions of "new traditional" students, a different educational paradigm is required in contrast to one that is premised on uniformity within the student community.

Such a paradigm ought to enable educators to foster engagement in all students as we transition from a focus on diversity to a commitment to a universally designed systematic approach that values variability (Meyer, Rose, & Gordon, 2014). To make this happen, those involved in fostering positive change in HEIs will require support on how to implement Universal Design for Learning (UDL) for all learners in their institutions.

Universal Design for Learning (UDL)

Universal Design for Learning is an educational framework based on research in the learning sciences, that guides the design and development of inclusive educational systems that accommodate and challenge all students, and foster the development of innovative technologies and critical next generation skills. Internationally, HEIs have embraced the core principles of UDL to increase accessibility and engagement, increase retention and attainment, and improve the outcomes of all students.

The term Universal Design was coined in the United States of America by architect Ronald Mace in 1988 who defined Universal Design as, "design of products and environments to be usable by all people, to the greatest extent possible, without the need for adaptation or specialized design" (Center for Universal Design, 2008). Buildings where all people could not enter were deemed, "architecturally disabling." UDL lends the same definition to learning.

If our HEIs are not designed to meet the needs of all students, without the need for adaptation, then our institutions, our classrooms, our curriculum and our teaching are disabling. The proactive nature of UDL acknowledges that educators cannot continue to retrofit our institutions to meet the needs of learners of all variability.

UDL provides educational policy makers and practitioners with a framework that deeply values variability and aims to make teaching and learning accessible and engaging for all learners. Universal Design for Learning (UDL) is a framework built on a set of three principles:

- *Provide multiple means of engagement:* Affect represents a crucial element to learning, and learners differ markedly in the ways in which they can be engaged or motivated to learn. In order to build engagement, there must be multiple options to foster both attention and commitment in all learners to address the unique variability in interest, effort and perseverance, and self-regulation strategies.
- *Provide multiple means of representation:* Representation guidelines remind us to provide multiple formats when teaching to activate all students' recognition networks. Historically, for example, reading and lecturing were popular teaching methods, yet such approaches potentially entail countless embedded barriers for many students.
- *Provide multiple means of action and expression:* It's imperative to engage students and represent content so it's accessible, but in order to determine if students have learned content, instructors must assess learning using multiple strategies so students have options regarding the type of assessment and ways in which they can present evidence of learning as well as attainment of learning objectives. Providing students with multiple means of action and expression ensures that students can incorporate critical next generation skills and authentic assessments in their learning journey.

The UDL Guidelines (2012), whose foundation includes over 800 peer reviewed research articles, provide benchmarks that guide educators in the development and implementation of UDL within each of the principles. These guidelines serve as a tool with which to critique and minimize barriers inherent in curriculum as educators aim to increase opportunities to learn (CAST, 2017). Essentially, the Engagement, Representation, and Action and Expression Guidelines correlate to the way our brains are organized for learning. This is why the framework itself is such a powerful learning tool. Figure 0.1 illustrates the interplay between the differing principles.

Conscious planning, using the three principles of UDL and the UDL Guidelines, provides a blueprint to design and deliver instructional goals, methods, materials, and assessments that meet the needs of all learners. Additionally, these principles and guidelines can be applied to all phases of student life pertaining to Higher Education; from pre-enrollment, to admissions, to campus culture, to pedagogy, to assessment, to space, resources, and educational mentoring, to social engagement and employment. Universal Design for Learning therefore provides an umbrella approach to meeting the learning requirements of all learners, while being specifically mindful to remove barriers of prejudice and exclusion so that we can realize greater levels of social and educational cohesion with the Higher Education sector.

The Universal Design for Learning Guidelines

CAST | Until learning has no limits

Provide multiple means of **Engagement**	Provide multiple means of **Representation**	Provide multiple means of **Action & Expression**
Affective Networks — The "WHY" of Learning	Recognition Networks — The "WHAT" of Learning	Strategic Networks — The "HOW" of Learning

Access

Provide options for **Recruiting Interest**
- Optimize individual choice and autonomy
- Optimize relevance, value, and authenticity
- Minimize threats and distractions

Provide options for **Perception**
- Offer ways of customizing the display of information
- Offer alternatives for auditory information
- Offer alternatives for visual information

Provide options for **Physical Action**
- Vary the methods for response and navigation
- Optimize access to tools and assistive technologies

Build

Provide options for **Sustaining Effort & Persistence**
- Heighten salience of goals and objectives
- Vary demands and resources to optimize challenge
- Foster collaboration and community
- Increase mastery-oriented feedback

Provide options for **Language & Symbols**
- Clarify vocabulary and symbols
- Clarify syntax and structure
- Support decoding of text, mathematical notation, and symbols
- Promote understanding across languages
- Illustrate through multiple media

Provide options for **Expression & Communication**
- Use multiple media for communication
- Use multiple tools for construction and composition
- Build fluencies with graduated levels of support for practice and performance

Internalize

Provide options for **Self Regulation**
- Promote expectations and beliefs that optimize motivation
- Facilitate personal coping skills and strategies
- Develop self-assessment and reflection

Provide options for **Comprehension**
- Activate or supply background knowledge
- Highlight patterns, critical features, big ideas, and relationships
- Guide information processing and visualization
- Maximize transfer and generalization

Provide options for **Executive Functions**
- Guide appropriate goal-setting
- Support planning and strategy development
- Facilitate managing information and resources
- Enhance capacity for monitoring progress

Goal

Expert learners who are...

Purposeful & Motivated	Resourceful & Knowledgeable	Strategic & Goal-Directed

Figure 0.1 CAST (2018) Universal Design for Learning Guidelines version 2.2

Source: CAST (2018). Universal design for learning guidelines version 2.2 [graphic organizer]. Wakefield, MA: Author.

Of course, it would be short sighted to maintain that a diversification agenda is not without its challenges, not least among these is the necessity to ensure that staff throughout the HE sector have access to the requisite resources and professional development enabling them to move beyond mere adaptation and to realize a vision of anticipatory inclusive practice. Additionally, as noted by Burgstahler (2015), significant gaps still remain in accessing in depth and critically informed insights about the ways in which UDL might be implemented to bring about inclusive organizational changes that have profound implications for enabling all learners to be equipped with the skills, knowledge and opportunities to realize their social and educational potential.

The authors in this publication are responding to the urgent need for a globally significant body of work that shares key theoretical and practical insights drawing on research and experience. The necessity for HEIs to learn from shared collegiate practices reflecting experiences from a diversity of settings in a variety of linguistic, geographical, and socio-cultural contexts has never been greater. In this text, global leaders in UDL implementation share concrete strategies for creating systems where all students can access, and at times, co-create, curricula, where they can collaborate in meaningful ways with their peers, and engage in authentic learning and assessment opportunities that will prepare them for the future.

Throughout the book, readers will be introduced to overarching themes of leadership and change management; working in partnership with key stakeholders; facilitating multiple identities and student engagement; transforming learning through redesigning the curriculum; content and praxis; universally designed assessments; and finally, using technologies to promote accessibility.

The strength and promise of Universal Design for Learning in the HE context is in its capacity to provide a vision for realizing a more rewarding, just and inclusive educational experiences for all students while being especially mindful of the educational experiences of students who traditionally may not have had a voice or visibility within the sector. As reflected in the chapter submissions to this book, that promise is currently being realized in many differing settings and in differing parts of the world. There is much yet to be achieved to realize the true potential of Universal Design for Learning to transform the educational experiences of all students, no matter where they may attend college or university, but we have started on the shared journey of exploration toward ensuring that our world is further enriched because of the inclusion of all students.

It is our hope that aspects of such an inspiring theoretical perspective might be applied in the context of leading whole organizational change processes aimed at ensuring curriculum, pedagogy, and assessment are increasingly accessible and engaging to a greater diversity of students in the context of higher education in international educational contexts.

References

Agencia Brasil (2015). Senado Aprova Lei de Inclusão da Pessoa com Deficiência. Accessed online December 11th 2017 from: http://agenciabrasil.ebc.com.br/politica/noticia/2015-06/senado-apr-lei-de-inclusao-da-pessoa-com-deficiencia

Arbaoui, L (2012). *Al karueein of fez: The oldest university in the world*. Morocco World News. Accessed online, January 18th 2018 from: www.moroccoworldnews.com/2012/10/59056/al-karaouin-of-fez-the-oldest-university-in-the-world/

Boyer, E. L. (2016). *Scholarship reconsidered: Priorities of professoriate* (Expanded 2nd; ed.). Hoboken: Jossey-Bass.

Brown, S. (2018). Personal correspondence following input at Researching Advancing and Inspiring Student Experience (RAISE) Conference, Manchester Metropolitan University, United Kingdom.

Burgstahler, S. E. (2015). *Universal design in higher education: From principles to practice*. Cambridge, MA: Harvard Education Press.

CAST. (2017). "What is UDL?" on UDL on Campus: Universal Design for Learning in Higher Education retrieved from http://udloncampus.cast.org/page/udl_about#l1970369

CAST. (2018). *Universal Design for Learning Guidelines version 2.2*. Wakefield, MA: Author.

Center for Universal Design. (2008). *About the center: Ron Mace*. Accessed online 11th January 2018 from: https://projects.ncsu.edu/ncsu/design/cud/about_us/usronmace.htm

Department for Education (United Kingdom). (2017). *Inclusive teaching and learning in higher education as a route to excellence*. Accessed online 18th January 2018 from: www.gov.uk/government/uploads/system/uploads/attachment_data/file/587221/Inclusive_Teaching_and_Learning_in_Higher_Education_as_a_route_to-excellence.pdf

Holmegaard, H. T., Madsen, L. M., & Ulriksen, L. (2017). Why should European higher education care about the retention of non-traditional students? *European Educational Research Journal, 16*(1), 3–11. doi:10.1177/1474904116683688

Hughes, K. (2015). The social inclusion meme in higher education: Are universities doing enough? *International Journal of Inclusive Education, 19*(3), 303–313. doi:10.1080/13603116.2014.930518

Krutkowski, S. (2017). A strengths-based approach to widening participation students in higher education. *Reference Services Review, 45*(2), 227–241. doi:10.1108/RSR-10-2016-0070

Marginson, S. (2016). The worldwide trend to high participation higher education: Dynamics of social stratification in inclusive systems. *Higher Education: The International Journal of Higher Education Research, 72*(4), 413–434.

Meyer, A., Rose, D. H., & Gordon, D. T. (2014). *Universal design for learning: Theory and practice*. Wakefield, MA: CAST Professional Publishing.

Stefani, L., & Blessinger, P. (Eds.). (2017). *Inclusive Leadership in Higher Education: International Perspectives and Approaches*. London: Routledge.

Tumuheki, P. B., Zeelen, J., & Openjuru, G. L. (2016). Motivations for participation in higher education: Narratives of non-traditional students at Makerere University in Uganda. *International Journal of Lifelong Education, 35*(1), 102–117.

UNESCO, UNICEF, the World Bank, UNFPA, UNDP, UN Women and UNHCR. (2015). Education 2030: Incheon declaration and framework for action for implementation of sustainable development goal 4. Accessed online January 2018 from: http://unesdoc.unesco.org/images/0024/002456/245656e.pdf

UDL and strategic leadership

A whole university approach to inclusive practice

Chapter 1

Universal Design for Learning – license to learn

A process for mapping a Universal Design for Learning process on to campus learning

Elinor Jeanette Olaussen, Ann Heelan and Kjetil Andreas Knarlag

Case study

Kari Haugen, a disability officer at a Norwegian University, was asked by the vice chancellor of education at her institution to coordinate a project where academics, administrators and colleagues in management were all going to work proactively in order to reduce disabling barriers and create better learning environments for all students. The project was given to Kari by the vice chancellor of education who wanted a quick solution to fulfill demands of inclusion, universal design and disability as stipulated in the Act relating to universities and university colleges (Norwegian Ministry of Education and Research, 2005). However, many stakeholders expressed skepticism about the project requirements and colleagues frequently voiced concerns about perceived high levels of work commitment that would go along with the project.

Some academic staff were skeptical arguing that they did not have any students with disabilities in their classes. Others could not find any time to develop new course material and did not see any barrier in a traditional lecture because "it has always worked that way". Management was worried about additional costs and how to prioritize competing concerns. Meanwhile, support staff from student services, who were used to working in an ad-hoc way to provide advice regarding adjustments in lecturers and for assessment methods to support individual students with disabilities, were worried they might become dispensable if this project became successful.

Despite their skepticism, the project continued and brought with it more student active learning. The students were assessed using a wider variety of assessment options during the semester and they had an increased focus on group work, in line with what is seen as pedagogical recommendations for a diverse student population.

Some students applauded the developments, while others, who preferred traditional lectures where they could listen to professors talk, were less convinced that the changes resulted in deeper forms of learning. In the new learning environment, they had to use more time to prepare for their classes and it also became more evident who participated in group work. Kari had to ensure that all of these stakeholders understood the reasons for the changes and that the project met its aims to embed a more inclusive experience for all.

Introduction

What are the mechanisms that assist educators to implement the philosophy, values and practice of Universal Design for Learning (UDL) among Higher Education colleagues, be they teaching staff or administrative staff? Why is it not seen as a priority when there is increasingly a significant diversity of students in higher education challenging the system? These are the questions that concern staff working in disability support offices and their students across Europe. This chapter will give some insight into how one ERASMUS+ funded project, Universal Design for Learning: A License to Learn (UDLL), tackled these questions.

ERASMUS+ is a European funded initiative that supports education, training, youth and sport in Europe. It provides a unique opportunity for organizations to work together on specific issues and develop their thinking with a view to exploiting their learning across borders. The partners in the project were Universell (lead partner and national coordinator for an inclusive learning environment and universal design in higher education in Norway), AHEAD (the Association for Higher Education Access and Disability in Ireland) and SIHO (Support Center for Inclusive Higher Education in Belgium). The three partners each have a national role in their county and share the objective of promoting full access and participation in further and higher education for students with disabilities. In collaboration with key stakeholders in higher education, the 18-month-long project from 2014 to 2016 aimed to develop a road map of Best Practice Guidelines for higher education staff (https://udll.eu) and a practical toolkit for introducing UDL for students (https://studenttoolkit.eu/).

Addressing disability in higher education in Europe

As UDL originally developed in an American context in the primary and secondary school level for pedagogically trained teachers (Meyer, Rose, & Gordon, 2014;

Novak, 2014), the UDLL project aimed to adopt and develop this learning into a European context and the higher education sector. According to recent European research, the number of students with disabilities in Europe varies substantially. The Eurostudent survey states that that the amount of students with impairments ranges from 7% to 39% of the student population (Hauschildt, Vögtle, & Gwosč, 2018). According to this investigation, around 5 to 8% of students are severely affected and their condition may be compounded by the lack of inclusive environment and individual support.

There is little doubt that student cohorts engaging in higher education across the EU today come from a diversity of backgrounds such as economic, cultural and linguistic affecting the way they learn, the way they best demonstrate knowledge and the way they are motivated to learn (HEA, 2015). Each learner is affected by different experiences, strengths, age and abilities, and while they have different perspectives and preferences, they all come with the expectation of learning.

In many universities, there is an ongoing cultural paradigm shift from a traditional teaching culture with a focus on lecturing and passive learning, towards a culture focusing on the learning itself. In this transformation, a significant challenge for universities is how to select, combine and implement different learning activities, into an optimal learning environment where each student reaches far beyond what is achieved through the individual and realizes the collective development of both students and faculty. In practice, we observe a development of modern teaching methods. An example is the "flipped classroom", where students are supposed to meet prepared to the teaching activities, and the teacher's role is more like a coach developing new learning and cooperative skills in a partnership with the students. Success presupposes a certain amount of personal efforts from both sides, and opens up for better learning for students with difficulties with traditional (passive) learning methods. Nora Tomas, a Norwegian student with only 30% vision, experienced increased learning outcomes and better grades when her teacher flipped his teaching practice. Suddenly, she was able to learn at her own pace and not limited by disabling barriers in her learning environments (Tomas, 2016). In this cultural shift teachers have an essential role and the choices they make will affect students' learning. However, the UDLL project revealed that many of the academic staff in higher education have limited pedagogical training as part of their education.

The current teaching format found in many HEIs is deeply embedded in the organizational culture, and individual teachers place much pride in the way they have taught over the last 20 years. Traditionally, individually incentives to change and improve teaching methods has been limited (NTNU & UiT, 2016). By culture, we mean the common belief systems and entrenched practices throughout the totality of the system and evidenced within different departments within the institutions. Organizational culture is enacted all the way from management to facilities; it includes the work of administration, academics and the behaviors of students (Kegan & Lahey, 2009).

As illustrated in the case, many factors may combine to make it difficult to stimulate change in a teaching environment that has remained unchanged for decades. The first mechanism for overcoming these challenges is to recognize that the main competence for identifying effective approaches lies outside the primary change actors, as this is an interdisciplinary problem (McClure, 2005).

From the UDLL project, we understand teaching culture in higher education as the combination of stakeholders' behaviors, beliefs, and interactions that affect learning. When addressing teaching culture, it is essential to keep in mind that within the different stakeholder population, people are highly diverse. One of the aims of the project was to acknowledge and embrace this diversity as a source of creativity and differing viewpoints. Further, we needed to be aware that the population within the different stakeholders would react differently to teaching and learning activities and efforts to improve teaching and student culture. In the EU project, we used the UDL framework (Meyer, Rose, & Gordon, 2014; Novak, 2014) and theories about "immunity to change" to address this aspect (Kegan & Lahey, 2009).

Immunity to change is an organizational development method, which describes how individuals and organizations may fail to change because of hidden commitments (Kegan & Lahey, 2009). The theory refers to how individuals' beliefs along with the collective mindsets in an organization create a natural but powerful immunity to change. As long as individuals have hidden commitments working behind the scenes, it doesn't matter what they try to do achieving their goal. They will continue to meet intransigence until they discover what mindsets are producing their behavior and unlock their immunity to change (Kegan & Lahey, 2009).

The UDLL project set out to challenge traditional academic thinking about how education can be designed to include a diversity of students (UDLL, 2016). It recognized that there is already a body of good inclusive practice emerging throughout the sector, but it acknowledged that this is happening in silos (Organisation for Economic Cooperation Development, 2011). The project actively engaged with key stakeholder groups to explore their views, ideas and perspectives on moving from a traditional culture of teaching and "one approach fits all" to a culture of inclusion and Universal Design for Learning (UDL). The goal was to provide a model that institutions could implement when introducing UDL onto their campus.

The key stakeholder groups were compounded of people from each of the three countries. The groups were:

- Students in Higher Education.
- Policy makers and senior management.
- Academic staff and other faculty members.
- Student support staff/administrative or teaching staff with that function.

The following section will describe the process of engagement and learning with each stakeholder groups, and discuss a holistic approach to how institutions must collaborate internally and interdisciplinary to ensure quality for all students in the teaching and learning process.

The process of engagement with stakeholder groups

The process of engagement with each stakeholder group was based on Appreciative Inquiry, a process designed by systems thinkers such as Argyris (2008), Senge (1999), Kegan and Lahey (2009) and others. In systems thinking, cycles of behavior repeat themselves time after time, making situations better or worse. Traditionally, higher education was available to a largely homogenous elite group of high achieving students for whom didactic teaching appeared to work. Now however, a larger proportion of the student population has become more diverse and this includes students with multiple and variant forms of disability. For these students, traditional pedagogy embeds many barriers to learning as evidenced by high dropout rates, poor evaluations and the high proportion of individuals who require adaptations to overcome impairments and meet learning needs.

Appreciative Inquiry (AI) could work as a helpful tool in order to transform traditionally cycles of behavior to match todays' educational landscape. AI is a method for studying and changing social systems, such as groups, organizations and communities, where the strengths of people working in the organization are identified and strengthened. AI "advocates collective inquiry into the best of what is, in order to imagine what could be, followed by collective design of a desired future state that is compelling" (Bush, 2011). When it comes to using AI as a tool for engaging the academic community in educational development, the most valuable part is probably the unconditional positive questions and its ability to engage, enthuse, energize and enhance learning communities (Ludema, Cooperrider, & Barrett, 2001; Kadi-Hanifi et al., 2014).

In approaching the stakeholder groups, both in the recruitment process and during the four focus group meetings, appreciative inquiry was the fundamental strategy. For three of the four stakeholder groups, there was an open invitation to apply for participation announced through the project partners' national websites and social media. This way, most participants had an intrinsic motivation to take part in the project. Participants applied to participate in the focus group meetings by answering an entry question. These questions were tailored to fit different stakeholder groups, all of them focusing on their strengths and success stories. The Appreciative Inquiry approach also had a huge effect during the workshops, when we asked questions that challenged the 'status quo' and focusing the group discussions on taking a 'Universal Design for Learning Approach' that would enable a greater diversity of students in their institutions.

The process of engagement with the stakeholder groups was an important and deliberate choice, supported by theories and research from Deci and Ryan (1985). They claimed that people's need for learning and development are related to whether a person is extrinsicly or intrinsicly motivated to engage in an activity. According to Deci and Ryan, external motivation is affected by external influences and the reward comes from the surroundings, such as the recognition one gets from others. When a person is motivated from within the activity is self-determined and the reward is in the activity itself. Research has shown that an inner motivation is important for people to engage in their own learning and development. Deci and Ryan believe that the inner motivation is spurred by interest and desire, but in order for it to last, it must satisfy three basic psychological needs: the need for self-determination, the need for competence and the need for belonging. This is also supported in the theories of Multiple Means of Engagement, where people become more motivated when they can be in charge of, and self-regulate, their interest in learning (Novak, 2014). Transferred to an organizational development perspective, it means that inner motivation can be promoted and developed when the learning process is self-determined, when the persons involved experience a sense of coping through increased competence and the feeling of a safe and holding learning environment.

An introduction to UDL was sent out to the participants prior all four focus group meetings ensuring a collective background to the theme and the project. Participants also got some reflective questions before the focus group meeting in order to start their thinking about their current and future role and practice.

All focus group meetings were led by a facilitator and supported by group facilitators and note-takers from the partner organizations. After each meeting, notes from the partner organizations were gathered and scanned trough in order to find commonalities between participants' experiences, focusing on mapping each stakeholder group's perspective, success stories and barriers in developing a universally designed learning environment.

Key stakeholder group 1: students

The first stakeholder group was students with disabilities from across the three countries, Norway, Belgium and Ireland. It was important to garner the views of students first, as their feedback was used to frame the content and questions for the remaining focus groups. Altogether, approximately 90 students applied to participate in the focus group meeting, and nine of them were chosen based on their reflective answers, representing some of the experiences within a range of disabilities (i.e. mental health difficulties, ADHD, chronic illness). The students were also chosen from a diversity of ages, genders and socio economic backgrounds.

When students applied to participate in the focus group, which was arranged in Dublin, they were asked: *If you could advise your younger self, when you were considering university, what advice would you now give?*

One of the main tendencies among the applicants' answers was that the experience of independence, autonomy and empowerment were key qualities for success. Most of the applicants expressed to have been more disabled in the past, and wanted to share their success stories to contribute to more knowledge about their handicaps and challenges to minimize prejudice in their surroundings.

In the focus group meeting, the activities were structured around success stories with questions like:

- Which class will you never forget?
- In what situations did you not at all have to be concerned about disabling barriers?
- What makes a good teacher for you?

The students were not interested in theoretical concepts such as universal design, but they wanted their stories and experiences to be seen and heard, and most importantly they wanted to know how to use their voice in a learning context among peers. They talked about having to repeat the same stories and questions for support staff repeatedly and a frequently heard question was "Could there be a system that just provides the support I require?" They also expressed the need for a closer relationship with teachers. Moreover, they wanted the teachers to "speak a language they understand" and use relevant and modern communication channels to reach them.

One month later, the student group were invited to a workshop with a larger group of first year students from an Institute of Technology in Ireland (IT Blanchardstown, Dublin). The objective was that the project group of students would lead the first year students to develop their thinking around UDL and they would jointly suggest methods to include students with disabilities in HEIs. The aim was also to develop material for the Student Toolkit, which intended to give students an introduction to UDL, empowering students to take part in developing a universally designed learning environment. The groups of students engaged in a highly innovative process and produced a poem, which gives insights into their experiences and thoughts about higher education:

> "In our hearts
> we stowed away hope
> humanity's oldest motivation
> and like flames inside out ribcages
> we hold our dreams,
> some almost extinguished
> some undiscovered like distant stars
> and all we ask from you is that
> you see this
> and give us a few things

Consistency
An environment that cares for
Our minds, our bodies, our souls
Somewhere to make friends
A system of mentors we can trust"

Positively changing students' immunity to change

Although the students wanted change in systems of higher education, they were focusing on individual accommodation and had difficulties in seeing their role, needs and strengths in a universally designed learning environment. As illustrated in the case in the introduction, individual accommodation seems to be a practice incorporated over many years, making it difficult to change students' mindsets for the benefit of other practices that work. Similarly, are alternative teaching methods, like flipped classroom and active learning something students will welcome with open arms when we know that they are unconsciously "trained" to sit as passive listeners in a traditional lecture? In all organizational development, we need to acknowledge that cultural shifts for students take time. Even though the students started the focus group meeting with a perception that their role in developing an inclusive education is very limited the student group developed their mindsets in these questions and ended up agreeing on three points of contribution.

Students' contribution in developing an inclusive education:

- Share knowledge about difficulties, needs and strengths in the learning situation.
- Show interest in developing lectures, assessments, exams and services the HEIs offer through providing feedback and evaluations.
- Care for fellow students' development, both personally and professionally: share notes, talk about gained learning and support others to their learning targets.

Reflection

For students:

- Think about a valuable learning moment as a student: who was there and what made it so valuable?
- What makes you motivated to learn?
- When do you "forget" your disability?
- How do you provide feedback to teachers and support services?
- How do you actively support fellow students?

Key stakeholder group 2 – faculty and teaching staff

Participants in the second focus group were teachers working in higher education from across a range of fields of study including teaching, engineering, nursing, arts and physics. Their motivation to participate came from an interest in developing their teaching with respect for inclusion. They also wished to meet colleagues across countries and discuss innovative teaching and learning practices.

As with the focus group meeting with the students, the teaching staff applied to participate in the focus group meeting. The faculty and teaching staff were recruited without addressing them as UDL experts; instead they were asked to answer a more comprehensive question to stimulate innovative thinking before the workshop:

- Think about your own practice and how you respond in an innovative way to diversity in the student population.
- What example of good practice are you most proud of?

In line with the Appreciative Inquiry approach, the questions for the academics were framed deliberately: instead of focusing on failure and things they couldn't cope with, we wanted to focus on their strengths and success stories. This approach also reduced the risk of the academics being reluctant to disclose their lack of knowledge of the terms of universal design, which was productive for the outcome from the focus group. As with the student group, the teachers were provided with an introduction to UDL before entering the workshop.

Altogether, nine teachers were selected to participate in the focus group meeting, which was arranged in Ghent in Belgium. The environment for the workshop was informal yet structured, and participants were encouraged to get to know each other over a dinner the evening before. This social interaction was important as trust engendered and better facilitated an ease of conversation, questioning and discussion the following day. The focus group facilitator asked questions based on the best past experiences of the group, while also looking to the future. Questions focused on three reasons for why they do what they do, three challenges they experience, and three ideas to get started on the UDL journey, and finally participants were asked to consider three ideas to motivate them to continue their commitment to change.

The focus group was a sharing point for stories about innovations and creative ways to be inclusive. It featured structured conversations with teachers about how they are managing diversity, and it captured and shared the details. In line with the AI process, the facilitator consistently prompted the respondents to clarify their ideas and this ensured the participants were actively engaged with positive stories from their work.

The use of the term UDL was substantially de-emphasized throughout the focus group. The workshop instead focused on the participant's experiences and the content of UDL without necessarily using the term UDL and perspectives were gathered from the group about the challenges they faced and their innovative solutions and practices. The group expressed a collective view that often, they as teachers felt constrained by the system to do things differently and that they had to maintain standards at the expense of being creative, while they did not believe the two were necessarily disconnected.

The group identified resisters to cultural change as fear of change itself. Academics are experts in their own field and may be reluctant to move into new areas such as using technology for fear of getting it wrong. They identified structural barriers towards a more inclusive approach; such as practices including the priority given to research over teaching in HEIs, rigid timetabling, inflexible systems of assessment and the allocation of resources to staff development. They felt that learning how to change their practice in order to become more inclusive was not an institutional goal, but left to the interests of individual staff to pursue in their own time. Looking back at the case at the beginning of the chapter, the teachers at least had collaborators and supporters across the institution to succeed with the faculty development. With the theories of Deci and Ryan (1985) and the theories of multiple means of engagement in mind, a safe and holding learning environment is of great importance in order to succeed with a change process. If teachers experience inclusive teaching practice as an institutional goal it is probably easier to prioritize the time and effort an UDL initiative needs and deserves.

In order to focus further as to how innovations and good practices could act as a road map to envision a more inclusive future, the group was presented with the following questions:

- "What was your best teaching moment so far?"
- "What did the students tell you about it?"
- "In the event that you were a blind student, what would your experiences be like within the subject area you currently teach?"

The responses were unanimous. Teaching is an emotional job that requires passion for your subject, good relationships with students and an appreciation for diversity with an openness to learning. The teachers in the focus group were challenged to write a quote based on discoveries and learning during group discussions. These are examples of the teachers "take home messages":

- "It is not about me as a teacher, but about the students and their learning". Carl Fredrik Sørensen, Norwegian teacher.
- "Studying is not competing, but learning from each other". Leif Houck, Norwegian teacher.
- "Whatever we are doing, if they are not learning we are just talking to ourselves". Marian McCarthy, Irish teacher.
- "It's not about knowing it all, it's about constantly seeking". Ellen Meersschaert, Belgian teacher.

Common among these quotes is the acknowledgement that in a modern and inclusive learning environment, the teacher is not the only one with all the answers. Knowledge is something teachers and students define and create together and neither of the two stakeholder groups will be fully trained learners; rather, they are lifelong learners (Aarsand et al., 2011). In practice, this presupposes a need for constantly seeking knowledge and greater learning for both groups, reducing teachers' control, while empowering the students as co-creators of knowledge at the same time. In the same way, Kari from the case study at the beginning of this chapter needs to empower, teachers to let go of control and encourage students to be more active in setting responsibility and direction for their own learning. According to the Universal Design for Learning Guidelines, one approach for teachers to realize this ambition and empower students to become strategic goal-directed learners is to provide multiple means of action and expression (Novak, 2014). If the teachers provide multiple ways of assessment, students have the possibility to choose a method that best caters to their strengths. During the process, teachers can guide appropriate goal setting and support the planning and strategy process. Knowing that both teachers and students have established roles and responsibilities for decades, they need time and scaffolding along the process in order to succeed.

There are many ways for students to reach academic and technical standards, and inclusion is about designing and delivering a curriculum for a diverse student population involving those with disabilities.

Positively changing teachers' immunity to change

Despite the fact that the academics who participated in the focus group were "early adopters" of inclusive education, they saw many resisters within their wider environments, and common among all of the barriers was a perception that changes were somehow "beyond their control". Long traditions with a teaching practice that "works" and a familiarization with a system of individual accommodations also made many teachers believe that introducing systematic changes are seen as someone else's responsibility. As we have seen, both in the case and among the teacher participants, the feeling of having "little control" could also be a sign of a fear of change. Even among early adopters, it takes courage, creativity and capacity to challenge tradition in order to bring about changes in a system which for decades may have been perceived as being "gold standard".

Many of the participants could make minor changes, but in order to develop inclusive education to the full, they needed support and change from other stakeholder groups, especially policy makers and management in HEIs. For the other stakeholder groups, teachers were seen as the only obvious contributors to change. Despite the fact that the teachers experience barriers to change, they realized that what they do as innovative and pedagogical initiatives also often includes better learning conditions for students with disabilities.

Academic staff's role in developing inclusive learning:

- Get to know your potential user group by providing multiple means of engagement. Be aware of any methodological access barriers and look for challenges in fulfilling a course.
- Provide multiple means of representation by planning teaching methods that best cater for different needs, learning styles and preferences (vary and be flexible).
- Provide multiple means of action and representation by choosing assessment methods based on what skills and characteristics you want your graduates to have.

Reflection

- Think about your own practice and how you respond in an innovative way to diversity in the student population. What examples of good practice are you most proud of?
- Think about redesigning your own educational practice with diversity in mind, to create an inclusive, accessible and welcoming learning environment for all students. Where would you start?

Key stakeholder group 3: policy and management at HEIs

The third focus group meeting were arranged in Norway's capital, Oslo. As participants in the three other stakeholder groups applied to participate in the project, the group of policy makers and management got a personal invitation to participate because we wanted to ensure key participants from all levels of management. Twelve managers, four from each partner country, participated in the focus group meeting, representing diverse backgrounds and roles differing between working nationally in developing or influencing Universal Design, working nationally in influencing or implementing Higher Education Policy and working in the management of a Higher Education institution. All the present participants were indeed representing important roles and perspectives to take the lead in the change towards a UDL environment. In order to stimulate their thinking, participants were asked to answer some preparatory questions before the focus group meeting. Questions included:

- What kinds of overall acts, regulations and expectations affect the ability within HEIs to ensure access for student diversity?
- How do you work to create/announce/implement these solutions in your context through your specific role?

This group was concerned with strategic challenges, with planning at different levels, and with the allocation of resources. The discussion identified key resistors to change and one in particular gained prominence: this was the silo nature of working in higher education, in which different faculties, departments and central units within a university worked in isolation while simultaneously, in many instances, competing internally for funding. The communication between these silos is in most cases woefully inadequate, and it is rare for different departments to join forces to collaboratively solve problems. This is a major barrier to success of UDL, as in many organizations 'inclusion' is perceived as being the sole responsibility of the disability offices. It was a unanimous view that changing this silo culture is not easy and there are many resistors such as fear of change, fear of an increasing workload, of having insufficient resources, of not having the knowledge or expertise, and perhaps most importantly, there was an assumption that the challenges due to diversity issues are solved elsewhere in the institution. In essence, many senior leaders felt it was 'someone else's problem'. To bring about change, these challenges have to be balanced by supports and scaffolds for staff regarding how to introduce UDL and how to change.

A key obstacle for introducing UDL as a generic and acknowledged tool for inclusion was, according to the management group, the lack of evidence-based proof besides occasional success stories. The workshop participants addressed several fundamental questions: Will UDL ensure that students are more satisfied, get better grades and have greater ability to fulfill higher education within a normal timeframe? Will the concept of UDL prove sustainable in a cost benefit analysis? The need for research in this field is indisputable, especially in the Higher Education context.

The facilitator identified that strategic change is emotional, and while we can introduce technical solutions to problems, they can be ignored, and the real barrier to change is how people feel about it. The starting point in any change initiative in higher education is the recognition of how people feel; what they think; their self-beliefs; their traditions, and once these have been acknowledged and taken on board, then we can plant the seeds of change.

Higher Education cultures consist of individuals with belief systems which reflect biases and assumptions about education. This includes staff who are advocates of traditional styles of education who see their role as researchers as the sources of knowledge. Others see active learning and student engagement as core components of learning and of education. Nevertheless, these beliefs can be tested and challenged, by making people more aware of their own thinking and inquiring with questions into the thinking of the group.

The management and policy maker workshop led to a "top-down-implementation-guide" as to how HEI leadership might best address diversity in the student population, based on UDL thinking (UDLL, 2016). A systemic approach with the support of key leadership will probably result in higher quality of teaching and learning, and better standards of services across the institution. Acknowledging the systemic nature of organizational change required in introducing UDL is the first key factor for success. The workshop participants were challenged to identify six ground rules for implementing UDL in Higher education (UDLL, 2016), which ended in these commitments:

- Develop an overarching institutional policy.
- Use the expert knowledge of the diverse users.
- Create clear and challenging vision.
- Form sustainable strategies at all levels.
- Develop action plans for implementation coherent with budgets and other important plans.
- Use/develop your system for evaluation and quality assurance in this field, and connect this to ordinary quality work for the institution.

This group identified their role as leaders at two important stages: first when articulating a vision for upcoming work for diversity and disability, and second, when it comes to starting these conversations across the institution. They also acknowledged a role in bringing different faculty and other key persons and functions together to collaboratively address the issue of diversity. Starting such conversations about diversity within the institution was seen as critical and these conversations can start with questions about how the organization can reach its strategic goals around inclusion.

The leader's advice to others was to incorporate good examples of collaborative success stories, and use them for future work:

- When have we worked collaboratively, when have we been successful?
- How can we increase cooperation between different stakeholders inside and outside the university sector?
- What is stopping us from stepping out of our silos?

Positively changing managements' immunity to change

Other stakeholders point at management as one of the most important stakeholders for changing the teaching practices, but like the previous stakeholders, management had difficulties in defining their own scope of action. While teachers claimed it would have been much easier if the management could lead the way and cheer for an inclusive teaching practice, management in the focus group did not necessarily feel they had this kind of 'power'. With support from the facilitator present at the workshop, the management and policy makers unlocked their ulterior motives that might prevent change, and they also highlighted some of the competing assumptions: their feeling of "lack of power" was a signal of an unconscious fear of failure. Academic institutions are above all measured on the quality and quantity of research, and to a lesser extent on innovations within pedagogical quality.

Important questions were addressed at the workshop, for example: if academic staff prioritize their teaching, how will it affect the quality of their research? Further, students who complete their studies and get good grades are seen as a reflection of an institution's quality, reputation and attractiveness. Will implementing UDL lower those standards, and can the HEIs vouch for students with disabilities if they got better grades using an alternative route? During group discussions, the participants discovered how they could turn around these beliefs and use this knowledge and UDL as a symbol of better quality for all. More concretely, UDL can be introduced as a framework that had the potential to strengthen the retention rate and develop higher standards and deeper learning for all students.

What is good leadership from a UDL perspective? Management contribution:

- Develop action plans for implementation.
- Use the expert knowledge of the diverse users and collaborates.
- Connect universal design guidelines to what the universities and university colleges are measured on.
- Equal education and pedagogy with research matters.
- Encourage cooperation across departments and between different stakeholders.

Reflection

- What visions and strategies exist at your institution to ensure an inclusive learning environment for all students?
- Who are key personnel to realize these visions, and how do you as a leader support them?

Key stakeholder group 4: disability and student support services

The collaborative workshop for student support services was held was held in Thronheim, Norway and constituted the most homogenous grouping of informants: all nine participants had the same kind of role within their institutions; they worked on a daily basis keeping in direct contact with students. However, while most of the participants worked centrally to support students with disabilities, some worked at a faculty or an institute. The group revealed years of experience with making individual accommodations for students. During their work, they have encountered resistance and skepticism from teachers and other administrative staff in providing individual accommodation for students with disabilities. The group reported that at times teaching staff were seen as the 'antagonists', who resisted their desire to support students adequately, for example it was not unusual to encounter teachers assuming that alternative assessment methods would lower the standards and affect the academic requirements in a study. The group also reported 'classic' sentiments of those who were resistant to inclusion on the basis that 'special arrangements' for some would be unjust and unfair for the majority of students without disabilities.

All selected members of this workshop had applied for their participation, like two of the other groups reflecting around two motivational questions:

- Looking at your work in supporting students with disabilities today, what challenges and success criteria do you see in developing a universally designed learning environment?
- How do you perceive your own role in the transition from working on an ad-hoc basis with individuals to planning proactively with universally designed solutions that provide better learning for all students?

In the recruitment process, the project learned that disability officers were motivated to apply for the focus group meeting by a desire to learn the right arguments for their cause and to acquire the knowledge and skills needed to support academic staff in realizing inclusive teaching practice. They also wanted to learn how colleagues in other countries worked with inclusion, and how they could take a systematic approach in including students with disabilities in ordinary solutions.

In the focus group, depending on the context, the purpose of the exercise and desired outcomes, participants were divided into both mixed international groups and national groups. Initially, international groups were established to become more familiar with other participants' roles and responsibilities. They were also encouraged to describe and reflect upon good student support moments and collaboration with other stakeholders. In the next exercise participants were placed in national groups to discuss challenges and barriers in developing a universally designed learning environment, to provide insights into best practice and to explore the future role of disability officers and their contributions to collaboration across departments. The purpose was to define national tendencies because the follow-up exercise – 'the café-table exercise' contained a discussion among commonalities between the countries. In the 'café-table exercise', the project partners, two from each partner country (2x3) had different responsibilities in the three groups. While one partner had the responsibility to introduce the discussion theme for the group and write notes from the conversation, the other partner followed the group consistently as a group facilitator.

Although the participants had years of experience with students, disabilities and reasonable accommodation, they had difficulties in transferring this competence in a universal approach to inclusion. They also have years of experience meeting resistance among teachers and management and expressed some kind of fear to actively step into another stakeholder's territory and suggest changes in time honored approaches to teaching.

According to the feedback, the main argument against UDL was the time-aspect and the challenges about how they could prioritize working with universal design for learning when they had used all their resources to find reasonable accommodations for individual students with disabilities. During the group discussions, the participants identified actions and resources in order to benefit more students. In an ideal UDL environment, only students with substantial difficulties in entering and accomplishing higher education would have to register with disability services for supports, while most students would be supported within the faculties. In this context, disability officers would be empowered to release resources into providing other actions and services to the institution, which would open them up for working for inclusion at a systemic level.

The most important identified action was to build relationships between departments inside the HEIs. If disability officers introduce UDL concepts to key colleagues and across the student welfare organizations, they might be able to develop a shared responsibility where different stakeholders could all begin to pull the same direction. Other suggested actions included digitalizing administrative services and considering what services could be provided more autonomously within the student body. Overall there were a few key insights that provide a foundation for future work. Eline Grouwels, disability staff, Belgium, suggested, "See solutions, not challenges", whereas Julie Tonge, disability staff, Ireland recommended that officers, "Support early adopters".

As for previous groups, the disability officers were challenged to identify recommendations to other stakeholders in designing a universally designed learning environment. Eva Ballo, disability staff in Norway shared that, "Even small steps make a big difference". Thorvald Abrahamsen, Norway, noted it was important for stakeholders to, "Make conscious and intentional choices".

Common for all these recommendations is a positive focus, an appreciative inquiry approach, encouraging both academic staff and management to take the first steps towards UDL by identifying success stories and by building upon them. An important piece of advice was to acknowledge that as an agent for change, one does not need to understand or implement the whole framework in order to act inclusively. Further, as long as all stakeholders take conscious and intentional choices, the change process has greater chance to succeed with bringing about systemically inclusive practice. This is because such work is pro-active instead of reactive and it is also 'active' instead of acting on autopilot – it positively interrupts the way we always have worked (Kegan & Lahey, 2009).

Remembering Kari, the disability officer in the case study, she had quite a challenge coordinating an organizational change at the faculty when all stakeholders expressed skepticism about participating in the grand change process. An important step in turning their mindsets consisted of addressing their assumptions and fears. For Kari, one way in which this could be achieved would be to adopt an appreciative inquiry approach focusing on small steps, early adopters and solutions, rather than focusing on the need to implement the whole framework at once.

Positively changing student services officers' immunity to change

For many years, disability officers have welcomed and worked for inclusion of students with disabilities to become an institutional responsibility, but when introduced to UDL, this group seemed to be skeptical as to what these changes might mean for the students, as well as being concerned about their future roles as disability officers. In an ideal UDL world, will the teachers succeed given the responsibility to support the students? The disability officers revealed actual concerns about this, and doubted that academics would invest time and effort to become inclusive and provide necessary support to the students with disabilities, knowing teachers often lack knowledge about their needs. Further, and quite fundamentally, the disability coordinators questioned whether a UDL approach could undermine their own position, meaning that the roles might ultimately then become redundant.

The participating disability officers had difficulties acknowledging how they might impact upon the development of UDL. They felt affirmed and competent in individual approaches and support, but had difficulties in transferring their experiences and knowledge into a universal approach. As with the other stakeholders, they primarily saw barriers in their surroundings.

During group discussions, participants uncovered a fear of adopting a role they could not cope with, and a responsibility that other stakeholders might not acknowledge as appropriate and valuable. Disability officers started the focus group meeting with the perception that they would become redundant in a UDL approach, but as they further explored the potential adoption of the approach, they discovered additional important initiatives and services that needed their attention and competence.

Disability officer's role in a UDL approach:

- Contribute in a proactive way to the development of the Universal Design policy across campus. This includes cooperating with management on the development of action plans for universal design implementation consciously reviewing Universal Design for Learning approaches.
- Cooperate with academic staff and the institution's center for teaching and learning to develop inclusive learning methods and assessment that cater for different learning styles and disabilities.
- Raise awareness and knowledge by providing training on best teaching practice with focus on the fields of disability, diversity and inclusive learning.
- Continue to support students with reasonable accommodation when universally designed initiatives are not sufficient.

> **Reflection**
> * Looking at your work in supporting students with disability today, what actions can you do in order to offer services that are universally designed for both students and staff?
> * Reflect upon different kind of reasonable accommodations that you have granted to students with disabilities that most students could benefit.

From silo thinking to a culture of inclusion

In the project, the four stakeholder groups discovered that it isn't one stakeholder group or one person who is responsible for the organization's culture, but rather, that patterns are created because of their collective behavior and attitudes. When this happens, they experienced a shift from a 'you and they perspective' to a 'we and I perspective'. Earlier, the blame was put on others when problems occurred. When 'we' slides in the foreground, pushing 'they' in the background, the participants discovered how their own behavior and attitudes contributed to maintain inexpedient and nonproductive patterns (Kegan & Lahey, 2009; Senge, 1999). In addition to discover their own role, they become aware of assumptions and biases they have of colleagues working in other departments inside HEI. New learning challenges the silo thinking and their meaning constructions, which make it easier to cooperate across departments and stakeholder groups, most of all, because they discovered their own role and how different stakeholders complete each other in developing an inclusive learning environment.

Conclusion

Why is it so hard to introduce the philosophy, values and practice of Universal Design for Learning to Higher Education staff? The Appreciative Inquiry approach with key stakeholder groups in higher education produced a wealth of rich responses from each stakeholder group. There was unanimous agreement across all groups about the barriers towards introducing a culture of Universal design for Learning, but regardless of roles, it became evident that all four stakeholders identify barriers beyond themselves within their wider environments that hindered them from using, implementing and adapting UDL as a tool for inclusion. However, the participants found it more difficult to acknowledge their own roles individually and unconsciously in maintaining some of the more traditional patterns, practice and developments. Since most participants in the focus group meetings applied to participate in the project they were positively disposed towards inclusion and curious about UDL as a topic, and they had an intrinsic motivation to learn more. It is a paradox that even motivated participants experience these kinds of challenges, and this learning needs to be taken into account when introducing UDL for all stakeholders.

Organizational development starts with the individuals. As soon as the staff individually work with their own mindsets, assumptions and choices, they will gradually influence a change in culture. For those who are tasked with bringing about systemic change, this requires knowledge and awareness about student diversity and students with disabilities, and an insight into the tools and best practices likely to bring about inclusive learning among all stakeholders. However, to ensure a universal design approach to diversity and disability matters, responsibility for inclusive learning should never be limited to the student support services. All the important stakeholders influencing the student learning must play their part. If support services and disability officers are the only one working for inclusive learning, we risk a culture where students with disabilities might continue to be 'students with special needs' when it in fact is a need for all students to present, demonstrate and engage in learning activities tailored to their strengths, needs and preferences. A proactive approach will gain better quality for all learners.

Common for all stakeholders was an immunity to change. They all know what they do today, but they do not know what these changes will cause as the process of change unfolds. A lesson learned is to start with the small steps. If an individual or a course or a whole organization wishes to act more inclusively, it's not mandatory to bring about a whole scale change process by implementing the UDL framework in its totality. Second, the term UDL does not have to be used in order to include students in pedagogical activities. Most important is to understand that students with different needs should be able to study on equal terms and have the opportunity to gain from their learning and to demonstrate that learning to themselves and to others.

For stakeholders in this project it was of great value to discover and acknowledge their own role within a wider context of organizational development. With raised self-awareness, the stakeholders identified positive and encouraging ways to move forward. The answers lie in the formation of positive strategic collaboration and alliances amongst key players within institutions from the top-down and bottom-up. A number of questions have emerged that higher education institutions and individuals should be asking themselves in relation to creating an inclusive mainstream learning environment.

- Is there a vision for a universally designed campus?
- Are departments aware and accountable for how they are responding to diversity?
- Are you creating space to collaboratively discuss with colleagues their perspectives and experiences of including a diverse student group in their area/subject?
- Is each department and faculty considering how they can use flexible and innovative teaching to enable *all* students to learn?

Moving towards UDL is a broader endeavor than having equality policies resting on a shelf. It requires deliberate cultural change across the institution. If Inclusion of diversity is everyone's job, then staff across the organization need to discover their role as well as be empowered and supported to build relationships across the organization. There needs to be a recognition that working collaboratively to share knowledge, good practices and ideas within the context of particular institutions is very effective in challenging the status quo. In order to accomplish this goal fully, each individual needs to take an active and responsible role in the development, and they need to trust the process.

References

Aarsand, L., Håland, E., Tønseth, C., & Tøsse, S. (2011). *Voksne, læring og kompetanse*. Oslo: Gyldendal Akademisk.

Argyris, C. (2008). *Teaching smart people how to learn*. Boston, MA: Harvard Business School Press.

Bush, G. R. (2011). Appreciative inquiry: Theory and critique. In D. Boje, B. Burnes, & J. Hassard (Eds.), *The Routledge companion to organizational Change* (pp. 87–103). Oxford: Routledge.

Deci, E. L., & Ryan, R. M. (1985). *Intrinsic motivation and self-determination in human behavior*. New York: Plenum Press.

Hauschildt, K., Vögtle, E. M., & Gwosc, C. (2018). *Social and economic conditions of student life in Europe: Synopsis of indicators. Eurostudent VI 2016–2018*. Bielefeld: W. Bertelsmann Verlage.

Higher Education Authority. (2015). *National plan for equity of access to higher education 2015–2019*. Retrieved from http://hea.ie/assets/uploads/2017/04/national_plan_for_equity_of_access_to_higher_education_2015-2019_single_page_version_01.pdf

Kadi-Hanifi, K., Dagman, O., Peters, J., Snell, E., Tutton, Caroline, & Wright, T. (2014). Engaging students and staff with educational development through appreciative inquiry, *Innovations in Education and Teaching International*, 51:6, 584–594. Retrieved from: www.tandfonline.com/doi/abs/10.1080/14703297.2013.796719

Kegan, R., & Lahey, L. L. (2009). *Immunity to change: How to overcome it and unlock potential in yourself and your organization*. Boston, MA: Harvard Business Press.

Ludema, J., Cooperrider, D., & Barrett, F. (2001). Appreciative inquiry: The power of the unconditional positive question. In P. Reason & H. Bradbury (Eds.), *Handbook of action research* (pp. 189–199). London: Sage.

McClure, B. A. (2005). *Putting a spin on Groups: the science of chaos*. Mahwah, NJ: Lawrence Erlbaum Associates.

Meyer, A., Rose, D. H., & Gordon, D. (2014). *Universal design for learning: Theory & practice*. Wakefield, MA: Cast Professional Publishing.

Norwegian Ministry of Education and Research. (2005). *Act relating to universities and university colleges*. Retrieved from: www.regjeringen.no/globalassets/upload/kd/vedlegg/uh/uhloven_engelsk.pdf

Novak, K. (2014). *UDL now! A teacher's Monday-Morning guide to implementing common core standards using universal design for learning*. Wakefield, MA: Cast Professional Publishing.

NTNU & UiT. (2016). *Innsats for kvalitet: Forslag til et meritteringssystem for undervisning ved NTNU og UiT Norges arktiske universitet.* Retrieved from: www. ntnu.no/documents/1263030840/1268058549/Innsats+for+kvalitet+-+Forslag +til+et+meritteringssystem+for+undervisning+ved+NTNU+og+UiT+Norges+arkt iske+universitet.pdf/aadea128-638f-4e2f-8516-5a2ffa54b87a

Organisation for Economic Cooperation Development. (2011). *Inclusion of students with disabilities in tertiary education and employment. Education and training policy.* Paris: OECD Publishing.

Senge, P. M. (1999). *Den femte disiplin: kunsten å utvikle den lærende organisasjon.* A. Lillebø (oversetter). Oslo: Egmont Hjemmets Forlag.

Student toolkit. (2016, October 20). Retrieved from: https://studenttoolkit.eu/

Tomas, N. (2016, November 3). *Flipped classroom – student perspective.* Retrieved from: www.youtube.com/watch?v=cNqhwxg0D6A, www.youtube.com/channel/ UCelV8HqIRp_S8WqWwqRSNhA/videos

UDLL – Universal Design for Learning in Higher Education – License to Learn. (2016). *A universal design for learning – License to learn – A best practice guideline.* UDLL Partnership: HOWEST (SIHO), AHEAD and NTNU (Universell), Ghent, Belgium.

Chapter 2

From national policy to university practice

Developing an inclusive learning environment within and beyond the United Kingdom

Geoff Layer

Case study

Sam studied three subjects for her A-level examinations (these are national examinations at the end of the secondary level/high school in the UK) and, because she had diagnosed specific learning difficulties, she had received some additional support. This support was in the form of a group teaching assistant supplied by her school. When she applied to university, she disclosed this learning difficulty but when she arrived at university to study for a BA (Hons) Business Studies degree, a disability coordinator explained to her that the support she had received at school was not available in higher education.

Sam was taught in a lecture with 200 other students and was in a seminar group with 20 others. She found it difficult to keep up in the lectures as she took longer to take notes as a result of her disability. Sam was a quiet student and found engaging in discussion in the seminar group difficult and took longer to make friends than some of her peers. So, unlike at school, she did not have people to talk to about her work.

Sam had to buy extra software for her laptop and, when she could not keep up in classes, she had to borrow notes from her classmates. She was however given additional time in her exams. Sam found university to be a real struggle but she was determined to succeed. Sam found the assessment tasks that students were given confusing, as she had not had to do anything like this before. Sam was wondering whether she belonged in higher education.

This is a real example of how a student felt about her life at university. Sam had received comprehensive information in the induction process and she had a personal tutor, but she was struggling to adapt. This case study could be in many universities within the UK and demonstrates the need to address not only the individual student, but the policy environment for supporting all students.

Introduction

This chapter seeks to explain how universities have changed, the need to continue that process of evolution towards a more student-centered environment and how the principles of Universal Design for Learning (UDL) can be used to create a more inclusive learning environment, in which everyone is supported to achieve.

Such an environment would not only support Sam, but would enhance the experience for all students. The detailed explanation of UDL is found elsewhere in this book; this chapter focuses on how universities are beginning to adapt to provide UDL in a seamless and applicable way to all students and learning situations. They are not there yet, but we need to understand how much they have changed and how much more change is needed to achieve greater inclusivity.

Universities and higher education (HE) have developed over the years in respect of their role, purpose and function. Within the UK, these developments have been driven by a combination of national policy drives but, more importantly, by the response of universities to different economic and social environments. This chapter looks briefly at: how universities have changed; the impact of those changes on disabled students; and the issues that have emerged in respect of differential outcomes for students. It then considers how the agenda has moved to one of greater inclusivity, incorporating some of the key aspects of UDL.

Throughout their history, universities have been perceived as the bastions of the establishment and the elite. The challenge has always been to make them more accessible and today's challenges simply move the debate forward. Higher education has responded by demonstrating a significant capacity to be able to develop and to cater for an increasingly diverse group of students. The opportunity to embed a more inclusive approach to education is one that needs to be taken.

The concept of a university has its roots in medieval times with the development of universities in Morocco and Bologna. Of course, invention, discovery and the pursuit of knowledge began well before then and did not require universities as we know them today. Socrates, Aristotle and Plato did not require universities and their facilities in order to develop their philosophies. In the UK, an early university developed through an ecclesiastical route in Durham, with the Venerable Bede (672–735) being key to the later development of the University of Durham. It was in this era that we saw the development of "seats of learning" based around the concept of a community of scholars. These were the early universities focused on the pursuit of knowledge and the sharing of that knowledge. It was not about the modern form of Credentialism, which is where a student is simply concerned with gaining the qualification as a means of moving a career forward. Here the key outcome is simply the achievement of the qualification and not the desire to learn, or the discovery of a subject and the pursuit of ideas. The next phase of development came in the mid-nineteenth century with Cardinal Newman and the view that the model of a university was essentially about broadening the mind and preparing people for the future. The Industrial Revolution highlighted the need for a more highly skilled workforce and the establishment of universities in the industrial towns and cities, focusing on a more utilitarian approach with the needs of the local economy in mind; for example, Sheffield with metallurgy, Leeds with textiles.

It is important to understand the history of higher education to both appreciate the challenges it has faced and the changes it has been through. These have created the opportunity to drive forward inclusive learning and UDL. Universities are now more open and receptive to developing their curricula and pedagogy in order to improve the experience and outcomes for all of their students. Such openness to change is critical to the case made in later chapters for the need to adopt UDL.

The background to change

The change that I focus on in this chapter is from the idea of a university as a "seat of learning" and "community of scholars" with a focus on the development of knowledge of the subject, to one whereby they focus on student learning, student experience and qualifications. This has been a rapid and significant period of change. Within the UK, the catalyst for this change was the Robbins report in 1963, which stated that "university places should be available to all who were qualified by ability and attainment" (Robbins, 1963). Robbins though was addressing the issue of who should be able to participate through the expansion of existing access, whereby the step change could only occur with the development of new provision and, whilst the Robbins philosophy created the culture for the expansion of higher education from 4% of the age group in 1962, it was through Wilson's "White Heat of Technology" (Wilson, 1963). Crosland's development of Polytechnics (Crosland, 1966)., Blair's mantra of "education, education, education" (Blair, 1996) and the continuing development of new universities and other HEIs that has led to a participation rate of approximately 43% within the UK today (Willetts, 2013).

Within this shift was the gradual process of the massification of higher education, as explored by Martin Trow (Trow, 1989), who developed an analysis of the growth in HEIs relating to social purpose. He referred to three stages of massification, in which he defined the stages of moving to mass higher education as starting at an "Elite" level in which up to 15% of the age group engage in higher education, as a system developed for what Trow refers to as the "ruling class", to prepare them for elite roles. As the participation level increases, then we move to a "Mass" system in which we see HEIs looking more at skill development and the preparation for a broader range of technical and economic elite roles, with participation rising towards 50%. After that, Trow states, comes the "Universal" system, which enables society to adapt to rapid social and technological change.

The approach to massification in the UK, and many other countries, came without major and strategic investment but through a process of both incremental and significant growth happening without the planned changes needed in student support and pedagogical approaches. At the same time, there was the desire to ensure greater social mobility through access to higher education. In Australia, this was to be found in "Fair Chance for All" (Department of Employment, Education and Training, 1990), in the USA through affirmative action, in South Africa through free tuition and in the UK through widening participation. Interestingly, both in Australia and the UK, the initiatives had a focus on increasing participation in HE of disabled students. The Higher Education Funding Council for England (HEFCE) funded its first set of disability initiatives in 1993/94 (Higher Education Funding Council for England, 1995).

Now the crucial aspect of Trow's analysis is how the universities responded to such expansion. Simply fitting in more students to the same pedagogical and support model provides not a mass approach but "crowded" higher education as the learning and teaching approach was designed for a smaller and more homogenous group. This means that universities needed to fundamentally address how they shift their curriculum approach. HEFCE sought to catalyze change through a focus on enabling and empowering developments in pedagogical approaches and student support, in order to enable universities to become more student focused and to open up the curriculum.

Initially, HEFCE funded a range of projects focusing on developing learning and teaching, enabling disabled students and widening participation. There was a focus on seeking to establish innovative practice. Then, in 2001, HEFCE addressed the bigger issue of seeking to encourage universities to develop a holistic approach to widening participation, disability and learning and teaching, by requiring comprehensive institutional strategies that linked these key issues together for effective enhancement, as shown in Figure 2.1.

Figure 2.1 A holistic approach to widening participation

This has been built on by the National Strategy for Access and Student Success, published by the government in 2014, 'Working in Partnership: Enabling Social Mobility in Higher Education', the final report of the Social Mobility Advisory Group published in 2016 and the Access and Participation Plan Guidance from the Office for Students (OfS) published in 2018.

Such change takes time and universities are still working towards this goal, but progress has been significant. For example, there has been notable investment by HEFCE and this has sparked a curriculum revolution involving a range of agencies and culminating in Centres for Excellence in Teaching and Learning (CETLs), with a £315 million investment from HEFCE between 2005–06 and 2009–10. Alongside this was further major investment in higher education by HEFCE to enhance both access and participation through what became the Student Opportunity Fund which, at its peak, led to £380m (GBP) per annum supporting this part of the HE mission (Higher Education Funding Council for England, 2017).

Reflection

- How has the evolution of HE in your context led to opportunities for pedagogical development and innovation?
- How would you suggest that regulators better provide for positive change in terms of widening participation in your national or university context?
- What might the next phase of development for HE look like when considering current global challenges?

It is important to note how relatively quickly this shift to a focus on the student has taken place, given that the concept of the university is 1,100 years old, but the drive for change only started in 1963 at a relatively pedestrian rate. However, the drive to enhance the student experience has been quicker and it is now at the heart of the Higher Education and Research Act 2017, which established the Office for Students.

As universities began to consider the impact of mass higher education and widening access, there was a plethora of national developments seeking to develop appropriate responses. HEFCE, alongside the Department for Employment and Learning (DEL) in Northern Ireland, funded significant developments in pedagogy through the Fund for the Development of Teaching and Learning (FDTL), which was established in 1995. This was followed by the Teaching Quality Enhancement Fund (TQEF), which was initiated in 1999 and which subsumed the FDTL and established the Learning and Teaching Support Network and it included the ground-breaking recognition that universities required Learning and Teaching Strategies and that these should be inextricably linked with strategies for Widening Participation (Higher Education Funding Council for England, 2001b). Currently, a key driver has been the National Student Survey (NSS), which is an independent survey of all final year undergraduate students in the UK and was introduced in 2005, with a 70% participation rate amongst students giving clear feedback over a sustained period of time. This has helped inform the development of a Teaching Excellence Framework (TEF), which is a national mechanism that rates universities against a mix of formulaic proxy metrics and which also considers contextual factors that influence student learning experiences and outcomes.

Students with disabilities

When we look at how students with disabilities have been supported in the UK over the last 30 years, the position is one that clearly necessitates a change in approach. The numbers of students declaring a disability has risen exponentially with a recent major increase in the numbers declaring a mental health issue. The data in Figures 2.2 and 2.3 comes from the Higher Education Statistics Agency (HESA, 2018), which covers all student enrolments across higher education.

The university sector has always responded to the need to support students with disabilities but this was typically developed on the basis of a need to support an individual student, through making a form of intervention in support systems. Interventions would vary from the physical adjustment of residential facilities to

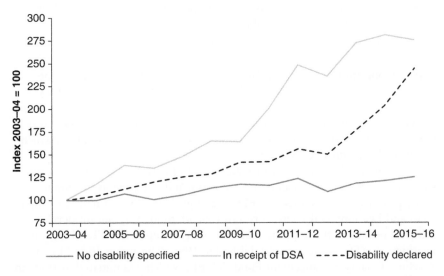

Figure 2.2 Change in HEFCE-funded HEI student numbers by disability, 2003/04 to 2015/16

Source: Taken from Williams et al. (2017)

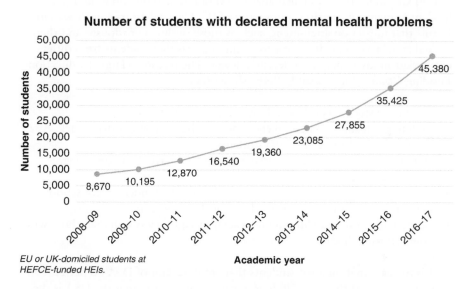

Number of students with declared mental health problems

EU or UK-domiciled students at HEFCE-funded HEIs.

Figure 2.3 EU or UK-domiciled students at HEFCE-funded HEIs

Source: Taken from HESA student record, 2008–2017

allowing extra time in examinations. Often, interventions would be coordinated from a specialist support team who would liaise with faculty staff over learning contracts for students, which would include commitments to the students, such as distributing lecture notes in advance for example. These reasonable adjustments have become part of everyday life in higher education and many of them were funded through additional support that the student receives from the Government's Disabled Students Allowance (DSA) scheme. The DSA covered additional costs up to maximum levels, following an individual assessment of need, and this had a significant positive impact for many students. This is a very different approach to other parts of the education system as, under this model, it is the individual student that receives the funding and not the institution.

The key issue for ensuring that we have an education system in which everyone has an equal opportunity to succeed is to consider how all students are supported in order to achieve the attainment and progression outcomes that they are capable of. If the outcomes for some groups are different than others and those differences cannot be explained by entry qualifications, subject studied, or other factors known to affect attainment and progression, then it raises serious questions around how universities need to change what they do to ensure that all students are able to maximize their potential. This is where institutions can make an important connection to the Universal Design for Learning (UDL) framework, where institutions proactively plan for and eliminate barriers to learning as opposed to merely responding to them.

HEFCE undertook a detailed analysis on differential outcomes in degree level attainment for certain groups within HE. The analysis took into account factors that impact on attainment, such as those outlined previously, and then looked at achievement. It is clear from this analysis that students from different backgrounds achieve at differential levels. The research (Higher Education Funding Council for England, 2015) shows that:

- Part time students do less well than full time students;
- White graduates are more likely to achieve better degrees than Black, Asian and Minority Ethnic (BAME) students;
- Graduates from the highest participation areas have the highest degree outcomes compared with graduates from other areas;
- State school graduates tend to achieve higher than independent school graduates with the same prior educational attainment;
- Graduates with disabilities tend to achieve slightly less well than those without reported disabilities.

It is the case that disabled students that are in receipt of DSA do better than those without, but that in itself does not necessarily mean that the DSA is the reason for their comparative success; it may be linked to a number of issues. It is also clear that if the key outcome is one of employability to enable greater social mobility, then again there are differential outcomes. In this instance, the situation is reversed with disabled students not in receipt of DSA doing better than those with it (Figure 2.4).

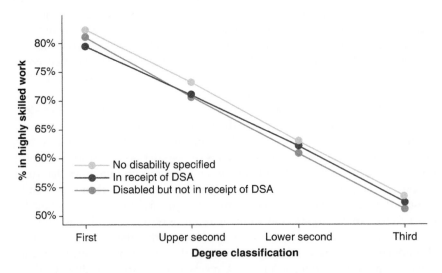

Figure 2.4 Employment outcomes six months after leaving HE, by disability status and degree classification

Source: Taken from Office for Students (2018)

Similarly, there are differences with respect to student satisfaction, with disabled students being less satisfied, particularly with course organization and management. The 2017 National Student Survey shows an average overall NSS satisfaction rate for those with a disability of 75.8%, compared to 84.2% for all student (Ipsos MORI, Office for Students, 2017).

The evidence is showing how the HE system is replicating rather than transforming society. It suggests that rather than universities acting as the catalysts for change and agents of social mobility in respect of disability, they instead mirror society. Irrespective of the legislative duty on universities through the Equality Act 2010, their role in our society requires them to address the moral and social demand for a more inclusive society. Put bluntly, disabled students with the same qualification base on entry to the degree course were not performing as well as students without a disability, they were less satisfied and were less likely to achieve high quality employability outcomes. This raises key questions both about the current support models and the approach of universities to learning and teaching. The evidence of differential outcomes across the sector makes a compelling case for change and highlights the need for urgent review of approaches and practice.

Reflection

- Consider how, at a national level, the focus on student voice (as exemplified for instance in the UK's National Student Survey), has impacted wider policy developments in access and participation.
- Consider the possible reasons for the significant increase in declarations of mental health problems between 2008/09 and 2016/17. What might the implications be for learning and teaching?

From medical to social models

The analysis of degree outcomes suggests that the DSA has a positive impact for those students in receipt of it. However, it has essentially become a deficit model within higher education as it provides support to be added on for the student according to their particular needs. This is effectively saying that in order for a disabled student to succeed, universities have to provide extra support, rather than simply ensuring that the curriculum and pedagogical approach enables success. The greater the focus on empowering learners as part of the process, the greater the engagement and achievement will be for all. In respect of disabled students, this was explicitly recognized in the Tomlinson Report (1997) into Special Educational Needs in the further education sector, when Tomlinson defined inclusive learning as 'the greatest degree of fit between the learner's requirements and the provision that is made for them'.

Although Tomlinson was reviewing provision for disabled students, it is clear that his model of inclusive education is one that can equally apply to all students in higher education. This is the basis of the social model and where UDL can be applied. It requires a shift from the deficit (or medical) model, wherein the student is regarded as requiring extra support to fit with the system, to the social model which values inclusivity and understands that the system needs to change to fit with the diversity of the student body. Universities in the United Kingdom have a statutory responsibility under the Equality Act (2010) to comply with legislation on the public sector duty:

> Having due regard to the need to advance equality of opportunity between persons who share a relevant protected characteristic and persons who do not share it involves having due regard, in particular, to the need to [. . .] take steps to meet the needs of persons who share a relevant protected characteristic that are different from the needs of persons who do not share it.
> (Legislation.gov.uk, 2010)

This built on earlier provision, the Disability Discrimination Act (1995), and the new position is that the legal duty is anticipatory by nature which makes it an invaluable tool for planning. As such, Universities need to be able to support all students and, for many of the support issues, they can make anticipatory adjustments in advance. It is this change that creates the next catalyst for change in respect of inclusive education and where UDL comes into play. While disabled student support centers fulfilled a really positive role in terms of the support they provided to students, they typically were not in a strategic position to influence culture change more broadly within the university. So, while they would be able to ensure that note-takers were available for students or that assessments were re-worded to make them more understandable for a particular student, they were not in a position to influence general practice around learning and teaching. It was in this way that the DSA, through its focus on specific needs of individuals, unintentionally contributed to a deficit model of provision and support for disabled students. It did not enable or encourage the development of inclusive practice but, rather, allowed for the provision of services to individuals. It often takes a shock to the system to generate change and, whilst that change may or may not be beneficial, it will take time to fully understand. Change though will also bring opportunity and it is important that we focus both on changes and also any opportunity that arises from it.

In 2015/16, the English Government announced a review of the DSA. From the Government perspective, it had become a blank check with escalating payments to individuals and institutions with legitimate claims for financial support. Institutions had generally established disabled student support centers in departments of Student Services, who would coordinate claims, negotiate support "contracts" with faculty staff and estates, as well as providing support. Often the budget for such work came from the DSA claims and the disabled student support center managed this whole process. So, when a consultation (Department for Business, Innovation and Skills, 2015) came out from the Department for Business, Innovation and Skills (BIS) proposing radical change and a reduction in what could be claimed, there was an outcry. It was seen as an attack on disabled students and as a challenge to inclusivity.

It was only after the initial outcry that the university sector was able to reflect and focus on the nature of the proposals. The new DSA guidance and regulation continued to support specific types of disabled student support but moved the agenda of inclusive education to, where it fundamentally belongs, within universities. The social model of disability suggests that someone's "disability" is caused by the way society is organized, rather than by an individual's difference, and it looks at ways of removing barriers that restrict life choices for all. This model finds that when barriers are removed, disabled people can be independent and equal in society, with choice and control over their own lives (Oliver, 2013). It does raise questions about the DSA approach. The social model refers to the barriers that we as a society have put in place that make life more difficult for disabled students, ranging from stairs, height of door handles, print font size, etc. Essentially, like Tomlinson before it, the new DSA position challenges universities within the UK.

The reliance on the DSA for funded individual support means that changes in pedagogy, curriculum design and teaching approaches have not really been addressed in order to address the diversity of our students. Universities have simply relied on the DSA to support students through our model. If we broadened the social model away from a focus on disability to being generally more inclusive, we can see opportunities for more accessible higher education and to bring UDL to the forefront of curriculum change. The argument for inclusivity can be likened to a choice: either a student joins "our club", or we seek to make the club more appropriate to include everyone. The consequences of the former can be seen from the case study at the outset of this chapter.

Significant research has been undertaken into the reasons behind differential outcomes for students and this has led to the development of curriculum and learner support frameworks in Figure 2.5. One major model was constructed by Cousins and Cureton following their research into the BAME attainment gap (Cousin & Cureton, 2012). This model was then adapted through further work commissioned by HEFCE.

Although Cousins and Cureton's work focused on the BAME attainment gap, the issues are much more widely applicable. The key to this argument is that it shifts the agenda from supporting an individual student through a process to one that enhances the support for all students. Table 2.1 lists and comments on specific initiatives that can be achieved as a way of moving towards greater inclusivity. By adopting some of the approaches included, the bottom segment in the HE 'Triangle Model' for supporting disabled students (shown later in this chapter) will change as universities will be more inclusive.

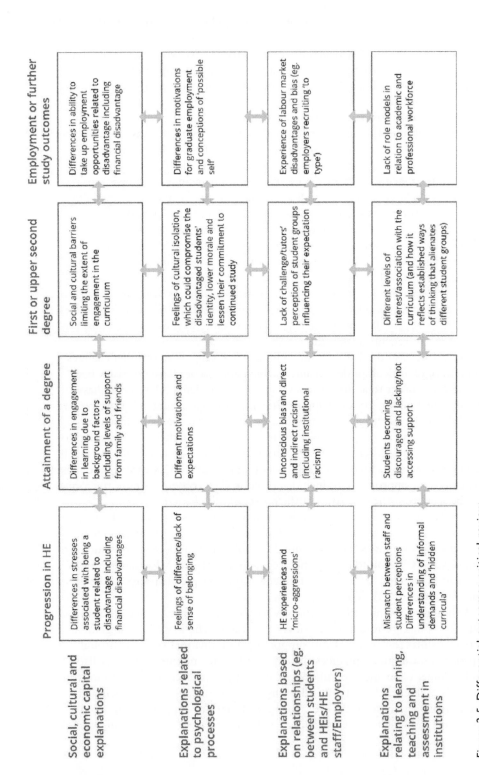

Figure 2.5 Differential outcomes critical review

Source: Taken from Mountford-Zimdars et al. (2015, p. 29)

Table 2.1 Key institutional strategies for widening participation

Current	Issue	Task	Benefits
For British Sign Language (BSL) users, assessment briefs are looked at on an individual basis for clarity.	Specialist intervention, which benefits the individual.	Staff development for all teaching staff on designing accessible, clear assessment briefs; Working with Deaf students; Using effective teaching and learning software.	All students.
For Specific Learning Difficulty (SpLD) students, laptops with specialist software are provided.	Specialist intervention, which benefits the individual and individual learning.	Place the software on open access PCs; Encourage students to tell staff what helps/hinders and adjust practice accordingly.	Students can work anywhere on-campus and more easily in group work; Students have agency in their own learning.
Feedback on assessment is generally variable.	Standardized and structured feedback.	Develop format with students; Create staff development program; Empower students to influence assessment.	All students.
Students could perform better in assessments.	Develop a curriculum that enables negotiated assessment activities.	Liaise with teaching staff and Professional, Statutory and Regulatory Bodies (PSRBs); Encourage use of negotiated assessments.	All students.
Depending on the disability, a student can record taught content using a Dictaphone recording app.	Specialist intervention that benefits an individual.	Embed lecture capture using agreed recording principles for staff and students.	All students have greater access to materials.

Addressing learner needs

There will still be a need for certain specialist support, British Sign Language interpreters, Braille materials, etc. but the focus for students shifts and is more about encouraging the success of all students, whether or not they are disabled. Or, if we look at it from a slightly different perspective, we can focus on the institution and how it needs to address the issue of students having a disability. Figure 2.6 seeks to show a pyramid of how universities need to address the issue of reasonable adjustment, with an indication of the scale of the progress towards greater inclusivity.

In this approach, the issue of inclusivity is addressed and, by strategically seeking to position the university within the broad inclusive approach, there is a reduced need to invest in specialist support as it seeks to address the needs of all students. The intention would be to grow the size of the bottom section which then demonstrates how the university is changing. In respect of disabled students, it is reasonably easy to predict that a number of students will have a Specific Learning Difference (SpLD) and that, instead of purchasing specific software for them, it is better for all simply to install that software on a range of open access PCs. The same principle applies to lecture capture technology. Rather than introducing only specific individual support, the university could invest in lecture capture so that all students have access to a recording of the lecture. Lecture capture often doesn't need to be interpreted and, in today's digital society, it is readily accessible; however more still needs to be done to produce text-based versions of the "lecture" as well as aural. Another example is the impact of the development of virtual learning environments (VLEs). Hardly in common usage 20 years ago, today they are the norm and students

Figure 2.6 The HE 'Triangle Model' for supporting disabled students

Source: Taken from Department for Education (2017, p. 16)

heavily rely on them for access to materials, chatrooms and support groups, etc. The impact that this approach has is that the bottom segment of the pyramid will increase in size as more needs are being met and the top segment will get smaller.

So, if we return to the Tomlinson perspective, we see that inclusive practice recognizes the diversity of students and enables all students to access content, participate fully and demonstrate their knowledge and strengths. This is where UDL comes to the forefront. It enables curriculum teams to focus on the needs of the learner, whatever their background, and to open up both the curriculum and the learning experience and opportunity. This requires building on some of the excellent innovative practice and rolling it out in a holistic manner across the institution. It is about re-thinking teaching, learning and assessment in terms of widening participation, rather than only additional support.

In respect of disabled students, there will always be a need to embed anticipatory reasonable adjustments and to ensure that some students receive additional support. The key however will be the development of a more independent learner. UDL principles then come into play with the design of the whole learning experience.

Reflection

- How can universities seek to change pedagogical culture through collaborative inter-departmental working practices?
- Consider how the social model of disability can be applied to the university sector to implement UDL effectively.
- What measures can be taken to introduce UDL for the benefit of all students, in addition to those suggested in the 'Addressing Learner Needs' table?

Conclusion and key concepts

By adapting the principles of inclusivity and implementing UDL, universities will change as will society. We should see increased staff awareness and training on how to support all learners with whatever issues they present. There may be a decrease in the number of students declaring a disability as the inclusive approach changes the need for support. It is important to recognize that the support needs will still be there but the inclusive UDL approach has minimized the need for specific individual support interventions. So conversely, success will be measured by reducing the numbers of students who are having additional support because it has been primarily mainstreamed.

This chapter has looked at a number of concepts. It has explained the historical base of university education, in which the individual has a major responsibility for their own learning. This is what is meant by the old adage of "reading for a degree" and, whilst the philosophy has moved on, often the services and approaches have not fully caught up with the change.

A second key concept is the importance to society of the issue of social mobility and that opening up higher education to individuals from differing backgrounds and moving away from homogeneity raises challenges. This means that university education has to change to reflect the needs of the learner.

A third key concept is the impact that a sudden change can have to create opportunity. The restructure and refocusing of the Disabled Student Allowance created shockwaves but that change has created the framework in which universities can look to change and provide the impetus for that change. Finally, this chapter has explained the concept of inclusive education and how it aligns with UDL as a framework in which the individual is able to be supported and to succeed.

References

Blair, T. (1996). *Labour Leader's Speech*. Blackpool, UK.

Cousin, G., & Cureton, D. (2012). *Disparities in Student Attainment (DISA)*. York: The Higher Education Academy.

Crosland, A. (1966). *A Plan for Polytechnics and Other Colleges*. London: Her Majesty's Stationery Office.

Department for Business, Innovation and Skills (2015). *Consultation on Targeting Funding for Disabled Students in Higher Education from 2016/17 Onwards*. London: Department for Business, Innovation and Skills.

Department for Education (2017). *Inclusive Teaching and Learning in Higher Education as a Route to Excellence*. London: Department for Education.

Department of Employment, Education and Training (1990). *A Fair Chance for All*. Canberra: Australian Government Publishing Service.

HESA (2018). Student Record, 2008–2017. Retrieved 20th August 2018 from www.hesa.ac.uk/collection/c16051

Higher Education Funding Council for England (1995). An HEFCE Report on the 1993–94 special initiative to encourage widening participation for students with special needs. Retrieved from www.hefce.ac.uk/pubs/hefce/1995/m2_95.htm

Higher Education Funding Council for England (2001a). *Strategies for Widening Participation in Higher Education: A Guide to Good Practice, Circular 01 / 36a*. Bristol: HEFCE.

Higher Education Funding Council for England (2001b). *Strategies for Learning and Teaching in Higher Education: A Guide to Good Practice, Circular 01 / 37*. Bristol: HEFCE.

Higher Education Funding Council for England (2015). *Differences in Degree Outcomes: The Effect of Subject and Student Characteristics, Circular 15/21*. Bristol: HEFCE.

Higher Education Funding Council for England (2017). Annual funding allocations for 2015–16. Retrieved from www.hefce.ac.uk/funding/annallocns/1516/lt/

Ipsos MORI, Office for Students (2017). National student survey 2017.

Legislation.gov.uk. (2010). *Equality Act 2010.* Retrieved from http://www. legislation.gov.uk/ukpga/2010/15/contents

Office for Students (2018). Differences in student outcomes. Retrieved from www. officeforstudents.org.uk/data-and-analysis/differences-in-student-outcomes/ disability/

Oliver, Mike. (2013). The social model of disability: Thirty years on. *Disability & Society,* 28:7, 1024–1026. DOI: 10.1080/09687599.2013.818773

Mountford-Zimdars, A., Sabri, D., Moore, J., Sanders, J., Jones, S., & Higham, L. (2015). *Causes of Differences in Student Outcomes: Report to HEFCE by King's College London, ARC Network and the University of Manchester.* Bristol: Higher Education Funding Council for England.

Robbins, L. (1963). *Report of the Committee on Higher Education.* London: Her Majesty's Stationery Office.

Tomlinson, J. (1997). Inclusive learning: The report of the committee of enquiry into the postschool education of those with learning difficulties and/or disabilities, in England, 1996. *European Journal of Special Needs Education,* 12:3, 184–196. DOI: 10.1080/0885625970120302

Trow, M. (1989). The Robbins trap: British attitudes and the limits of expansion. *Higher Education Quarterly,* 43:1, 55–75.

Willetts, D. (2013). *Robbins Revisited: Bigger and Better Higher Education.* London: The Social Market Foundation.

Williams, M., Pollard, E., Langley, J., Houghton, A., & Zozimo, J. (2017). *Models of Support for Students with Disabilities, Report to HEFCE.* Brighton: Institute for Employment Studies.

Wilson, H. (1963). *Labour's Plan for Science.* [Speech at the Labour Party Annual Conference]. London, UK: Victoria House Printing Company.

Chapter 3

Universal Design for Learning and strategic leadership

A whole university approach to inclusive practice

Abigail Moriarty and Phil Scarffe

Case study

The number of disabled students in HEIs in the UK has gradually increased with a notable rise in the proportion of individuals with mental health conditions and specific learning difficulties. De Montfort University (DMU) currently has 17% of its overall student population (23,000) with a declared disability. This is the third highest across all UK HEIs. Over recent years, funding models for supporting students with a disability have changed (Department for Business, Innovation and Skills, BIS, 2014), with the shift of responsibility moving towards the HEI provider and away from central Government. This move provided DMU with the opportunity to move away from a medical model and to embrace a real social model of student support. Where often the perceived 'problem' of being 'disabled' belongs with the individual rather than society disabling them.

The implementation of an institutional wide Universal Design for Learning (UDL) framework through a strategic change programme provided the basis for this reform. Moreover, UDL has been implemented for a wider student profile, and not just those with disabilities, this shift has enabled a truly universal institutional approach. UDL has become a critical foundational catalyst for change that enables a multifaceted approach. Academics and a diversity of professional services work in partnership to deliver a change process based on a 'middle-out' approach. Often in HEIs the middle managers have a particular position of knowledge and influence. They are close enough to the front line and have a critical understanding of operational realities and are also senior enough to have the trust and relationships with senior leaders. The key principle shared is that, by engaging effectively with middle managers in defining and deploying the UDL change, this change becomes dynamic and institutionally embedded, senior managers may still be involved, particularly in regards to sharing a strategic vision, but middle leaders and 'UDL champions' are given particular responsibility and authority to make the positive changes happen (Cummings et al. 2005).

Introduction

This chapter provides a rationale for English HEIs to seek more joined up and strategic approaches to mainstreaming of social perspectives and practices when it comes to inclusion. The chapter presents a comprehensive study of how De Montfort University (DMU) has strategically adopted a UDL approach to meet the demands of external change forces and to realise its own goals of providing an inclusive social and educational experience for all of its students. This approach relied upon a sensitivity to local considerations and was developed using the power of middle leadership to effect change.

The policy and legislative context of inclusion in English HE

Academics often claim that they either work to, or would like to work with a 'social model' of disability. A social model holds that disability is a consequence of individual and societal attitudes, and consequently the way in which organisations, such as HEIs, conduct their business. The Union of the Physically Impaired Against Segregation (UPIAS) was an early disability rights organisation in the United Kingdom. It established the principles that led to the development of the social model of disability, wherein a sharp distinction is made between impairment and disability, this approach gained academic credibility through the work of Finkelstein (1980), (Barnes, 1990) and more recently Oliver and Barnes (2011). The social model is often contrasted to a medical model as outlined by World Health Organisation (WHO) (1980) in the International Classification of Impairments, Disabilities and Handicaps (ICIDH). This identifies a person's health condition or impairment as 'the problem' and concentrates efforts on 'fixing' them (see Figure 3.1).

The criticism of the ICIDH (WHO, 1980) coupled with the emergence of the social model, prompted the WHO to commission a revised explanation of disability. The endorsed International Classification of Functioning, Disability and Health (WHO, 2002) resulted in a more holistic definition of disability (Ingstad cited in Albrecht, Seelman and Bury 2001). However, the UK Disability Discrimination Act (Legislation.gov.uk, 1995) amalgamated into the

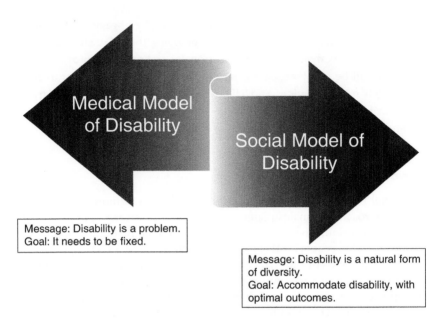

Message: Disability is a problem.
Goal: It needs to be fixed.

Message: Disability is a natural form of diversity.
Goal: Accommodate disability, with optimal outcomes.

Figure 3.1 Medical vs social model of disability

2010 Equality Act (Legislation.gov.uk 2010), continues to still **define** disability using a medical model framework; having conditions limiting a person's ability to carry out normal day-to-day activities. The Equality Act (Legislation.gov. uk, 2010) does codify the array of UK policy and regulations to mandate equal treatment in access to services, employment and education regardless of the nine protected characteristics, including disability (see Table 3.1).

In the case of disability, HEIs have a duty to make reasonable adjustments for disabled students to overcome barriers to their learning caused by their disability. The duty to make reasonable adjustments is not a minimalist requirement of simply ensuring that some access is available to disabled students; it is, so far as is reasonably practicable, to approximate the access enjoyed by disabled students to that enjoyed by the rest of the student body. The detail reflected in the technical guidance for further and higher education providers (Equality and Human Rights Commission, 2012), sets out the Act's requirements in relation to provision of education and access to benefits, facilities or services, both educational and non-educational. It is questionable to what extent the HEI sector has actively engaged with this guidance. Clearly many institutions have done a great deal in relation to disability, but whether any could realistically claim to have met their legal obligations is a moot point. The requirements certainly go significantly further than is commonly perceived, and in a sense, perhaps, that

Table 3.1 Protected characteristics identified under the Equality Act 2010

Age
Disability
Gender reassignment
Marriage and civil partnership
Pregnancy and maternity
Race
Religion or belief
Sex
Sexual orientation

should always be the case, there being little point to equality legislation if it does not go further than public understanding and attitudes.

As identified in the previous chapter by Layer, there have been significant changes in the ways that Disability Student Allowance has been awarded to students and this has had an impact on how universities are approaching planning for inclusion. In 2014–2015 DMU students received in the region of £13.2 million (GBP) a year of individual support funding from the DSA, but the changes to the system reduced this funding by around £5.2m per annum. This reduction covered, for example, note takers and non-specialist equipment. More disabled students are applying to universities and many are successful at DMU in their applications. According to Higher Education Statistical Agency (HESA) (2018) the national average of disabled students going to university in 2016–2017 equated to 12%, whereas DMU saw a steady increase to 17%, with some programmes reaching 56%. The 2016 DSA changes meant that most of the £5.2 million of funding which had been removed would now either have to be met by the institution, or alternatives found, in accordance with the Equality Act (Legislation.gov.uk, 2010). It is within this context that DMU adopted a two-year strategic programme of positive whole organisational change.

Reflection

•   How does the UK legislative context compare and contrast with developments in your area?

Moving from external dependence to internal autonomy

A measured approach was taken with DMU Senior Executive staff when discussing the ramifications of this funding shortfall on the student experience, highlighting this as a shared responsibility, rather than a loss of funding affecting just one part of the university. All decision-making with these key stakeholders was informed, which required detailed information on student satisfaction, financial implications and university reputation, but without any hyperbole or rhetoric. As such, a strategic programme of change to mitigate against a negative impact on the disabled student was employed across the institution.

A systemic whole university approach

It is important to note that DMU did not match the DSA funds on a like-for-like basis, but rather concentrated on a collaborative approach to the development of an inclusive student environment and curriculum through the purposeful adoption of UDL. This required a substantial focus on the advancement of inclusive teaching and learning practice, and this led to a holistic and organisational adoption and adaption of UDL principles and practices (Rose and Meyer, 2000, 2006). The UDL attribute of change management is just one part of a wider programme of change that came under the remit of an overarching and interrelated change processes entitled the Disability Enhancement Programme (DEP). This initiative consists of a number of project streams that complement the broader development of UDL; these are explored further in Table 3.2.

Comprehensive vs incremental university change

The following section provides an overview of the planned institutional UDL change process and its operationalisation. A senior management top-down

Table 3.2 Broader infrastructure that supported UDL developments

1 Institutional roll out of commonly used assistive software available for all. Examples include Inspiration and Mind Genius+; supported by the employment of an assistive software trainer for all students. This also involved installation of relevant equipment and software that is available for all students to access.
2 The library has a 'Click and Collect' service, and accessible format service and electronic resource lists. As well as remodelling some of the learning environment to provide more quiet spaces for disabled students to use.
3 The disability support service established a DSA assessment centre (DMU-CAN).
4 A 'helper' provision provided the less specialist aspects of student support. For example, assistance for student when accessing learning spaces and accommodation, such as carrying bag and equipment to classes.
5 Review of disabled student accommodation was undertaken. With quiet themed accommodation established aimed primarily at addressing some of the sensory issues that Autistic students report. In addition, this also benefits students with mental health conditions and other disabilities, where sleep and fatigue are an issue.

approach was avoided. To engage the 'hearts and minds' of staff and to sustain the ongoing development of UDL, change had to come from the staff itself.

The impetus to deliver a whole scale UDL curriculum was time sensitive; the pedagogic infrastructure needed to be completed in one academic year in readiness for students starting the university in 2016–2017. A 'slow burn' option was not available. The application of UDL at DMU was not another 'bolt on' initiative but rather viewed as the enactment of a set of principles guiding lecturers as they planned and delivered their teaching to students. Rather than retrofitting teaching for students via adjustments, special compensation and modifications, the principles of UDL prompt teachers to embed anticipatory adjustments in the design of curricula that is flexible, adaptable to multiple forms of engagement and therefore facilitates student learning. However, the distinct application of UDL at DMU differs from other UK HEIs. The principles of UDL **apply to all students** whether they have a distinct disability (Rose and Meyer 2000) or not. This initiative does not just focus on those 17% of students at DMU with disabilities. Instead, it built on the educational perspective that what is essential for some students is most likely to be beneficial for them all (Smith and Harvey, 2014). A UDL curricula serves a wide mix of learners, in fact the literature review from Al-Azawei et al. (2016) indicates that UDL based teaching and learning reduces barriers to learning for both 'abled' (itself a contentious term) and 'disabled' students.

The DMU-UDL project followed the Managing Successful Programmes (MSP) approach and governed by the PRINCE2 methodology (an acronym for PRojects IN Controlled Environments) over an 18-month period. PRINCE2 is a de facto process-based method for effective project management emphasising the division of a project into manageable and controllable stages (Kerzner, 2017). This very process driven approach supports the project leader as an academic Director of Teaching and Learning, rather than as a Project Manager. Ownership of the project takes place at multiple levels. The institutional adoption of UDL cuts across all stakeholders. It involves academic, professional services staff and the current and future student body. It is more than the application of a new 'policy' but a different way of working, teaching and learning for all involved, and it fundamentally shifted pedagogy of the institution and challenged the convention of many.

A top-down vs bottom-up change tactic was considered but the preference for wider impact attainment ultimately led to adoption of a 'middle-out' approach (Figure 3.2). According to Cummings et al. (2005) middle-out is a way of advocating, and most importantly delivering, strategic outcomes in HE. This requires senior management support with an appetite for transformation but with the engagement of individual staff members to champion and carry out the change. A full project team supported by six specialist work stream leads was overseen by a hierarchy of governance.

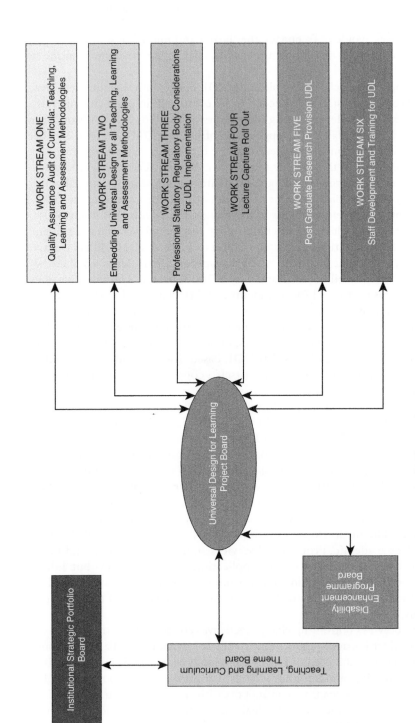

Figure 3.2 The middle-out way to institutional UDL development

Source: Cummings et al. (2005)

Reflection

- What are the characteristics of a successful top-down approach to HE strategic change and then think about a bottom up?
- Reflect on your own experience of a top-down diktat for change that has not been successful. Identify reasons why this was not successful.

All of the groups identified here worked collaboratively but some had work to do before others could follow. The work streams were dependant on the institution's philosophical understanding and operational commitment to what UDL meant for the university. Uprooting a framework broadly based and developed in the USA (Rose and Meyer 2000) into a UK university without consultation would have been perceived as something being done *to staff* rather than *with the staff.* The institution endorsed a 'DMU UDL position statement' that incorporated, but also contextualised to our own setting, the key elements of multi-model student representation, engagement and expression from the original CAST (2011) guidance. This adapted approach made it more 'home grown' and as such staff saw their own teaching within a resulting framework that positively influenced staff engagement for early adoption. The individual work streams identified here are further discussed in the forthcoming sub sections.

Work stream I – quality assurance audit of curricula: teaching, learning and assessment methodologies

The quality assurance audit involved a systematic modular level review of the entire curriculum against the agreed DMU UDL position statement. This process identified areas for teaching, learning and assessment enhancement to meet the UDL expectations through an appropriate module modification. Some of these developments were minor and did not go through the university teaching quality assurance requirements. For example, the inclusion of alternative teaching methods to deliver the module content in a more diverse way complemented existing practice. Whereas other changes were deemed to be more substantial and therefore they required a full module modification in accordance to the revised UK Quality Code for Higher Education (UK Standing Committee for Quality Assessment 2018). The revised UK quality code is the cornerstone of quality in UK HE; focusing on improved accessibility and a guarantee of regulatory fitness for purpose protecting the public and student interest.

All of the modules at the university were involved in the audit ($n - 2000$ modules) and audit events were overseen by Faculty leads of Teaching Quality to ensure due process and rigour. Most of the substantive changes concentrated on the development of a more diverse assessment methodology, moving away from the end of year examination to incremental assessment points using innovative approaches. This was a retrospective audit of existing curricula. To sustain ongoing scrutiny, this work stream instigated a UDL theme into all future quality assurance processes, teaching enhancements and external reviews.

Reflection

- If you conducted a UDL audit of your own teaching, what would be the strengths, and what would be the area of requiring development?

Work stream 2 – embedding universal design for all teaching, learning and assessment methodologies

The audit of the DMU curriculum not only identified areas of pedagogic development for UDL, but it also acknowledged existing good practice. This was vital in sustaining the ongoing enhancement to teaching practice. Many subject areas already identified with the UDL framework expectations; *'it's just what I do'* they would say. However, CAST (2018) strongly advocate that UDL is not something that one 'does'. It is a framework for viewing teaching and learning practices so learners have options and choices to challenge themselves and provide the opportunity to develop as an autonomous learner. To move towards this proactive approach with academic staff, six UDL Champions were appointed across the institution. They supported and further developed UDL practice and promoted existing scholastic innovation. Hargreaves and Ainscow (2015) have identified the pivotal role that such 'middle leaders' play in championing innovation and being the early adopters for inclusive change for their own teaching – which subsequently influences the practice of others. All of the UDL Champions shared common traits of enthusiasm, passion and sense of collegiate belief in UDL.

Work stream 3 – professional statutory regulatory body (PSRBs) considerations for UDL implementation

DMU has a strong relationship with many PSRBs; these are a diverse group of professional and employer bodies, regulators and those with statutory authority over a profession or group of professionals. PSRBs engage with HEIs to accredit courses that meet professional standards. Examples of PSRBs are the General Medical Council, the Architects Registration Board and the British Association of Art Therapists.

This working group explored suggestions from PSRBs that might have been perceived to inhibit UDL adoption. However, despite some academics in these subject areas identifying PSRB barriers, further scrutiny acknowledged any such interpretations of the professional perquisites were a legacy interpretation by the staff themselves rather than from any statue. For example, a PSRB expectation for '*an examination of student knowledge*' had historically been interpreted to mean students had to sit a single unseen exam at the end of a module to demonstrate their understanding. This assessment method would only have the 'normed' student in mind and would not consider the diverse needs of all students. Whereas allowing the student to gain ongoing summative feedback before a final formative assessment is an iterative feedback and feedforward loop and fulfils the PSRB expectation for '*the examination of student knowledge*'.

Reflection

- Are there professional bodies such as PSRBs that provide partnership arrangements within your university? How might their role hinder or advance the adoption of a UDL approach in your setting?

Work stream 4 – lecture capture roll out as DMU replay

In recent years, web-based technologies to support teaching and learning have increasingly been used in HE. One widely used method is the recording of staff lectures delivered during face-to-face teaching which can be subsequently reviewed online by students (O'Callaghan et al., 2017). The institution rolled out this system as 'DMU Replay', using Panopto as a video content management system for uploading, managing and sharing video and audio files with students on their Virtual Learning Environment (VLE). DMU provided all students with anytime access to audio and/or visual material that lecturers recorded before, during or after a taught session. Significant capital funding enabled all teaching spaces to be equipped with recording equipment along with the deployment of multiple servers and on-site storage.

Of all of the UDL initiatives at DMU, the development of DMU Replay was by far the most contentious with academics but one with the most positive impact on students. The university already had an *opt-in* approach where staff could choose to record their teaching sessions and share them with their students; this was primarily used for modules with a blended learning approach. The university policy to mandate the use of DMU Replay from 2017 for all 'staff led teaching' was a much firmer strategic approach but this clearly showed leadership commitment to adopting a whole organisational UDL approach. The DMU Replay policy outlined the capture of staff audio and the screen-capture of slides as a minimum threshold. Disabled students have made audio recordings of classes for years and many have had personal scribes to take notes in these sessions. The impact of the DSA funding changes at DMU were mainly around individual support arrangements for the students with learning differences. This was the provision of note takers and non-medical helpers for students that equated to a large proportion of the £5.2 million shortfall. The investment in DMU Replay significantly mitigated against this and has multiple recognised benefits for all students as reflected in Table 3.3.

Some concerns were raised by academics on the use of DMU Replay, such as its potential to negatively impact upon student attendance and engagement, and restricting the style and structure of lectures. The producers of the DMU Replay policy developed interventions to overcome these perceived barriers and worked closely with academics and students to understand their concerns. An institutional definition of 'staff led' teaching was agreed. Using the centralised timetabling process, these sessions were captured on DMU Replay. Predominantly, 'staff led teaching' consisted of large group sessions conforming to a traditional 'lecture style' approach, but it did not preclude the use of DMU Replay for demonstrations, seminars or tutorials. It was left to individual academic judgement to determine the appropriateness of capturing other non-staff led approaches. The policy encouraged students to identify to staff if they wanted the recording to be paused so they could contribute to the session without being recorded; the term 'in confidence' was to be used by students and signs in all teaching spaces instructed this. In the 18 months since the DMU Replay policy has been in place, no students have used this opt out preference. Equally, there is not an obvious impact on student attendance, students do not attend classes for a variety of reasons and is not dependent on whether DMU Replay is used or not. Furthermore, Nashash and Gunn (2013) indicate that the availability of recordings does not encourage students to miss classes and not attend.

Some staff still held firm opinions that the use of DMU Replay would negatively affect their teaching performance and, as such, the policy built in the option for staff to use an agreed 'equitable alternative' to DMU Replay. This enabled staff to use alternative forms of audio and screen-capture strategies for staff led teaching sessions but not via the Panopto platform. To date colleagues have not availed of this option primarily due to the additional timing and resource implications. However, this staff option remains available for those

Table 3.3 The benefits of lecture capture technology for students (Based on Newcombe, 2017)

- Re-visit subjects closer to assessment points to support revision
- Catch up with missed sessions
- Re-visit complex ideas and concepts
- Allow student to work at their own pace and take control of their own learning
- Support students for whom English is a second language
- Support students who have a wide range of accessibility needs
- Provides flexibility and reassurance for students who, for example, are carers and may not be able to get to lectures all of the time

who do not wish to make use of DMU Replay. To support the use of the DMU Replay service, 1,000 academic staff members attended DMU Replay technical training and had access to staff help guides and videos available online. This was further supported by the availability of roaming helpers that offered hands on support in the classrooms for academic staff when first using the technology.

Reflection

- How might the benefits of recording lectures be best shared with academic colleagues who are resistant to such approaches?
- If you had all of these colleagues supporting the innovative use of such technologies, how would you persuade senior staff to fund an institutional wide initiative?

Work stream 5 – postgraduate research provision and UDL

The audit to establish current UDL practice at DMU involved both undergraduate and postgraduate modules and resulted in significant module modifications and development. The postgraduate research provision was managed through a separate work stream via the university graduate office. It involved scrutiny of how PhD supervision was conducted and how the DMU UDL position could be further enhanced. As such, changes were adopted in the supervision and assessment of PhD students. For example, the development of a low sensory environment for Viva examinations and the standard audio recording and sharing of notes from supervision sessions.

Work stream 6 – staff development and support for UDL

Traditionally, university lecturers have undergone little or no formal preparation for their role as teachers. They are recruited for their subject expertise and research scholarship. The HESA and the Higher Education Academy (HEA) (2016) published sector-level data on academic teaching qualifications in HEIs. In England 36% of staff has no academic teaching qualifications; therefore, over a third of university teachers are not taught 'how' to teach. This does not mean they are not accomplished teachers, but there may be gaps in any underpinning conceptual principles that would support a differentiated approach to student learning such as the enabling framework provided by UDL. There was an organisational recognition that in order to strengthen the pedagogical principles and practices of UDL it was vitally important to focus upon enabling colleagues' access to requisite knowledge, skills and values professional development. A focus on the core professional capabilities of all colleagues was also reinforced by changing external policy factors.

The introduction of the UK Teaching Excellence and Student Outcomes Framework (TEF) (HEFCE 2017a), which used a series of proxy measures to make judgements about the recognition of high quality teaching became an important consideration for all UK based HEIs. For years, it has been suggested that in many UK HEIs teaching has been less valued than research (Cadez et al., 2017). The TEF aims to address this issue and to make teaching and research, in universities, of equal status and to provide students with better information on teaching standards. The TEF awards for teaching excellence are Gold, Silver and then the lowest, Bronze (HEFCE, 2017a). The TEF (HEFCE, 2017a) uses results from 'Teaching on my course' (questions 1–4) and 'Assessment and feedback' (questions 8–11) of the National Student Survey (NSS, 2017), a UK wide annual student satisfaction questionnaire. The results to these questions are the student perceptions of *'quality teaching'*, and Davies et al. (2012) does question student ability and awareness to determine the quality of university teaching. Students indicate they want to be taught by staff who are enthusiastic and knowledgeable about their subject, empathetic, approachable, helpful and patient, and encourage students to develop their full potential (Bradley et al., 2014). All teachers will support these sentiments, however there is an ongoing discourse among academics regarding the ways in which teaching quality might be most effectively identified and shared, for example as reflected in discussions about the TEF, which is open to a myriad of interpretations (Land and Gordon 2015). Does a gold, silver or bronze award, mimicking the Olympics, truly reflect teaching excellence in HEIs? Wood and Su (2017) indicates this dialogue is empty rhetoric for teaching practice. However, despite the contentious nature of discourse surrounding TEF, it is clear that it has sharpened the minds of educational leaders within HEIs especially regarding the nature of what might constitute quality learning and teaching and how such 'quality' might be strengthened through further professional development.

For senior colleagues at DMU the fundamental principle was to develop a shared collegiate understanding of UDL amongst academic and professional service staff, and this could be synthesised as quite simply, the 'what, why and how' of UDL. This was the foundation stone of developing the pedagogy and enhanced teaching practice across the institution. There were no assumptions that staff already knew about UDL or they had already necessarily welcomed the introduction of UDL into their working lives.

The first area of change was to ensure UDL was evident throughout the in-house academic staff development offering. All existing staff learning opportunities were revised and relaunched with an obvious UDL stamp and feel. Staff were undergoing a UDL learning experience without even realising it because it had become part of the university's DNA. Furthermore, the areas of UDL teaching practice identified in the original curriculum review were packaged and made available as bitesize online resources for staff to use as exemplars. Also, as exemplified here, they were used to accompany a pathway of mandatory sessions for all academic staff:

i   *An introduction into Universal Design for Learning* – These were com-
     posed of small group sessions as well as an on-line interactive session, which
     provided the fundamentals of UDL at DMU.

ii   *Developing your UDL practice* – This required staff to bring a sample or
     exemplar from their practices constituting of a single learning opportunity,
     a module or even a whole programme of study. A UDL lens was used to
     interrogate the example provided to demonstrate how it could move along
     the UDL continuum of multi-modal approaches in student representation,
     engagement and expression (CAST, 2018). This focused on operational
     change and development rather than full scale repositioning of conceptual
     pedagogy. It detailed practical steps staff could make to develop their UDL
     practice in the short and medium term.

iii *DMU Replay* – This introduced a high-level introduction to the use of the
     DMU Replay software to enable practices that support multi-modal peda-
     gogies of UDL. This professional development session has a clear academic
     and technology focus. It included functional instructions on how to use
     the software but also focused on broader issues of Intellectual Property and
     Copyright. This session led onto more advanced DMU Replay develop-
     ment. Including 'basic to advanced editing', 'recording at your desk' and
     'using voting technology in class'. These clearly aligned to CAST (2018)
     UDL Guidelines (1.1) in offering ways of customising the display of infor-
     mation for students.

Alongside this activity was a coordinated and high profile institutional launch
on UDL involving:

- what this meant strategically and operationally to DMU along with its
  ongoing commitment
- why the university has decided to go down this path and the implications
  for staff and students
- ongoing staff support with pedagogy when adopting UDL as well as the
  recognition that many staff were already 'UDL*able*'
- the investment technology would receive to enable UDL developments.

All of the UDL staff development activities at the university aligned with the
UK Professional Standards Framework (UKPSF) for teaching and supporting
learning in HE. The UKPSF is a nationally recognised framework for benchmarking teaching and learning support to drive improvement in, and raising
the profile of, learning and teaching in HE. The DMU process for staff to gain
UKPSF recognition involved an evidencing of how UDL was reflected in their
own teaching practice. As acknowledged earlier, a substantial proportion of
academics in HE, and at DMU, did not have a recognised teaching qualification and HEFCE are supporting the publication of staff teaching qualifications
for review by prospective and existing students. Undergraduate students in the

UK have rights as a consumer from their university as outlined by the Competition and Markets Authority (CMA, 2015). As such all HEIs have to provide all students with clear and transparent information on course content, delivery and assessment, including academic staff teaching and learning qualifications such as UKPSF accreditation.

Furthermore, a new Postgraduate Certificate for Learning and Teaching in Higher Education (PCLTHE) was developed and aimed at all new or early career lecturers and teaching staff who had less than three years full-time teaching experience at DMU. This resulted in a 60-credit programme, entirely delivered through UDL teaching examples, using multi-disciplinary and interactive workshops to reflect experience of work-based practice. Individual academic supervision supported participants to reflect on their own teaching and further UDL development. The UKPSF and PCLTHE are both recognised teaching qualifications submitted to HESA, a UK Government department, on an annual basis. HEIs have a statutory requirement to report data to the HESA on students, staff and graduates as well as academic departments and course outcomes. This multi-tiered approach in developing staff knowledge, understanding and therefore practice is a long-term commitment to UDL and continues in the institution today.

Reflection

- How can you engage staff in UDL staff development opportunities?
- Reflect on your own most recent staff development activity. As a participant how, compatible was this experience to the UDL Guidelines? Guidelines can be accessed at http://udlguidelines.cast.org/

Conclusion: the impact of UDL at DMU

The true ambitions for UDL at this institution are reflected within the adapted maturity model (Fixsen et al., 2009; CAST, 2011) (see Figure 3.3). The 'explorative', 'prepare' to current 'integration' stage has been achieved to some extent through this project. However, there are still areas of prospective UDL developments that require up scaling to achieve optimum sector impact.

Further work is required to identify the broader pedagogic influence on student experience and educational outcomes such as continuation and attainment, nevertheless there is strong anecdotal evidence that in the 18 months since the UDL project began the university has managed to make a significant impact on student learning and on collegiate professional capacity. Organisationally, there has been a relatively effective transition from relying on DSA funding to providing for an anticipatory inclusive programme for all students. Academic and support staff continue to inform their inclusive practices by accessing ongoing professional enhancement and by engaging in research in the field of UDL.

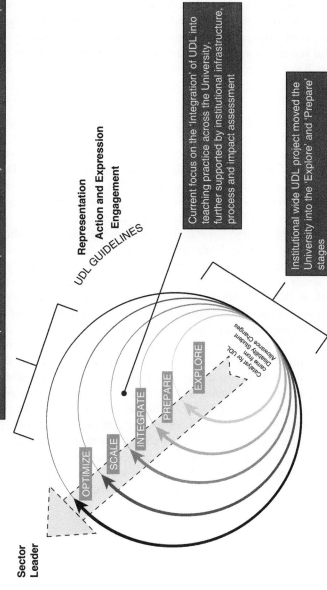

To 'Scale' and 'Optimize' UDL requires the University to Influence wider UK sector adoption

Representation
Action and Expression
Engagement

UDL GUIDELINES

Current focus on the 'Integration' of UDL into teaching practice across the University, further supported by institutional infrastructure, process and impact assessment

Institutional wide UDL project moved the University into the 'Explore' and 'Prepare' stages

Sector Leader

OPTIMIZE

SCALE

INTEGRATE

PREPARE

EXPLORE

Catalyst for UDL came from Student Disability Allowance Changes

Fixsen et al. (2009) & National Center on Universal Design for learning (2011)

Figure 3.3 Fixsen graphic

Reflection

- DMU has used UDL as a truly universal approach to teaching and learning and not just for these students with disabilities. How could this 'universal' approach be adopted within for own organisation?
- Map out the necessary work streams you would require to adopt this 'universal' institutional method, see Figure 3.2 to give you a few ideas.

This chapter has outlined the 'big bang' approach to institutional adoption of UDL, a locally adopted UDL framework was developed to underpin inclusive practice for the whole student cohort and not just to those students with disabilities. This approach exemplifies the true 'universality' of UDL, as the whole university community benefits and also has been shared as UK sector good practice in Institute for Public Policy Research (2017) and Institute for Employability Studies (2017). The institutional strategic development of UDL was not a 'fad academic project', it required a true partnership throughout the university community, with academics and professional services staff working collaboratively together. In order to achieve that systemic focus, vision and support from senior leadership has been a critical ingredient leading to the success of UDL at DMU. A clear leadership commitment was made to the pedagogy and support for the UDL developments. Additionally, the use of local discipline based 'champions' and middle leaders to advance an understanding and practice of UDL provided a strong foundation upon which to build a collaborative approach to curriculum and pedagogy change management. This middle-out, rather than top-down or bottom up, approach to educational change was effective in the planning and monitoring of progress. The role of technology also proved a powerful tool to advance complementary attributes of inclusive teaching practice. Taken together, the differing strands of UDL all combined in complex and interweaving ways to ensure that a systemic rather than individualised approach to inclusive practice continues to inform organisational culture and practice. Ultimately, such efforts provide promise to transform the lives of those who now have access to the means of evidencing their learning potentials.

References

Al-Azawei, A., Serenelli, F. and Lundqvist, K. (2016) Universal design for learning: A content analysis of peer reviewed journal papers from 2012–2015, *Journal of the Scholarship of Teaching and Learning*, 16 (3), 39–56.

Barnes, C. (1990) *Cabbage Syndrome: The Social Construction of Dependence*, London, The Falmer Press.

Bradley, S., Kirby, E. and Madriaga, M. (2014) What students value as inspirational and transformative teaching, *Innovations in Education and Teaching International*, 52 (3), 231–242. DOI: 10.1080/14703297.2014.880363

Cadez, S., Dimovski, V. and Groff, M. Z. (2017) Research, teaching and performance evaluation in academia: The salience of quality, *Journal of Studies in Higher Education*, 42 (8), 1455–1473.

CAST (2011) *UDL Guidelines 2*. [On-Line] www.udlcenter.org/aboutudl/udlguidelines/downloads [Retrieved 21 December 2017].

CAST (2018) *Universal Design for Learning Guidelines Version 2*. [On-Line] www.cast.org/our-work/about-udl.html#.Wvh0WoWcGhc [Retrieved 21 March 2018].

Competition and Markets Authority (2015) *Higher Education: Short Guide to Consumer Rights for Students*. [On-Line] www.gov.uk/government/publications/higher-education-a-short-guide-to-consumer-rights-for-students [Retrieved 21 March 2018].

Cummings, R., Philips, R., Tilbrook, R. and Lowe, R. (2005) Middle-Out Approaches to Reform of University Teaching and Learning: Champions striding between the "top-down" and "bottom-up" approaches, *International Review of Research in Open and Distance* Learning, 6 (1). ISSN: 1492–3831.

Davies, R. A., Hope, M. J. and Robertson, A. D. (2012) *Student-Led Teaching Awards,* York, Higher Education Academy.

Department for Business, Innovation and Skills (2014) Higher education: Student support: changes to Disabled Students' Allowances (DSA) Written Ministerial Statement by David Willetts, Minister for Universities and Science, on future changes to Disabled Students' Allowances. [On-Line] www.gov.uk/government/speeches/higher-education-student-support-changes-to-disabled-students-allowances-dsa [Retrieved 21 December 2017].

Equality and Human Rights Commission (2012) *Equality Act 2010 Technical Guidance on Further and Higher Education,* London, Department for Education.

Finkelstein, V. (1980) *Attitudes and Disabled People,* New York, World Rehabilitation Fund.

Fixsen, D. L., Blasé, K. A., Naoom, S. F. and Wallace, F. (2009) Core implementation components, *Research on Social Work Practice,* 19 (5), 531–540.

Hargreaves, A. and Ainscow, M. (2015) The top and bottom of leadership and change: Successful large-scale reform efforts – one in northern England, another in Canada – bolster the approach of "leading from the middle", *Phi Delta Kappan,* 97 (3), 42.

Higher Education Funding Council for England (2017a) *The TEF.* [On-line] www.hefce.ac.uk/lt/tef/ [Retrieved 22 December 2017].

Higher Education Statistical Agency (2018) Figure 4 – HE Student enrolments by personal characteristics 2016–2017. [On-line] www.hesa.ac.uk/data-and-analysis/sfr247/figure-4 [Retrieved 21 January 2018].

Higher Education Statistics Agency and the Higher Education Academy (2016) Report on Research and Data Analysis on Academic Teaching Qualifications Bristol, HEFCE.

Ingstad, B. 'Chapter 35: Disability in the Developing World', cited in Albrecht, G. L. Seelman, K. and Bury, M. (2001) *Handbook of Disability Studies,* Thousand Oaks, CA, Sage Publications.

Kerzner, H. (2017) *Project Management: A Systems Approach to Planning, Scheduling, and Controlling* (Twelfth Edition) NY, USA, John Wiley & Sons.

Land, R. and Gordon, G. (2015) *Teaching Excellence Initiatives: Modalities and Operational Factors*, York, Higher Education Academy.

Legislation.gov.uk (1995) *Disability Discrimination Act 1995*. [On-line] www.
legislation.gov.uk/ukpga/1995/50 [Retrieved 21 December 2017].

Legislation.gov.uk (2010) *Equality Act 2010*. [On-line] www.legislation.gov.uk/
ukpga/2010/15/contents [Retrieved 21 December 2017].

Nashash, H. A. and Gunn, C. (2013) Lecture capture in engineering classes: Bridging gaps and enhancing learning, *Educational Technology and Society*, 16 (1),
69–78.

National Student Survey (2017) [On-line] www.thestudentsurvey.com/about.php
[Retrieved 30 January 2018].

Newcombe, M. (2017) Lecture capture – can it help 'hard to reach, *Journal of
Educational Innovation and Change*, 3 (1). [On-line] https://journals.gre.ac.uk/
index.php/studentchangeagents/article/view/602/pdf [Retrieved
1 February 2018].

O'Callaghan, F. V., Neumann, D. L., Jones, L. and Creed, P. A. (2017) The use
of lecture recordings in higher education: A review of institutional, student and
lecturer issues, *Education and Information Technologies*, 22 (1), 399–415.

Oliver, M. and Barnes, C. (2011) *The New Politics of Disablement* (2nd ed.), Tavi-
stock, Palgrave.

Rose, D. H. and Meyer, A. (2000) Universal design for learning, *Journal of Special
Education Technology*, 15 (1), 1–12.

Rose, D, H. and Meyer, A. (2006) *A Practical Reader in Universal Design for
Learning*, Cambridge, MA, Harvard Education Press.

Smith, S. J. and Harvey, E. E. (2014) K-12 online lesson alignment to the principles
of universal design for learning: The khan academy, *Open Learning: The Journal of
Open, Distance and E-Learning*, 29 (3), 222–242.

UK Standing Committee for Quality Assessment (2018) *The Revised UK Quality
Code for Higher Education. The Quality Assurance Agency for Higher Education.*
Gloucester, UK.

Wood, M. and Su, F. (2017) What makes an excellent lecturer? Academics'
perspectives on the discourse of 'teaching excellence' in higher education,
Teaching in Higher Education: Critical Perspectives, 22 (4). DOI: 10.1080/
13562517.2017.1301911

World Health Organisation (1980) *International Classification of Impairments, Disabilities, and Handicaps: A Manual of Classification Relating to the Consequences
of Disease*, Geneva, WHO.

World Health Organisation (2002) *International classification of functioning, disability, and health. ICF.* World Health Organization, Geneva.

Section 2

Working in partnership with key stakeholders to engage all students

Chapter 4

Transforming the professor
Motivating university students in every discipline through design

Kimberly Coy

Case study

Spring semester began and the education professor met with a new group of learners who were almost certified teachers. These students had received their undergraduate degrees and then spent an additional 18 months taking courses as post baccalaureate students in order to meet the requirements of the State of California to obtain teaching certificates. This group was now working as student teachers in classrooms and taking their final evening course. The course content was covering diverse and special education learners and inclusive classroom management. The professor was planning a course rich in both content and experience featuring Universal Design for Learning.

The professor was excited with her planned UDL curriculum, and expected the students would enjoy their experience. There were multiple ways students could choose to access the curriculum, multiple ways for students to respond to formative and summative assessments. Flexibility was at the core, the professor hoped that learning in a UDL environment of their own would encourage these future teachers to create a UDL experience for their students. It looked positive until a few weeks in the professor noticed one student was disengaging. Sean began to leave early every class and arrived late. Some three weeks into the semester he had not turned in an assignment. During in-class activities he would lightly mock the activity, or even the other students. The professor felt like she was trying to wrangle a pre-teen student who experienced some defiant behavior characteristics. What was going on?

The professor made a decision, it was time to try to arrange the course with Sean's needs at the center, and to see if the UDL framework could help her redesign parts of the course for Sean to be more successful. The professor began with what Sean had been communicating. She made a list:

- He told the class repeatedly that did not like the assignment options, he only wanted to write traditional papers;
- He had so far refused to use the social media platform;
- By his comfort with oppositional behaviors the profession surmised he may have honed these skills over a lifetime in school;
- He did not participate in class discussions except to derail from the topic;
- He had a small child he was clearly devoted to, and a wife he loved;
- He was street-smart and successful in highly structured environments;
- He did not understand how UDL looked in practice beyond classroom options for seating.

How could examining and using the UDL framework help the professor meet Sean's needs and break down some of the barriers the class presented for him?

Introduction: a United States West Coast University

On the west coast of the United States, the California State University system consists of 23 campuses with a total enrollment of almost 500,000 students. These campuses educate a very diverse group of students who are often first to college in their families, they tend to be multilingual with English being a second language, and many are eligible for grant supports because their family incomes are within the poverty designation. This chapter examines the efforts on one campus to meet the educational needs of this diverse group of students. It does so by exploring how professors and instructors use the Universal Design for Learning Framework.

The university concerned is Fresno State University, it is set in the central interior of the State of California known as the Central Valley and it is part of the California State University. In 2017, 68% of the students attending the university were the first in their family to attend college. Approximately 60% of the students attending are from families who qualify for grants because of low income status. Adding to this rich diversity, over 70% of the students are multilingual with English not being their first language. The U.S. Department of Education designates this university as both a Hispanic-Serving Institution and an Asian American and Native American Pacific Islander-Serving Institution. In addition, there are also students with a wide range of learning disabilities, and although there are services available to support their educational needs, students are not required to disclose identified disabilities in order to attend classes and complete degrees.

Reflection

- Each higher education system encompasses a unique set of demographics. Reflect on your institution's student characteristics. Most universities have a dedicated department or website where this information can be found. Check out the one you work in, or find out about another institution you think may be similar.
- Reflect on student demographic characteristics that might surprise you. It could be the amount of commuter students, or the average age of the undergraduate students in your institution. How might these students view some of the aspects of your university as a barrier?
- Reflect on the unique experiences students at your university bring to class each day that are different from your own. What barriers and opportunities does this variability create for designing the learning environment?

A brief literature review to support UDL in university settings

For HEIs Universal Design for Learning (UDL) is a relatively new educational focus. In fact there is still ongoing debate as to how to conceptualize what UDL is (King-Sear, 2009). While definitions for UDL exist within the literature (Rose, Meyer, & Hitchcock, 2005; Meyer & Rose, 2005) and federal guidelines, including the Higher Education Act of 2008 (U.S. Department of Education, 2008) and the Every Student Succeeds Act (ESSA) (U.S. Department of Education, 2015), the search has only just begun to fully illustrate what educational actions constitute UDL with educators and students (Hitchcock, Meyer, Rose, & Jackson, 2002).

There is a desire within the UDL community to understand what it means to design, implement, and measure UDL (Edyburn, 2010; King-Sears, 2009; Meo, 2008), and yet for the most part this is still elusive. There are some limited studies available – for example, when UDL principles were embedded into a university level nursing course the students reported feeling more in control of their own learning by making choices around the way in which they accessed information, and the choices they were given to process and consolidate understanding of discipline content (Kumar & Wideman, 2014). In addition, the disabilities department in the Canadian university featured in the research reported less intervention on behalf of students with reported learning disabilities. Further, In Capp's meta-analysis of effectiveness, there is a recognition that implementation of the UDL framework improves the learning process for all students (2016: 795) nevertheless, the study qualifies that the result is provisional due to the low number of studies analyzed (n=18). This chapter proposes to look at what UDL looks like in practice for higher education students through professors' efforts to transform their own approaches to teaching at the University level.

At Fresno State University

In order to provide successful opportunities to its diverse group of learners, Fresno State has been engaged in several university wide initiatives to support faculty in teaching. Three initiatives in particular highlight UDL as part of the optional training offered. Two of these are supported by the Center for Faculty Excellence at Fresno State. This Center provides faculty development to increase teaching effectiveness through training in the uses of academic technologies.

One interesting program is titled "DISCOVERe". This is part of the mobile technology program to maximize the use of technology on campus to support student learning. The focus of DISCOVERe is to support faculty to create and provide learning experiences in the classroom setting that increase student innovation and engagement in order to have learning activities meet higher learner outcomes. This was not initially designed as a UDL initiative, but instead with a focus on technology to encourage and support faculty as they taught diverse students.

One example of a change that occurred as a result of this program is how one of the professors in the business school joined the DISCOVERe program because he realized that his students were not learning the course content through his lectures. He had attended faculty training, realizing he needed support to change his teaching. He hoped by using technology that he could engage his students in the content. What he did not expect to learn was that it was the pedagogical approach, as framed by UDL that supported him in reaching his goals with his students. His case study is the second case in this chapter.

Online learning and teaching is another path Fresno State is using to introduce educational pedagogy to support all faculty. Online courses in particular are growing in prevalence in higher education. The design process in online courses is interesting because the design is done at the beginning of the course, due to the necessity of conceptualizing how the technology will be used. For example, Universities need to choose learning management systems to use well in advance of the professor creating the course. And the professor needs to let students know well in advance if a fully online course will involve the need for synchronous instruction so students can prepare time and technology to participate. One study by He (2014) looked specifically at the purposeful use of UDL in the design and implementation of an online teacher education course. The results of this study affirmed that leaning into design of a course with UDL principles increased students' satisfaction with their awareness of their own learning, as well as confidence in content acquisition.

The Center for Faculty Excellence offered a certificate program that required Professors to participate in a blended learning curriculum with cohorts meeting both online and face to face. The goal was for faculty and instructors to gain skills and knowledge necessary to teach a variety of students in an online or hybrid setting. While not initially setting out to use the UDL framework, the feedback of early participants demonstrated that faculty were struggling with using the technology. As the certificates were developed over time, more emphasis was placed on the UDL framework approach for designing and implementing course work.

A final program is focused specifically on Faculty designing courses at the graduate level. Faculty participate in a one week blended-learning summer session. Participants spend half of the week in a digital or online version of the content, both in synchronous and asynchronous spaces, and the other half of the week face-to-face. This course has been progressively focusing on the UDL framework, both in the delivery of the course and the content and pedagogy offered to faculty.

While this is still early days in transforming a large University, it is interesting that each of these initiatives and programs, designed to help Professors and instructors meet the needs of a very diverse student body, are leaning more purposefully into UDL.

Reflection

- Reflect on the nature of work-related trainings you have been involved in. Was there a difference in your satisfaction when you were able to have several options to choose from? How did the timing, setting, and personal affect your experience?
- How do you feel about Universal Design for Learning being a secondary goal to the trainings offered at this University? Do you think this might make it more accessible to the learners in this environment, or will it diminish the importance of UDL?
- Reflect on the decision makers in your institution. Do you have access to the people who create faculty support systems? How flexible are they in their thinking about learning?

The disruptive nature of UDL

The professor in case study #1 worked to make adjustments in one course to support the journey of a disengaged student. The forthcoming case study #2 highlights a professor who participated in the DISCOVERe program. He began the journey to understanding that his students did not learn the way he learned in college. In each case, the professors learned about using the UDL framework to support the educational goals of the course within one of the University initiatives. The guidelines and checkpoints gave the professor permission to enact change. The next part of this chapter focuses on specific examples of UDL in University course design and implementation.

Purposeful, motivated learners

In the first case study, the professor designed the course in advance and purposefully reflected on the nature of the assignment choice options she had created for the course. She required students to only choose a traditional paper once during the semester, the rest of the assignments needed to be from a list offered. Alternatively, students were encouraged to come up with an alternative assessment idea that the professor could accept. The list included a poster, diorama, power point presentation, video, graphic organizer, as well as some options involving digital tools such as smore.com, seesaw, and screencast-o-matic. Sean had said several times that he was annoyed that only one traditional paper would be accepted during the semester.

The professor set about creating class time so that she could have some one-to-one time with Sean, before he scooted out early, she took the time to sit with him and explain the rationale behind the assessment choices. She asked Sean to look at the assignments where this rule applied and explain if he thought the assignments were difficult. He quickly responded "no", the assignments were not difficult. They included an interview with a parent of a student with special learning needs, a lesson observation that included students with special learning needs, and an Individual Educational needs Plan (IEP) meeting observation. Sean was annoyed that his choice to write the traditional paper he was most comfortable with was taken away. The professor agreed, he was right, she gave back his choice to write a paper. In addition, she explained that one of the goals for these assignments was to give Sean and his classmates a way to understand the world of students with special needs by experiencing a course from a UDL perspective. That meant optimizing choices whenever possible, so when he had his own classroom as a teacher, Sean could understand how students might feel when given choices.

The professor went about explaining individual choice and autonomy of assessment choice, and explicitly pointing out the relevance, value, and authenticity of the structure of assignments and their assessment protocol. She acknowledged that this was different from Sean's previous academic experience and shared her understanding of how this might cause him some distress. Going forward each time the class met they were going to be given time to work with each other to formulate their assignments while integrating the digital choices. Sean would have support if he chose a different assignment option, and so would the rest of the class.

Sean and the education professor's story highlights the UDL principle of engagement. The Professor was striving to set the stage for learners to be purposeful and motivated in order to leverage mastery of content and curriculum in meaningful ways to enhance their own efforts when they were teachers. In the UDL Guidelines (2018), the necessity to address students' affective and cognitive engagement is identified as central for further learning to take place. In the next section, the guidelines and checkpoints within Engagement are highlighted with specific examples applied to this teacher education program. The wording from the UDL guidelines are included in italics. This is intended to illustrate the ways in which University professors can make choices when designing the structure of courses focusing on the content goals.

Spark excitement and curiosity for learning

To *empower learners to take charge of their own learning* the professor kept the assignment structure choices and encouraged, but did not require, students to choose outside of their comfort zone. The professor was explicit in explaining why this led to course goals. This enhances the students' ability to *connect learning experiences that are meaningful and valuable*. In order to *foster a safe space to learn and take risks* class time to complete assignments with support from both the professor and the other students was provided.

Tackle challenges with focus and determination

Some class meetings were run as small learning centers that the students rotated through in order to *set a vision for the goal and why it matters*. One center was always open to "ask the professor anything". During one class session, Sean spoke about one of the children in his class exhibiting off task behavior. Sean was frustrated, and the professor couldn't alleviate Sean's frustration. Finally, the professor explained that what was really important was for Sean to demonstrate kindness toward the student, Sean took the advice on board. The professor said that the other students would learn from Sean's patience as he demonstrated kindness towards the child concerned. Everyone would benefit.

Giving Sean permission to treat his current student with kindness also allowed Sean to think of his former self with kindness. Other students sitting at the table with Sean and the professor added in their points of view and this helped to *cultivate a community of learners* both for Sean, the other students, and the professor who was able to learn as well. The professor was able to *guide learning by emphasizing the role of effort and process.* Interestingly, toward the end of the conversations Sean admitted he has been a similar student. The professor then followed Sean's lead and talked about additional structures and behaviors he could use to support that student.

Harness the power of emotions and motivation in learning

In order to allow students to *set personal goals that inspire confidence and owner-ship of learning*, the professor sent students individual updates on progress, and also assisted students to coordinate their calendars with their other time demands. While this could certainly work under the guideline of executive functions, by acknowledging all of the responsibilities the students needed to accomplish during this semester, the professor was also communicating that she believed they had the personal coping skills and strategies they would need to be successful. Students provided feedback to each other based on forma-tive work they prepared. This activity of peer feedback enabled the students to *develop and manage healthy emotional responses and interactions.* Towards the end of the semester, the professor encouraged the students to reflect on their achievements when they had earned enough points for their own grade goal *increasing awareness around progress toward goals and how to learn from mis-takes.* For example, if they had earned enough points for a B grade, and they were satisfied with that grade, they were invited to stop working. The professor reasoned the goal of achieving their potential through UDL was the real goal, rather than focusing on grade points. Sean stopped when he earned a B grade.

Reflection

- In this case study the professor seems to really tune into the needs of one student, and changes several important parts of the course to meet his needs. Do you think this was an appropriate response? How might other students have felt about this?
- Reflect on students or learners you may have worked with or taught in the past. Did you have a student similar to Sean? How did you handle students who left class early, or displayed some of the other behaviors Sean demonstrated?
- Do you work with colleagues that also exhibit behaviors that are oppositional? How have you seen other leaders deal with these challenges?

Sean's feedback at the end of the semester was exceptionally positive. Also important was the feedback the Professor received some months later from an administrator at the school where Sean was working at his first teaching position. The administrator told the professor how impressed he was with Sean's enthusiasm and understanding of Universal Design for Learning in the classroom.

Case study 2: Are relationships enough?

Dr. Bennett was in his second year of a tenure track faculty position, and he knew he was facing challenges. As a professor in the School of Business he taught three courses each semester in addition to holding additional committee duties and having a research agenda. He was a person who was successful in large part due to his charismatic personality. Dr. Bennett was easy to approach, enthusiastic, and people, both faculty and students, wanted to be around him. He a had a natural gift for humor, and seemed kind to everyone. He also loved his content area discipline. He worked in the business world for a time before getting his doctorate and transitioning to academia and he wanted to share what he knew from the world of work with others.

However, he had faced two significant challenges. Firstly, his students were giving him poor course reviews. At a primarily teaching University this was a problem in his quest for tenure. Secondly, he really did not think his students were learning the content. Unused to experiencing this level of difficulty in his past work, Dr. Bennett was both disappointed and confused. This is when he decided to join University technology and online training. He wondered if he was out of touch with the level of technology his students were looking for in educational settings. He was also wondering if he could get his students to engage in the content more if they used technology. As he began the trainings, he admitted he was looking for that **one** technology, or that **one** app that would transform his courses, the student outcomes, and consequently his course ratings. Relying on the force of his personality and ability to relate to a wide variety of people, while before successful, was not enough here.

Resourceful, knowledgeable learners

It took Dr. Bennett several attempts to understand that it was the course delivery he was designing that was the problem, not the technology. He would participate in trainings and ask repeatedly for the best app, or best program to use with his lectures. One program he wanted to use was Nearpod (practical advice about how to use this program is available on YouTube). During the time Dr. Bennett was participating in the DISCOVERe program, the technology was taught to faculty first, then the pedagogy behind it was presented. Dr. Bennett got "stuck" at the technology part. He could not conceptualize how to use this technology tool with his lectures. Watching him struggle was really frustrating to the program facilitators. This is when they reached out to UDL experts, and asked for some presentations to the group about this framework. After one session addressing the concept of neurodiversity, Dr. Bennett shared: "My students don't learn with lectures the way I did, what am I going to do?". What follows are many of the ideas Dr. Bennett worked on, and a few of the changes he implemented. Again, the UDL language is in italics.

Dr. Bennett first began to consider how best to enable students to Interact with flexible content that doesn't depend on a single sense like sight, hearing, movement, or touch. He decided to put some of his key lectures on video. He then asked the Center for Faculty Excellence to caption the videos and made them available to his students. This use of flexible materials with settings that can be adjusted based on needs and preferences enabled students to listen repeatedly to lectures, as well as providing them with access to written text. Dr. Bennett also began to be open to the idea of sharing information in more ways than sound and voice alone. Pinterest literally opened a new world for him, and consequently his students. He loved the graphic organizers. To organize much of this information, he used the University's Learning Management System in new ways. He was able to store and share information in more ways than images and text alone. His discussion boards included both his own and his students' reflections on the readings and lectures.

Business courses rely upon numbers and symbols to communicate information. Dr. Bennett began to explore the idea of using a case study approach with a real-life example familiar to the students in his courses. During an exchange with some of his colleagues while attending one of the faculty training initiatives, he learned about a new warehouse complex coming to Fresno. A distribution center was being built and would lead to employment for almost 2,000 people. He was talking about how much he wanted to tour the new facility, and he wondered what this would mean to the people of the area. He wondered whether these jobs were really better for workers. Dr. Bennett was so engaged with this development that one of his colleagues encouraged him to incorporate it into his courses. Dr. Bennett loved the idea, he was going to *make the patterns and properties of systems like grammar, musical notation, taxonomies, and equations explicit* by looking specifically at the distribution center. Such a case study would enable him to *communicate through languages that create a shared understanding.*

This approach would also make learning come alive *with simulations, graphics, activities, and videos.* By providing instruction to support learner choices on how to access specific content: video, graphic organizers and podcasts, the professor was provided with the opportunity to learn alongside the students while sourcing new resources. Inviting guest lectures to talk about the project and putting those lectures on video with captions would also free up some time for Dr. Bennett to focus on another new idea: giving students feedback through video instead of text. Taken together, these approaches enable the use of *translations, descriptions, movement, and images to support learning in unfamiliar or complex languages*

Dr. Bennett then sought to support students with endeavors to *construct meaning and generate new understandings*. In order to build connections to prior understandings and experiences, Dr. Bennett spent more time on explaining his own background work experiences. Stories connected to him drew positive interest from his students. With this narrative technique he was able to draw lines between the content he was teaching, and the broad learning goals he had for his students. He was able to accentuate important information and how it relates to the learning goal. Another way he supported this practice was to design class sessions in a predictable rhythm. For example, once a week Dr. Bennett would explicitly address goals and objectives. Subsequent class sessions were spent reviewing the goals and connecting how new information supported attainment of individual learning objectives.

One last change Dr. Bennett was willing to try was the idea drawn from an article written by Rose, Harbour, Johnston, Daley, and Abarbanell (2006). This article explained how Rose and colleagues worked to deliver a course at Harvard using a UDL inspired design. The case overview of the process of incrementally changing a course that had previously been heavily lecture oriented, to one that was framed by UDL inspired Dr. Bennett. One change Rose and company made was to have designated note takers every lecture or discussion. These note takers would then publish their work for the whole class to see, and therefore *support the process of meaning-making through models, scaffolds, and feedback*. Students were able to see the wide variety of ways they looked at lecture content and feel more comfortable with their own divergent thinking. Dr. Bennett was also able to reflect on his own lectures by seeing in almost real time what students had learned. With a UDL informed approach, Dr. Bennett was now well equipped to make positive inclusive changes.

Key learning and conclusion

Several areas of key learning are highlighted by the Fresno State University experience, and the attempts of the education professor and Dr. Bennett to transform their teaching approaches to meet the needs of their diverse students. One is that even when planning with UDL, mistakes can be made. As Sean pointed out to the education professor, through his off-task behaviors, students really need to see and understand the pedagogical goals of the course so they can overcome their own personal barriers. Sean needed to see why he should try new and unfamiliar ways of demonstrating his own knowledge before he could put aside his oppositional behavior and engage with the learning.

Another key learning opportunity was looking at introducing UDL as a "booster" to higher education initiatives already in place, such as the use of technology, or the use of lower cost open access materials to support students' learning from texts. The previous chapter by Moriarty and Scarffe takes a thorough look at how a HEI plans and implements a complete UDL adoption. They highlighted how several facets of the University community benefited from an institutional approach. Perhaps one day in the not too distant future universities with such diverse student bodies, like Fresno State in California, will attempt such an approach. Until then, using UDL to play a supporting role can strengthen existing practices.

And finally, a word regarding metacognition – University students are still learning how to learn, when university professors transform the way they think about learning, learning events change. When Dr. Bennett was ready for change, he proactively sought solutions. When he finally saw that it was his own thinking that needed to change, he was ready to access and implement facets of the UDL framework. As he shared his own thinking with people around him support and guidance was given in a manner that he was ready to accept and use. As he shared his own thinking with his students, a transformational change in his educational process began.

Reflection

- Reflect on your own thinking around how you support others in the higher education environment. Do you encourage them to share their own thinking processes?
- How can you effect change both locally, and in your own teaching or administrative practice in small ways?
- Review the UDL framework, looking specifically at one checkpoint and discuss how this one attribute might be used to prompt change in learning, teaching, or assessment?

References

Edyburn, D. L. (2010). Would you recognize universal design for learning if you saw it? Ten propositions for new directions for the second decade of UDL. *Learning Disability Quarterly*, *33*, 33–41.

He, Y. (2014). Universal design for learning in an online teacher education course: Enhancing learners' confidence to teach online. *MERLOT Journal of Online Learning and Teaching*, *10*(2), 283–297.

Hitchcock, C., Meyer, A., Rose, D., & Jackson, R. (2002). Providing new access to the general curriculum: Universal design for learning. *Teaching Exceptional Children*, 8–17.

King-Sears, M. (2009). Universal design for learning: Technology and pedagogy. *Learning Disability Quarterly, 32*, 199–201.

Kumar, K. L., & Wideman, M. (2014). Accessible by design: Applying UDL principles in a first year undergraduate course. *Canadian Journal of Higher Education, 44*(1), 125–147.

Meo, G. (2008). Curriculum planning for all learners: Applying universal design for learning (UDL) to a high school reading comprehension program. *Preventing School Failure, 52*(2), 21–30.

Meyer, A., & Rose, D. H. (2005). The future is in the margins: The role of technology and disability in educational reform. In D. H. Rose, A. Meyer & C. Hitchcock (Eds.), *The universally designed classroom: Accessible curriculum and digital technologies* (pp. 13–35). Cambridge, MA: Harvard Education Press.

Rose, D. H., Harbour, W. S., Johnston, C. S., Daley, S. G., & Abarbanell, L. (2006). Universal design for learning in postsecondary education: Reflections on principles and their application. *Journal of Postsecondary Education and Disability, 19*(2), 135–151.

Rose, D. H., Meyer, A., & Hitchcock, C. (Eds.). (2005). *The universally designed classroom: Accessible curriculum and digital technologies.* Cambridge, MA: Harvard Education Press.

U.S. Department of Education. (2015). *Every Student Succeeds Act.* Retrieved from https://www.ed.gov/essa

U.S. Department of Education. (2008). *Higher education opportunity act – 2008.* Retrieved from http://www2.ed.gov/policy/highered/leg/hea08/index.html

Chapter 5

The transition to higher education

Applying Universal Design for Learning to support student success

Danielle Hitch, Petra Brown, Susie Macfarlane, Janet Watson, Mary Dracup and Kate Anderson

Case study: Academic skill development as a shared responsibility

The widening participation agenda has enabled increasingly diverse cohorts of students to enter higher education. A teaching team in a School of Health and Social Development had recognized that students were entering the course with a wide range of academic preparedness, and acknowledged that the acquisition of academic skills was crucial to their successful transition into higher education. They undertook a project to understand student and academic perceptions of their roles in the learning experience, and develop a framework of academic skill progression specifically adapted to transition into higher education.

The framework incorporated many of the principles of Universal Design for Learning to enable both students and academics to understand the why, what and how of learning academic skills. An explicitly student centred, strengths (rather than deficit) based approach was adopted to ensure skill development that met individual needs and enhanced personal coping strategies. Engagement was also promoted via the explicit alignment of academic skills with the professional competencies students are expected to achieve by graduation.

The need for multiple means of representation was met by the adoption of epistemological equity practice (Sefa Dei, 2008), which values diversity in experience and learning preferences and actively works to incorporate them into the learning process. The existing knowledge, skills and agency of students transitioning to higher education are respected and activated. The development of students' academic skills was conceptualized as a process that required iterative and interweaving actions, rather than a single pathway. Responsibility for academic skill development was recognized as a joint responsibility shared between students, academics and academic skills staff; and collaboration, communication and negotiation were vital to the project (Goldingay et al., 2012).

Introduction: supporting success and transition through Universal Design for Learning

Transition to higher education can be understood as "change navigated by students in their movement within and through formal education" (Gale & Parker, 2014, p. 737). This process may begin during the final year of secondary school, with programs and curricula that familiarize students with university expectations, discourse and culture. Schools that better prepare their students in this way have been found to positively enhance students' progression into HE (Krause, Hartley, James, & McInnis, 2005). However, this chapter is concerned with transition as it occurs across the first year experience within higher education – a formative period in which the university has direct influence.

This chapter draws on Nelson and Kift's (2005) conceptualization of transition pedagogy as a scaffolded approach to meet the "continuum of student needs" that occurs throughout their first year of higher education through to the beginning of second year. While this time frame includes enrolment procedures and orientation programs, our discussion focuses on how teaching and learning experiences impact on transition, with specific attention to curriculum design and delivery and student academic support. Essentially, transition concerns adjusting to and settling into university life and becoming conversant with the digital and academic literacies required to be self-directed, active and engaged learners in chosen disciplines of study. The challenges of transition are mediated by profound transformations in the higher education landscape, which include demand-driven funding, widening participation, the dramatic growth of teaching technologies and concurrent shifts to online/blended learning environments (Baik, Naylor, & Arkoudis, 2015).

Given the diverse backgrounds from which Australian students now hail, many are ill-prepared for, or unfamiliar with, university (Nelson & Kift, 2005) – it can be a foreign land, even for domestic students. Students face a daunting array of information, institutional structures and new technologies, and this may be compounded by other life circumstances, such as relocating away from social support networks, health concerns, financial pressures and family and workload commitments (Baik et al., 2015; Brooker, Brooker, & Lawrence, 2017; Kift, 2015; Nelson & Kift, 2005).

Learning how to manage and balance competing demands on student time and develop new competencies is pivotal to smoothing the pathway to tertiary success. Therefore, a "transition pedagogy", which foregrounds first year curriculum as a central mechanism to engage, support and enhance success and retention, provides a scaffolded approach to assist students' transition over time, by enabling both knowledge and skill development (Kift, 2009).

As described in previous chapters, Universal Design for Learning (UDL) applies the universal design approach to technology and built environments to the dynamic processes of teaching and learning (Hall, Meyer, & Rose, 2012). UDL has been defined as "a scientifically valid framework for guiding educational practice" that "provides flexibility in the ways information is presented" and "reduces barriers in instruction, provides appropriate accommodations, supports, and challenges" (*Higher Education Opportunity Act 2008* (USA)). UDL differentiates itself from other universal design frameworks by incorporating the results of neuroscience and learning research, and utilizing the capabilities of information technology to facilitate learning design.

The UDL framework aims to address learner variability by organizing instruction and designing curriculum around three principles, each of which corresponds to one of three classes of brain networks that together facilitate learning: recognition, strategic and affective (Hall et al., 2012). Providing multiple means of representation, which develops resourceful and knowledgeable learners, supports recognition learning. Providing multiple means of action and expression, which develops considered and goal directed learners, supports strategic learning. Finally, providing multiple means of engagement, which develops purposeful and motivated learners, supports affective learning. UDL aspires to give all individuals the opportunity to learn, through providing a "blueprint for the creation of instructional goals, methods, materials and assessments that work for everyone" (National Center on Universal Design for Learning, 2014). It also seeks to take advantage of the capabilities of contemporary technology to deliver flexible resources and instructional practices, which can be adjusted for need within a single curriculum (Hall et al., 2012). This framework is most effective when the principles are utilized to develop curriculum from the ground up, rather than being retrofitted to existing content.

Conceptualizing student success during transition

Over the last decade, with widening participation and a significant increase in student numbers, the discourse and practices of higher education have changed from the deficit language of attrition and failure, to that of retention and success (Wood & Breyer, 2017). Universities that are open to the majority are required to focus on students' learning, progress and success, but the notion of what constitutes student success is a contested and evolving one.

Traditionally, student success is conceptualized from the institution's point of view, driven by reporting requirements and funding. A study of 31 Australian higher education institutions (Coates, Kelly, & Naylor, 2016) identified the most commonly reported measures of success focused on: learning (possessing the knowledge and skills for practice); academic achievement (passing subjects, grade point average and course progress); retention and course completion; and employability in the field following graduation.

However, perspectives on what counts as success may differ between and among higher education institutions, academics, employers and students. How student success is conceptualized in a particular historical moment can determine national policy and funding levers, university strategic goals and metrics, beliefs and practices about what constitutes student learning and achievement, and the forms of engagement and participation available to students. There may be tension, for example, between an educational experience aimed at achieving institutional goals (such as developing students' graduate attributes), and one that engages students as active participants in their learning and enables them to meet their individual goals.

A broader understanding of student success is now emerging that focuses on students' transition and sense of belonging (Lizzio, 2006; Wood & Breyer, 2017), engagement with others (Thomas, Hill, O'Mahony, & Yorke 2017), personal and professional growth (Wood & Breyer, 2017) and capabilities to transform their identity, adapt to disruptive change and navigate multiple career paths (Barnett, 2004; Gale & Parker, 2014).

A situated framing of student success characterizes student success not solely as academic achievement or employment, but as the quality of students' relationships with the institution, higher education, other students, and themselves as learners. Interactions that connect students' learning to their lived experience and developing identity fosters their sense of belonging (Hockings, Cooke, & Bowl, 2010), and the belief they can achieve. Ultimately, this supports students' motivation to continue their studies and their appreciation of lifelong learning. Student success can therefore be understood as the development of socio-cultural capabilities, such as reflective practice, socio-cultural practice (e.g. help seeking, seeking feedback) and critical thinking, along with the university-specific literacies, practices and discourses required to achieve success (Lawrence, 2005). Students' transition to higher education requires their engagement in conversations, practices and communities that will support their success. Students' success is therefore dependent on their participation in communities of practice that foster their personal sense of capability, connectedness, purpose, resourcefulness and participation in academic practices and culture.

Reflection

- Reflect on your personal experiences of transition, as both a student and an educator. What do you consider to be the key challenges faced by students at this phase of their higher education journey?

- How is students' transition into higher education supported at your institution? Are there specific programs or information provided to meet the needs of new students?
- Reflect on how you conceive of student success in your current role. How is success defined for students transitioning into higher education in your local context, and by whom? How is it evidenced, and how it is "measured"?
- In discussion with first year teachers, professional staff and students, consider 1) the opportunities for transitioning students to safely acknowledge, express and draw on their diversity as a resource for themselves and for others, 2) how transitioning students engage in dialogue, interactions and partnerships that foster their belonging and enculturation in academic culture and practices, 3) what opportunities students are provided for active participation in designing what and how they learn and 4) how transitioning students may engage in UDL.

This chapter will begin by providing an overview of current international evidence for the use of UDL to engage, teach and assess transitioning students. Two case studies will then be provided, which describe how UDL has been implemented in the Australian higher education system at Deakin University with this group of students. The challenges of this implementation will be reflected upon in detail, as will how the markers of success are defined and evaluated.

Current perspectives on Universal Design for Learning at the transition to higher education

As demonstrated throughout this book, significant developments in the use of UDL are occurring in higher education globally. These initiatives have targeted all phases of the student journey, however the specific context of the transition to, and within, higher education is only just emerging as a focused area of inquiry. The nexus between Universal Design for Learning, transition and success is increasingly recognized as a crucial space for higher education practice and development. A range of UDL approaches have been applied and evaluated specifically with transitioning higher education students internationally, demonstrating how the principles work in this context.

Studies have found a range of positive outcomes, such as the positive response of Greek university students to an accessible study guide, explicitly designed using the UDL framework (Tzivinikou, 2014). Other studies have also demonstrated positive outcomes from taking a course-wide (involving multiple units) approach to UDL during the transition to higher education. In a Canadian first year science unit, the majority of students reported positive perceptions of

UDL strategies particularly around assessment choice after they were embedded throughout the course (Kumar & Wideman, 2014). A further 74% appreciated the opportunity to share their student profile at the beginning of the course as a means to raise both their own and their teacher's awareness of their learning needs (Kumar & Wideman, 2014, p. 134). On a larger scale, students in a "gateway" course called Introduction to Psychology in the United States were surveyed on their perceptions of UDL practices by academics (Schelly, Davies, & Spooner, 2011). Pre-course survey findings were used to provide targeted training in UDL to teaching staff. Post-course, students responded positively to the significant increase in the use of specific UDL practices by teachers they perceived, particularly in regard to multiple means of representation.

An initiative from Australia likewise shows positive outcomes when applying UDL with students' transition to higher education. In a recent study, the UDL framework was applied as part of a pilot project in an information skills unit designed to support students from equity groups during transition into higher education, at a university college (Dinmore & Stokes, 2015). The pilot included a communication strategy for all teaching staff, review of learning materials to identify opportunities for multiple means of representation, alterations to learning experiences to enable multiple means of action and expression, and explicit connections between learning, lived experience and degree aspirations. The redeveloped unit achieved the highest pass rate of units offered within the college that semester, and 97% of students reported feeling satisfied with the unit (Dinmore & Stokes, 2015, p. 14).

Providing a faculty perspective on the application of UDL in a first year undergraduate unit in the United States, Higbee (2015) highlights how this approach is helpful to all students, and furthermore, that its implementation at a course level ensured all students had the opportunity to benefit. Higbee describes how strategies such as consciously creating a welcoming classroom, highlighting the essential components of the unit, making expectations explicit and encouraging students to use natural supports complemented the provision of resources in multiple formats. A student evaluation of this approach was very positive, and Higbee reports the same approaches are still being applied in the unit ten years later, indicating their potential sustainability over time.

A small but fairly consistent evidence base therefore exists to support the notion that UDL practices can support personal capability, purpose and resourcefulness for students transitioning to higher education. Their ability to support enculturation into higher education and connectedness is yet to be explored, but would be worthy of future research. However, implementing UDL practices during the transition to higher education is not without its challenges. Nielsen (2013) described her application of UDL at a classroom level in a composition unit. She ensured there were multiple methods of representation in resources, reduced risks and threats by interacting with students and also introduced opportunities for choice within assessments. Despite these measures, Nielsen observed that first year classrooms are "fraught with growing pains"

(2013, p. 18), and underlined the need for students to build their capacity in digital literacy to take advantage of some resources. She also reflected on the time required to develop new or adapted resources, and noted that finding the time to retrofit UDL into existing courses can be very difficult in the context of competing workplace demands.

Reflection

- Reflect on efforts to implement UDL in higher education in which you have been involved or have observed. What were some of the benefits and challenges to using UDL strategies that you experienced or noticed? Do any of the initiatives described provide an evidence base for what you are seeing implemented?
- Choose one UDL strategy or approach being implemented in your local setting (either currently or that is intended for the future). What is the intended impact or outcome of using this strategy or approach? Which data sources and methods could you use to evaluate the impact or outcome?

Case study: building students' pedagogical literacy for improved engagement

Disability, Diversity, and Social Inclusion is a first-year unit, with an average yearly enrolment of 200 students. The unit explores the application of universal design in a broad range of environments, including education. The student cohort is heterogeneous (including high-school graduates, workers and carers), and the different expectations that inform their transition to higher education can pose challenges for an inclusive education experience. In recognition of this diversity, and based on evidence that this unit had a higher than average fail rate, a number of universal design strategies were implemented in 2015. These strategies included multiple modes of content delivery (detailed notes, recordings and live delivery), and multiple avenues for student expression (face-to-face seminars, peer mentoring groups, discussion boards and flexible assignment submission formats). However, feedback indicated many students found the number and variety of opportunities available overwhelming, provoking a high number of queries from students to the unit team. In addition, these strategies did not have the intended impact on engagement and participation rates, which remained low.

The following year, the unit team decided to make the rationale for the UDL strategies more transparent to students. Students are now provided a small amount of information about UDL in week one, with concrete examples related to the unit's content and learning activities. In recognition of their transition experience, the unit team encourages students to explore the range of options on offer, and over time establish patterns of engagement that best suit their own learning needs.

In week five, students are expected to critique the UDL approach, grounded in their own personal experiences of a universally designed curriculum. This reflection process is intended to consolidate the students' understanding of universal design, but also provides the unit team with important feedback. For example, the unit team discovered that "listeners" in the cohort tended to consume the unit podcasts during activities such as driving, cleaning or exercise. This prompted the re-packaging of previously bite-sized audio recordings into longer files for uninterrupted listening. Another pattern the unit team identified was that some students, including those with language or learning difficulties, engaged with audio and video content simultaneously to support comprehension. In response to student reflections and engagement patterns, the unit team also altered the format of assessment instructions and reinforced the recommended learning pathway through presenting weekly online content.

Evaluation of the unit's redesign using UDL has identified a noticeable increase in students' observed and self-reported use of unit resources. Students responding positively to the statement "*I make best use of the learning experiences in this unit*" increased by 14% from 2015 to 2016, and positive responses to "*I think about how I could learn more effectively in this unit*" increased 20% in the same period. The impact on student success is indicated by the finding that unit fail rates have dropped from 12% (2015) to 6% (2017), and the percentage of students earning a distinction or higher has increased from 38% to 52%. The rate of assessment task submission has also increased, as has student participation in weekly online discussion board threads (which rose by 9.1% in the two years to 2017), and the proportion of students who read at least one post (which rose 8% in the same period). The quality of students' comments demonstrates that they are reflecting more deeply on their learning experience, and their content is now often framed by UDL concepts (e.g. resource flexibility and modes of engagement available).

Pedagogical literacy is an emerging concept, referring to the capability of educators to reflect on their teaching and appraise educational literature to deepen their professional knowledge and enhance their practice (Maclellan, 2008). To date pedagogical literacy has most commonly been associated with the learning of teachers, rather than teaching students the principles underpinning their learning. For instance, Maclellan proposed "the construction of written representations about teaching and learning can be powerful catalysts for teacher education students' own learning" (2008, p. 1987). The unit team's observations suggest that increasing the conscious awareness and understanding of UDL principles among students of disciplines other than education also puts them in a better position to appraise and leverage its strategies and tools. Within weeks of commencing *Disability, Diversity, and Social Inclusion*, students become vocal, critical, and discerning consumers of their educational resources. Exposing and explaining UDL to transitioning students from a range of disciplines could prove an effective and transformational approach, with the potential to impact their learning, engagement and success across their units of study and beyond their first year of higher education.

Reflection

- Consider a subject or course that you have been part of. What degree of pedagogical literacy did learners in that context typically display? How aware do you think they were of the rationale behind UDL or other curriculum design features of the course?
- What might be the immediate and longer-term benefits of educating students about how UDL is being applied in teaching in your own discipline?

Case study: balancing multiple representation, too much information and too many choices

AIX160 or *Introduction to University Studies* is a foundation unit designed to help university students develop the basic skills and knowledge they need to succeed in their studies. The unit was redeveloped in late 2014 by a collaborative team of academic and professional university staff, which included a project manager, learning designer, UDL consultant, unit chairs (past and present), library staff, Division of Student Life staff and an Institute of Koorie Education representative. This redevelopment was prompted by the perception that the previous iteration of this unit had become out-dated, and required development to embed digital literacies and a more internationalized curriculum.

The team aimed to embed the development of academic skills and literacies and digital literacy skills into the new iteration of the unit, using the UDL principles to frame the curriculum (Blake, Brown, & Watson, 2015). An audit of the existing curriculum against UDL guidelines and checkpoints (Center for Applied Special Technology, 2014) highlighted opportunities to redevelop and create new, more inclusive resources and activities. On reflection, the team experienced some difficulties in using the UDL framework as a guide for curriculum development and evaluation, noting that: "The UDL framework is large, wide-ranging and complex; and some elements overlap or are poorly defined" (Dracup, 2016). However, UDL is compatible with other frameworks of curriculum and resource design, and the team also drew on the UK Higher Education Academy inclusive curriculum principles and the constructive alignment model (Biggs & Tang, 2011), enabling a multidimensional approach to the unit's redesign.

A team including academics, librarians and student academic advisers delivered the redeveloped unit to a cohort of 268 students in early 2015, across three campuses and online. Following this inaugural delivery, evaluation took place to determine the effectiveness of the improved curriculum (particularly for equity groups) and identify possible future improvements. The evaluation sought to determine how the application of UDL had impacted on student engagement and learning. As indicated earlier in this chapter, the number and nature of factors that affect student engagement, learning and success make it impossible to establish or quantify causal relationships between approaches such as UDL and these outcomes (Naylor, Baik, & James, 2013). However, it is possible to gather relevant evidence by proxy methods, such as computer usage logs and student achievement via grades (Phillips, McNaught, & Kennedy, 2012). Valuable insights from both students and teachers can also be gained through qualitative methods, such as interviews and surveys (Merriam, 2009), and therefore a mixed methods approach was adopted for the evaluation.

The evaluation findings (Dracup, 2016) indicated that the 2015 cohort of students who experienced the redesigned curriculum achieved improved overall performance compared to 2014 students, which indicated it had helped students develop key transition-to-university skills. Students in all target equity groups achieved higher success rates, and the pass rate was 7.7% higher than in the previous year (Dracup, 2016). Also, the retention rate of students who completed the unit was 7.1% higher than their peers who completed other units. Notably, the retention rate was 9.3% higher for low-socio-economic status students and 8.7% higher for regional/remote students. Students' comments reinforce this finding, suggesting that designing curriculum and resources around UDL principles resulted in dynamic and powerful learning experiences. In particular, student feedback on quality and variety of unit resources was overwhelmingly positive, for example: *"The learning resources used in this unit are excellent"* (student survey comment); *"It would be a good example for a lot of other units: some of them have very little in the way of different media forms"* (focus group comment).

However, the evaluation found that students' preferences did not always match UDL guidelines. While many students appreciated the range of resources provided to support learning, many also responded that these were almost *"too much"*: *"Comprehensive almost to the point of overkill. So much information in a relatively short time frame, it was sometimes hard to absorb all I wanted to"* (student survey comment). A TESOL expert echoed this observation in an independent analysis; *"In general, I note that although there are engaging activities, videos and many links to further resources (and this is what makes the unit such high quality) – there is a high volume of information each week to process".*

In addition, while most students welcomed the subject choices in the major assignments, some students and teachers expressed concern about a lack of clarity and increasing complexity associated with these tasks. Some students commented they lacked resources or support to take best advantage of the opportunity to choose their topic, readings and arguments without guidance, for example:

"I struggled a lot trying to read the articles, especially ones for the assignment because I found it was such a weird assignment topic . . . I didn't know what they wanted me to find and it, it threw me a lot . . . and then trying to find points that backup with it . . . I struggled so much with that" (focus group comment).

Therefore, a significant finding from this evaluation was the tension between UDL guidelines for multiple representations of knowledge (i.e. in the unit learning resources) and multiple means of action and expression (i.e. in choices given for activities and assessments), and the transitioning students' need for clear direction and minimal distraction. Members of the redevelopment-teaching-evaluation team concluded that providing a highly supportive environment that anticipates diverse student needs must also include opportunities for students to develop self-reliance and efficacy at independently finding information (Dracup, 2016). Since its inaugural delivery and subsequent evaluation, ongoing unit improvement has sought to address concerns raised in the evaluation report, including streamlining the organization of resources, and more recently, making the rationale of the curriculum explicit, noting UDL as a framework that informs the inclusive curriculum design of the unit in an introductory video and transcript. While no further formal evaluation has taken place, the student success rate and student satisfaction over five trimesters has remained consistently at or above the faculty and university averages.

Reflection

- Reflect on a learning experience you have had in which a wide range of choices in terms of media types or areas of interest to pursue in an assessment task may have worked against your learning. What sort of mechanism or guidance would have helped you to make the best choices?
- If you have been involved in designing learning experiences for relatively large numbers of students in transition to higher education, in what ways have you balanced providing well-supported choices with ensuring tasks are easily understood?

Reflecting critically on UDL to support student success during the transition to higher education

Ideally, an optimal transitional experience entails a holistic whole-of-university approach. This brings together student support services and staff capacity building, along with curriculum design, in an integrated, sequenced, consistent, relevant, explicit and learner-focused manner (Kift, 2009; Nelson & Kift, 2005; Nelson, Creagh, Kift, & Clarke, 2014). However, such an approach takes time to develop (Brooker et al., 2017) and embed university-wide. It requires partnerships and collaboration across divisions and faculties, executive and senior level endorsement, as well as buy-in from professional and academic staff. A further challenge is thus "bridging the gaps between academic, administrative and support programs" (McInnis cited in Nelson & Kift, 2005, p. 226), to provide the optimal context for universally designed curriculum.

Looking forwards, Kift (2009) foregrounded third-generation approaches to transition that could entail whole-of-institution change guided by a coordinated strategy. This could address some of the workplace challenges identified by Nielsen (2013), but it is not widely practised at present as highlighted in a recent desktop audit and survey of Australian universities (Hitch, Macfarlane, & Nihill, 2015). This study found inconsistent evidence across the sector of professional development activities that support inclusive teaching practices. Around a third of Australian universities referred to inclusive teaching or UDL in policies or procedures, however the majority of professional development available for teaching staff consisted of one-off workshops focused on accommodating specific groups of students. Without a coordinated approach supported by all organizational levels in higher education organizations, the potential for UDL to enhance students' transition to higher education may not be fully realized.

UDL is undoubtedly a complex phenomenon, where guidelines and domains overlap, and are interdependent when put into practice. The principles and guidelines of UDL were designed to be sufficiently flexible to account for myriad education contexts, which have supported their global proliferation as described in this book. However, this flexibility can also lead to a lack of conceptual clarity and an overwhelming sense of its many potential applications. As the second case study illustrates, making the UDL framework explicit to students can support their success when transitioning into higher education, but they may not yet have developed sufficient personal abilities and capacities, and socio-cultural understanding of academic culture, to take full advantage of it.

Our experiences with UDL have also highlighted that the framework cannot be used in isolation. There are a number of other frameworks relevant to higher education (such as constructive alignment, social justice models, etc.), and UDL can be adapted to integrate successfully with these alternative theoretical perspectives. This makes UDL particularly suitable in multidisciplinary educational teams, as both a common ground and site for discipline-specific contributions.

While UDL has much to recommend it at the transition phase of the student journey, there are also modifications required in this context. During transition, students are dealing with a range of additional stressors and demands that may reduce their ability to engage with multiple means of engagement, representation, action and expression. They are also required to become far more independent learners than they may have expected to be previously; and in the current environment, they are unlikely to be receiving the whole-of-institution approach to either UDL or transition pedagogy that has been recommended as best practice. As highlighted in the third case study, too much of the flexibility and choice that UDL promotes can be just as problematic as too little for the transitioning first year student.

The rigorous evaluations undertaken in our case studies have enabled us to proceed with UDL in the transition setting in an informed and evidence-based way. However, as with any evaluation of educational experiences (Phillips et al., 2012), these are best planned from the inception of UDL initiatives and often require additional resourcing. Just as universal design in the built environment has been criticized for having an insufficient evidence base (Heylighen, 2014), our understanding of UDL during transition to higher education must continue to build over time to ensure we are using this approach to its best advantage.

Conclusion

The experience of implementing UDL in curricula to support students transitioning to higher education described in this chapter highlights the need for its adaptation to this specific phase of the student journey. There is sufficient flexibility within the UDL framework to enable it to be thoughtfully modified in this manner, and also align with the many other theories and policy frameworks that inform transition pedagogy. Evidence from Australia, and indeed globally, provides support for the application of UDL during the transition to higher education as a means of supporting student success.

However, the inclusion of students in the process of designing how and what they learn remains an underdeveloped aspect of the use of UDL in higher education. The case studies and research cited in this chapter involve students as participants in, and critics of, UDL-informed curriculum design. The Students as Partners movement is growing in the higher education sector in Australia and globally (Healey, Flint, & Harrington, 2014; Matthews, 2016), offering students the opportunity to take a more agentic role in the design of universally accessible and relevant curriculum. The next step in applying UDL during the transition to higher education could be the formation of collaborative partnerships between students and educators, to co-create practices and cultures of learning targeted at the needs, capacities and capabilities of those beginning their journey in higher education.

Further reading

Transition Pedagogy
http://transitionpedagogy.com/

References

Baik, C., Naylor, R., & Arkoudis, S. (2015). *The first year experience in Australian universities: findings from two decades, 1994–2014.* Melbourne: Melbourne Centre for the Study of Higher Education (CSHE), University of Melbourne.

Barnett, R. (2004). Learning for an unknown future. *Higher Education Research and Development, 23*(3), 247–260.

Biggs, J., & Tang, C. (2011). *Teaching for quality learning at university* (4th ed.). Maidenhead: Open University Press.

Blake, D., Brown, P., & Watson, J. (2015). *Faculty of Arts & Education inclusive curriculum design project report.* Geelong: Deakin University.

Brooker, A., Brooker, S., & Lawrence, J. (2017). First year students' perceptions of their difficulties. *Student Success, 8*(1), 49–62.

Centre for Applied Special Technology. (2014). *What is UDL?* Retrieved from www.udlcenter.org/aboutudl/whatisudl

Coates, H., Kelly, P., & Naylor, R. (2016). *New perspectives on the student experience.* Parkville: University of Melbourne. Retrieved from http://melbourne-cshe.unimelb.edu.au/__data/assets/pdf_file/0011/1862228/New-Perspectives-on-the-Student-Experience_240316_updated.pdf

Dinmore, S., & Stokes, J. (2015). Creating inclusive university curriculum: Implementing universal design for learning in an enabling program. *Widening Participation and Lifelong Learning, 17*(4), 4–19.

Dracup, M. (2016). *Applying UDL in an 'Introduction to University' unit: Evaluation report.* Geelong: Deakin University.

Gale, T., & Parker, S. (2014). Navigating change: A typology of student transition in higher education. *Studies in Higher Education, 39*(5), 734–753.

Goldingay, S., Macfarlane, S., Hitch, D., Hosken, N., Lamaro, G., Farrugia, D., Nihill, C., & Ryan, J. (2012). *A multidimensional framework for embedded academic skill development: Transition pedagogy in social work.* Geelong, Australia: Deakin University.

Hall, T., Meyer, A., & Rose, D. (2012). *Universal design for learning in the classroom: Practical applications – what works for special-needs learners.* New York: Guilford Publications.

Healey, M., Flint, A., & Harrington, K. (2014). *Engagement through partnership: Students as partners in learning and teaching in higher education.* York: Higher Education Academy.

Heylighen, A. (2014). About the nature of design in universal design. *Disability & Rehabilitation, 36*(16), 1360–1368.

Higbee, J. L. (2015). The faculty perspective: Implementation of universal design in a first year classroom. In S. Burgstahler (Ed.), *Universal design in higher education: From principles to practice* (pp. 101–116). Cambridge, MA: Harvard Education Press.

Higher Education Opportunity Act 2008 (USA) Sec 103. [a] (24). Retrieved from www.gpo.gov/fdsys/pkg/PLAW-110publ315/html/PLAW-110publ315.htm

Hitch, D., Macfarlane, S., & Nihill, C. (2015). Inclusive pedagogy in Australian universities: A review of current policies and professional development activities. *The International Journal of the First Year in Higher Education*, 6(1), 135–145.

Hockings, C., Cooke, S., & Bowl, M. (2010). Learning and teaching in two universities within the context of increasing student diversity: Complexity, contradictions and challenges. In M. David (Ed.), *Improving learning by widening participation in higher education* (pp. 95–108). London: Routledge.

Kift, S. (2009). *Articulating a transition pedagogy to scaffold and to enhance the first year student learning experience in Australian higher education*. Canberra: Australian Learning & Teaching Council.

Kift, S. (2015). A decade of transition pedagogy: A quantum leap in conceptualising the first year experience. *HERDSA Review of Higher Education*, 2, 51–86.

Krause, K. L., Hartley, R., James, R., & McInnis, C. (2005). *The first year experience in Australian universities: Findings from a decade of national studies*. Melbourne: University of Melbourne.

Kumar, K. L., & Wideman, M. (2014). Accessible by design: Applying UDL principles in a first year undergraduate course. *Canadian Journal of Higher Education*, 44(1), 125–147.

Lawrence, J. (2005). Addressing diversity in higher education: Two models for facilitating student engagement and mastery. *Research and Development in Higher Education*, 28, 243–252.

Lizzio, A. (2006). *Designing an orientation and transition strategy for commencing students: Applying the five senses model*. Queensland: Griffith University.

Maclellan, E. (2008). Pedagogical literacy: What it means and what it allows. *Teaching and Teacher Education*, 24(8), 1986–1992.

Matthews, K. E. (2016). Students as partners as the future of student engagement. *Student Engagement in Higher Education Journal*, 1(1), 1–5.

Merriam, S. (2009). *Qualitative research: A guide to design and implementation* (2nd ed.). San Francisco, CA: Jossey-Bass.

National Center on Universal Design for Learning. (2014). *What is UDL?* Retrieved from www.udlcenter.org/aboutudl/whatisudl

Naylor, R., Baik, C., & James, R. (2013). *A critical interventions framework for advancing equity in Australian higher education*. Report prepared for the Department of Industry, Innovation, Climate Change, Science, Research and Tertiary Education. Melbourne: Centre for the Study of Higher Education, University of Melbourne.

Nelson, K., Creagh, T., Kift, S., & Clarke, J. (2014). *Transition pedagogy handbook: A good practice guide for policy and practice in the first year experience at QUT* (2nd ed.). Queensland: Queensland University of Technology.

Nelson, K., & Kift, S. (2005, July 3–6). Beyond curriculum reform: Embedding the transition experience. In A. Brew & C. Asmar (Eds.), *HERDSA 2005*. Sydney: The University of Sydney.

Nielsen, D. (2013). Universal design in first year composition – Why do we need it, how can we do it? *CEA Forum*, 42(2), 3–29.

Phillips, R., McNaught, C., & Kennedy, G. (2012). *Evaluating e-learning: Guiding research and practice*. New York: Routledge.

Schelly, C. L., Davies, P. L., & Spooner, C. L. (2011). Student perceptions of faculty implementation of universal design for learning. *Journal of Postsecondary Education and Disability*, *24*(1), 17–30.

Sefa Dei, G. (2008). Indigenous knowledge studies and the next Generation: Pedagogical possibilities for anti-colonial education. *Australian Journal of Indigenous Education*, *37*, supplement.

Thomas, L., Hill, M., O'Mahony, J., & Yorke, M. (2017). *What works? Student retention and success*. York: Higher Education Academy.

Tzivinikou, S. (2014). Universal design for learning – application in higher education: A Greek paradigm. *Problems of Education in the 21st Century*, *60*, 156–166.

Wood, L., & Breyer, Y. (2017). Success in higher education. In L. Wood & Y. Breyer (Eds.), *Success in higher education: Transitions to, within and from university* (pp. 1–19). Singapore: Springer.

Chapter 6

Using professional learning communities to redesign learning environments in HEIs

Liz Berquist and Jane Neapolitan

Case study

A leadership team led by an assistant provost and consisting of department chairs and deans from multiple colleges meets regularly to discuss instruction at a mid-sized public university in the Northeast United States. Of recent concern is the increase in student attrition, particularly in first generation college students, students of color and students whose primary language is not English. Upon examining exit interviews of students leaving higher education, faculty determine that course content, accessibility and lack of engagement with instructors are among the primary reasons for students deciding not to return to campus.

An analysis of these barriers leads faculty to identify improved instruction as an area of focus. Interestingly, the group came to the conclusion that the majority of faculty members have been trained in content, and while they are experts in their field, many have not been trained in pedagogy. The campus leaders wonder how they can provide additional professional development to their faculty in order to proactively meet the needs of the learner variability that exists within their institution. Faculty members understand it is their ethical and moral imperative to teach each learner who registers for the course, regardless of the skill set that they are bringing to the classroom.

One strategy to meet the need of this changing population is to identify the factors that can be controlled by the instructor. Universal Design for Learning (UDL) is a framework that encourages instructors to first consider the variability that exists in their

learning environments and then design proactive learning environment supports. This proactive planning process is new to many
faculty, who were trained to teach to the "average" student. The
leadership team decides to design a series of professional learning
opportunities to proactively address the challenge of learner variability through UDL.

Introduction: national context of UDL and higher education

Universal Design for Learning (UDL) is defined in the Higher Education
Opportunity Act of 2008 (HEOA) of the U.S Department of Education as a
scientifically validated framework for supporting all learners through flexible
curriculum. In the field of higher education, UDL has traditionally been applied
to two areas: pre-service teacher education and the support of post-secondary
students with disabilities. In recent years, HEIs have become increasingly interested in the potential of the UDL framework to support instructors tasked with
designing accessible and engaging learning environments.

Rappolt-Schlichtmann, Daley and Rose indicated that "there has been
exponential growth in interest surrounding the UDL framework, primarily
within education policy and practice" (2012: 1). This growth can be attributed
to the uniqueness of the UDL framework, which is grounded in equity based,
inclusive practices. UDL encourages educators to identify barriers that learners
may experience and to remove those barriers proactively. Instead of focusing on
changing our learners, UDL focuses on designing learning environments that
are flexible (Berquist, 2017). The UDL guidelines are actionable strategies for
applying the UDL framework. These guidelines can help faculty members to
identify patterns in learner variability and proactively offer options for engagement, representation, action and expression.

While interest in UDL is growing in higher education, faculty rarely have
formal training on how to proactively incorporate the guidelines into their
practice. This chapter will provide an overview of how leadership can design
professional learning opportunities for faculty members in HEIs through a
professional learning community format aligned to CAST's phases of UDL
implementation (National Center on Universal Design for Learning, 2012).
Attention will also be given to strategies specifically developed to support adult
learners. This professional learning structure can be applied to across multiple environments in HEIs, from community colleges to four-year institutions.
Community colleges generally are two-year programs that offer an associate's
degree. Credits from community colleges can then be transferred to a four-year
institution to earn a bachelor's degree.

Identifying faculty professional learning needs: university context

Towson University is a public institution located outside Baltimore, Maryland with 22,000 undergraduate and graduate students, it is the largest public institution in the Baltimore area. For many teaching universities, a track record of good teaching is often assumed but not always articulated in such a way that it becomes shared across the institution. Over the past 10 years, Towson University's student population has doubled in size and has become more racially and socially diverse. To a lesser extent, faculty have also become more diverse with many having worked in business, health care, P-12 education, and the arts and sciences before making their way into academia. A large proportion of them are non-tenure track or part-time. With the growth of academic departments, an increase in teaching and advising responsibilities, and an increased emphasis on scholarly production, protected time for reflecting on one's teaching in the company of colleagues seems challenging. Fortunately, many departments and colleges continue their traditions for supporting faculty professional learning within their disciplines. However, as colleges and departments grow, the focus on curriculum and pedagogy may become specialized rather than widened.

Reflection

- What is the nature of your own university, has its demographic changed in recent years, and how has this impacted on professional development requirements?
- What scope is there for cross faculty engagement with professional learning in your setting?
- What types of professional learning may meet best meet the needs of your faculty?

Building a professional development network using professional learning communities

The Universal Design for Learning Professional Development Network (UDL PDN) was developed to introduce faculty to the Universal Design for Learning (UDL) framework and to build capacity in the design and delivery of courses that applied UDL to instruction. The Office of Academic Innovation (OAI) sponsored the UDL PDN, ensuring that that the UDL PDN was a campus-wide, multidisciplinary project that brings faculty from multiple colleges together across the university. The UDL PDN used a professional learning community (PLC) model for exploring the UDL guidelines and principles and applying them to teaching. There are numerous iterations of a PLC; the UDL PDN is guided by Dufour's (2006) definition of a professional learning community (PLC) as an ongoing process in which educators work collaboratively in recurring cycles of collective inquiry and action research to achieve better results for the students they serve. UDL PDN members worked together in job-embedded settings to explore advances in the learning sciences and flexible curricular materials as they develop an understanding of UDL and its application to instruction in higher education.

The goal of the UDL PDN was to align instructional practices with the UDL framework, to enhance instructional practice through collaboration with colleagues in professional learning communities and to show positive change in faculty beliefs, knowledge and skills related to UDL. The design of the UDL PDN is aligned to CAST's stages of UDL Implementation (see Table 6.2 on page 110). UDL implementation is an iterative process that includes exploration, preparation, integration, scaling and optimizing and is characterized by

Table 6.1 Six foundations for adult learning

Adult Learning Foundation	Strategies for applying adult learning foundation to the design of a UDL PDN
Emotions: Adults must feel safe to learn	Provide multiple opportunities to explore and prepare for UDL implementation prior to actual implementation
	Allow faculty to self-select enrollment in a learning community
	Assign a peer coach to each learning community to provide job-embedded support and non-evaluative feedback
History: Adults come to learning experiences with histories.	Ensure that dedicated time is available to uncover existing conceptions about teaching and learning
	Recognize and celebrate instructional strategies that are already aligned to the UDL framework
Knowing why: Adults need to know why we have to learn something.	Make a clear connection to the work of the learning community and the goals of the University
	Encourage early adopters to share success stories as a rationale for participation
Self-direction: Adults want agency in our learning.	Provide choice in learning: face to face, online, webinars, guided exploration of resources.
	Design learning community sessions to include open discussion and collective problem solving
Internalizing learning: Adults need practice to internalize learning.	Build in opportunities for faculty to practice new instructional strategies in a supportive environment
	Design learning walks or classroom to classroom visits that allow faculty to see new learning in practice
Problem-centered learning: Adults have a problem-centered orientation to learning.	Encourage learning community members to bring authentic problems of practice to meetings
	Make a commitment that all deliverables will be based upon a defined need and will be able to be used by faculty immediately

ongoing evaluation and improvement (Ralabate, 2013; Fixsen, Naoom, Blasé, Friedman, & Wallace, 2005), these phases are further explored next.

Applying adult learning theory to a professional development network

Campus leaders grounded their work in the foundations of adult learning (Knowles, 1984). This approach to the development of the UDL PDN encouraged coaches to consider the six foundations of adult learning (see Table 6.1) as they developed learning experiences for their professional learning communities. The foundations of adult learning were applied to the project in its entirety and to each phase of implementation. For example, we know that adults must know why they need to learn something; it is essential to ensure that we provide a rationale for our work. Campus leadership was clear that the goal of the UDL PDN was to support faculty as they designed instruction to meet the challenge of the learner variability that exists in their classrooms. We also know that adults want agency in their learning. UDL PDN members were offered multiple options to engage in learning: components of the UDL PDN included face to face and online professional development, just in time support provided by a UDL facilitator, campus-wide professional learning opportunities, and tool and resource sharing. At the PLC level, coaches focused on changing the beliefs, knowledge and practices of individual faculty. Adult learning theory informed this work. For example, coaches were cognizant that adults come to any learning experience with history (Knowles, 1984). With this knowledge, coaches dedicated time to exploring the existing conceptions of faculty and the impact that these conceptions have on the design of learning environments. Table 6.1 presents the foundations and additional examples of application to the UDL PDN.

Applying Adult Learning Theory to a Professional Development Network

> ### Reflection
>
> - Consider the foundations of adult learning in Table 6.1. How can knowledge of adult learning enhance application of UDL in HEIs?
> - What strategies might you employ in your setting?

Applying phases of UDL implementation to a professional development network

In addition to applying adult learning theory to the design of the UDL PDN, campus leaders also used their knowledge of CAST's phases of UDL implementation to ensure that professional learning experiences were designed to meet the needs of faculty variability.

Explore

During this phase, campus leaders investigate UDL as a framework for curriculum design and decision making, raise awareness about UDL among key decision makers, and determine interest and willingness to pursue UDL implementation. This phase is characterized by investigation of UDL as a potential implementation framework. The Office of Academic Innovation (OAI) was established at Towson University (TU) for the purpose of supporting faculty to use innovative teaching practices assisted by technology integration. The goals of Towson University's UDL Professional Development Network (UDL PDN) were (1) to provide TU faculty with a flexible curriculum framework that would support a common language for planning, implementing and reflecting on pedagogies founded on research; and (2) creating an interdisciplinary professional learning community for sustaining the effort.

Prepare

In this phase, campus leaders should be able to state their vision for UDL implementation and develop an action plan to meet that vision. Goal setting, identification of supports and resources and the development of measurable outcomes characterize this phase. Having met to discuss UDL with university leaders from the Office of the Provost, Disability Support Services, the Office of the Registrar, and Academic Advising, the Assistant Provost was convinced a campus-wide UDL effort would help faculty improve their teaching in order to affect student success. With support and encouragement from the university leaders, the Assistant Provost set out to develop a plan to bring UDL to all faculty.

OAI sponsored a workshop to introduce faculty members to the UDL framework. The purpose of this workshop was to provide faculty with an overview of UDL, to identify implications for strengthening instruction in higher education and to recruit interested individuals to become UDL coaches. Following the introductory workshop, prospective coaches (solicited from any faculty demonstrating interest) completed applications and requested approval from their department Chairpersons and Deans. Prospective Coaches' Applications were reviewed by OAI and the first UDL training for Coaches began. Coaches met monthly to expand their knowledge of UDL and also participated in a book study of Meyer, Rose, and Gordon (2014).

The UDL Coaches were guided by a facilitator who focused on introducing the elements of the UDL framework and offered examples of UDL in classroom practice. Shortly thereafter, the notice went out to all faculty (including tenure track, non-tenure track and part-time) about the new UDL PDN. Interested faculty completed a simple form that asked why they were interested in UDL and what they hoped their students would gain from its application. Interested faculty were also required to obtain the signatures of their department Chairperson and Dean to ensure that administrators supported faculty's participation. Each faculty would be given a modest stipend for applying UDL principles to at least one teaching artifact, such as an assessment, digital learning object, project, assignment or an entire syllabus. Faculty would be required to share their work at a campus-wide "speed dating" type event and encouraged to upload their artifacts on UDL Connect, a collaborative, open website aimed at connecting UDL implementers. This intense focus on preparing for UDL implementation through goal setting, long range planning, resource mapping and foundation setting was a crucial step in the success of the UDL PDN.

Integrate

During this phase, campus leaders provide professional learning opportunities to develop faculty expertise, create processes and resources to support integrating UDL with practices that already exist, and create procedures and protocols for reviewing and evaluating outcomes. Another key strategy includes establishing professional learning communities (PLCs) that use an inquiry process to collaboratively learn how to employ UDL practices in higher education. For example, faculty would come to PLC meetings with authentic problems of practice and work together to identify barriers and proactive solutions.

As a result of the first year of exploration and preparation, a number of faculty who had shown a special interest in UDL volunteered to serve as peer coaches for the next iteration. In consultation with the faculty expert, OAI decided to raise expectations by designing a more intentional program of professional development that included smaller learning communities coached by experienced UDL faculty. Five PLCS engaged a total of 50 faculty drawn from all 6 colleges across the university. PLCs were led by trained Towson faculty coaches who meet regularly with their PLCs throughout the academic year to share and discuss information about UDL and create modifications or new components for their courses. These components included an extensive range of strategies and approaches from revisions of course syllabi, readings, activities, quizzes and exams, to more complex multimedia objects that can be used in face-to-face courses, blended courses, and fully online. PLC members also had the opportunity to participate in a three-day summer UDL institute, co-sponsored by the Baltimore County Public Schools.

A doctoral student from the Instructional Technology program in the College of Education was also hired by OAI to serve as a facilitator for the online UDL PDN. Adding an online component to the UDL PDN allowed faculty to interact without having to be in the same physical location. A UDL toolkit was developed and shared with other TU faculty at campus-wide UDL meetings and at invitational meetings in academic departments and demonstrated that UDL was aligned with commonly-used best teaching practices (this is available from the University website under a document entitled "Faculty Friendly Ideas and Strategies for Implementing UDL").

Scale

During this phase, campus leaders enhance effective processes and organizational supports, expand practices throughout the system, and promote a community of practice to support shared learning across the system. This phase is characterized by adoption of UDL as a system-wide curriculum and decision-making framework.

Five years after its inception, the UDL PDN continued to grow, supported by the Office of Academic Innovation (OAI). This phase is aligned to the University's strategic plan to close the achievement gap for first generation and economically disadvantaged students as well as students from underrepresented groups. While both undergraduate and graduate faculty members are eligible to apply for the UDL PDN, preference is given to those faculty who teach courses that serve our at-risk students. By continuing to build UDL cohorts, the OAI hopes to increase the number of faculty trained to use UDL concepts and best practices in their teaching, thus increasing the number of UDL-enhanced courses across the University. In addition, the UDL PDN engages faculty in the scholarship of teaching and learning. Cohort members have the option to engage in action research about the impacts of UDL-enhanced courses through inquiry-oriented communities of practice. It is important to note that this work was not without its challenges. Inevitably, changes in university priorities and budget cut-backs slowed down the momentum of the UDL PDN. Midway through the project, the formal cohorts went on hiatus, but occasional UDL information sessions continued.

In year four of implementation, OAI added the UDL PDN to its strategic initiatives for the purpose of quantifying some of its impacts on student success and faculty development. The goal for the next three years was to increase the number of new faculty participants to 30 with an end product of 60 UDL-oriented syllabi. Over 60 syllabi were collaboratively reviewed and revised for courses in the arts and sciences, business, fine arts, education and health care. Being able to identify the specific courses where UDL is applied will help track the number of students on the receiving end. It is hoped that some targeted and in-depth studies of the impacts of UDL can be identified for further exploration in the coming years. As in the former iterations, experienced UDL faculty would continue to serve as mentors and consultants to the participating faculty. Through a series of group meetings and one-on-one consultations as needed, faculty participants worked on revisions of their syllabi and uploaded them to a community site on Blackboard (the university's Learning Management System). Meanwhile, the number of faculty users and the number of students affected are expected to increase.

Optimize

The UDL PDN at Towson University is just beginning to explore strategies for maximizing continuous improvement. During this phase, campus leaders strategically predict and plan for internal and external change that could impact UDL implementation, embed processes that allow for innovation while maximizing continuous improvement, and cultivate and enhance a UDL culture. This phase is characterized by continuous adjustment, innovation and refinement to optimize sustainability of UDL as a system-wide decision-making and instructional framework.

In addition to increasing the number of faculty engaged in UDL teaching practices and the number of courses modified via UDL principles, OAI sought to assess the application of UDL and share insights about UDL with other faculty. In 2017, a 16-item questionnaire constructed by OAI was sent to 135 faculty who had participated either in the UDL PDN or had independently sought assistance from OAI for using UDL. Questions covered the extent to which faculty had applied UDL, overall perceptions of student performance in UDL-modified assignments, and kinds of assignments or activities in which UDL had been used. The majority of the faculty responded they had used UDL to modify both individual- and group assignments in class, homework assignments, and individual projects/performances/portfolios. To a lesser extent, UDL had been applied to group projects/performances/portfolios and to papers, quizzes, tests and exams.

Nearly 80% of the respondents felt the revisions they made using UDL had met or surpassed their goals for increasing student motivation. Also, nearly 75% felt the use of UDL had met or surpassed their goals for increasing overall student knowledge and resourcefulness. Nearly 70% agreed that UDL had met or surpassed their goals for overall student performance on quizzes, exams, assignments and projects. Additional comments emphasized increases in student engagement with the course material, peer-to-peer interactions, and interactions with the instructor. Opportunities to demonstrate mastery of material was also cited as a benefit as well as taking ownership of one's learning.

Approximately 80% of the respondents stated they had shared information about UDL with other teaching professionals. More than half had shared information about UDL with faculty and/or administrators in their program, department, college, or university; and nearly one quarter had shared information via presentations to audiences outside TU. Approximately 10% had shared information in published works they had authored or co-authored. Additional comments about sharing insights included, "I like the UDL philosophy, but changing decades worth of teaching styles takes a long time. Little changes are happening each semester. One assignment or one class at a time". Another professor succinctly stated, "We all need more time and opportunity to talk to each other". This emphasis on collaboration and shared inquiry is a hallmark of the UDL PDN and an example of how faculty are now working to thoughtfully and proactively consider the needs of the learner variability that exists within their institution as they design and deliver instruction.

Table 6.2 Phases of UDL implementation (informed by CAST 2012)

	Phase	Goal
Explore	Raise awareness of UDL, identify need or reason to change practice	Articulate why you should be able to integrate UDL
Prepare	Identify needed supports, map resources, identify measurable outcomes	State vision for UDL and develop an action plan to reach that vision
Integrate	Application and evaluation of UDL	Successfully integrate UDL into learning environment
Scale	Promote design using UDL, enhance implementation, expand practices	Successfully scale UDL to additional faculty, courses, departments
Optimize*	Predict and plan for internal and external change that could impact UDL implementation, embed processes that allow for innovation while maximizing continuous improvement, and cultivate and enhance a UDL culture	Adjust strategic implementation based on data in order to ensure that UDL is sustainable as a system-wide decision-making and instructional framework

*Case study in this chapter is just beginning to enter this phase

---

Reflection

- Consider the phases of implementation. Where is your university? What lessons can you learn from the work of the UDL PDN?
- Identify strategies within each phase that could help move your work forward.
- How might you form a professional development group within your own setting?

Conclusion

This chapter describes how campus leadership can develop a process to design professional learning communities that meet the needs of adult learners and progress through the phases of CAST's UDL implementation process. The UDL PDN at Towson University is one example of applying both adult learning needs and the phases of UDL implementation to a multi-year project. The UDL PDN at Towson can provide other HEIs with lessons learned for implementation. Next steps will include expanding upon the first survey to include tracking of selected individual courses and more in-depth interviews with faculty about what they have learned as UDL participants. Additional efforts will be made to investigate the application of UDL by faculty who teach online and have been trained to use TU's adaptation of the University's Quality Matters Rubric for online course design. As online course offerings increase at the university, applying UDL principles to distance education will further deepen UDL's influence for improving teaching and learning in multiple modalities. There is no prescribed number lock step process for implementing UDL in higher education; it is most important to consider the needs of faculty and a proactive, flexible design that provides for variability in faculty and to provide time and strategic planning for positive change to take place.

References

Berquist, E. (Ed.). (2017). *UDL: Moving from exploration to integration*. Wakefield, MA: CAST Professional Publishing.

CAST (2012). *UDL implementation strategy guide*. Wakefield: MA: Author.

DuFour, R., DuFour, R., Eaker, R., & Many, T. (2006). *Learning by doing: A handbook for professional learning communities at work*. Bloomington, IN: Solution Tree.

Fixsen, D. L., Naoom, S. F., Blasé, K. A., Friedman, R. M., & Wallace, F. (2005). *Implementation research: A synthesis of the literature*. Tampa: University of South Florida, Louis de la Parte Florida Mental Health Institute, NIRN (FMHI Publication #231).

Knowles, M. (1984). *Andragogy in action: Applying modern principles of adult learning*. San Francisco, CA: Jossey-Bass.

Meyer, A., Rose, D. H., & Gordon, D. (2014). *Universal design for learning: Theory and practice*. Wakefield, MA: CAST Professional Publishing.

National Center on Universal Design for Learning. (2012). *UDL implementation: A process of change* [Online seminar presentation]. UDL Series, no. 3. Retrieved from http://udlseries.udlcenter.org/presentations/udl_implementation.html#

Ralabate, P. K. (2013). Collaborative planning using universal design for learning. *ASHA Perspectives*, 15(1), 25–30. Rockville, MD: ASHA.

Rappolt-Schlichtmann, G., Daley, S. G., & Rose, L. T. (Eds.). (2012). *A research reader in universal design for learning*. Cambridge, MA: Harvard Education Press.

Facilitating multiple identities and student engagement

Chapter 7

Instructional design with UDL

Addressing learner variability in college courses

Kavita Rao

Case study

Elza teaches courses in a Masters of Social Work program at a large public university in the United States. Her department has developed several online and hybrid programs in addition to their existing on campus programs intended to appeal to diverse students who are seeking graduate degrees. The typical demographic of Elza's courses, both online and on campus, include culturally and linguistically diverse students, first generation learners, and adult learners who enroll in school part time while working. Elza is aware of the diversity and circumstances of her students and tries to be a responsive and supportive instructor.

In her end-of-course evaluations, students often comment that they feel overwhelmed by the reading assignments and amount of writing required. In addition, some students comment on the fact that course expectations are unclear to them. Over the years, Elza has reduced the number of articles she assigns. She feels reluctant to eliminate more because she wants to maintain high expectations and standards. She uses several short writing assignments as assessments, expecting students to be able to synthesize information and articulate their understanding and mastery of content. Elza notes that about one-third of the students enrolled in her courses have challenges with the writing assignments, in areas ranging from mechanics and clarity of writing to depth of expression.

Every semester, a couple of students drop out due to the inability to juggle the demands of the course with other obligations. Considering the common challenges and barriers she sees semester-after-semester, Elza wonders how she can redesign her courses to facilitate her students' success. She considers using an instructional design process to systematically redesign her courses to more proactively support her diverse learners.

Introduction

Instructional design (ID), a systematic process of creating instructional experiences, lies at the heart of developing effective lessons and courses. Broadly, various systems of instructional design include these five stages: Analysis, Design, Development, Implementation, and Evaluation (Morrison, Ross, Kemp, & Kalman, 2010). The ID process is a systematic way to design and implement courses aligning learner needs with pedagogical decision-making.

Although ID is essential to course development, university-level instructors often do not have formal training on how to systematically use these processes when they develop courses. Instructors generally use teaching methods and formats that they have encountered as students or have seen colleagues using. These days, instructors may be tasked with teaching courses in various formats such as online, blended, and face-to-face. When tasked with teaching courses in a new or different format, it can seem expedient to transfer activities and materials from one format to another (for example, from one's face-to-face course to their online course). By using an ID process, instructors can make more thoughtful decisions about pedagogical practices, providing supportive and engaging learning environments in the formats they teach.

This chapter provides an overview of how instructors can benefit from undertaking a systematic ID process as they develop courses. The ID process lets instructors consider how they can most effectively use various pedagogical practices to meet their objectives for a course. The systematic process also allows instructors to begin with a needs assessment that includes consideration of the learners they will be teaching and to proactively design instruction to address student needs and preferences. This process can be applied to online, blended, and face-to-face courses.

Learner variability and Universal Design for Learning

Learner variability is the norm in today's classrooms. Refuting the notion that there is an "average learner," the concept of learner variability emphasizes individuals can become expert learners in varied ways (Meyer, Rose, & Gordon, 2014). There is no one path to mastery; all students can benefit from having flexible options and choices as part of the learning process. Meyer and colleagues describe the implications of learner variability for educators:

> We now understand from scientific research that brains and even genes are highly responsive to their environments. Individual differences in our brains are not innate or fixed but developed and malleable, and context has huge impact. This is the best news yet for educators who have the opportunity to provide environments that facilitate positive growth, or learning, for all students.
>
> (p. 81)

Instructors can design instructional experiences that address learner variability, proactively building in flexible choices, supports, and scaffolds that facilitate the learning experience for all. Learner variability is systematic and predictable, making it possible for instructors to design learning experiences that will benefit many students instead of designing for each individual student (Meyer et al., 2014). To design for variability, instructors can begin by preempting common barriers to learning, identifying students' attributes and preferences, and by investigating specific areas and needs for supports that students have in their courses.

UDL is defined in the Higher Education Opportunity Act of 2008 (HEOA) of the U.S Department of Education as a scientifically validated framework for supporting all learners through flexible curriculum. The HEOA emphasizes the need to use UDL to provide supports for students with disabilities at a post-secondary level. In addition to proactively providing support for students with disabilities, UDL can be used to enhance access to curriculum and instruction for all learners. Researchers describe various ways apply UDL guidelines to post-secondary course design to enhance student support and increase accessibility (Dell, Dell, & Blackwell, 2015; Gradel & Edson, 2009; Rao, Edelen-Smith, & Wailehua, 2015; Rao & Tanners, 2011; Scott & Temple, 2017). The term "access" commonly connotes the provision of support to students with disabilities to ensure that they receive appropriate accommodations and modifications. The use of UDL extends the concept of access to all students who can benefit from the design features that take into consideration that individuals learn in varied ways. This broader definition includes "cognitive access," a consideration of flexible options and scaffolds that can help students master knowledge and skills in a course.

In the literature, UDL researchers address various levels of access within courses. Dell et al. (2015) present the University of Arkansas' Ten Steps of Design of Online Courses. These ten steps include considerations of text readability, color choices, presentation design, and use of captions and transcriptions, which are consistent with UDL guidelines for *providing options for perception* and *options for comprehension* (associated with Multiple Means of Representation). Researchers describe UDL-based strategies that can be incorporated during the learning process, such as supports that can be provided to help students conduct a research project (Gradel & Edson, 2009). Articles on universally designed courses also illustrate how researchers can use various digital tools, scaffolds, and interactive strategies to add flexibility and enhance clarity in a course (Rao & Tanners, 2011) that are consistent guidelines for providing *options for expression and communication* (associated with Multiple Means of Action and Expression) and *providing options for self-regulation* (associated with Multiple Means of Engagement). Researchers also emphasize the importance of clear and consistent navigation in a course (Rao et al., 2015; Scott & Temple, 2017), which aligns with the idea of *providing options for comprehension* by highlighting key areas and *provide options for supporting executive function* (associated with Multiple Means of Action and Expression).

Identifying barriers, preferences, and support needs

During the ID process, the first step is to consider the intended learners. With this as a starting point, instructors can begin to make pedagogical design decisions. When considering instructional design with a UDL lens, this first step includes not only considering who the learners might be but also identifying potential barriers for learners. Although instructors may not know exactly who will enroll in their courses, they have some idea of the characteristics of students who take a particular course or enroll in a program. Instructors can often discern some common challenges for students once they have taught a course or worked with particular groups of students. Although each student will have individual strengths, preferences, and needs, there will be commonalities that can be addressed through a systematic design process. Because learner variability is systematic and predictable (Meyer et al., 2014), instructors can consider the common barriers for students and begin to address those during course design.

It is important to note here, that in addition to predictable variability, there are students who require specific accommodations. Using UDL does not eliminate the need to provide specific modifications when needed. For example, for a student with a sensory impairment (e.g., visual impairment or deaf/hard of hearing), the UDL options may reduce the need for modifications if the instructor has already provided text-based captions to videos and auditory options for various resources. However, some students may need additional specific modifications or accommodations to ensure access to all aspects of the course.

The following sections describe ways in which instructors can address variability and support students who enroll in post-secondary programs with diverse educational backgrounds and life experiences, such as the students who enrolled in Elza's classes in the opening vignette. This includes culturally and linguistically diverse students, first generation college students,

students with disabilities, and adult learners. These students bring with them various experiences and strengths but can also benefit from supports to help them juggle multiple obligations, access academic content, and understand academic expectations. For example, adult learners may return to school to gain new or advanced training in a field while concurrently working and managing other obligations. First generation learners are the first in their families to go to college and may not have the family support or background knowledge on how to navigate academic expectations. While UDL-based course design can provide supports for all learners, this chapter addresses specific ways in which instructors can reduce barriers and integrate supports students with diverse backgrounds and abilities (Johnson, Taasoobshirazi, Clark, Howell, & Breen, 2016; Schuetze, 2014). Common barriers for these students can include:

1   Excessive reliance on text (reading and written assignments)
2   Ambiguity about expectations

(Eady & Woodcock, 2010; McLoughlin & Oliver, 2000; Rao, Eady, & Edelen-Smith, 2011; Rao et al., 2015)

These barriers can arise as a function of the pedagogical practices instructors regularly use in courses. With an awareness of the challenges that some pedagogical practices can create for students, instructors can design courses that provide flexibility and build in options that support students to persist and succeed with coursework.

When faced with these barriers, some students report feeling less confident about their ability to complete a course or a program. Students might internalize these feelings of underconfidence and start to feel a sense of failure in their attempts to undertake post-secondary coursework, assuming they are personally not qualified or capable enough to be in these university level courses. This can lead to a lack of persistence on the student's part and eventual attrition from the course. Table 7.1 provides additional information on the types of issues that students have reported for each category of barrier.

In addition to barriers, it is important to consider students' potential preferences. Instructors might be aware of preferences that the students who typically enroll in their courses have and can use that information to design future courses. For example, some students prefer collaborative work while others prefer working individually. Some may prefer having structure within an open-ended task. It can be useful to survey students on their preferences to find out what sorts of options students choose and benefit from having. This sort of information can be collected through short inventories (e.g., a three-item survey using Google forms) that give instructors insights on options that students use. Although instructional design decisions are made before a course begins, instructors can consider the patterns they see in student preferences and build in options for a current course or for future courses based on students' feedback.

Table 7.1 Common pedagogical barriers

Barriers	Specific issues
Excessive reliance on text	• The volume of reading can be overwhelming. • Students may not be familiar with the types of texts being assigned (e.g., scholarly research articles). • Due to the heavy volume of reading, students may find it difficult to comprehend and/or to identify key points. • Assessments that rely heavily on writing (essays, reports) can be challenging.
Ambiguity about expectations	• It is confusing to navigate through the course (especially for online courses). • It is difficult to discern what the course expectations are from the syllabus or directions provided. • The professor's expectations for assignments are unclear. • Feedback provided on assignments does not give students information on how to improve work.

Reflection

- Identify learner variability factors in a typical course you teach.
- What are some aspects of curriculum and instruction that can create barriers for your students?
- What are preferences and needs of the students you teach?
- What types of student diversity do you have in your classroom (e.g., factors may include cultural and linguistic backgrounds, socioeconomic backgrounds, educational experiences)?

The next step of the planning process is to consider the instructional components of a course, in relation to barriers and preferences. This is the point at which the UDL guidelines can provide guidance and ideas for incorporating elements that support students.

Intentional design: instructional design with UDL

Undertaking an intentional design process to consider one's pedagogical practices is essential to developing a universally designed course. By proactively designing a course to address variability, UDL-aligned strategies can be used in purposeful and systematic ways. By being thoughtful and intentional, instructors can address barriers and embed strategies meaningfully and in ways that can support student needs. The instructional design process can also reduce the potential for strategies to be used in inefficient or ineffective ways. For example, instructors might provide flexible methods for students to respond (using text, audio, or video). Some strategies, when overused or not integrated to support a specific purpose, can become wearisome to students. UDL-based instructional design allows instructors to integrate supports in a thoughtful and deliberate way. When instructors make design decisions taking into consideration how a strategy can support student mastery of learning objectives, it is more likely that the strategy will be useful and effective for students.

The instructional design process with UDL entails (a) considering learner variability and identifying potential barriers, preferences, and needs and (b) using the UDL Design Cycle (see Figure 7.1) to course components by identifying goals, applying UDL to assessments, and applying UDL to methods and materials to support students in reaching the goals.

The following sections provide more detailed information and examples of how to undertake these steps.

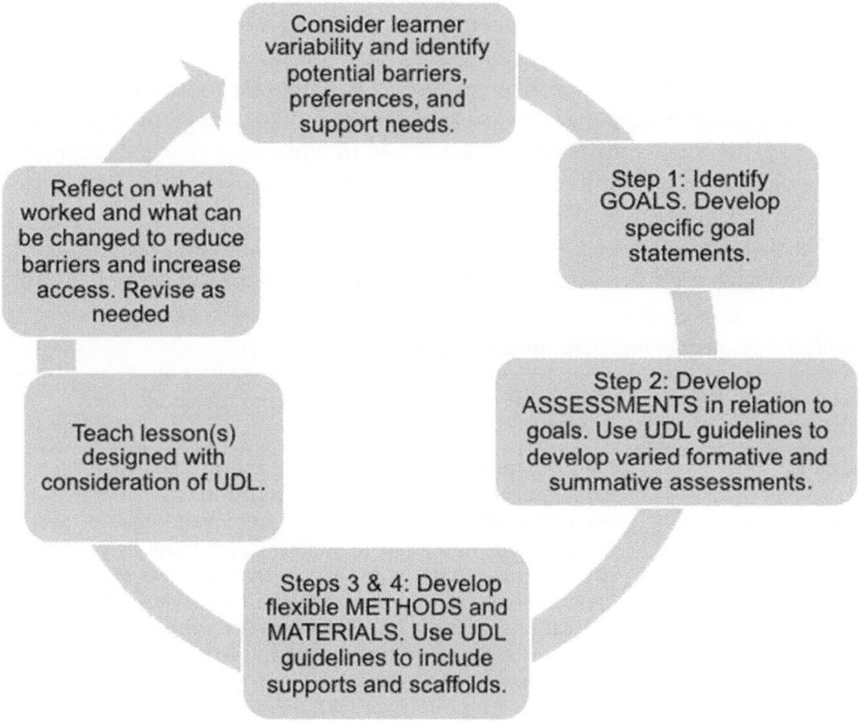

Figure 7.1 UDL Design Cycle

Applying UDL to instructional components

One way to approach course development is to think about what needs to be taught in relation to four major components of lessons and units of instruction: Goals, Assessments, Methods, and Materials (Meyer et al., 2014; Rao & Meo, 2016). Regardless of the content or skills we teach, all faculty start with goals or objectives, have ways to assess student learning, and use a variety of instructional methods and materials. UDL can be applied to any of these components by the instructor as appropriate for the instructional unit they are teaching. Table 7.2 presents the questions that instructors can consider for each component.

Instructors can start by chunking down a semester long course into three to four distinct instructional modules. The number of modules can be determined by the instructor and based on the natural topical breakdown of the course. The first module of a course may include an overview of the main concepts, followed by modules that focus on specific aspects of content. The final module may be one in which the students synthesize or apply knowledge from the earlier modules. For example, a course on research methods may start with a module on research methodologies in general, be followed by modules that address specific methodologies for two to three weeks each. The final module could include activities for students to apply a methodology to a project of their own. Using this modular approach, the instructor can break design down into manageable chunks and ensure that the activities of each module integrates supports as needed. The instructor can also consider how to integrate a variety of support strategies, ensuring that they do not seem redundant or overused, within each module as well as across all the modules of the course.

The first step of instructional design with UDL is to identify instructional goals for each module. Based on these goals, the instructor can apply UDL to

Table 7.2 Considering UDL for course components

Instructional Components	Questions to ask when considering flexible components and UDL
Goals	Based on course objectives, what are the skills and concepts that you want students to master?
Assessments	How can students demonstrate understanding and mastery of the identified goals in varied ways? How can formative and summative assessments be used to give students flexible ways to demonstrate their knowledge?
Methods	How can instruction be designed with supports and scaffolds that help students acquire the content and demonstrate what they have learned? How can flexibility and choice be incorporated into instruction?
Materials	What resources, materials, and tools can be used to provide multiple means to represent and express information and concepts or to engage with content?

other three components – assessments, methods, and materials – for each module. Within a module, the instructor can apply UDL to different components as appropriate.

UDL does not have to be applied to aspects of a course concurrently. In fact, as instructors become familiar with UDL and try to design a course with some UDL-based elements, it can be useful to start by applying UDL to one module and selecting a specific component to begin with (e.g., creating a more flexible assessment). UDL can be applied to additional modules and components over time. The ID process and the UDL Design Cycle can be iterative. After implementing a course with some UDL-based elements, instructors should reflect on those elements, retain the ones that were effective for students, and apply UDL to other components as needed for future courses.

When designing a course, it is most important to make design decisions based on the content being taught. The instructor can identify how to most effectively teach that content and where to introduce support and flexibility with UDL. There are no prescribed number of guidelines that an instructor must use; instead it is important to consider instructional goals and identify how to apply UDL guidelines to the course components to reduce barriers and to increase flexibility and engagement.

Reflection

- Consider a course you teach. What are some common barriers for students (e.g., areas that are challenging for students to comprehend or master)?
- Identify one module within a course you teach (a series of lessons) that you could redesign with the UDL Design Cycle. This could include the lessons you teach over a multi-week period and the assessment given at the end of a series of lessons.
- Use the guiding questions in Table 7.2 to define where you can integrate UDL-based strategies for the module you identified.

Examples of UDL application

When designing with UDL, instructors might ask, "Where do I begin?" The prospect of overhauling a course to integrate various flexible options can be daunting for instructors who are tasked with developing and implement multiple courses along with other commitments as they develop and implement courses. Although some universities provide workshops and professional development opportunities for faculty to learn about universal design, in many cases faculty design their courses without access to much information or professional development on instructional design or UDL.

Although it can seem daunting at the start, there are ways to systematically begin using UDL during the course design process. One way to begin using UDL is by starting small – selecting pieces of a course to modify. Ideally, an instructor can look at the big picture and design the whole course, but realistically, adding flexibility to components bit by bit will also achieve the same end result of making courses more accessible and engaging to students. One asset of UDL is that it is not prescriptive. The 31 checkpoints of UDL provide a "menu of options" that can be applied in ways that are most relevant and useful to a given instructor. With some information on the UDL framework, faculty will be able to integrate flexible and engaging options into their course design, choosing a few of the checkpoints to apply to selected components. This non-prescriptive nature of UDL application can also pose a challenge for instructors seeking to design with UDL; some may prefer to have concrete models and examples of UDL-based course components that they can integrate into their courses.

The following sections present some ways in which instructors can address the barriers described in Table 7.1. These strategies can be adapted as relevant for individual instructors. Although some examples of UDL-based strategies are presented, they represent just some of the ways that that UDL can be applied. The following examples illustrate how an instructor can use the UDL Design Cycle while planning a course and making instructional design decisions. These strategies can be applied to all course formats – face-to-face, online, and hybrid courses.

Excessive reliance on text. One common barrier is the text-heavy nature of college coursework. Students may struggle with the volume of reading for many reasons, such as not being able to keep up with all that is required, having difficulty with comprehension of academic texts/scholarly articles, or finding it difficult to identify key points due to the complexity of text and the unfamiliarity with new content/concepts.

Faculty who strive to maintain high standards may be reticent to "dumb down" the course by requiring fewer or simpler text. As experts in their fields, faculty have often selected texts that are essential for students to read in order to learn the course material. Faculty can rightfully expect students to tackle challenging text and to keep up with readings once they enroll in an academic course or program. Using the UDL Design Cycle, they can design ahead of time and provide supports to help students manage the amount of text they are expected to read and to comprehend key information. Having identified the barrier, instructors can consider their goals and then decide to apply UDL to their methods, materials and/or assessments.

For example, an instructor's goal may be for students to complete all readings and comprehend core concepts in the readings. The instructor can provide supports in varied ways to reach this goal. The instructor may choose to provide flexible options in their methods or materials as noted in Table 7.3. Table 7.3 also denotes the alignment between the instructor's design choices and the relevant UDL guidelines and checkpoints.

Table 7.3 UDL-based strategies for reading assignments

Goals:
1 Students complete all assigned readings each week (textbook and additional scholarly articles)
2 Students comprehend core concepts in the assigned readings
3 Students begin to synthesize ideas across texts

Methods:

- Highlight key aspects that students should look for as they read a text. If using articles, include a short summary describing the article relation to the current topic being addressed in class.

- Include a short assignment related to the reading, in which students pick a few key points and write some sentences about the reading; review the students' key points to assess who may need assistance and redirection with comprehension.

- Make some of the readings optional. If you assign several articles in one week, identify the essential ones as required readings; anything that is not essential can be optional reading. This allows students who struggle with volume of text and comprehension to focus on essential information.

- In an online course, include synchronous sessions and provide guidance for students to discuss essential points from the readings together; have students summarize the discussion as a group or individually. These discussions can be ungraded to ensure that they provide support without adding pressure.

Materials:

- Provide text in digital format (or make students aware of how to download digital format of texts, e.g., a digital textbook)

- Encourage students to use text-to-speech features, built into devices, to listen and read concurrently

- Use a collaborative document (e.g. Google Docs, Padlet) to have students share key points about a reading with instructor or each other

UDL Guideline: Provide options for comprehension
- Highlight patterns, critical features, big ideas, and relationships
- Guide information processing, visualization, and manipulation
- Maximize transfer and generalization

UDL Guideline: Provide options for expression and communication
- Build fluencies with graduated support for practice/performance

UDL Guideline: Provide options for recruiting interest
- Optimize individual choice and autonomy

UDL Guideline: Provide options for sustaining effort and persistence
- Foster collaboration and community

UDL Guideline: Provide options for perception
- Offer ways of customizing the display of information
- Offer alternatives for auditory information
- Offer alternatives for visual information

UDL Guideline: Provide options for physical action
- Optimize access to tools and assistive technologies

Courses that rely heavily on written assessments can also pose a challenge for non-traditional students who may need extra supports during the writing process. Instructors may expect students to have a minimum level of writing proficiency and to be able to communicate ideas via writing, especially in online courses where information is largely communicated by text rather than verbally. However, students struggle with writing for various reasons. For example, students with learning disabilities may experience challenges with organizing their thoughts and clearly drafting written text. Students who speak the language of instruction as a second language may find it harder to express what they know in writing. Students without solid foundations in writing at a college level may also experience issues of confidence in relation to writing, thinking of themselves as "bad writers" when they receive feedback that their written assignments do not meet expectations. Table 7.4 presents some strategies an instructor can use to provide address these barriers, in this case by applying UDL to assessments and methods.

With all the supports listed in Table 7.4, instructors can choose to use them as appropriate for the students in their courses. Providing some support to build a sense of confidence and to help learners persist can go a long way for many students.

Ambiguity about expectations. Students may find it difficult to understand the structure and expectations of instructors. If a student is enrolled in multiple courses, they may find that instructors have varied ways to post materials, communicate deadlines, and interact. This can be an issue especially for students enrolled in multiple courses online. Although instructors might have a clear scheme about what they are presenting and how, the student may feel confused for varied reasons. Students may require more time to complete assignments due to learning disabilities or juggling multiple obligations and commitments. Table 7.5 delineates some ways that instructors can enhance clarity and provide checks to ensure that students are not confused.

Conclusion

This chapter describes how instructors can undertake a process to design courses in ways that reduce barriers and support students in mastery of course goals. Using a systematic process of instructional design with UDL, instructors can plan for learner variability from the outset, ensuring that students with varied backgrounds and experiences feel supported in a course. The process itself is flexible and can be applied in ways that resonate for each individual instructor. The most important part is to design intentionally, with a consideration of what you intend to teach and how to help students both "access" and "master" the content and skills they are learning.

Instructors can feel free to make instructional design decisions that resonate with their philosophy of teaching and match their pedagogical styles. Some instructors might feel that certain supports mentioned in this article are not

Table 7.4 UDL-based strategies for written assignments

Goals:
1 Students will express their understanding of key concepts in an essay format
2 Students will engage in discussion in the online forum, demonstrating their synthesis of key concepts and by presenting persuasive arguments and written feedback in response to peers' discussion comments

Assessments:

Assessments	UDL Guideline
• Have students build a set of slides outlining key ideas over the course of the module; If the slides are created in a collaborative environment (e.g., Google Slides) instructors can periodically review the students' work. For the final written assessment, students use the slides as a structure to write the essay.	UDL Guideline: Provide options for expression and communication • Use multiple media for communication • Use multiple tools for construction and composition • Build fluencies with graduated support for practice/performance
• Give students option to submit supplemental files using other modes of expression, for example, presenting information orally (or with an audio or video recording).	

Methods:

• Post models of what is expected in a written assignment, including a discussion post and an excerpt from an essay. Models can also illustrate non-examples, what would constitute a weak essay	UDL Guideline: Provide options for expression and communication • Build fluencies with graduated support for practice/performance
• Clearly delineate expectations using a checklist or rubric of what an acceptable or exceptional written product includes; when grading an assignment, note which areas of the criteria the student met/did not meet	UDL Guideline: Provide options for sustaining effort and persistence • Increase mastery-oriented feedback
• Provide specific feedback on areas that can be improved or modified; if appropriate for the assignment, allow student to make the modification to earn additional points	UDL Guideline: Provide options for self-regulation • Promote expectations and beliefs that optimize motivation

Table 7.5 UDL-based strategies to reduce ambiguity

Goals: 1 For all course formats: Students will have a clear understanding of expectations, deadlines, and upcoming assignments 2 For online courses: Students will successfully navigate the online course environment and be able to find and use all key tools 3 Student will meet deadlines for all assignments during the semester	
Methods: • At the beginning of the semester, provide an overview of your course structure. For an online course, this can be done by creating a short video or narrated powerpoint that highlights your expectations and where/how to find key areas of the course. • For online courses that include synchronous (virtual class) meetings, begin or end the meeting with a quick check in about whether students have questions about upcoming assignments; end the synchronous session with info on the upcoming weeks and ask students if they have questions. For traditional face-to-face courses, end the class with an overview of what is expected the following week. For all course formats: Have virtual office hours – be available online at a regular time when students can log in if they have questions.	UDL Guideline: Provide options for perception • Offer alternatives for auditory information • Offer alternatives for visual information UDL Guideline: Provide options for expression and communication • Use multiple media for communication • Use multiple tools for construction and composition • Build fluencies with graduated support for practice/performance
Materials • Reduce clutter from documents that provide information about course expectations, such as the syllabus. If the syllabus is lengthy, place the key information about course expectations up front or create an overview of major assignment dates/expectations. • Choose tools carefully and use tools consistently within the course management system; for example, post announcements regularly on the main page about upcoming deadlines. • Too much or random information can also be confusing; consider sending out one email a week with all course info summarized for that week. • Encourage students to email or contact you as preferred if things are unclear.	UDL Guideline: Provide options for comprehension • Activate or supply background knowledge • Highlight patterns, critical features, big ideas, and relationships UDL Guideline: Provide options for executive functions • Guide appropriate goal-setting • Support planning and strategy development • Facilitate managing information and resources

for them; there is no set way to address barriers and instructors should feel free to choose strategies that work for them. Even if UDL-based strategies cannot be applied to every single element of a course, by applying UDL to even a few components of a course, instructors can broaden the range of students who will be supported and engaged by increased flexibility and choice in a course.

Additional resources on UDL-based course design

- UDL on Campus website – Course Design webpage: udloncampus.cast. org/page/planning_landing
- MERLOT Case Stories at elixr.merlot.org
- Universal Design in Higher Education – Promising Practices: www. washington.edu/doit/resources/books/universal-design-higher-education-promising-practices

References

Dell, C. A., Dell, T. F., & Blackwell, T. L. (2015). Applying universal design for learning in online courses: Pedagogical and practical considerations. *The Journal of Educators Online, 13*(2), 166–192. https://doi.org/ISSN 1547-500X

Eady, M. J., & Woodcock, S. (2010). Understanding the need: Using collaboratively created draft guiding principles to direct online synchronous learning in Indigenous communities. *International Journal for Educational Integrity, 6*(2), 24–40.

Gradel, K., & Edson, A. (2009). Putting universal design for learning on the higher ed agenda. *Journal of Educational Technology Systems, 38*(2), 111–121. Retrieved from http://baywood.metapress.com/index/0673J2M1157820K3.pdf

Johnson, M. L., Taasoobshirazi, G., Clark, L., Howell, L., & Breen, M. (2016). Motivations of traditional and nontraditional college students: From self-determination and attributions, to expectancy and values. *The Journal of Continuing Higher Education, 64*(1), 3–15. https://doi.org/10.1080/07377363.2016.1132880

McLoughlin, C., & Oliver, R. (2000). Designing learning environments for cultural inclusivity: A case study of indigenous online learning at tertiary level. *Australian Journal of Educational Technology, 16*(1), 58–72. https://doi.org/10.14742/ajet.v16i1.1822

Meyer, A., Rose, D. H., & Gordon, D. T. (2014). *Universal design for learning: Theory and practice.* Wakefield, MA: CAST Professional Publishing.

Morrison, G. R., Ross, S. M., Kemp, J. E., & Kalman, H. (2010). *Designing effective instruction* (6th ed.). Hoboken, NJ: John Wiley & Sons.

Rao, K., Eady, M., & Edelen-Smith, P. (2011). Virtual classrooms for rural and remote. *Phi Delta Kappan, 92*(6), 22–27.

Rao, K., Edelen-Smith, P., & Wailehua, C. U. (2015). Universal design for online courses: Applying principles to pedagogy. *Open Learning: The Journal of Open, Distance and E-Learning, 30*(1), 35–52. https://doi.org/10.1080/02680513.2014.991300

Rao, K., & Meo, G. (2016). Using universal design for learning to access academic standards. *Sage Open*, *6*(4), 1–18. https://doi.org/10.1177/2158244016680688

Rao, K., & Tanners, A. (2011). Curb cuts in cyberspace: Universal instructional design for online courses. *Journal of Post Secondary Education and Disability*, *24*(3), 211–227.

Schuetze, H. G. (2014). From adults to non-traditional students to lifelong learners in higher education: Changing contexts and perspectives. *Journal of Adult and Continuing Education*, *20*(2), 37–55. https://doi.org/10.7227/JACE.20.2.4

Scott, L., & Temple, P. (2017). A conceptual framework for building UDL in a special education distance education course. *Journal of Educators Online*, *14*(1). Retrieved from https://eric.ed.gov/?id=EJ1133749

UDL in apprenticeships and career training programs that serve youth with untapped talent

*Sam Catherine Johnston and
Eleanor (Ellie) Castine*

Case study

The sun is rising as Marcus kisses his still-sleeping kids goodbye. He grabs his toolbox and heads off to the local community center. He arrives early to the site and greets José, his site supervisor. Merely six months ago José was wondering if Marcus would do okay in this program, given that he hadn't finished high school. Yet, over the years, José has learned the importance of not letting school success predict job performance within the job training program. Today, Marcus is walking his fellow trainees through the concepts of elevation and bearing to optimize the position of a solar panel. They will be installing solar panels on the roof of the community center. Since early on in the program, Marcus has learned quickly by watching his peers, listening to his site supervisor, and engaging with a team to problem solve. Although Marcus has done well, José wishes the training manuals were less of a barrier. He frequently finds himself turning to YouTube videos to show a skill before the trainees use it on the job, and these models seem to be effective for a number of them. Marcus is most happy about the idea that he is paid to learn. Without the income, he would be unable to participate in this program, and he would be no closer to his dream of one day becoming an engineer.

Introduction

There are an estimated 4.6 million youth aged 16–24 in the United States who are out of school and out of work. This represents one out of every eight youth and young adults in the USA, which is higher than numerous other advanced nations (Burd-Sharps & Lewis, 2018), These young people, often referred to as opportunity youth in the United States, are predominantly from low-income backgrounds, approximately one third are African American or Latino, and 27% have no High School diploma (Burd-Sharps & Lewis, 2018). In Latin America, one in every five youths aged 15 to 24 is out of school and out of work (de Hoyos, Rogers, & Szekely, 2016). Referred to as ninis in Latin America, the rate of disconnection in Latin America is closer to the world average than the United States, which is better than the Middle East and North Africa, where one in three are out-of-school and out-of-work. Outside of the U.S., the majority are female from poor, urban neighborhoods who have left school due to an early marriage or teen pregnancy. Yet, the rise in the number of ninis is due to men who have had more trouble obtaining jobs as female labor participation increases while few jobs are created (de Hoyos et al., 2016).

Out-of-school and out-of-work youth is a universal problem. *The Economist* (2013) compiled data from various sources and estimates that across the globe, there are 290 million youth out of school and out of work. Referred to by the OECD as NEETS (not in employment education or training), this is a population of young people that have been failed by "one size fits all approaches" in K-12 education, by chronically under-resourced schools and communities, and by uneven opportunities for education, training and employment. Without different pathways to college and career, these young people are often unable to secure employment beyond low skill minimum wage jobs (Tucker, 2004) and consequently, our society wastes an enormous talent pool.

Some argue that providing more career training, particularly in technical occupations, is one sound way to address youth unemployment, growing income inequality and the mismatch between available jobs and the skills young people possess (Symonds, Schwartz, & Ferguson, 2011; Lerman, 2012). Career training encompasses a broad range of programs yet generally these programs share a common focus on skills training for entry into a specific industry. Career training certificate programs can take between a year to a year and a half and can prepare learners for entry-level positions into a specific field such as criminal justice, health care or information technology (U.S. Career Institute, 2017). Career training can also involve longer programs such as registered apprenticeships. Registered apprenticeships are designed to move an apprentice from entry-level to occupationally proficient in a specific industry. An individual business, often in conjunction with a labor organization, sponsors a registered apprenticeship program and an apprentice learns through a combination of supervised work-based training and related classroom learning often lasting four years. Upon successfully completing the apprenticeship, the apprentice is issued an industry-recognized credential that validates occupational proficiency in an apprenticeable occupation (U.S. Department of Labor, 2018b).

Labor force data would suggest career training is a sound investment. A projected 14 million jobs in the United States are currently available for people with associate's degrees or occupational certificates. Moreover, more than 25% of people with occupational certificates earn a higher income than those with bachelor's degrees (Symonds et al., 2011). Many nations aim to bridge the gap between young people's skills and employment by increasing apprenticeships and other forms of career training (Generation Jobless – Youth Unemployment, 2013). Internationally, vocational career training that leads to qualification in hundreds of well-paying and well-regarded occupations, is an integral part of the education system from late adolescence onwards (Symonds et al., 2011). For example, in Germany, half of the youth population enter dual education and training as a route into 326 professional trades. The focus is on integrating work-based learning with education early resulting in young people that are labor force ready (Niranjan, 2018). Drawing upon Germany's model, in 2010 South Korea developed the network of Meister Schools, which have curricula that were developed in collaboration with industry partners to help prepare youth to work in advanced jobs (NCEE, 2018; UNESCO, 2018).

Youth with disabilities are a segment of the youth population that are particularly vulnerable to being underprepared for the labor force and ultimately unemployed. As Table 8.1 illustrates, young people with disabilities in the United States are at least twice as likely to not complete High School, not enroll in postsecondary education and not persist in postsecondary education as young people without disabilities (McFarland et al., 2018).

This is a phenomenon that exists outside of the United States as well. Across 27 countries, a staggering 60% of the working-age population with disabilities are not in the labor force compared to just 25% of those without disabilities (OECD, 2009).

Table 8.1 National data on education and employment by disability status (Data from 2013–2017)

	People with disabilities	People without disabilities
Never completed high school	22%	8%
Not enrolled in postsecondary upon graduation from HS	34%	16%
Left postsecondary prior to completion of first year[1,2]	25%	13%
Percentage of population between 16–64 that is **not participating in the labor force**[3]	68.8%	23.6%

1 McFarland et al., 2018.
2 Hinz, Arbeit, & Bentz, 2017.
3 Bureau of Labor Statistics, 2018.

Reflection

- What factors do you think have contributed to high youth and young adult unemployment?
- What are some consequences of youth and young adult unemployment specifically?
- What opportunities do you see to bridge the gap between the skills young people have and those the labor force needs?

Growing investment in career training postsecondary opportunities

In the United States, there is growing recognition of the importance of improving educational and career training opportunities for youth. The Workforce Innovation Opportunity Act (WIOA) of 2015, the legislation that governs and funds the public workforce development system in the United States, provides more than $873,000,000 annually to direct service youth workforce development activities, with 75% of this money going to college and career preparation of out-of-school youth. Out-of-school youth includes youth that have left school before graduating from High School as well as youth that have a High School diploma but lack basic skills and are under employed or unemployed (U.S. Department of Labor, 2017).

At the Federal level, the United States is also investing heavily in the apprenticeship model for career training. In its 2016 budget, the Department of Labor invested approximately $84,000,000 in the YouthBuild program and $1,597,825,000 in the Job Corps program, national pre-apprenticeship training programs designed to help out of school youth gain their high school equivalency as well as occupational skills (Department of Labor, 2016a). These programs are designed to increase opportunity youths' eligibility for apprenticeship programs as well as college. WIOA is also heavily invested in strengthening the transition to career training and employment for youth with disabilities (US Department of Labor, 2017; LEAD Center, 2016).

Apprenticeship training programs have grown significantly as an alternative to attending a two or four-year college in order to access careers. There were 375,425 registered apprentices in 2013 and 505,371 in 2016 with 1,200 new registered apprenticeships in 2016 alone (Employment and Training Administration, 2018). Apprenticeships provide a pathway to high-wage jobs within industries that have significant projected growth. For example, the Bureau of Labor Statistics (2013) predicts 1.6 million new construction jobs by 2022, where some of the main apprenticeable occupations lie. Apprenticeships are also a cost-effective route to enter the workforce and secure well-paying jobs: apprentices engage in classroom training and on-the-job training for which they are paid; 89% of apprentices are employed after completing their program with an average starting wage of $65,000; and apprentices earn industry credentials equivalent to two-or-four-year college degrees (U.S. Department of Labor, 2016b). Studies of employers hiring apprentices indicate a high return on this investment (Helper, Noonan, Nicholson, & Langdon, 2016; Lerman, Eyster, & Chambers, 2009). Finally, new agreements between community colleges and sponsors of registered apprenticeships allow for apprentices to attend and complete a degree at a two or four-year higher education institution upon completion of their apprenticeship programs (US Department of Labor, n.d.).

There is evidence that out-of-school and out-of-work youth and youth with disabilities can and do succeed in well-designed career training programs. For example, YouthBuild USA, the pre-apprenticeship career training program mentioned, predominantly serves African American and Latino young men from low-income backgrounds. Interim findings from a randomized controlled trial of YouthBuild USA found that participation in a YouthBuild program increased the rate at which opportunity youth completed High School, enrolled in college, engaged in vocational training, volunteered, and led to a small increase in earnings more than two years post program enrollment (Miller, Millenky, Schwartz, Globe, & Stein, 2016). Similarly, a rigorous impact evaluation of Job Corps, the nation's largest residential job training program for opportunity youth, found positive impacts on educational attainment and earnings as well as lower involvement with the criminal justice system (Schochet, Burghardt, & McConnell, 2008). Project SEARCH provides youth with significant disabilities with a one-year employment training program that occurs in the workplace. Outcome research on the program has found that more than 68% of program graduates secure competitive integrated employment (Christensen, Hetherington, Daston, & Riehle, 2015). While there is still a need for research on longer term employment outcomes, and a need to examine what kinds of work young people are obtaining as a result of participation in these programs, findings are promising.

While this growth in investment in career training may be helping opportunity youth and youth with disabilities to access employment, there is reason to believe that more attention should be paid to the curricular design of these programs so all learners have a better chance of getting through. In a recent external evaluation of Job Corps, suggestions were made for improving the design of the program including focusing on developing a growth mindset, introducing more positive youth development practices, communicating high expectations and creating a trauma-informed environment (Lee, Schochet, & Berk, 2018). YouthBuild USA has already begun to implement Universal Design for Learning in its teacher training (Emerick & Marshall, 2017). At the apprenticeship training level, Argyres and Moir (2008) conducted a study in Massachusetts and found that completion in apprenticeship programs is on average 42% for apprenticeship programs delivered by unions and 25% for non-union programs. Sponsors of apprenticeship programs in the Boston area indicate that performance in the classroom or on-the-job is frequently a reason for non-completion (S. Johnston personal communication with union apprenticeship programs in Massachusetts, 2017). A greater focus on supporting all apprentices to succeed through to program completion would result in significantly different employment prospects. Ninety-one percent of employees/ apprentices that complete a registered apprenticeship are employed nine months after completion (U.S. Department of Labor, 2018a).

Reflection

- What elements of Universal Design for Learning, if any, do you think would be beneficial to the curricular design of career training programs?

Universal Design for Learning applied to career training programs

Universal Design for Learning, a framework pioneered at CAST for the design and implementation of inclusive educational and training practices, could be a key approach to improving postsecondary career training opportunities in the United States and elsewhere. Applying UDL to pre-apprenticeship programs, apprenticeships, as well as other opportunities that better link education and the workforce, could broaden who participates in these programs and whether or not they successfully complete them. UDL holds promise in this arena because it is a framework that emerges from a focus on particular groups of learners – historically those with disabilities – that were not well served by one size fits all approaches to education. Yet, what the UDL framework throws into relief is the repeated finding that systematically planning and designing for variability in how people perceive information, demonstrate understanding, and are engaged, can create practices that are more effective for everyone (Meyer, Rose, & Gordon, 2014). Research and development on UDL is supported by multiple federal agencies, state departments of education, individuals and foundations. The Department of Labor, the primary workforce development entity in the United States, has advocated for Universal Design for Learning through its grant programs. For example, the Department of Labor required that UDL be used by all grantees that received funding through its two-billion-dollar TAAC-CCT training program designed to help displaced workers engage in career training that would prepare them for well-paying occupations with a significant regional or national labor shortage (Employment and Training Administration, 2018). In the summer of 2018, UDL was included in the reauthorization of the legislation that governs Career and Technical Education in the United States (GovTrack.us, 2018).

Considering how UDL can serve as a framework for the design of career training programs is timely. Efforts are underway to diversity pre-apprenticeship and apprenticeship training programs as well as the occupations that hire apprentices. As of 2016, the Department of Labor's Equal Employment Opportunity regulations state that individuals with disabilities are a group that cannot be discriminated against in apprenticeships, and the Office of Management and Budget has started to ask apprenticeship programs to gather on a voluntary basis data on the number of apprentices they train that have disabilities (Employment and Training Administration, 2018). The Department of Labor invested $90,000,000 to diversify apprenticeships with a focus on recruiting and retaining people of color, women and people with disabilities (U.S. Department of Labor, 2016a). Universal Design for Learning (UDL) in particular with its focus on systematically designing for a broader range of learners from the outset, could be a critical factor to ensure that more young people successfully transition to well-paying and meaningful occupations through career training programs.

Finally, an effort to integrate UDL into pre-apprenticeship, apprenticeship and other programs that provide career training either alongside or independent of college, may actually also inform how UDL could best be integrated into two and four-year college as that system is also rapidly changing. The Office of Educational Technology (2017) National Education Technology Plan Higher Education Supplement describes a new normal student in postsecondary education, which may not be a high achieving 18-year-old high school student coming directly to postsecondary education but may instead be a person working or parenting while pursuing college either full or part time. These "new normal" students require multiple and varied opportunities, including online opportunities, to develop expertise both inside and outside of formal education institutions across their lifetime (Office of Educational Technology, 2017)

Reflection

- What challenges do you think might arise in using Universal Design for Learning within apprenticeships and other career training programs?

The work ahead

CAST, the nonprofit that pioneered UDL, is engaged in an organizational effort to ensure that "learning has no limits" whether it be in schools, pre-apprenticeships, apprenticeships, the new non-traditional college system or the workforce. CAST's engagement with other organizations committed to full inclusion of learners historically relegated to the margins, has grown exponentially over the past five years. We are currently working at the local, regional and national level in K-12 schools, youth serving workforce development organizations such as YouthBuild, juvenile justice settings, with forward looking institutions of higher education that deliver career training, and directly with employers and industry associations. In partnering with both students that have not been successful within traditional systems and the program providers that offer them new ways of accessing education and careers, we hope to inform the road map for redesigning postsecondary opportunities so all young people have equal opportunities to access and succeed in meaningful careers.

In this chapter and in our effort to wade into these waters to date, we find that the three UDL principles – provide multiple means of representation, provide multiple means of action and expression, and provide multiple means of engagement – are remarkably robust. Universal Design for Learning principles have been applied to career training programs such as YouthBuild, workforce development programs designed to help individuals with disabilities upskill and access careers such as the Disability Employment Initiative at the Department of Labor, in workforce focused community and technical college programs, and in settings educating incarcerated youth.

What does merit analysis in terms of UDL's application to career training, is the four dimensions that UDL considers to be a curriculum, that is goals, methods, materials and assessments. Given that the thinking about how UDL applies to these four curricular components was developed within the context of traditional K-12 education – the original context for UDL – we ask ourselves whether they can continue to be described in the same ways that they have been? This chapter is a first effort to reconsider how we might apply these four curricular components to career training programs in the United States.

Goals

Within traditional classrooms, goals are learning expectations set by teachers that are informed by the broader educational standards (CAST, 2011). These goals tend to sit along a linear path. For instance, students in secondary school continuously work to fulfill objective requirements in order to ultimately graduate with a high school degree. UDL addresses the fixed nature of these goals by noting that "goals themselves are articulated in a way that acknowledges learner variability and differentiates goals from means" (CAST, 2011, p. 7). This offers a great starting point, but goals are still largely bound by traditional expectations of how education unfolds (time based) and where it takes place (traditional classroom). The way goals have been conceived of within UDL does not account well for education that combines work-based and classroom-based learning as in pre-apprenticeship or apprenticeship programs. Nor does the work around applying UDL to learning goals address the tension between these learning goals and life goals such as raising children and feeding and housing them, which, is a reality for many young people that pursue education and prepare for careers in their late teens and twenties. A first question we must ask when thinking about learning goals is: how will this goal account for an individual's past experiences and align with their future plans (Wigfield & Eccles, 2000).

The goal setting process

The easiest way to ensure that goals are useful to the learner is to treat the learner as an equal partner in the goal setting process. What outcomes are most important to the learner? Collaboratively answering these questions helps to foster self-determination, encouraging individuals to feel in control of their own lives and in turn eager to work towards their goals (Parsi, Whittaker, & Jones, 2018). Adults in particular have been found to learn more effectively when actively engaged in the learning process and this engagement starts with goal setting (Kolb, 1984). Knowles' four principles for adult learning should inform goal setting in career training programs as well as the other three curricular components of UDL: methods, materials and assessments. Knowles outlined that: adults needed to be involved in the planning and evaluation of their training/education; experience provided the basis for learning; learning topics needed to be immediate relevant and/or impact job or personal life; and learning was problem-centered rather than content-centered (Knowles, 1980), UDL does not assume that learners can independently set appropriate goals for themselves, yet it also does not call for goals to be imposed on the learner. Goals need to be co-constructed to help build self-awareness and to ensure that they align with one's identity, both personally and professionally.

As opposed to having content or performance goals, UDL posits that the goal is to develop expert learners, and as a result set higher expectations (CAST, 2011). We know that expectations are a significant predictor of retention and persistence in postsecondary education (Tinto, 2010). However, opportunity youth or youth with disabilities in career training programs often come to these programs with a history of negative experiences in traditional education where the adults have had low expectations of them and they have experienced repeated school failure as well as stigma, typically a product of an individual's race, ethnicity, and/or disability status (Parsi et al., 2018). Furthermore, goals have been regularly thwarted for a variety reasons, including lack of access to resources. For instance, Marcus introduced at the beginning of this chapter, would have enjoyed a pre-engineering class to nurture his interest in becoming an engineer, but that was not offered at the school he attended.

Given a history of adverse experiences in education, many young people come to expect that others will not support their goals, which further decreases their motivation and lowers their expectations about themselves (Tinto, 2012). Therefore, having a say in the goal setting process creates opportunities for students to not only recognize their own needs but also advocate for themselves to ultimately combat stigma and low expectations and to work with providers of career training to address systemic barriers to training and employment that have very little to do with the individual learner's efforts. In order to create goals that are meaningful as well as realistic and attainable, it is critical to identify an individual's skills, career interests, and strengths. The assessment of these areas is now a requirement under the Workforce Innovation and Opportunity Act (WIOA) any program receiving WIOA funds to deliver services to youth. Furthermore, individuals report feeling less positive about pursuing goals that others set for them and only a transitory sense of accomplishment when they achieve such goals (Snyder, Feldman, Shorey, & Rand, 2002).

One important factor that predicts the accomplishment of goals is hope. Snyder (1995) defined hope as "the process of thinking about one's goals, along with the motivation to move toward (agency) and the ways to achieve (pathways) these goals" (p. 355). Hope theory suggests that both the agency and pathway for goals are essential components to develop high levels of hope. In other words, hope is a cognitive-motivational set for achieving goals by developing, initiating and keeping viable routes open (Snyder, 1994). Hope plays a critical role in the development of motivation and influencing human behavior and individuals who demonstrate higher levels of hope are more likely to come up with various strategies, consider potential barriers, and generate solutions to accomplish their goals (Kenny, Walsh-Blair, Blustein, Bempechat, & Seltzer, 2010; Snyder et al., 2002). Infusing hope into a collaborative goal setting process is critical if goals are to be achieved. This shared goal setting process focuses goals on problems that can be addressed through training and learning opportunities, rather than on learning content without regard to context (Knowles, 1980).

The nature of goals

In career training programs for youth that have faced adversity, focusing exclusively on curricular learning goals or even goals around becoming an expert learner is too narrow of an approach. If the goal is prescribed to the learner and fails to align with their broader life context and values, not only is the process of goal setting voided but the goal itself is also futile. If Marcus is unable to provide food for his children, the completion of the career training program will not be of value to him. Therefore, opportunities should be sought to align learning goals with job and life goals (Knowles, 1980).

YouthBuild does this well by teaching construction skills (i.e. an occupational goal), and applying these skills to building affordable housing, which meets an essential community need and positions the young person as a community leader. Importantly, YouthBuild participants are also paid for the time they spend at YouthBuild, thereby lowering a system level barrier to education and career training, namely, the income a young person would have to forgo to participate in any unpaid career training program. Finally, YouthBuild programs regularly coordinate their efforts with other systems and people engaged with the young people. This includes treatment facilities for recovery from drug or alcohol use, the juvenile justice system, family support structures such as pre-schools, and informal supports such as churches, families and friends. The goal setting process then is first and foremost around the whole person, their values and their life and career training needs. Important but secondary goal setting happens around standardized curricula and assessments, such as the prepara-tion for, taking and passing of the exam to gain a High School equivalency, a necessary prerequisite for college entry, apprenticeship programs and numerous careers.

Weighing the importance of goals is twofold. It requires attending to the significance of the goal on an individual level as well as the significance of the goal on a societal level. Goals need to be meaningful to the individual but also relevant both in the short term and the longer term. For example, obtaining a high school credential is associated with better future earnings, life satisfaction, lower levels of depression and substance abuse, compared to those who do not obtain a credential, suggesting that this credential carries personal and profes-sional relevance (Heckman, Humphries, & Mader, 2010; Sealey & Noyes, 2010). However, that goal is long term and therefore needs to be balanced with meeting goals such as getting on-the job training and industry recognized cer-tificates that are often more immediately gratifying and relevant to young peo-ple, particularly those that had negative experiences in traditional high schools. Consider Marcus' path, although he is interested and motivated to reach his long-term goal of becoming an engineer, it is important to be accomplishing small goals along the way to provide a sense of accomplishment and self-efficacy. For goals to be universally designed, time needs to be spent understanding the various roles that an individual has in the many contexts they operate in (Meyer et al., 2014). More research is needed to better assess the goal setting process in career training programs with a more diverse group of young people.

Reflection

- What opportunities does considering goal development in the career training context provide for you to reconsider how you develop goals with/for learners?

Methods

"Methods are generally defined as the instructional decisions, approaches, procedures, or routines that expert teachers use to accelerate or enhance learning. Expert teachers apply evidence-based methods and differentiate those methods according to the goal of instruction" (CAST, 2011, p. 7). Within work, learning happens in the process of engaging with others to frame, examine and resolve complex problems (Fischer, 2011). In a pioneering study of apprenticeships around the world, Wenger (1998) and Wenger, McDermott, and Snyder (2002) explained that most of the learning occurs among apprentices themselves, rather than through explicit teaching of master to apprentice (Lave & Wenger, 1991). They described learning within apprenticeships as a "community that acts as the curriculum" for the apprentice. Methods in many forms of work-based learning rely on quality relationships where learners can form strong enough bonds to share one another's experiences practicing skills and can collaborate effectively to understand and solve problems. A primary goal of instruction in career training is to initiate the learner into the social processes that allow for their continued acquisition of occupational skills.

Methods that foster social learning

"UDL curricula facilitate further differentiation of methods, based on learner variability in the context of the task, learner's social/emotional resources, and the classroom climate" (CAST, 2011, p. 7). Career training relies heavily on peers learning from and with one another. A primary focus for practitioners applying UDL to career training then should be to help learners with widely different characteristics engage with one another in order to build occupational skills. UDL methods in the context of career training might need to be informed by the theory and applied research into communities of practice, where careful attention is paid to social learning processes and how to design effectively for them, in particular to advance occupational skills.

If career training is going to be a vehicle for opportunity youth to access well-paying occupations, practitioners applying UDL in career training programs that work with this population need to learn from culturally responsive teaching approaches (Aceves & Orosco, 2014; Gay, 2010; Ladson-Billings, 2009; Nieto, Bode, Kang, & Raible, 2008). In culturally responsive teaching, teachers see the students' cultural and linguistic resources as assets to use within learning rather than things to exclude from the learning process. This includes students' personal experiences, cultural, racial and linguistic experiences and interests (Aceves & Orosco, 2014). Moreover, culturally responsive teaching tends to emphasize instructional methods that encourage students to work collaboratively and to learn from one another (Aceves & Orosco, 2014).

Similarly, career training programs engaging youth with disabilities should understand ableism, a set of beliefs as well as practices that devalue people with disabilities, discriminate against them, and assume they need to be fixed in order to succeed in education or employment (Center for Disability Rights, 2018). In order to move beyond ableism and use methods that value and teach everyone, career training programs should examine the research currently being done at the intersection of inclusion and disability studies (Baglieri, Bejoian, Broderick, Connor, & Valle, 2011; Baglieri & Shapiro, 2012).

Aligning methods to goals, materials and assessments

In thinking about methods in career training programs, those invested in UDL also need to ask how goals, materials and assessments align with methods in this context. Often, what an individual learns cannot be distinguished from the relationship or the community where the learning took place. Consider materials as an example. In career training, skills and knowledge are often acquired through work, engaging with peers, or seeing models of skills in action. In our work at CAST that involves work-based learning and career training, we have brought UDL into methods and materials that fit with a social view of how learning happens. For example, we have come to regularly integrate universally designed multi-media cases into our projects. Cases combined with case-based teaching as a method, allow learners to engage with one another in order to visualize practice and reproduce a problem (Leonard, 2010). Cases, because they often focus on people and their practices, allow for the learner to think about the broader real world context for acquiring skills.

Within career training programs that rely on social processes for learning and given that "UDL methods are adjusted based on continual monitoring of learner progress" (CAST, 2011, p. 7), learners, not just teachers, need to be able to monitor one another's progress and adjust how they teach one another accordingly. In some of our work at CAST, skills we would previously have taught just to teachers, we now extend to students as well. For example, we have provided students with skills and tools to provide one another with mastery-oriented and wise feedback, so they too can play a role in encouraging one another to continue to engage with challenging tasks.

Reflection

- How can you increase opportunities for peer-to-peer learning?
- How might you scaffold peer-to-peer learning for a learner who struggles to engage with peers?

Materials and tools

"Materials are usually seen as the media used to present learning content and what the learner uses to demonstrate knowledge" (CAST, 2011, p. 8). UDL materials offer multiple media and supports. They also support organization, planning and analyzing information and they engage different learners through offering choice and different levels of support and challenge (CAST, 2011). The digitization of materials has made more materials readily available in many parts of the world and has made materials transformable. This is generally a win for UDL as "within the UDL framework, the hallmark of materials is their variability and flexibility" (CAST, 2011). Most materials in postsecondary education today come in, or have, a digital version. Digital text allows for embedded supports such as text to speech so the text can be read aloud, resized or dropped into a translation engine in order to get the content in a different language. Furthermore, print and even text is no longer the dominant medium in our education system (Johnston & Rose, 2017). Simulations, video, images and audio all now compete with text or collaborate with text to convey information.

Creating accessible materials and tools

A primary concern is that a barrier lowered for one group of learners (i.e., less text is good for students with dyslexia or students that are Deaf or Hard of Hearing) may result in a barrier being erected for another group (i.e., video is not a great medium for people who are legally blind). Increasingly, the lack of centralization or standardization in materials that are in education systems, particularly in less traditional delivery approaches for postsecondary education such as pre-apprenticeships, apprenticeships or online postsecondary courses, raises concerns about the quality and accessibility of materials for all learners and for accountability in providing materials in an accessible format.

As a baseline, anyone who is making or selecting materials for postsecondary learners should know how to ensure they are accessible (National Center on Accessible Educational Materials, 2018). Accessible means "students with disabilities must be provided the opportunity to: acquire the same information; engage in the same interactions, and; enjoy the same services as students without disabilities with substantially equivalent ease of use" (Office for Civil Rights, 2011). This means that curricular developers for international trade unions responsible for the materials used in union apprenticeship programs, developers creating manuals for the occupational safety and health administration (OSHA) that are used in career training programs, and vocational trainers selecting materials on the fly to show a new technique in installing solar panels on a roof, should all have a basic skill set in making materials accessible. Towards this end, CAST runs the National Center on Accessible Educational Materials (AEM Center) that provides capacity building around procuring and producing accessible educational materials and technologies. The AEM Center mandate is to increase the capacity of postsecondary and workforce development stakeholders to use accessible materials and technologies. The AEM Center would be a helpful resource for José, Marcus' supervisor, to reach out to in order to increase the accessibility of the manuals he knows are difficult for Marcus and other learners to understand.

Career training programs should also pay attention to legal settlements with the U.S. Department of Justice entered into by postsecondary institutions to resolve allegations that the institution violated the Americans with Disabilities Act (ADA) by using inaccessible materials and/or technologies. The United States has been a leader in using the judicial system to ensure that technology used to deliver content, as well as the content itself, is accessible. These judicial settlements are important because they put significant pressure on educational materials and technology producers to ensure that they adhere to laws on accessibility. For example, Miami University of Ohio recently entered into a settlement with the Department of Justice to resolve allegations that the university violated the Americans with Disabilities Act (ADA) by using inaccessible classroom and other technologies. In the settlement, the University agreed to overhaul its technology procurement practices (U.S. Department of Justice, 2016). To understand the significance of this, consider the butterfly effect metaphor. When a butterfly flaps its wings, it can be a precursor to a tornado several weeks later. When Miami University of Ohio changes its technology procurement policy, YouTube, because it wants to continue to be one of the technologies used within the University system to deliver course content, hires several accessibility experts. As if by magic, the automatic captioning functionality in YouTube or the capability to filter out any uncaptioned videos using the search feature is vastly improved. This then makes it much easier for a trainer or teacher to create or procure videos that are captioned and transcribed.

A second significant legal settlement with the U.S. Department of Justice was a result of the American Association for the Deaf (AAD) suing Massachusetts Institute of Technology (MIT) and Harvard University, the creators of EdX, an open educational resources platform used to deliver postsecondary education content freely over the web (the courses are often referred to as Massive Open Online Courses or MOOCs). The AAD sued EdX because many of the MOOCs on the platform were inaccessible to individuals who were Deaf or Hard of Hearing. In the legal settlement, EdX agreed to address accessibility concerns found in its delivery platform, conduct annual accessibility audits and develop guidance and training for content providers. As a result, this settlement places the responsibility for accessibility on both the technology provider creating the platform to deliver content and on the professor creating content or materials (U.S. Department of Justice, 2015).

What these settlements make clear, is that this new era of decentralized materials offered in many different formats delivered through various platforms requires multiple stakeholders to take responsibility for accessibility. Teachers, trainers and even fellow students creating or procuring content need a basic set of skills to ensure that all learners can effectively use the materials in a course or program. Vendors offering technology delivery vehicles or content to postsecondary programs and institutions need to be following best practices in accessibility.

Creating universally designed materials and tools

Accessibility is only a foundational layer for materials and technologies that employ UDL. To make materials effective for a broader range of learners, one would need to integrate a number of UDL guidelines including use of plain language, highlighting critical features, gradually releasing information, providing background knowledge, building in options for progress monitoring and supports for goal setting, planning and organizing information. While those considerations cover some of the existing UDL guidelines, there is another fundamental area of consideration especially when working with opportunity youth as well as with youth with disabilities on career training. Materials need to be aligned with method such as culturally responsive teaching (Aceves & Orosco, 2014; Gay, 2010; Ladson-Billings, 2009 Nieto et al., 2008) and use the students' racial, linguistic, cultural and life resources within the learning process (Aceves & Orosco, 2014).

Opportunity youth as well as youth with disabilities have rarely had materials in school that validate who they are, their experiences in the world, or the communities they come from. YouthBuild Philadelphia regularly engages in hip hop listening sessions, lyric analysis and other activities to engage young people around what is of value to them (Akbar, 2018). This culturally relevant approach acknowledges the centrality of a young person's identity and experience in career exploration (Porfeli & Lee, 2012). Consider how often the lyrics in hip hop address barriers to employment in the descriptions of illegal ways to acquire income in order to survive. Using hip hop as a resource provides an opportunity to address system level barriers to employment for opportunity youth and consider how to confront those in the course of career exploration and training.

Bringing in resources that have currency with young people is one way to have materials that are culturally relevant. Another is to bring into materials people – peers, role models – that are from the same racial, ethnic, cultural and/or linguistic background as the youth engaged in career training. Mindful of the fact that in career training programs, much of the learning happens through relationships, rather than by engaging with content. In our work with out of school youth around STEM career exploration, we bring in video portraits of role models who have successful STEM careers and that are from the same cultural, racial, ethnic, economic or linguistic backgrounds as the young people we are working with. When Marcus completes his training program, he would be a great candidate to share his story or showcase his work to add to the learning materials for future learners in his training program.

Reflection

- In your context, how might you go about understanding the accessibility of the materials and technologies you use to teach/train?
- What steps could you take to make sure that your materials are responsive to the particular learners that you have?

Assessments

With the appropriate goals, methods and materials in place, we then need to ask, are learners making measurable and meaningful progress toward their goals? In the same way that students are more motivated to pursue goals when they are of personal value to them, their performance on assessments can be improved by increasing engagement and the usefulness of assessments themselves (Rose et al., 2018). Assessment broadly is the way in which information is collected about an individual's performance using different methods and materials (CAST, 2011). Current systems are set up to suggest that there is an "ideal-type point of reference", which fails to appreciate that these systems are still value-laden and indicate what is and is not important (Hanesworth, Bracken, & Elkington, 2018; McArthur, 2016, p. 973). The goal of assessment within the UDL framework is "to improve the accuracy and timeliness of assessments, and to ensure that they are comprehensive and articulate enough to guide instruction – for all learners" (CAST, 2011, p. 8). Achieving this objective in all postsecondary settings including career training programs accommodates learner variability, encourages equity, and creates ample, varied opportunities for learning and career success (McArthur, 2016; Smith, Leconte, & Vitelli, 2012).

Relationship as central in assessment

The importance of relationships has been discussed in goals, methods and materials. Relationships are also central to the assessment process as it is through the relationship that the question of "by whom and for whom" as it relates to assessment can be addressed (McArthur, 2016). Assessments are intended to be mutually beneficial to help both the learners identify their strengths and opportunities for growth while also allowing those supporting the learners to identify ways to enhance their instruction and the learning environment (Rose et al., 2018).

The youth population being provided with career training opportunities includes a significant number of young people that have not had success with one size fits all approaches or with the adults – teachers, principals – delivering those one-size-fits-all approaches. This fact increases the importance of having assessments that are individualized to the learner to promote engagement and a sense of ownership (Parsi et al., 2018; Smith et al., 2012). Similar to the work on effective goal setting, a primary way to personalize assessment is through involving the learner and getting to know them well (Smith et al., 1994). Building this relationship lends itself to a more holistic approach to assessment, which is especially necessary with vocational assessments (Smith et al., 1994). Understanding the learner's strengths, interests and access to information helps to harness their motivation, which in turn improves the results of the assessments (Russell, 2011). UDL presumes that no matter how well designed an assessment is to measure its intended subject, it also captures elements of engagement, emotions, stereotype threat, and more (Rose et al., 2018). However, with a deeper understanding of a learner's knowledge and skills, UDL assessment can minimize these barriers and more accurately measure their knowledge, skills and engagement (CAST, 2011). Returning to Marcus' experience, José directly asked him and each of his students what kind of feedback was most and least useful. After providing feedback, he would encourage Marcus to share what kinds of thoughts and feelings came up to help him ensure that it came across in the way that he intended and could clarify anything that seemed misconstrued. Asking the learners directly what they find most and least helpful in feedback, how they intend to use the feedback, and what thoughts, feelings and behaviors arise in response to feedback is a simple way to ensure that the relationship is preserved if not strengthened and the learners move closer toward their goals (Ahmed Shafi, Hatley, Middleton, Millican, & Templeton, 2018).

Assessments in career training programs should provide multiple means of representation, multiple means for action and expression, and multiple means of engagement to enhance a learner's self-determination, which is beneficial to all when these skills genuinely align with a learner's interests and goals (Field, Martin, Miller, Ward, & Wehmeyer, 1998). For example, an individual's ability to engage with others is fundamental within the workplace as it forms the foundation for many interpersonal skills such as trust, communication, collaboration and teamwork. Measuring all of these different skills on an individual level is inconsistent with the way they are taught. Yet, giving the learner multiple methods to choose from as to how they can demonstrate these skills could not only more accurately illuminate their performance but the choice also promotes their self-determination. In sum, learners need to be active participants in deciding what needs to be assessed, how those factors will be measured, and how assessment results will be used (Field et al., 1998; Ahmed Shafi et al., 2018). Through collaboration, those supporting the learner can model the importance of self-determination while identifying what is of value to the learner and tailor the experience accordingly.

In an institution-centered system, the purpose of assessment is to get correct answers in order to obtain a grade. This is a tremendous shame because research consistently suggests that assessment has an extraordinarily potent impact on learning (Boud & Falchikov, 2007; Maclellan, 2001; McArthur, 2016; Taras, 2008). Within a student-centered learning system, the goal is to create many opportunities for ongoing feedback, as feedback has been shown to be the variable with the greatest impact on achievement (Hattie, 2009). However, the impact of feedback is highly inconsistent because not all feedback is of the same quality and it often fails to be delivered effectively (Boud & Molloy, 2013, Evans, 2013). For such feedback to be useful, it needs to come from individuals who the learners trust (Cohen, Steele, & Ross, 1999). Typically, the teacher is the source of feedback. However, within career training models of postsecondary education, various individuals are able to provide feedback ranging from the site supervisor, community partners, peers, or automated computer-based systems (Carless & Boud, 2018; Parsi et al., 2018). No matter who the feedback is coming from, how learners are assessed and the way in which feedback is given will determine whether the feedback is absorbed or dismissed (Carless, 2013). Feedback needs to go beyond an individual prescribing to the learner ways to improve alongside telling them their strengths and weaknesses (Carless & Boud, 2018; McLean, Bond, & Nicholson, 2015). The learner needs to not merely be a recipient of information. Rather, the learner must be actively involved in the process by appreciating feedback, making judgments about the information, managing their affect, and in turn, taking action (Carless & Boud, 2018).

Specifically with regard to affect, learners often react negatively and feel defensive, especially when feedback is critical (Robinson, Pope, & Holyoak, 2013). Without the proper tone and a clear message that the learner is cared about, feedback may be seen as a threat to the learner's identity, especially those from marginalized groups (Carless & Boud, 2018; Lipnevich, Berg, & Smith, 2016). By adolescence, learners from marginalized backgrounds are very aware of negative stereotypes held about their group (McKown & Weinstein, 2003). These personal experiences with bias foster the development of mistrust of both those providing feedback, assessments and the education system as a whole (Brown & Bigler, 2005). A lack of trust ensures that feedback, especially of a critical nature, is seen as bias instead of information that can in fact help a learner improve (Cohen et al., 1999). However, when both individuals – feedback provider and recipient – firmly believe that they are operating with good intentions and aim to truly benefit one another, the opportunity to view feedback with a positive lens is created (Bryk & Schneider, 2002; Cohen et al., 1999; Yeager et al., 2014). Prioritizing the importance of building and nurturing these relationships to reduce inequities that persist today is imperative to establish "a psychological climate that fosters trust and engagement" (Yeager et al., 2014, p. 822).

The use of wise feedback refers to strategies that work to focus on the humanity of someone from a stigmatized group and counter the related stereotype threat and racial bias by validating and assuming their knowledge and skills instead of doubting them (Cohen et al., 1999; Goffman, 1963; Steele, 1997). Feedback should build upon a learner's background and be provided in varying formats (Hanesworth et al., 2018). Wise feedback then can convey high expectations and is specific and useful to the learner. Additionally, feedback should be mastery-oriented, conveying to the learners that effort and practice are the necessary components to be successful, instead of intelligence. The goal is to encourage perseverance, help to enhance their self-efficacy and self-awareness, and improve their sense of agency to seek support when challenged (CAST, 2011). Such feedback should be specific, substantive and informative as opposed to comparative. Having an e-portfolio where young people can gather evidence of skill acquired in real time can provide evidence of student learning that a teacher or job trainer can easily give wise or mastery-oriented feedback for.

Nature of assessments

In these postsecondary contexts in particular, assessments need to be not only informed by UDL but the type of assessments are also fundamentally different than in traditional contexts. These settings necessitate that assessments are more relevant for work-based learning and are designed in a way that does not erect barriers in the same way that traditional assessments have.

> Learners might show understanding of content through demonstration or performance, such as an internship. . . . Settings for teaching may vary to include the community or a job site. Student peers or community partners might serve as instructors. Through this flexible, experience-oriented approach, personalized learning encourages students to get engaged and take ownership of their learning.
>
> (Parsi et al., p. 5)

In today's world, technology allows us to have information instantaneously and these learners are accustomed to using devices and this sense of immediate gratification. As such, assessments should leverage technology and be timely and reciprocal so that the information gathered is used to improve instruction, not just place a student on a continuum (Smith et al., 2012). One example of an assessment used in career training that engages students through participation and reflection and provides ample opportunities for feedback is an e-portfolio. For Marcus, the e-portfolio would give him a clear picture of his strengths and weaknesses and allowed him to work with his supervisor José to tailor his experience in order to reinforce his strong areas while also seeking opportunities to ensure he was able to receive more practice and training in weaker areas. With so many students to keep track of, José also appreciates having all of the information in one place, making it easy to access and assess each student's competency levels at a given point in time and over the course of their training.

Through a National Science Foundation grant, CAST is developing just such an e-portfolio for students at YouthBuild to use so they can document their learning of science, technology, engineering and math competencies (STEM) and facilitate the transfer of lessons from the classroom, from the job site and from their engagement with the community into a personalized and portable environment where they can have their skills assessed by the adults working with them at YouthBuild as well as by prospective employers or college admissions staff. Within the e-portfolio, the students can decide the way in which they would like to demonstrate their STEM competencies (e.g., take a video, annotate an image, obtain a testimonial from a trusted adult) and the adults working with them can provide feedback. The young people also tag the things they have put in their portfolio with relevant STEM competencies tags. They can then see over time based on their use of tags, what STEM competencies they are building and they can also pull up specific artifacts in their e-portfolio to demonstrate their learning and skills related to those tags. This approach to assessment is largely formative rather than summative. The summative information (i.e., use of tags over time) is derived from the formative information (i.e., tags used for each instance that something was uploaded into the e-portfolio). In this way, the summative information does provide a snapshot of what has been assessed formatively. This is a more viable approach to both formative and summative assessment for young people that have often fared poorly on high stakes summative assessments that are often disconnected from what they know and can do.

Reflection

- What skills do you need to develop to enhance the type of feedback you are providing to learners and ensure such feedback is being received well?
- What steps can you take if a learner consistently appears to have difficulty with feedback uptake?

Case study revisited

Imagine Marcus within a career training program that was universally designed. In such a program, Marcus might be able to drive with his kids to work and drop them off at the high-quality early learning center tied to the career training program, before he arrives early to the job site. José, his site supervisor, might be waiting at the job site with a captioned and transcribed video modeling solar panel installation. He would have that video pulled up on his IPad along with a handout with the big ideas for understanding load bearing and elevation. The trainees could choose to view the video, the handout or use both to remind them of key concepts they had practiced the week before to get ready for this installation job. Marcus could start the day working alongside his peers, giving and receiving mastery-oriented and wise feedback to stay motivated through challenging aspects of the work. At lunch time, the director of the community center and members of the community, would provide lunch to the trainees, and take fifteen minutes to thank each trainee for helping to make the community center environmentally sustainable and cost efficient. At the end of the day, Marcus would be able to login to his personalized e-portfolio and update it with a short, annotated video he took with his phone to show that he had learned to install solar panels and indicate through tagging this upload that he used mathematical reasoning, teamwork, measurement and tool safety skills. Within 48 hours, José could provide Marcus with feedback on his uploaded, annotated and tagged video and with Marcus' permission send the e-portfolio entry over to a friend that had a job opening in a green construction company. José could also provide Marcus with some information about how to enroll in a new hybrid (half face-to-face and half online) civil engineering course at the local community college.

Conclusion

UDL is a promising approach to improve the design of career training programs that enroll youth with disabilities and opportunity youth. Such improvements could allow for a more diverse group of young people to get into these programs and more importantly through and on to well-paying jobs. To bring UDL into these environments, practitioners in the field and researchers need to revisit some of the assumptions around a UDL curricula – that is the goals, methods, materials and assessments in any learning environment. UDL curricula need to be aligned with the context and the people participating in career training programs. Furthermore, to bring UDL more directly into career training programs, UDL practitioners need to engage in more conversations with practitioners framing culturally relevant teaching and culturally sustaining pedagogy, especially those using this pedagogy with opportunity youth. Greater engagement in conversations with those applying disability studies concepts to career training programs is also needed. This chapter offers some ideas and potential steps in providing goals, methods, materials and assessments that are both universally designed and relevant, truthful and engaging for youth that have been marginalized in traditional education settings.

References

Aceves, T. C., & Orosco, M. J. (2014). *Culturally responsive teaching* (Document No. IC-2). Retrieved from University of Florida, Collaboration for Effective Educator, Development, Accountability, and Reform Center website: http://ceedar. education.ufl.edu/tools/innovation-configurations/

Ahmed Shafi, A., Hatley, J., Middleton, T., Millican, R., & Templeton, S. (2018). The role of assessment feedback in developing academic buoyancy. *Assessment & Evaluation in Higher Education, 43*(3), 415–427.

Akbar, A. (2018, May 31). *Dreams unfold, nightmares come true.* Presented at the Annual Coalition of Schools Education Boys of Color Conference. Boston, MA.

Argyres, A., & Moir, S. (2008). Building trades apprentice training in Massachusetts: An analysis of union and non-union programs, 1997–2007. *Labor Resource Center Publications.* Paper 2. Retrieved from https://scholarworks.umb.edu/cgi/viewcontent.cgi?article=1001&context=lrc_pubs

Baglieri, S., Bejoian, L., Broderick, A., Connor, D., & Valle, J. (2011). (Re) claiming "inclusive education" toward cohesion in educational reform: Disability studies unravels the myth of the normal child. *Teachers College Record, 11*, 2122–2154.

Baglieri, S., & Shapiro, A. (2012). *Disability studies and the inclusive classroom.* New York: Routledge.

Boud, D., & Falchikov, N. (2007). Introduction: Assessment for the longer term. In D. Boud & N. Falchikov (Eds.), *Rethinking assessment for higher education: Learning for the longer term* (pp. 3–13). London: Routledge.

Boud, D., & Molloy, E. (2013). Rethinking models of feedback for learning: The challenge of design. *Assessment & Evaluation in Higher Education, 35*(3), 291–300.

Brown, C. S., & Bigler, R. S. (2005). Children's perceptions of discrimination: A developmental model. *Child Development, 76*(3), 533–553.

Bryk, A. S., & Schneider, B. (2002). *Trust in schools: A core resource for improvement.* New York: Russell Sage Foundation.

Burd-Sharps, S., & Lewis, K. (2018). *More than a million reasons for hope: Youth disconnection in America today.* Brooklyn, NY: Measure of America. Retrieved from www.measureofamerica.org/youth-disconnection-2018/

Bureau of Labor Statistics. (2013). *Employment projections – 2012–2022.* Retrieved from www.bls.gov/news.release/archives/ecopro_12192013.pdf

Bureau of Labor Statistics. (2018). Persons with a disability: Labor force characteristics 2017. *U.S. Department of Labor.* Retrieved from www.bls.gov/news.release/disabl.nr0.htm

Carless, D. (2013). Trust and its role in facilitating dialogic feedback. In D. Boud & E. Molloy (Eds.), *Feedback in higher and professional education: Understanding it and doing it well* (pp. 90–103). London: Routledge.

Carless, D., & Boud, D. (2018). The development of student feedback literacy: Enabling uptake of feedback. *Assessment & Evaluation in Higher Education.* doi: 10.1080/02602938.2018.1463354

CAST. (2011). *Universal design for learning guidelines version 2.0.* Wakefield, MA: Author.

Center for Disability Rights. (2018). Retrieved on January 15, 2018 from http://cdrnys.org/blog/uncategorized/ableism/

Christensen, J., Hetherington, S., Daston, M., & Riehle, E. (2015). Longitudinal outcomes of project SEARCH in upstate New York. *Journal of Vocational Rehabilitation, 42*, 247–255.

Cohen, G. L., Steele, C. M., & Ross, L. D. (1999). The mentor's dilemma: Providing critical feedback across the racial divide. *Personality and Social Psychology Bulletin, 25*(10), 1302–1318.

de Hoyos, R., Rogers, H., & Szekely, M. (2016). *Out of school and out of work: Risk and opportunities for Latin America's Ninis.* Washington, DC: World Bank. Retrieved from https://openknowledge.worldbank.org/handle/10986/22349

Emerick, S., & Marshall, J. (2017). Tight on goals, flexible on means: Universal design for learning empowers opportunity youth. *Digital Promise.* Retrieved from https://digitalpromise.org/2017/03/13/tight-goals-flexible-means-universal-design-learning-empowers-opportunity-youth/

Employment and Training Administration. (2018). Registered apprenticeship national results fiscal year (FY) 2017 (10/01/2016 to 9/30/2017). *U.S. Department of Labor.* Retrieved from www.doleta.gov/OA/data_statistics.cfm

Evans, C. (2013). Making sense of assessment feedback in higher education. *Review of Educational Research, 83*(1), 70–120.

Field, S. S., Martin, J. E., Miller, R. J., Ward, M., & Wehmeyer, M. L. (1998). Self-determination for persons with disabilities: A position statement of the division on career development and transition. *Career Development for Exceptional Individuals, 21,* 113–128.

Fischer, G. (2011). *Social creativity: Exploiting the power of cultures of participation.* Proceedings of SKG2011: 7th International Conference on Semantics, Knowledge and Grids, Beijing, China, October (in press). http://l3d.cs.colorado.edu/~gerhard/papers/2011/SKG-China.pdf

Gay, G. (2010). *Culturally responsive teaching: Theory, research, and practice* (2nd ed.). New York: Teachers College Press.

Generation jobless – Youth unemployment. (2013, April 27). *The economist.* Retrieved from www.economist.com/international/2013/04/27/generation-jobless

Goffman, E. (1963). *Stigma: Notes on the management of spoiled identity.* Englewood Cliffs, NJ: Prentice-Hall.

GovTrack.us. (2018). *S. 3217–115th congress: Strengthening career and technical education for the 21st century act.* Retrieved from www.govtrack.us/congress/bills/115/s3217

Hanesworth, P., Bracken, S., & Elkington, S. (2018). A typology for a social justice approach to assessment: Learning from universal design and culturally sustaining pedagogy. *Teaching in Higher Education, 24*(1), 1–17. https://doi.org/10.1080/13562517.2018.1465405

Hattie, J. (2009). *Visible learning: A synthesis of over 800 meta-analyses relating to achievement.* London: Routledge.

Heckman, J. J., Humphries, J. E., & Mader, N. S. (2010). The GED (No. w16064). *National Bureau of Economic Research.* Retrieved from www.nber.org/papers/w16064.pdf

Helper, S., Noonan, R., Nicholson, J. R., & Langdon, D. (2016). The benefits and costs of apprenticeships: A business perspective. *US Department of Commerce.* Retrieved from www.esa.gov/sites/default/files/the-benefits-and-costs-of-apprenticeships-a-business-perspective.pdf

Hinz, S. E., Arbeit, C. A., & Bentz, A. (2017). *Characteristics and outcomes of undergraduates with disabilities.* Washington, DC: National Center for Education Statistics. Retrieved from https://nces.ed.gov/pubsearch/pubsinfo.asp?pubid=2018432

Johnston, S. C., & Rose, D. H. (2017). Print and its disabilities. In E. L. Meyen & Y. Bui (Eds.), *Exceptional children in today's schools: What teachers need to know* (5th ed.). Austin, TX: ProEd.

Kenny, M. E., Walsh-Blair, L. Y., Blustein, D. L., Bempechat, J., & Seltzer, J. (2010). Achievement motivation among urban adolescents: Work hope, autonomy, support, and achievement-related beliefs. *Journal of Vocational Behavior, 77*, 205–212.

Knowles, M. S. (1980). *The modern practice of adult education: From pedagogy to andragogy.* Wilton, CT: Association Press.

Kolb, D. A. (1984). *Experiential learning: Experience as the source of learning and development.* Upper Saddle River, NJ: Prentice-Hall.

Ladson-Billings, G. (2009). *The dreamkeepers: Successful teachers of African American children* (2nd ed.). San Francisco, CA: Jossey-Bass.

Lave, J., & Wenger, E. (1991). *Situated Learning. Legitimate peripheral participation.* Cambridge: University of Cambridge Press.

LEAD Center (2016). *Reviewing your state's WIOA unified or combined state plan from a disability perspective* (WIOA Title I Requirements). Retrieved from www.leadcenter.org/system/files/page/title-I-guide.pdf

Lee, J., Schochet, P. Z., & Berk, J. (2018). *The external review of Job Corps: Directions for future research.* Report submitted to the U.S. Department of Labor. Washington, DC: Mathematica Policy Research. Retrieved from www.dol.gov/asp/evaluation/completed-studies/JC-Evaluation-Design-Options.pdf

Leonard, D. (2010). *Lecture on the art and craft of discussion leadership.* Cambridge, MA: Harvard Business School.

Lerman, R. I. (2012). Can the United States expand apprenticeship? Lessons from experience. *IZA Policy Paper No. 46.* Retrieved from http://ftp.iza.org/pp46.pdf

Lerman, R. I., Eyster, L., & Chambers, K. (2009). *The benefits and challenges of registered apprenticeship: The sponsors' perspective.* Washington DC: Urban Institute. Retrieved from www.urban.org/research/publication/benefits-and-challenges-registered-apprenticeship-sponsors-perspective

Lipnevich, A. A., Berg, D., & Smith, J. K. (2016). Toward a model of student response to feedback. In G. T. L. Brown & L. Harris (Eds.), *Human factors and social conditions in assessment* (pp. 169–185). New York: Routledge.

Maclellan, E. (2001). Assessment for learning: The differing perceptions of tutors and students. *Assessment & Evaluation in Higher Education, 26*(4), 307–318.

McArthur, J. (2016). Assessment for social justice: The role of assessment in achieving social justice. *Assessment & Evaluation in Higher Education, 41*(7), 967–981.

McFarland, J., Hussar, B., Wang, X., Zhang, J., Wang, K., Rathbun, A., . . . Bullock Mann, F. (2018). *The condition of education 2018* (NCES 2018–144). U.S. Department of Education. Washington, DC: National Center for Education Statistics. Retrieved from https://nces.ed.gov/pubsearch/pubsinfo.asp?pubid=2018144.

McKown, C., & Weinstein, R. S. (2003). The development and consequences of stereotype consciousness in middle childhood. *Child Development, 74*, 498–515.

McLean, A., Bond, C., & Nicholson, H. (2015). An anatomy of feedback: A phenomenographic investigation of undergraduate students' conceptions of feedback. *Studies in Higher Education, 40*(5), 921–932.

Meyer, A., Rose, D. H., & Gordon, D. (2014). *Universal design for learning: Theory and practice.* Wakefield, MA: CAST Professional Publishing.

Miller, C., Millenky, M., Schwartz, L., Globe, L., & Stein, J. (2016). Building a future: Interim findings from the YouthBuild evaluation. *MDRC*. Retrieved from www.mdrc.org/sites/default/files/YouthBuild_Interim_Report_2016_508.pdf

National Center on Accessible Educational Materials. (2018). *Home page*. Retrieved from http://aem.cast.org

NCEE. (2018). *South Korea: Career and technical education*. Retrieved from http://ncee.org/what-we-do/center-on-international-education-benchmarking/top-performing-countries/south-korea-overview/south-korea-school-to-work-transition/

Nieto, S., Bode, P., Kang, E., & Raible, J. (2008). Identity, community, and diversity: Retheorizing multicultural curriculum for the postmodern era. In F. Connelly, M. He, & J. Phillion (Eds.), *The SAGE handbook of curriculum and instruction* (pp. 176–198). Thousand Oaks, CA: Sage.

Niranjan, A. (2018, June 4). What is Gerany's dual education system and why do other countries want it? *DW*. Retrieved from www.dw.com/en/what-is-germanys-dual-education-system-and-why-do-other-countries-want-it/a-42902504

OECD. (2009). *Sickness, disability, and work: Keeping on track in the economic downturn*. Retrieved from www.oecd.org/els/emp/42699911.pdf

OECD. (2018). Youth not in employment, education or training (NEET) (indicator). Retrieved from https://data.oecd.org/youthinac/youth-not-in-employment-education-or-training-neet.htm doi: 10.1787/72d1033a-en

Office for Civil Rights [OCR]. (2011). *Frequently asked questions about the June 29, 2010 dear colleague letter*. Washington, DC: U.S. Department of Education. Retrieved from http://www2.ed.gov/about/offices/list/ocr/docs/dcl-ebook-faq-201105.html

Office of Educational Technology. (2017). *Reimagining the role of technology in higher education: A supplement to the national education technology plan*. Washington, DC: U.S. Department of Education.

Office of Management and Budget, Voluntary Self-Identification of Disability Form CC-305. Retrieved from www.dol.gov/ofccp/regs/compliance/sec503/Self_ID_Forms/VoluntarySelf-ID_CC-305_ENG_JRF_QA_508c.pdf

Parsi, A., Whittaker, M. C., & Jones, L. E. (2018). *Agents of their own success: Self-advocacy skills and self-determination for students with disabilities in the era of personalized learning*. New York: National Center for Learning Disabilities. Retrieved from www.ncld.org/wp-content/uploads/2018/03/Agents-of-Their-Own-Success_Final.pdf

Porfeli, E. J., & Lee, B. (2012). Career development during childhood and adolescence. *New Directions for Youth Development, 134*, 11–22.

Robinson, S., Pope, D., & Holyoak, L. (2013). Can we meet their expectations? Experiences and perceptions of feedback in first year undergraduate students. *Assessment and Evaluation in Higher Education, 38*(3), 260–272.

Rose, D., Robinson, K. H., Hall, T. E., Coyne, P., Jackson, R. M., Stahl, W. M., & Wilcauskas, S. L. (2018). Accurate and informative for all: Universal Design for Learning (UDL) and the future of assessment. In S. N. Elliott et al. (Eds.), *Handbook of accessible instruction and testing practices* (pp. 167–180). Cham, Switzerland: Spring International Publishing AG.

Russell, M. (2011). Personalizing assessment. In T. Gray & H. Silver-Pacuilla (Eds.), *Breakthrough teaching and learning* (pp. 111–126). New York: Springer Publishing.

Schochet, P., Burghardt, J., & McConnell, S. (2008). Does Job Corps work? Impact findings from the National Job Corps study. *American Economic Review*, *98*(5), 1864–1886.

Sealey, P., & Noyes, A. (2010). On the relevance of the mathematics curriculum to young people. *The Curriculum Journal*, *21*, 239–253.

Smith, F. G., Leconte, P. J., & Vitelli, E. (2012). The VECAP position paper on universal design for career assessment and vocational evaluation. *Vocational Evaluation and Career Assessment Journal*, *8*(1), 13–26.

Smith, F. G., Lombard, R., Neubert, D., Leconte, P., Rothenbacher, C., & Sitlington, P. (1994). The position statement of the interdisciplinary council on vocational evaluation and assessment. *The Journal for Vocational Special Needs Education*, *17*(1) (Fall, 1993), 41–42.

Snyder, C. R. (1994). *The psychology of hope: You can get there from here.* New York: The Free Press.

Snyder, C. R. (1995). Conceptualizing, measuring, and nurturing hope. *Journal of Counseling & Development*, *73*, 355–360.

Snyder, C. R., Feldman, D. B., Shorey, H. S., & Rand, K. L. (2002). Hopeful choices: A school counselor's guide to hope theory. *Professional School Counseling*, *5*(5), 298–307.

Steele, C. M. (1997). A threat in the air: How stereotypes shape intellectual identity and performance. *American Psychologist*, *52*(6), 613–629.

Symonds, W. C., Schwartz, R., & Ferguson, R. F. (2011). *Pathways to prosperity: Meeting the challenge of preparing young Americans for the 21st century.* Cambridge, MA: Harvard Graduate School of Education. Retrieved from https://dash.harvard.edu/handle/1/4740480

Taras, M. (2008). Assessment for learning: Sectarian divisions of terminology and concepts. *Journal of Further and Higher Education*, *32*(4), 389–397.

Tinto, V. (2010). From theory to action: Exploring the institutional conditions for student retention. In J. C. Smart (Ed.), *Higher education: Handbook of theory and research* (pp. 51–89). New York: Springer Publishing.

Tinto, V. (2012). *Completing college: Rethinking institutional action.* Chicago, IL: University of Chicago Press.

Tucker, M. S. (2004). High school and beyond: The system is the problem – and the solution. In R. Kazis, J. Vargas, & N. Hoffman (Eds.), *Double the numbers: Increasing postsecondary credentials for underrepresented youth* (pp. 47–60). Cambridge, MA: Harvard Education Press.

UNESCO. (2018). *TVET country profile: Republic of Korea.* Retrieved from https://unevoc.unesco.org/wtdb/worldtvetdatabase_kor_en.pdf

U.S. Career Institute. (2017). *What is career training?* [blog post]. Retrieved from www.uscareerinstitute.edu/blog/what-is-career-training

U.S. Department of Justice. (2015, April 2). *Justice Department reaches settlement with edX Inc., provider of massive open online courses, to make its website, online platform and mobile applications accessible under the Americans with Disabilities Act.* Retrieved from www.justice.gov/opa/pr/justice-department-reaches-settlement-edx-inc-provider-massive-open-online-courses-make-its

U.S. Department of Justice. (2016, October 17). *Miami University agrees to overhaul critical technologies to settle disability discrimination lawsuit.* Retrieved from: www.justice.gov/opa/pr/miami-university-agrees-overhaul-critical-technologies-settle-disability-discrimination

U.S. Department of Labor. (2016a). *Budget in brief.* Retrieved from www.dol.gov/sites/default/files/documents/general/budget/2016/FY2016BIB.pdf

U.S. Department of Labor. (2016b). *Fact sheet: National apprenticeship week celebrates advancements in apprenticeship.* Retrieved from www.dol.gov/apprenticeship/NAW/pdf/Final_DOL_NAW_Factsheet.pdf

U.S. Department of Labor. (2016c). *US Labor Department announces final rule to help employers diversify workforce, provide apprenticeship opportunity for all Americans.* Retrieved from www.dol.gov/newsroom/releases/eta/eta20161216

U.S. Department of Labor. (2017). *FY 2017 budget in brief.* Retrieved from www.dol.gov/sites/default/files/documents/general/budget/FY2017BIB_0.pdf

U.S. Department of Labor. (2018a). *Apprenticeship toolkit: Advancing apprenticeship as a workforce strategy.* Retrieved from www.dol.gov/apprenticeship/toolkit/toolkitfaq.htm

U.S. Department of Labor. (2018b). *What is registered apprenticeship?* Retrieved from www.doleta.gov/OA/apprenticeship.cfm

U.S. Department of Labor. (n.d.). *Registered apprenticeship-college Consortium Frequently Asked Questions (FAQs).* Retrieved from https://doleta.gov/oa/pdf/RACC_FAQs1.pdf

Wenger, E. (1998). *Communities of practice: Learning, meaning, and identity.* Cambridge: Cambridge University Press.

Wenger, E., McDermott, R., & Snyder, W. (2002). *Cultivating communities of practice: A guide to managing knowledge.* Cambridge, MA: Harvard Business School Press.

Wigfield, A., & Eccles, J. S. (2000). Expectancy-value theory of achievement motivation. *Contemporary Educational Psychology, 25,* 68–81.

Yeager, D. S., Purdie-Vaughns, V., Garcia, J., Apfel, N., Pebley, P., Master, A., . . . Cohen, G. L. (2014). Breaking the cycle of mistrust: Wise interventions to provide critical feedback across the racial divide. *Journal of Experimental Psychology: General, 143,* 804–824.

Chapter 9

Pedagogy of seasons and UDL

The multiple temporalities of
learning involving the university as
a whole

Elizabete Cristina Costa-Renders

Case study

My name is Pedro and I study with João, we're friends who met while
studying on a computer networking course in São Paulo, Brazil. For
some time, I have observed and learned from my friend João's university experiences. Together we learned that Professor Carlos designed
his courses so every student could excel. He spoke aloud as he wrote
on the board and he provided all of the resources a couple of days
in advance. Like João, I recorded his sessions on my cell phone. This
professor had a lot of patience. He explained the content and skills
in different ways. But we had another professor who assumed João
wouldn't be able to solve calculation problems and he was left out
of some of the group activities. Our electronics classes were with
professor Sílvia. When João needed additional support, after class,
she stayed behind and went through the content. She also drew the
material in relief and could write in Braille, using the tips from Virtual
Braille (USP, 2017).

At certain times, João also relied on Davi, his disability support
tutor. Davi accompanied him all the time and would describe the
program codes presented, since, as a blind person, João couldn't use
a mouse to complete the tasks. Felipe the laboratory technician was
also a huge support in the learning process. We had Linux classes and,
at that time, João was not familiar with the accessibility resources for
this operating system. Felipe researched a Linux version of the accessibility codes for Linux and then he ensured we had access to these
codes. The second part of Linux classes was much more complex,
because they involved on-screen drawings and the drawing tools were

only visible on the screen, unfortunately, there wasn't any assistive technology available to make these drawings accessible via code, so João needed Davi to check the design techniques and describe them. When João couldn't handle the software by himself, it was down to us, his classmates, to describe the drawings on his screen.

In everyday university life there were many barriers to learning. For example, there wasn't a high-quality screen reader in the laboratory computer and that's why Davi would read everything João typed. Davi also took responsibility for checking João's written program codes. Examinations were some of the most challenging and stressful times. The test information that was shared visually didn't come with any alternative accessibility format, and that's why another tutor, Sérgio, a journalism student, accompanied João to explain what had to be done.

João and I managed to finish the course together and along the way we learned really well together. Between challenges and successes, we depended on professors and students who chipped in so that João and I developed the best learning strategies we could. We will keep on learning, because we believe learning extends beyond professors and students in the university; it's not possible to talk about gaining insight without considering how learning experience is gained within a space where many people interact, with many objects at lots of differing times – it's complex but we aim to continue navigating along that journey.

Introduction

This case study explores findings from my doctoral research; the names mentioned are fictitious but their experiences ring true and illustrate the complexity of being disabled while attending higher education. These insights are particularly important because, having worked for ten years in Brazil as an advocate for inclusion in HEIs, I can share that implementing the principles and practices of Universal Design for Learning (UDL) is a daily struggle encompassing both physical and epistemological barriers. Nevertheless, the inclusion of people with disabilities has provoked important movements for the transformation of HEIs into more accessible and creative spaces as envisioned by application of the UDL framework. The intentional crafting of this case study to the fore illustrates how, by their presence, people with disabilities contribute significantly to the emergence of UDL principles in Brazilian universities. This chapter considers, therefore, how their presence, and their claim of 'different corporalities', effects, and potentially transforms, the HEI experience for both students and teachers.

The philosophical foundation for this chapter is premised on the notion of the university as an open, dynamic and contested spatial and temporal field, it is a transit space that is affected by the movement of differences, these come together and diverge to create coherent and, at times, conflicting ways of being within the institutional space and time. Second, it is understood that inclusive education constitutes a utopian horizon, for this innovative imagining provokes, through ethical research, a desired resolution to the question, 'how can we create a university so that everyone is successful?' This chapter also introduces a third concept that explores the extent to which the use of UDL principles can help create a conceptual framework that underpins a workable paradigm for inclusion in higher education.

Pedro and João's experiences exemplify the many intentions and actions in the emerging necessity to remove barriers and to recognize the validity of UDL principles in a university's quest for movement towards inclusion. Starting from this perspective, the chapter progresses using the following core principles:

1   Accessibility and UDL conceptions and methodologies to challenge notions of monocultures in the university;
2   The pivotal contribution of people with disabilities in fashioning accessibility and UDL in higher education;
3   Pedagogy of Seasons and UDL: the necessary consideration of simultaneous plurality.

I Accessibility and UDL: conceptions and methodologies to challenge notions of monocultures in the university

The application of UDL in the field of education constitutes a relatively recent phenomenon particularly for HEIs (Meyer & Rose, 2002; Rose & Meyer, 2006). In Brazil, the research base for UDL application is somewhat negligible. A review of the Brazilian Digital Library of Theses and Dissertations [Biblioteca Digital Brasileira de Teses e Dissertações], using the indexers "Universal Design for Learning" and "education", revealed only two works in this field. When indexers are changed to "accessibility" and "education", this number increases significantly, and some 1,237 research studies are found. However, upon inserting the indexer "higher education", this number decreases to 198 studies. The same research conducted using a search of the nationally significant CAPES Journal Portal [Portal Periódicos CAPES] provides similar findings. There were some 1,605 articles with reference to "accessibility" and "education", but only 552 articles related to "accessibility" and "higher education". Further, when using the indexers "universal design for learning" and "higher education", as well as "universal design for learning" and "education" there is not a single research study.

There are however some publications in the field of distance education studies (Sondermann & Albernaz, 2013) and in a broader review of the literature, one article has identified that there were 23 Brazilian publications incorporating "the principles of UDL as a foundation" (Prais, 2017: 14, 483). It might be surmised that, despite the growing body of research literature concerned with the broad concept of 'inclusion', the application of the UDL Framework has not, as yet, been embedded into practice. In a national situation where the teaching-learning process is more likely to bring us closer to the reality of people with a disability and their necessity to confront and overcome barriers (presence/claim), we should wonder why the relevant application of UDL principles has not posed a more pressing urgency in terms of research.

Reflection

- Do you agree that the presence of people with disabilities in the university represents, in and of itself, a claim for things to be done differently? In what ways might this be manifested in your own setting?
- How might such alternative 'ways of being' (the presence of persons with disabilities) contribute to emerging and innovative ways of thinking and doing things differently within your own setting?

The case study testified that the daily life of universities is a constant and dynamic space for negotiating the use of senses, creating and reinventing knowledge and it is also a pivotal place of action for all students considering their differences and capacities. For example, during the classroom routine when spatial reorientation was required, it not only led to a curricular change for João, the experience also broadened the knowledge base for all, including teachers.

Within the dynamic processes of facing barriers and negotiating new meanings and practices, it is possible to perceive that difference ipso facto leads to the demand for accessibility. Thus, the presence of a disabled person (with his or her difference) demands new ways of learning and opens the way for the application of UDL principles in the university. This is in essence beneficial for all students because it opens the range of paths to knowledge in everyday studies. For example, listening to a student with cerebral palsy who speaks more slowly creates new demands to learn through listening. A person who wishes to share his notes with a deaf student creates the demand for translation. In the latter example, the teaching of sign language by deaf students to hearing students enables them to learn a new language. These and other situations can emerge from the coexistence between different subjects in the educational environment and this creates a space for realizing the UDL principles through action and interaction.

So how has that presence and demand changed in Brazil over the years? In the early 2000s, universities began to witness the enrollment of students with disabilities and since 2005, there has been a significant increase in the number of students with disabilities in HEIs. According to the *Instituto Nacional de Estudos e Pesquisas Educacionais*, the enrollment of students with disabilities increased dramatically from 5,078 to 35,891 (BRASIL/INEP, 2016) over a period of 13 years. Certainly, this is a notable increase, but there are still barriers to welcoming students with disabilities into our universities. The number 35,891 corresponds to only 0.45 % of the total enrolled number of students in Brazilian HEIs (BRASIL/INEP, 2016). Nationally however, some 23.9% of the total population of 46 million people (IBGE, 2010) have identified as having some for of disability.

It is in this wider context that students João and Pedro experience the complexities of navigating their ways through ideas of 'inclusion' and how accessibility may be managed. João was one of the pathfinders in a journey full of epistemological, physical and interactional barriers. Research conducted by the 'Advisory Team for Pedagogical Inclusion', the staff responsible for the development of university accessibility within the author's university, revealed some critical incidents as communities strived to create an inclusive university. For example, in the case of blind students' access to their learning – course reading materials proved to be hugely problematic. Among some of the immediate questions posed by students were: 'Which text format is preferable for blind students, Braille or digital'? 'Who can teach us how to produce these alternative text formats'? Most of the time, the ones who responded to these questions through action were students themselves. They taught professors and managers the alternative ways for writing and reading. This happened in such an intense and dynamic way that the first blind students also started working within the university systems, especially within the library and information sectors. João, for instance, ended up working in the information technology and communication department, checking the accessibility conditions for virtual learning environments. After that, he helped to teach other students how to use these resources.

The general situation was quite haphazard, for instance, in terms of studying strategies, some blind students used assistive technology tools with ease while others were building competence with new ways of learning. Some knew and preferred the use of Braille, while others had no knowledge of Braille whatsoever, nor were they familiar with the software to facilitate computer screen reading. In certain situations, it appeared that there were conflicting approaches, for example individuals and universities may have used different software systems, additionally there were conflicts between student preferences between face-to-face and/or the use of online learning modalities. Some students showed more interest in digital text due to the accessibility, speed and multiple representations this format offered them. Whatever their diversity of contexts and backgrounds, students encountered one constant, this was what might be termed the 'pedagogic monoculture'.

Monocultures are modes of social reproduction that are typified by absence, they are a 'one size fits all' perspective effacing the legitimacy of difference and instead elevating and affording presence only to the historically legitimized and privileged normed 'able bodied' student. A pedagogical approach based on monoculture produces barriers in the processes of teaching and learning, for example by reducing language learning interactions to a core code of reading and script writing and thereby denying the role of Braille or sign language interaction. On the other hand, UDL principles confront monocultures as they advocate interaction through multiple ways and means for accessing and representing knowledge.

Reflection

- In your experience, how does 'monoculturalism' present a barrier to learning?
- What kinds of monoculturalism is most prevalent in universities?
- In your opinion, how do UDL principles and practices challenge monocultural practices in higher education?

No two students learn in the same way and one of the major variances in learning relates to time. In order to support application of the UDL principles, as this confounds a monocultural perspective, this chapter proposes a metaphorical adoption of 'the pedagogy of the seasons', since this refers to multi-temporalities in the teaching-learning process. The presence and demand (for adaptation and alteration) of people with disabilities in the daily life of the university brings to mind the important challenge this has made to accepted realities. Presence and demand have contributed significantly to the destabilization of the classical hierarchical dichotomies between normal and abnormal or capable and incapable. The starting point for the pedagogy of the seasons is to articulate the emergence of flexible times and spaces for the construction of knowledge. This approach considers different perceptions of the world and confronts the monoculture of linear time in the university. This argument highlights the relevance of a cyclical curriculum which, organized in stations of knowledge, allows for the consideration of simultaneous plurality and it also encourages epistemological reflection within the academic community as explored for example in the work of Cooper (2006).

Why use the 'Pedagogy of Seasons' Metaphor?

The seasons of the year clearly show that light and the sun get to all parts of the planet, but not with the same intensity or at the same time. Similarly, all knowledge gets to everyone at different times and spaces respecting the ecology of "knowledges" and temporalities. The seasons are inserted into an annual calendar, but don't settle in 'chronos', they shift in terms of planetary movement and differ, in each hemisphere (solstices and equinoxes).

Research is required to explore the temporalities and spaces of learning that don't fit neatly into predetermined pedagogical times which are constrained by narrow perceptions of how curriculum might be enacted. Just as there are variables in the continuous movement of the seasons that enable conditions for life on our planet, for example the average temperatures that influence the temperatures of our oceans, so too educationalists need to consider the variations and work required to cater for individualized learning according to the dynamics informing curricula design and implementation.

Universities tend to work within monocultural frameworks and because João was not part of the 'normal' experience as typified in a monocultural environment, he faced multiple forms of exclusion (in both space and time) and his presence and legitimacy at university was questioned. For example, He ran into the monoculture of reading printed text and writing in ink, with the monoculture of space visual signalization (physical and virtual) and with the monoculture of the evaluation formats and time.

Despite operating within broad legal frameworks that legislate for design of inclusive educational policies, clear gaps become visible when the lived experiences of students are researched through narrative approaches. This illustrates that the implementation of policy frameworks tends to be reactive, lethargic, complex and, they are sometimes, contradictory. Too often what tends to happen is that inclusive policies are reduced to a series of restricted services offered within the narrowest interpretation of the legislation rather than seeing the legislation as a potential springboard for innovation and inclusivity. When considering these factors, it is worthwhile reflecting on how such a proposed flexible approach might fit within national regulatory frameworks.

One of the most important pieces of legislation related to inclusion in higher education is Decree N.3284 of 2003, this statute provides a restricted view of inclusion related to three identifiable student cohorts; those with a physical disability, those with a visual disability and students with a hearing disability. Additionally, subsequent pieces of legislation related to the use of sign language (Decree N. 5626 of 2005) and extending accessibility within wider society (Decree N. 5296 of 2004) have paradoxically strengthened a monocultural approach. By determining singular approaches to accessibility conditions, these documents disregard the variability of students and insist on a homogenous categorization of people and stipulate a delimiting provision of services.

Within both legislative and pedagogical domains, there is a mutual and unhelpful restriction of resources that defines how educational spaces can be perceived in terms of inclusivity. In this context, HEI Accessibility Centers, which are responsible for the development and continuous improvement of accessibility at the university, as provided for within Decree N.7611 of 2011 (BRASIL, 2011) have limited their services to a restricted interpretation of what constitutes 'special education', providing services and resources exclusively to people with disabilities, and those who are termed as having 'global developmental disorders', as well as to people who are termed as being 'gifted and talented', though these notions are, in and of themselves, also highly contested. In 2015, the Inclusion Law (Law N.13.146 of 2015) provided an even narrower interpretation of inclusion specifically defining the statute of the person with a disability as follows: "a person with a disability is considered to be a person with a long-term physical, mental, intellectual or sensory disability, which, in interaction with one or more barriers, may obstruct their full and effective participation in society on an equal basis with others people" (*Agência Brasil*, 2015).

In a context where inclusion policies and practices are reductionist and essentialist in their perceptions of diversity and learner variance, it is timely to explore the potential for application of UDL principles within higher education because, as identified by Meyer and Rose (2005, p. 11), "students 'on the margins', for whom current curricula are patently ineffective, can actually lead the way to true reform because they help us understand weaknesses in our educational system and curricula that impede teaching and learning for all". Such a perspective challenges the notion that those with power know best for those who are marginalized. Rather, by placing the experiences of students at the heart of the decision-making processes, traditional and reductionist monocultures are disrupted.

Contributions of people with disabilities: towards multi-temporalities in the university

The sensory experiences of those with disabilities occur in various ways, this is what inspires the concept of multiple temporalities and multiple learning spaces. This is, in essence, a pedagogical approach required for all learners but it takes on particular significance for those with disabilities. So we need to re-evaluate how learning and teaching takes place, for instance in the domains of reading and writing and how they are manifested in space and time. Reading a text in Braille reformulates space and time differently from reading an ink-based text. The written words, to the blind, will show up, letter by letter, at their fingertips, in a different sensorial field.

Conversational sign reading by students who are profoundly deaf requires the patient and more considered exercise of linguistic translation from the immediate oral form into sign language. This requires a search for synonym words and symbols involving a symbolic exchange between these different linguistic forms. Further, a person with a motor disability can write on a regular keyboard, with the support of assistive technology, or with assistance from an orthosis or other device. However, this takes differentiated space/time from the commonly established notions for text production in the learning space.

By adapting to the 'pedagogy of the seasons', learning occurs within a cyclical movement, where it is possible to align systems of responsibility with systems of diversity. Difference demands consideration of the intensity within which knowledge is generated and shared and it necessitates the use of collaborative 'stations' or reflective moments to evaluate educational processes and their impact upon learning. At each station, the content offered could be the same, but the intensity of the requirements would be different, gaining greater complexity at each session, this mirrors the movement of the seasons.

As argued by Costa-Renders (2016) the presence of individual 'human corporeality' – the shape and demands of the body – should better inform any pedagogical approach, so that community consideration of people with disabilities and their varied learning requirements generates a claim or demand that alters 'taken for granted' foundations for knowing and learning within the university community. Once homogenization and monocultures of learning have been problematized, the approaches to teaching, learning and assessment better lend themselves to the collaborative adoption of UDL principles (CAST, 2011).

In the case study, for instance, João extended the use of multiple representations (for example through extending the need for written and tactile images and by including the need for audio description of images), and he also paved a way for the multiple means of action and expression (for example, by typing the codes instead of using the mouse and by developing his own approaches and tools for learning). Furthermore, he showed autonomy and resilience when faced by insecurity and anxiety, requesting different supports throughout his course (including being able to access learning resources and through tutoring in the laboratory). This illustrates how the presence of persons with disabilities lends itself to a more universalist, rather than reductionist, approach to policy and practice; a concept that is further explored in the following section.

Reflection

- How might the metaphor of 'the Pedagogy of the Seasons' have relevance within your own setting?
- What resources are needed to respect the different 'temporalities' and spaces in the process of teaching and learning for all?
- How can educational policies guarantee different supports and multiple representations in the teaching-learning process?
- How might the adoption of UDL principles at university support inclusive educational practices?

2 The pivotal contribution of people with disabilities in fashioning accessibility and UDL in higher education

The inclusion of people with disabilities in university requires a critical reflection upon the centrality of human corporeality in the design of pedagogical approaches. Educational experiences are not merely concerned with a functionalist or utilitarian provision of specialized educational assistance, rather effective pedagogy, and more general well-being in the wider social world, purposefully considers the multiple ways in which human corporeality and variance affects education, demanding alternative ways of being and learning. Drawing on the research of Sanchez (2005), alternative pathways for learning are provided when anticipatory considerations of physical, interpersonal and attitudinal accessibility underpin the formation of learning in a diversity of pedagogical environments. The impact of this presence/claim begins to affect the paradigmatic nature of educational experiences within learning environments (Mantoan, 2005). What transpires is an iterative and cumulative process starting from a notion of physical presence that calls for adaptations to traditional dominant modes of knowledge transference and moves towards effective inclusion entailing continuous, collaborative and persistent actions that remove barriers and create conditions for social and curricular accessibility. This is reflected, for example, in Figure 9.1 below, which illustrates changes in curricular accessibility at the Universidade Methodista de Sao Paulo (UMESP).

For the purposes of sustainability, there is a need to re-conceptualize prescriptive models of educational design considering both space and time. As illustrated, the presence/claim of people with disabilities also confronts the hegemony of institutional time, pointing out that the:

> Notions of time cannot be easily unified through a unique universal representation, because time incorporates dimensions of spatiality which are characterized by our unique sensing of the world that holds us, it remains problematic and it is not easily unifiable within human experience
>
> (Assmann, 1998, p. 221).

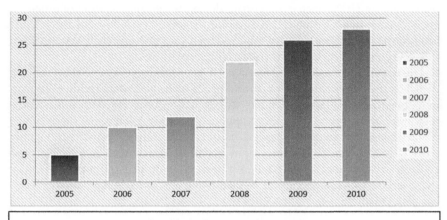

Graphic 1, Costa-Renders, 2018

Figure 9.1 Trends in curriculum changes to accommodate students with disabilities

Whether we are conscious of it or not, and whether we like it or not, our lifetime experiences, inform part of our university experiences. From halls to classrooms, from square benches to libraries and laboratories, learners experience "being" in their own ways whether this is recognized, or not, and whether it is responded to, or not. These experiences emerge and make way for "knowledge" and acknowledgements in the university. Our lifetime experiences and narratives are all about the human condition of "being more" (Freire, 2005) which, also elicits the possibility of "being less" through limiting situations or conditions that are imposed by systems of effacement or oppression. As shared by Freire, "in contrast to other animals who are unfinished, but not historical, people know themselves to be unfinished; they are aware of their incomplete nature. In this incomplete status and this awareness lie the very roots of education as an exclusive instrument for liberation" (Freire, 2005, p. 84). There is a need to clarify that this chapter, concerned as it is with analyzing a pedagogical movement, can only be partially effective because its impact is as yet unfinished and it is as open as the human condition and education itself.

Costa-Renders (2016) argues that the presence/claim of people with disabilities in the university confirms that a 'one size fits all' approach is ineffective because it is conceptually unsound. Thus, a unitary experience of deafness does not exist, nor does one exist for those who are blind, nor are binary divisions between 'a person with a disability' and 'a person without a disability' helpful ways to conceptualize curriculum design and enactment. Difference and vulnerability are anthropological conditions that exist along a continuum within a diversity of contexts and spaces, this is what Cook and Rao (2018) refer to as 'variability' in UDL. Such a perspective demands the consideration of differences outside of a hierarchical classification of ability/disability and also it lends itself to the ethical inquiry as to how best we can create university systems so that everyone is successful in their learning.

The paradigm of inclusion, based on UDL principles (CAST, 2011), demands the continuous reformulation of academic and administrative systems in higher education (Costa-Renders, 2010). This process involves consistent interplay between reflection and action, incorporating a consideration of curriculum, based on students' learning requirements and their capacity to identify barriers and to suggest solutions for overcoming impediments to learning. Such processes also need to be reflected in systems of leadership and management so that they are increasingly capable of identifying and overcoming limitations to learning (Madureira & Nunes, 2015).

Reflection

- How does the presence of persons with disabilities impact upon learning, teaching and assessment within your own setting?
- How might the voice and experience of students be better accommodated in order to ensure that all students succeed?
- What are the main challenges for collaboration between administrative and pedagogical teams within HEIs and how might they be overcome?

---

3 Pedagogy of seasons and UDL: the necessary consideration of simultaneous plurality

Potential paradigm shifts, such as that provided by UDL, also provide new space to identify suitable metaphors for re-conceptualizing our educational experiences. Thus, the 'Pedagogy of Seasons' (Costa-Renders, 2016) provides an opening to incorporate human agency and narrative within the developing fabric of curriculum re-formation. The centrality of human corporeality (variance) and values are positioned to the core recognizing the diversity of ways that an educational world is both sensed and experienced. On a day-to-day basis, university inclusion of people with disabilities points to the necessary centrality of human corporeality in educational processes, from the articulation of conditions necessary for accessibility to the development of shared alternative pedagogical paths that encourage multi-temporalities. It is not a functionalist, reductionist or utilitarian concern for those exclusively with special educational needs, but rather a perception of the multiple ways in which human corporeality and cognitive variance affects education, requiring alternative ways of being and learning.

UDL (CAST, 2011) proceeds with a didactic intentionality marked by a necessity to eliminate barriers through making way for access, representation and expression in the teaching-learning processes. This perspective is complemented by the Pedagogy of Seasons, which proposes that change is not linear but rather dynamic and cyclical, it is also highly susceptible to environmental and cultural variables, in the sense that differentiation has to purposefully mindful of all persons at all times whilst paying attention to the unique contexts of setting and person. Change processes require flexibility, as well as consistency in making way for conditions of curricular accessibility for all learners. When removing barriers and promoting conditions for accessibility, there is also a need to reflect upon the ways that UDL can respect time frames for realization of learning.

Reflection

- How can curriculum development be better designed so that it meets the diverse needs of learners over different time frames?
- How can lecturers and professors implement the curriculum changes suggested by students?

The Pedagogy of Seasons (Costa-Renders, 2016) recognizes that while variance may be somewhat predictable, it is also quite specific requiring the reconceptualization of how space and time for learning respect and reflect the need for multi-temporalities that operate in a cyclical curricular movement informed by real time narrative learning (Goodson et al., 2010). Narrativity is a dynamic dialogic engagement between students and teachers that promotes learning from learners' individual life stories and brings to the fore a relational affective dimension that demands an element of flexibility when adopting the UDL principles for implementation (Sanchez, 2005). In the process of building an accessible curriculum, it considers, and seeks to rectify, possible tensions between the need for personalization and universalization as well as the tension between pedagogical time and lived temporalities within the different subject domains.

Because Pedagogy of Seasons respects the multiple and varied attributes of human learning within specific spaces, it is possible to invert curriculum beginnings according to each learner's wishes and requirements thereby creating different knowledge building seasons, where multiple possibilities and abilities are acknowledged (Costa-Renders, 2016). Accordingly, the intensity of challenge should be different in each season, this pedagogical approach encourages a gradual movement of attainable goals identified through dialogue and enhanced through ever-greater autonomy and resilience (CAST, 2011). This model is premised on respect for multi-temporalities as well as calling for flexibility within learning spaces, both must be respected and recreated on a daily basis to continuously foster this pedagogical process. The process contributes to the permanent recognition of differences and to ever more informed emergences of learning for students and teachers alike. What has not been grasped first time around, for one reason or another, can be offered again, in the same way that the cyclical movement of the seasons of the year provides opportunities for nature to renew itself. Thus, learning is enacted in a cyclical movement through the time/space nexus.

The considerations of time and space lead us to the issue of 'simultaneity' and rhythm in the teaching-learning process. Based on Bakhtinian studies, Faraco (2010) affirms that "the rhythm by its regularity and predictability, closes, shapes, molds, predetermines". Therefore, the creating act is an interruption of rhythm. As Faraco shares, "By the rhythm I can only be owned; in it I live as if under anesthesia" (Faraco, 2010, p. 20). In education, we can draw comparisons with the limitations and barriers imposed by the linear nature of school marked by the clock (*chronos*) and by space that is used to control difference in its yearning for homogeneity. In the scenario of an educational institution guided by the classificatory and selective logic, rhythm is part of a gear that doesn't allow deviations, interruptions and variations. It leads us to the automaton, being composed of a mechanism that imposes determined movements, ultimately this is a denial of education being a more ontological vocation (Freire, 2005).

There is a strong argument that the "most resistant domination in relations are the ones based upon temporal hierarchies" (Santos, 2008, p. 27), thus, to cater for diversity, it is necessary to break with the monoculture of linear time in higher education. However, this is not an easy task. Such difficulty will only be overcome with a mutual learning that frees "social practices from the statute which is has to date provided entitlement through a hegemonic temporal canon" (Santos, 2008, p. 110). Would it be possible to expand the present time and contract the future in higher education? In realizing such a goal, Santos suggests that an expansion of time would come about through a "border practice that happens in the boundary between a past which really existed and a past which had no license to exist" (Santos, 2008, p. 91). This affirmation leads us back to the case study, when Pedro and João narrate the confrontations and advancements within the many learning seasons in a university. In that context, it seems that disability, as a deviation, pushed the continuous appearance of other temporalities in the university.

Applying this concept to a visually impaired student would entail learning from that student about her preferences for reading text, establishing where there may be a preference for Braille, or for using apps for text reading. Similarly, in terms of study strategies, some students will skillfully use technology and electronic accessibility tools, while others may require assistance in using them. In the midst of all this, in certain situations, conflicts may arise between the use of different software, between the mode of educational engagement whether distance or face to face. Ambivalence provides a counterflow to the uniformity of time and can be a constant in the process of educational inclusion. If "none of the patterns learned could be appropriate in an ambivalent situation – or more than one standard could be applied . . . the result is a sense of indecision, irresolution, and therefore loss of control" (Bauman, 1999, p. 10).

Reflection

- How might discipline content be differentiated to ensure that learning objectives are achieved with a variable group of students?
- What services and colleagues might be encouraged to work collaboratively in order to develop a support network for meeting students variable learning requirements?
- How can we recalibrate differences between pedagogical time required by students with a university's more traditional perception of 'linear time'?

The Pedagogy of Seasons strives towards mitigating some of the rhythmic constraints derived from the dominant paradigm It is necessary to consider constant and cyclical movement, rather than a linear one. Learning for all, entails working epistemologically for accessibility and provides for imaginative anticipation in its multiple dimensions. With this mind, inclusive pedagogy is built upon foundations of: simultaneous plurality, narrative learning and paradigmatic transition.

Some concepts that form a foundation for the Pedagogy of Seasons

- **Simultaneous plurality** (Assmann, 1998): It problematizes the imposition of 'chronos' or linear time, by engendering different ways of sensing the world and anticipating multiple implications of corporeities, temporalities and space as they influence teaching-learning processes.
- **Narrative learning** (Goodson et al., 2010): This conceptual framework seeks to shift the focus of learning from the prescriptiveness of a strongly defined curriculum to accommodate personal narrative styles and, thereby, encouraging engagement and motivation in the learning process. At its heart is a consideration of learners and their dynamic life histories.
- **Paradigmatic transition** (Sanchez, 2005): This approach is premised on the capacity of learners and educators to force a rupture with pre-existing paradigms existent within traditional schooling and enable development of new ways of learning.

Assmann raises two strands related to the nature of time and how it influences learners and the learning experience: "on the one hand, the presence of time (acts) as an arrow in all fields of nature and history; but, on the other hand, lies the experience of time as opportunity, individual and collective, the latter implies simultaneous plurality" (Assmann, 1998, p. 221). Here he problematizes, the predominance of linear time (*chronos*) which subordinates time of opportunity (*kairos*). The former produces delimiting institutionally established, rhythmic monocultures; whist the latter encourages relationships and care for learning.

The fact is that inclusion, and here we can also read adoption of UDL, necessitates a change of educational paradigm that generates a reorganization of school practices: planning, class formation, curriculum, evaluation and management of the educational process (Mantoan, 2008, p. 37). The presence of people with disabilities in university interrupts linear and chronological time by pointing out the need for other temporalities and spaces that enable human learning and growth. Knowing the world without visual images, passing through the time of learning with the tactile and auditory memories, as well as knowing the world only by visual images rather than auditory ones, provides a dynamic and sharp panoramic vision, such existence illuminates new times and spaces to be explored within pedagogical time. Educational inclusion requires a new relationship between chronological time and lived time (*kairos*), where there is space for becoming respectful towards human differences giving time to subject learning while also recognizing the lived experiences of learners.

Respect for multi-temporalities requires that we respect stillness, pause and slowness in the process of knowledge building. For instance, people with cerebral palsy have much to teach us in this regard. Their corporeality necessitates another reading of time in the processes of communication, especially through oral communication. Time slows in the conscious exercise of word articulation, in the training of the listener to become attuned to differing rhythms and tones of speech, and in the pleasure of communicating what is desired, finally, coming together the communication between speaker and listener creates a respect for diverse forms of oral communication brought about by human corporeity. Considering this form of learning, educators also need to question whether and to what extent the UDL principles (CAST, 2011) also consider simultaneous plurality. For example, how would this plurality sustain itself in the progressive constitution of resourceful/knowledgeable, strategic/goal-directed and purposeful/motivated learners as described in *Guidelines 2.0*?

Which temporalities underlie the UDL principles? After all, the three principles sustain themselves in multiplicity. Namely; Principle I: Provide multiple means of representation (the "what" of learning); Principle II: Provide multiple means of action and expression (the "how" of learning). Principle III: Provide multiple means of engagement (the "why" of learning). (CAST, 2011, p. 5). This epistemological tension is shown when *Guidelines version 2.0* (CAST, 2011) and *Guidelines version 2.1* (CAST, 2014) are put side by side. It is noted that there is an advancement in version 2.1 (CAST, 2018) as this one breaks with the principles linearity by removing directional arrows and sequential numbers. In this version, the multiple dimensions of the teaching and learning process are highlighted and the graphical drawing allows for greater flexibility in this process.

Experiencing management of the inclusive processes in a Brazilian university, I noticed that advancements were intermittently interrupted by pauses and retrogression which caused great frustration and anguish. Many times, especially the administrative inflexibility (marked by the rhythmical monoculture and homogeneity) dissuaded the actions that would have emerged from UDL principles. Would these interruptions be a consequence of the contradictions coming from the dominant paradigm? Or are these interruptions inherent to the implementation process of the UDL principles in times of a paradigmatic transition?

In seeking to enhance educational praxis, Assmann suggest that "institutional time should strive towards an institutional atmosphere that stimulates a greater synchronization between chronological times and lived times" (Assmann, 1998, p. 23). Such a perspective also allows for a flexible adaptation of the UDL principles as they too could stimulate synchronisity between chronological and lived times, also allowing for pauses and revisiting of past learning. Such learning is a particularly welcome feature of the promise within *Guidelines version 2.1* (CAST, 2018). Taken together the principles could act in concert with the Pedagogy of Seasons enabling an opening to the concept of learning continua that respect individuality, corporality, simultaneous plurality and a curriculum informed by the power of student narrative and identity. This is reflected in the continuous cycle of interplay between UDL and the Pedagogy of Seasons as identified in Figure 9.2.

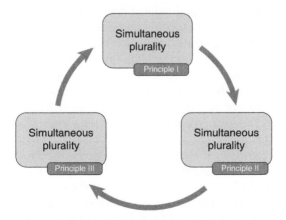

Figure 9.2 Interfaces between UDL and Pedagogy of Seasons

Reflection

- How can students' daily lives be related more closely to discipline content studied at the university?
- Provide some examples of how the presence of persons with diverse learning requirements might affect the 'temporalities of pedagogy' within your own setting. Share how the learning outcomes might be enhanced for all students as a result.

The interplay between the Pedagogy of Seasons and the role of the UDL principles encourages an engagement with Faraco's theorizing as he points out that Bakhtin founded his conceptualization of time malleability while considering the necessity to encounter 'the other' in an altered form of time. Here, he speculates that "Bakhtian time, is open to a constant change, indetermination, and possibility" (Faraco, 2010, p. 20). Such a reconceptualization of how educators engage with time brings praxis closer to the Pedagogy of Seasons. Openings and new possibilities for learning emerge through meeting and striving to incorporate the lived experiences of others within the curriculum. This pedagogy, along with an incorporation of UDL principles, works for the creation of a new conceptualizations regarding space-time within the university fostering the emergence of another possible university, the university for all.

Conclusion

Exploring the application of UDL methodologies within the context of Brazilian higher education has revealed that the concept of accessibility appears both in educational research studies and in national policies. Nevertheless, there is prevalence towards epistemological reductionism and categorization, especially within the regulatory framework such that actions premised on the notions of universal design for learning are negligible. In this context, it is important to question whether there is scope for the UDL principles to underpin a radical conceptual leap that may lead to a re-mapping of the methods and strategies that could lead to new pathways for accessibility in Brazilian universities.

The chapter also looked at how people with disabilities have, through their presence and claims for recognition, altered the ways in which learning has taken place in many HEIs. This could be further strengthened with the adoption of UDL principles so that through the interplay between individual experiences and the overarching framework the potential arises to transform the university into an inclusive space. Being mindful of the multiplicity of perspectives inherent in the UDL Framework, the academic, and action oriented, claim emerges that UDL has real potential to challenge the hegemony of monocultures within Brazilian universities. However, in a mutually dynamic fashion there is a realization that Brazilian research and cultural realities can also prompt new questions for the pedagogical movement proposed by UDL.

In drawing together differing strands of learning to enhance inclusion in HEIs, this chapter introduces the Pedagogy of Seasons, which strives toward consideration of simultaneous plurality to better enable accessible curricula. This core concept problematizes the imposition of linear chronological time marked by an institutionalized rhythm which forecloses pedagogical variance. Instead, the chapter argues that university time and space has the capacity, in a Freireian sense, to be guided by its learners as it strives to create an enabling space for "being more". A key conceptual touchstone for this pedagogical approach is based on learning that springs from learners' lived narratives. In being able to read about the experiences of João and Pedro, our lives as educators are enriched. We learn better how to promote simultaneous plurality, how to encourage paradigmatic transition as, in kairos, our collaborative actions create a new, always more inclusive, university.

Reading suggestions

- CAST (2014). *Universal Design for Learning guidelines version 2.1* [graphic organizer]. Wakefield, MA: Author.
- Freire, P. (2005). *Pedagogy of the oppressed*. London and New York: Continuum.
- Goodson, I. F., Biesta, G., Tedder, M., & Adair, N. (2010). *Narrative Learning*. London and New York: Routledge.
- Reily, L. (2004). *Escola Inclusiva: linguagem e mediação*. Campinas-SP. Papirus.

References

Agência Brasil (2015) *Senado aprova Lei de Inclusão da Pessoa com Deficiência*. Retrieved from http://agenciabrasil.ebc.com.br/politica/noticia/2015-06/senado-aprova-lei-de-inclusao-da-pessoa-com-deficiencia

Assmann, H. (1998). *Reencantar a educação: rumo à sociedade aprendente*. Petrópolis, RJ: Vozes.

Bauman, Z. (1999). *Modernidade e ambivalência*. Rio de Janeiro: Jorge Zahar.

BRASIL (2011). *Decreto n. 7.611, de 17 de novembro de 2011*. Dispõe sobre a educação especial, o atendimento educacional especializado e dá outras providências. Retreived from: www.planalto.gov.br/ccivil_03/_ato2011-2014/2011/decreto/d7611.htm. Accessed: 27 July 2016.

BRASIL, INEP (2016). *Censo da educação Superior 2016*. Brasília. Retrieved from: http://portal.mec.gov.br/index.php?option=com_docman&view=download&alias=71211-apresentacao-censo-educacao-superior-2016-pdf&category_slug=agosto-2017-pdf&Itemid=30192. Accessed on: 17/02/2018.

CAST (2011). *Universal Design for Learning guidelines version 2.0*. Wakefield, MA: Author.

CAST (2014). *Universal Design for Learning guidelines version 2.1* [graphic organizer]. Wakefield, MA: Author.

CAST (2018). *Universal Design for Learning guidelines version 2.2.* Retrieved from http://udlguidelines.cast.org

Cook, S. C., & Rao, K. (2018). Systematically applying UDL to effective practices for students with learning disabilities. *Learning Disability Quarterly, 41*(3), 179–191. doi:10.1177/0731948717749936

Cooper, K. (2006). Beyond the binary: The cyclical nature of identity in education. *Journal of Curriculum Theorizing, 22*(3), 119.

Costa-Renders, E. C. (2010). O movimento das diferenças na educação superior. *Inclusão Revista de Educação Especial.* Brasília: MEC, ano *5*(2), 49–54.

Costa-Renders, E. C. (2016). *A inclusão na universidade: As pessoas com deficiência e novos caminhos pedagógicos.* Curitiba: Prismas.

Faraco, C. A. (2010). O espírito não pode ser o portador do ritmo. The spirit is incapable of being the bearer of rhythm. *Bakhtiniana, São Paulo, 1*(4), 17–24, 2°.sem. 2010.

Freire, P. (2005). *Pedagogy of the oppressed.* London and New York: Continuum.

IBGE (2010). *2010 Population Census.* Retrieved from https://ww2.ibge.gov.br/english/estatistica/populacao/censo2010/

Madureira, I., & Nunes, C. (2015) *Desenho universal para aprendizagem: Construindo práticas pedagógicas inclusivas.* Retrieved from: http://repositorio.ipl.pt/bitstream/10400.21/5211/1/84-172-1-SM.pdf. Accessed on: 09/03/2017.

Mantoan, M. T. E. (2005). *Inclusão Escolar: O que é? Por quê? Como fazer?* São Paulo: Moderna.

Mantoan, M. T. E. (2008). *O desafio das diferenças nas escolas.* Petrópolis, RJ: Vozes.

Meyer, A. & Rose, D. (2002). *Teaching every student in the digital age.* Alexandria, VA: ASCD.

Prais, J. (2017). *Desenho universal para aprendizagem nas produções brasileiras.* Retrieved from: http://educere.bruc.com.br/arquivo/pdf2017/27318_13667.pdf. Accessed on: 09/09/2017.

Rose, D. H., & Meyer, A. (2006). *A practical reader in universal design for learning.* Cambridge, MA: Harvard Education Press.

Sanchez, P. (2005). Educação inclusiva: um meio de construir escolas para todos no século XXI. In: MEC. *Inclusão Revista da Educação Especial.* N. 1, out. 2005. Retrieved from: http://portal.mec.gov.br/seesp/arquivos/pdf/revistainclusao1.pdf. Accessed on: 09/03/2017.

Santos, B. S. (2008). *A gramática do tempo – para uma nova cultura política.* São Paulo: Cortez.

Sondermann, D. C. V., & Albernaz, J. M. (2013). O universal design for learning. *Revista Papers, 1.*

USP (2017). *Braille virtual.* Retrieved from: www.braillevirtual.fe.usp.br/. Accessed on: 09/03/2018.

Chapter 10

Not just about disability

Getting traction for UDL implementation with international students

Frederic Fovet

Case study: addressing the rapid internationalization of higher education

A mid-size Canadian campus is attempting to assert its place within the competitive race currently occurring among Higher Education Institutions (HEIs). With declining demographics within each province, it becomes increasingly important for universities to attract International Students. This influx is in fact quite simply the key to survival. On this campus the stakes were acknowledged early on and the International Development Office has succeeded in securing a constant high volume stream of applicants from Asia in particular. The percentage of International applicants is currently reaching 22%, a rate which is phenomenal in a university that remains mid-size, fairly rural and is not situated in a major urban center. The first battle has been successfully won but over the last two years a new hurdle has presented itself: with one fifth of students arriving from overseas, classrooms are becoming diverse to the point of challenging instructors and making them question their pedagogical approach. In some Graduate level courses, the percentage of International students can be as high as 80%.

A recent survey of teaching staff by the teaching union reported that a majority of instructors feel out of their depth. Not only is oral and written expression within academic parameters a challenge for many of these second language learners, but a cultural gap is tangible when it comes to understanding the mechanisms of group work, the implicit expectations relating to assignments, the reliability of sources and ways to access them, as well simply as the etiquette around communication with teaching staff.

Senior administration remains determined to continue raising the level of International intake until it passes 25% within the next 12 months. They are however increasingly conscious of the tension this is creating in terms of teaching and pedagogy, and have created a committee to examine the process of pedagogical change within a landscape of Globalization. The stakeholders at this round table include faculty members, faculty support services, student services personnel (in particular representatives of the International Office) and student representatives. The aim of this group is to make hands on recommendations to senior administration with regards to transforming pedagogy across campus to address diversity. Senior administration wish, within six months of the production of the recommendations, to issue faculty with guidelines on how best to prepare and coach teaching staff to embrace in a sustainable fashion a phenomenon which is to become the trend rather than the exception.

It is from this case study and this context that many of the examples will be drawn within this chapter. It is also to this situation the reader will be brought back to, in order to examine the potential usefulness of UDL within his or her own campus and institution. It will be argued that this rapid internationalization is a global challenge faced by all 21st century post-secondary campuses and that UDL should increasingly be examined within this lens, as it may well prove successful in offering solutions.

Reflection

For staff:

- What is the percentage of International Students on your campus?
- Do you work with International Students in your current capacity?
- Have you ever considered examining the impact of UDL with International Students as an angle?
- What is your stance when examining UDL?
- Do you have a perspective on UDL that is disability specific?

For students:

- Are you an International Student who is struggling with pedagogy that is not geared towards your specific expectations?
- Do you feel your campus is reflecting on the process of change that is required for pedagogy to meet the needs of International Students?
- Have you encountered teaching staff who referred to UDL when reflecting on the needs of International Students?

Introduction: examination of the landscape in which this reflection emerges

The rapid internationalization of Higher Education has undoubtedly been one of the most striking features of the field over the last decade (Machin & Murphy, 2017). Globalization has been a constant variable across most parts of industry, a trend fed and supported by neo-liberal economic values and goals; few areas of public service, however, have been affected by globalization as rapidly and as dramatically as Higher Education Institutions (HEIs). Seemingly, Higher Education is embracing ideals and values of international collaboration, global access to knowledge and diversity (Hershock, 2010). More pragmatically, in a landscape of ruthless competition, economic survival for most campuses means a proactive commitment to internationalization (Altbach & Knight, 2007). Most North American campuses are aiming to achieve a fifth of enrolment coming from overseas; many are seeking to achieve a percentage even higher than this.

This rapid internationalization has led to pedagogical tension and challenges (Robertson, 2010). First, faculty and instructors have felt, for the last decade, increasing pressure within this neo-liberal landscape: resources are scarce, expectations are rising while employment security for many is progressively disappearing. This creates a first point of friction as a majority of teachers view internationalization as little more than a revenue exercise. This can lead to discontentment and unwillingness to adapt pedagogical methods to address this trend. Second, this rapid internationalization can cause genuine unsettlement and doubt for even the most committed of educators. The striking feature of this internationalization of the HEI classroom is that it has happened suddenly and without much planning or strategic foresight from the classroom perspective. Issues with language fluency are causing pedagogical difficulties never before experienced in Higher Education. This relates to mastery of academic writing and presentation skills, but also the grasp of the numerous implicit messages contained in the evaluation format, the etiquette of group work, or even the intricacies of formal communication with a faculty member.

This is not however the sole challenge: ethnocentrism, for instance, is rife in post-secondary education, an environment that for decades has perpetuated its own implicit values and practices, without having to be confronted about this inherent traditionalism. It can be fairly said that the internationalization of the Higher Education classroom represents the first overt challenge to the sage on a stage model. Lastly, there is a perhaps more fundamental issue emerging which relates to a more experiential dimension in the Higher Education experience of these International Students. The majority of applicants are seeking a degree, but also seeking employability. These students have explicit expectations with regards to the real world applicability of the course content they are being offered, and this can seem daunting to many post-secondary instructors, since Higher Education, as a field, is only just starting to deconstruct its 'ivory tower' stance and reflect on the relevance of its teachings in a context of employment and employability.

For all these reasons, a search for quick solutions is under way on many North American campuses to reduce or even eliminate the tension that has otherwise become tangible as a result of internationalization. Various approaches are being explored – many still focusing on support services rather than in classroom pedagogy. UDL offers a clear potential in this context and this text will detail the various ways the UDL framework can serve as a viable and sustainable lens for post-secondary instructors seeking to create inclusive conditions for International Students.

One faculty on the East Coast Canadian campus discussed here has been successful in securing a high level of International enrolment. This has been the Faculty of Education in which I am employed. It is the context within which the present personal reflection situates itself. One MEd program has been specifically created to attract International applicants. Its enrolment has increased steadily over the last three years and it now represents one of the main streams in graduate education. Despite the financial relevance of this program and its steady growth, tension has been palpable and practical pedagogical issues have emerged fairly regularly: students are often ill-prepared for the challenges and implicit expectations of Canadian graduate education; the learning curve is two-fold for these students. It consists of acquiring graduate skills rapidly, just like every other student, but also involves gaining idiomatic fluency, as well as a working understanding of socio-cultural expectations. The task is arduous. Add to this the fact that resources have grown scarce and workloads for instructors have increased rapidly, and the stage is set for potential conflict, misunderstanding, tension and dissatisfaction on all sides.

This is the picture which was beginning to form within this department, and this is the context within which Universal Design for Learning (UDL) was floated as a potential solution, and progressively discussed more and more explicitly among faculty and support staff. It has proven to be a game changer and has helped quickly shift mindsets and erode the growing tension that had been previously felt.

Research has begun to emerge around the phenomenon I have just described in terms of tension caused by a rapid Internationalization, a phenomenon which has been felt across Canada. Thus far, however, scholars have focused on the social implications of the rapid internationalization of campuses (Zhang, 2016). Campuses have reflected on cultural competency within student services (Zhou & Zhang, 2014), and on administrative ethnocentrism (Manning & Muñoz, 2011), or even on issues of employability for these International Students post graduation (Arthur & Flynn, 2013). Few studies, however, have so far explored the issue of multicultural tension in pedagogy, enquired into the disconnect that many International students feel in the Higher Education classrooms of the host country, or examined the issue of retention and academic success within this rapid expansion of internationalization in both undergraduate and graduate classes. Yet there is little doubt that these students are often having difficulties adapting to their new academic setting, and navigating with success the expectations of instructors in environments that are entirely novel to them. This is where the UDL model becomes directly pertinent and offers concrete solutions.

How widespread is UDL in the field of multicultural education?

There is a striking paucity of research around the use of UDL within the context of multicultural education in Higher Education. Historically the UDL literature has focused primarily on students with Disabilities. This is understandable when one considers that legislation, in both Canada and the US, has placed early pressure for the inclusion of students with Disabilities (Pooran & Wilkie, 2005). The use and relevance of UDL with regards to diverse learners generally has been in many cases an afterthought as, to this day, inclusive provisions for these students are considered best practices but do not represent a legal burden. Things are changing though, and the Center for Applied Special Technology (CAST) has certainly recently been explicitly louder about the fact that it asserts UDL has relevance for students of all profiles, not just learners with Disabilities. So just how widespread is the literature on UDL and multicultural education at this stage of the shift in mindset?

UDL and multiculturalism

As mentioned in the previous paragraph, CAST has explicitly altered its discourse and branding to highlight the fact that UDL is relevant for all learners and not just learners with disabilities (Roschelle, Courey, Patton, & Murray, 2013). Still prominently mentioned are gifted learners, and much of the current K-12 literature highlights this notion of two groups on the 'edges': with learners with exceptionalities at one end and gifted learners at the other. UDL is seen as framework which allows educators to bridge this otherwise unmanageable dichotomy in the makeup of the inclusive classroom (Moore, 2016).

Cultural diversity still very much lies one the edges of the UDL discourse currently. Some overlap does appear in the literature between UDL and Culturally Sustaining Pedagogies (Alim et al., 2017; Waitoller & King Thorius, 2016). Culturally Sustaining Pedagogies indeed are teaching approaches that seek to sustain linguistic and cultural plurality in social fabric with a view to supporting social justice. It is clear that conceptually UDL may well serve these goals and connect seamlessly with this pedagogical stance. Pragmatically though, at this stage, cultural diversity remains fairly inconspicuous in the UDL literature when it comes to guidelines to practitioners or hands on tools for reflection. This angle is also often altogether absent from the contemporary K-12 (early childhood to end of secondary school) literature on inclusion. There is a dusting of exploratory literature on UDL and multiculturalism (Chita-Tegmark, Gravel, Serpa, Domings, & Rose, 2012), much of it still focused on the K-12 classroom and ways of addressing issues raised by immigration rather than internationalization per se (Sadowski, 2014). The deficit model therefore remains deeply rooted.

When it comes to Higher Education, the literature on UDL and Multiculturalism is even slimmer. Higbee has now long broached the subject and she does advocate for an institutional shift in mindset (2008), but she remains a lone voice, and pieces on cultural diversity and UDL in the post-secondary sector remain mostly conceptual (Hackman, 2008). At other times, cultural diversity – as it pertains to UDL – is still interpreted as ethnic and racial diversity within the home country rather than focus on the challenges experienced by International Students (Madyun, 2008).

Exploration of the need for reflexive capacities around pedagogy within a context of intense globalization

There is abundant parallel literature, on the other hand, tackling the issue of multiculturalism in Higher Education pedagogy but, generally speaking, it adopts a Critical Pedagogy stance and focuses specifically on issues of power, race and systemic discrimination (Clark, Kleiman, Spanierman, Isaac, & Poolokasingham, 2014). This is an interesting and rich angle but one that lies rather far from the concerns of UDL. At best the Critical Pedagogy discourse leads to concerns around cultural competency (Chun & Evans, 2016; Leask & Carroll, 2013), a dimension that is less immediately concrete than UDL's focus on diversity and flexibility in classroom practices. Indeed, while the UDL and Critical Pedagogy discourses are aligned on some points – particularly when it comes to the desire to develop 'expert learners' who are critical, autonomous and intrinsically motivated, Critical Pedagogy remains founded on a political reflection that goes further than UDL. UDL seeks classroom transformation whereas Critical Pedagogy aims for transformative action that disrupts institutions and seeks to rectify wider social power imbalances. Importantly, for our purpose in this chapter, the literature on Critical Pedagogy in Higher Education has yet to refer to or use the UDL terminology. Critical Pedagogy, in general terms, remains conceptual to a degree whereas UDL really aims to offer instructors immediate hands-on solutions for instruction and assessment.

Ethnocentricism – what is it?

It is important to explore this notion within the literature review as it will remain important through the chapter and weave itself throughout this reflection on UDL. Ethnocentricism is the phenomenon whereby individuals tend to create interactions, provide services, or build expectations using a lens that is anchored in their own cultural values and implicit norms (Hammond & Axelrod, 2006). In doing so they create a dialogue that is one-sided and imposes the value system and cultural stance of one stakeholder while ignoring those of the other parties (Yamagishi & Suzuki, 2009). In the classroom this manifests itself through pedagogy that lacks reflection about the learner's needs, expectations and own cultural preferences. It tends to lead to instruction and assessment practices that carry implicit messaging for the learner who is an insider, and create challenges for learners who our 'othered' by the design of the learning experience (Brown & Holloway, 2008).

Intersectionality

One final concept needs to be addressed and defined in this literature review and that is the notion of Intersectionality. The terms 'intersectionality' has two common uses in literature. Both are associated with Critical Theory but are still very distinct in flavor and relevance. Both meanings of the word will become relevant to this analysis and be used in this chapter.

The first interpretation of the word relates to the notion of an oppression that is cumulative rather than unidimensional (Shin et al., 2017). A learner for example could be marginalized for having a disability but also for being Indigenous. This use of the term will be relevant to the exploration within this chapter. Often indeed International Students are seen and supported on North American campuses in strikingly unidimensional ways. These learners are perceived as 'International' first and foremost and become associated with a number of difficulties staff and faculty expect to see materialize. Very rarely, however, do we think of these International Students as experiencing marginalization on other grounds: because of a disability, because of their gender or sexual orientation, etc. It will be essential for instructors to reflect on Intersectionality to genuinely understand the complex and multilayered campus experiences International Students have on a daily basis.

The second distinct interpretation of Intersectionality describes the way minority groups which have very little shared lived experience can nevertheless come together in their political aspirations, because of the perception of marginalization they consciously share (Carastathis, 2013). The voices of these groups can thus come together and make collective demands (May, 2015). This is an interesting concept too for the purpose of this chapter, and it will be used in the closing section when future developments are considered; it will be suggested that by coming together and understanding the challenges they share in the classroom, International Students and Students with Disabilities can formulate a common discourse, one that advocates powerfully for the implementation of UDL on our campuses.

Reflection on the relevance of the UDL principles in this landscape

The methodology used for this part of the chapter is auto-ethnography since I draw here on my own experience and reflection regarding the usefulness of the three UDL principles when attempting to create inclusive classroom conditions for International Students taking graduate courses (Trahar, 2009; Ellis, Adams, & Bochner, 2010). This exploration has taken place over a two-year period during which I have been involved in teaching MEd courses in classes mainly composed of International students. My professional experience and trajectory are unusual and this perhaps explains the innovative stance I bring to UDL and multicultural education. I have previously been a K-12 teacher working in the field of inclusion with students affected by social, emotional and behavior difficulties (SEBD). Within this professional context I was relying heavily in UDL in my practice. I also, for the duration of my PhD, took on the position of unit manager within a disability service provision office on a large Canadian campus. During these four years, I was equally heavily involved in Disability Studies, and UDL again was a framework that provided support and clarity for much of my work. When first taking on a faculty position, applying UDL to the Higher Education classroom was therefore very much a reflex. Observing its usefulness and impact with International Students was a logical next step.

The data presented here briefly is phenomenological in nature and does not purport to quantify the satisfaction of International Student with the UDL strategies implemented. In this respect further research is required to evidence this angle. Phenomenology seeks to examine the lived experiences of subjects confronted with specific phenomena in order to analyze the constructs these individuals create in a process of meaning making (Groenewald, 2004). My phenomenological reflection as an instructor, however, remains very pertinent as an indicator of the degree to which UDL implementation is able to reduce the tension felt by faculty within a climate of intense internationalization of classrooms.

The three UDL principles will be used as upcoming section headings in order to roughly classify the observations I made within my own practice over these two years working and collaborating with International Students, as well as the professional reflection I carried out through this time. Of course, the UDL principles overlap in many ways and certain strategies and tools can be categorized under several of the UDL headings. It is used for convenience of presentation rather than as a strict and rigid classifying method.

Multiple means of representation

There have been several practices that have reduced the friction that can be experienced when International Students are faced with implicit expectations that they do not always immediate grasp. The following UDL reflection allows instructors to deconstruct traditional assumptions that can be perpetuated within the Higher Education classroom.

Technology in the classroom

A simple application of the UDL principle focusing on representation is to encourage students to use technology in the classroom in order to offer them access the support strategies that suit them and meet their needs. There is a tangible dichotomy in current post-secondary practices around technological use in the classroom, particularly laptop and mobile phone use. These are integrated successfully in many classrooms (Poling, Smit, & Higgs, 2013) while still banned as a matter of policy by many instructors (Grove, 2017). Technological use is important for many students and the stakes are high in terms of active learning outcomes. International Students, however, more than most require easy in class access to technology as part of their adaptation process. International Students will often – during class time – search the internet for concepts they have not encountered before, seeking deep learning by engaging with resources that are connected to the notions being introduced to them, and simultaneously often improving their fluency by using digital dictionaries and other linguistic support sites. This allows for multiple means of representation throughout instruction and is key to the inclusion of these students.

Systematic in-depth use of digital learning environments

Digital Learning Environments (DLEs) can include a variety of electronic learning platforms which are purchased by campuses and integrated into course delivery, whether it is face to face or through online means (Baker, 2017); these are referred to as Learning Management Systems (LMSs) in North America and as Virtual Learning Environments (VLEs) in the UK and certain other European countries. Again, effective and systematic use of a Learning Management System (LMS) platform is useful for all students, but will prove crucial when it comes to integrating International Students quickly and successfully into the classroom. A UDL use of these platforms, targeting the inclusion of International Students, will include for instance systematically and thoroughly displaying all course material, PowerPoints, directives, and assessment instructions, etc. It will also include providing these resources in multiple media: text, video, podcasts, etc. This will allow students autonomy as they access the material, view it and master it in advance, and compensate with autonomous work for any challenge, be they linguistic or cultural, they might otherwise face in the classroom when viewing this material for the first time.

Rethinking assignment directives

Assignments probably represent the area where the risk of ethnocentrism on the part of the instructor is the most tangible. Even when the teacher is aware of the danger and reflects extensively on how to reformulate and rethink assignments to avoid this pitfall, it seems to be human nature to assess the way we have been assessed and to therefore perpetuate modes of assessments that carry implicit messages. These are inherently understood far better by the cultural insider than by the International Student. The issue of implicit messaging in assignment directives is an arduous task to successfully unpack and it takes time to resolve. For example, I used to ask graduate students routinely to journal their reflection throughout a course as a form of assessment. In the course of my second semester teaching in an International stream the ethnocentric nature of this exercise became all too apparent to me: students having completed their undergraduate degree outside Canada had often never been exposed to this type of exercise and did not readily possess the skills I assumed them to have in this regard. This is where UDL comes into play and offers instructors a structured way of analyzing barriers and identifying solutions. Rubrics often have to be redrafted with International Students in mind, making all expectations explicit. In order to genuinely offer multiple means of representation in assignment directives, instructors working with International Students may have to go beyond a simple redrafting of instructions. Modeling is often the tool that best allows for this diverse representation with regards to the expectations. Modeling can take two forms: instructors can, if time allows, produce samples they have themselves drafted – which can be posted on the LMS platform for easy consultation. Alternatively, the author has in the past adopted the practice of asking past students their permission to use work demonstrating varying degrees competence to be used as samples in subsequent semester. This is the strategy which best complements the palette available to an educator reflecting on UDL and 'multiple means of representation' when it comes to the challenges International Students may experience in trying to grasp implicit expectations.

Reflection

For faculty:

- Are you using the Digital Learning Environment (DLE) available in your institution to its full potential when it comes to International students and their access to content?
- What are some of the assumptions you may be perpetuating with regards to the way International students grasp your evaluation format?

For staff:

- When supporting International students, are you considering sensitizing instructors to the implicit expectations they may have?
- How might you encourage faculty member to 'unpack' expectations that may be implicit and not immediately apparent to International students?

For students:

- When you are experiencing formats, directives or expectations that are not congenial to you, how might you be able to make the instructor aware of this?
- If a DLE is used optimally by an instructor, in which ways might you be able to draw from this platform to gain better access to learning?

Multiple means of action and expression

Curriculum co-creation

The most effective way of bridging cultural gaps in the classroom is to encourage students to voice their expectations and needs. Using curriculum co-creation (Taylor & Bovill, 2017) is a powerful tool to allow students to have input on the course, based on their identity and background. It fits naturally with the UDL notion of multiple means of action and expression as it places the student in a unique position to rethink their role in the classroom. It also allows International Students to develop awareness around their own challenges and to play a key role in identifying solutions. The use of curriculum creation can seem daunting but can be implemented fairly simply (Bovill, Cook-Sather, Felten, Millard, & Moore-Cherry, 2015; Bergmark, 2016). This can amount to dedicating a class at the start of a course to discussing in depth the objectives and the format of evaluation. This inevitably creates a more democratic climate and offers learners the freedom to take on new meaningful roles and responsibilities within the class. For those having less time available within their course structure, or for the instructors dipping a toe and trying curriculum co-creation for the first time, a first step might alternatively be to pick a specific class during the course, and to plan the unfolding of that specific unit through active and reciprocal dialogue.

Fragmentation of assessment

Assessment represents, as we have already seen, an area that is fraught with challenges for International Students. Even when implicit expectations are unpacked and eliminated, there may still remain something very daunting in submitting work, in a format and in an academic setting that are entirely novel, when these assignments may be worth such a large amount of points. If the instructor only sets a limited amount of assignments but they are each worth a large amount of points, there is then a danger that misunderstanding, or underestimating, expectations might result in a fail on the whole course. Fragmenting and diversifying methods of assessment becomes the UDL strategy that best eliminates this barrier. International Students will find it less daunting to tackle several assignments that may be in their sum total just as complex, but which are formulated as separate tasks worth less points. In essence this allows these students to renegotiate their relationship to assessment; by offering multiple tasks rather than a single unidimensional window into the depth of the student's learning, this process normalizes failure and presents it as an acceptable part of the formative assessment process, while allowing International Students the space to rectify their aim and makeup for initial mistakes before the course ends.

Use of formative assessment

In the same vein, the UDL principle focusing on action and expression can be used in a further way to eliminate barriers for International Students as they struggle to grasp the stakes and goals of assessment. Using formative assessment systematically is key in creating inclusive classroom conditions for these students. Allowing pre-submission of all assignments in particular is a very UDL way to transform the relationship the learner has with the task. This allows the learner flexibility, in terms of action and expression, as they transform their role and mode of interaction with the instructor. Submitting assignments is now no longer a one-dimensional process that leaves them fairly helpless once a mark is attributed. Instead it opens the way for learners to gain autonomy and self-reliance. They gain control over the task as they are provided with interim feedback and can then decide to deepen their understanding or explore the question from other angles. The author has found that this is particularly pertinent for International Students. Pre-submission, submitting a first draft of an assignment to an instructor for review before the final marking, is not always appealing to home students; it implies – and this is of course a quick generalization – further work and, in the traditional culture of North American Higher Education, is sometimes seen as somewhat of a gamble: 'Is it worth investing more time when I am not guaranteed a better grade?' In this sense, formative assessment has not yet taken root in our Higher Education institutions. The author's work with International graduate students over the last two years has, on the other hand, shown them to be willing to submit drafts several consecutive times if needed. Response to formative feedback is welcomed and used effectively.

Alternate formats of submission for assignments

Alternate formats of submissions are discussed at length in Higher Education but it would be realistic to state that they have not yet, in practical terms, taken hold as daily classroom practices. While diversity in the nature of assignments (i.e. submissions other than term papers) is slowly increasing, few Higher Education instructors at this stage feel comfortable offering students the freedom to submit the same assignment in various formats. Traditions are painfully difficult to erode in the post-secondary sector and the conventional diet of assessment is fairly narrow and strikingly repetitive. Exploratory phenomenological work carried out by the author in this area also warns against superficial interpretations of what 'alternate formats' might mean (Fovet, 2016). When interviewed on this issue many graduate students voiced concern – if not frustration – that instructors, when they are receptive to the idea of breaking out of the traditional 'term paper' format, fall victim to another pitfall: simply replacing term papers by presentations and group work. Students observe that this is often done without genuine reflection on accessibility or inclusion, and at times result in the creation of other barriers. Faculty will often push back arguing that it is arduous to write rubrics that are suitable for various alternate formats of submission, or even that they may feel ill-equipped when assessing work submitted in formats with regards to which they possess little expertise. For example, faculty may be uncomfortable or unwilling to explore the use of animation, art projects, and video productions. There is undoubtedly a fair amount of professional development to be carried out with faculty before this sort of UDL reflection will take root in Higher Education. In the meantime, support work with International Students certainly demonstrates that allowing the submission of work in varied formats goes a long way to removing barriers. Allowing students to submit assignments in podcast and video format in particular allows some International student to overcome challenges in academic writing, offers greater freedom for them to demonstrate their skills in ways that are congenial to them, and does a great deal to boost self-confidence and feed intrinsic motivation.

Reflection

For faculty:

- Where would you begin as you 'unpack' issues related the ethnocentric nature of your assessment as they are currently designed?
- What are the specific fears preventing you from redesigning these tasks with more flexibility?
- How might UDL, and the 'Multiple means of action and expression' principle specifically, support you in this ongoing professional reflection?

For students:

- If you face assessment methods which inherently create challenge because of your linguistic or cultural perspective, how might you make your instructor aware of this issue?
- How specifically would you like to see assessment practices evolve in order to reflect the cultural diversity of your classroom?
- How would you articulate this wish to a faculty member in order to convince them of its urgency?

Multiple means of engagement

UDL also encourages educators to reflect on barriers to learning and to offer flexibility in the area of engagement – what CAST scholars classify as the 'affective dimension of learning' (Daley, 2014). The way this UDL principle is addressed in Higher Education is ambiguous; in many ways, engagement is a dimension that is actively discussed in 21st century teaching and learning. Quite distinct from UDL, theoretical trends such as experiential learning, active learning and project-based learning have been models that have led the field to reflect on what transformative 21st century might be – or need to become; these models have explicitly tackled the notion of engagement and forced a rethink. This dialogue has begun and few educators can ignore the issue. The UDL principles, however, require and invite a certain rigor and conceptual thoroughness in addressing engagement from a design perspective in daily classroom practices. It would be difficult to claim that, as a field, Higher Education has genuinely undertaken the pedagogical transformation required. These are perhaps notions that are commonly encountered in research papers and one might therefore understandably presume that such practices would be common place now in classrooms. It is not the case. Yet these transformative steps can be quite effective even when they are initially small. They are again of striking pertinence when it comes to International Students. Next appear a few suggestions that have been explored by the author and that provide simple, hands on application of the UDL principle focused on engagement.

Hybrid learning experiences

UDL encourages educators to offer learners multiple means of engagement within the classroom. Offering these multiple means of engagement can be at times more complex than appears and it undoubtedly represents a significant degree of reflection on the part of instructors. When it comes to International Students, however, I suggest based on my experiences in this context that creating a hybrid mode of interaction with learners over the length of a course provides a relatively easy way to offer this flexibility. A hybrid mode of interaction is an interface with the learner that does not limit itself to one media. It will combine diverse means of interaction with the learner. This could merely involve providing rich and multilayered dimensions for interaction; it could simply amount to a seamless merging of existing modes of communication: face to face teaching, office hours, accessibility via phones, email communication, creation of LMS forums, active use of a course hashtag on Twitter, etc.

Indeed, International Students are often inherently caught up in hierarchical dynamics – often transposed from their own previous experiences in Higher Education in their home countries – which can over-entangle them in fears and general reticence when interacting with instructors that are so powerful they end up jeopardizing learning outcomes. Add to this the wider issues of cultural shock and homesickness and the need to break through the isolation felt by these students becomes pressing. UDL offers readily applicable tips when it encourages the creation of multiple means of engagement. Reflecting on this and providing International Students with multiple interfaces with instructor and peers – is a very effective way to encourage the International Student to rethink their assumptions around communication, to break through fears and cultural inhibitions, and to eventually transform their perception of self. Students have at times commented to the author on how they felt 'transformed' and 'liberated' at the end of a course when UDL was implemented, reflectively, in this way.

Experiential connections to real world concerns

We have discussed earlier in this chapter how International Students often query the immediate real world relevance of course content, perhaps more so than home students. It is undeniable that for many International Students the selection of a course overseas represents an essentially mercantile transaction, one they hope to see linked to immediate outcomes, particularly in terms of employability. As a result, International Students are perhaps more open about their expectations with regards to the experiential connections they expect to see between the course content and real world priorities. This is an element which is particularly challenging for Higher Education as whole, since as a sector it tends to still pride itself on its intellectual detachment and its ambitions which it sees as distinct from the pressures of employment. As a result, globalization is disturbing many faculty members and this creates yet another justification to push back when faced with increasing waves of internationalization. Yet, UDL offers simple ways to tackle these expectations of International Students with regards to experiential opportunities, in a proactive and supportive way. One method the author has used in his own practice is to grab the bull by the horns – so to speak – and to systematically start all classes with a discussion around media sources: real world press segments, news clips, or web videos which explicitly tackle the themes of the class. This offers students – and particularly International Students – multiple means of engagement. Rather than approach a topic conceptually and through textbook reading, they have the opportunity to develop a pragmatic relationship to the topic first if they wish – something that often quickly and successfully satisfies their thirst for an experiential dimension.

Proactive development of cultural parameters and milestones

UDL scholars advocate for the development of the 'expert learner'; being offered multiple means of engagement is key for International Students when it comes to developing a critical awareness within their new academic setting and to acquiring quickly the cultural parameters and points of reference that will enable this growth and development. Higher Education courses can be narrow in scope and presume prior knowledge, and more importantly cultural competence. Using UDL with International Students will often mean creatively seeking ways to allow these students to develop their general awareness of the host culture while also fulfilling the course requirements. One such creative way developed by the author on his MEd courses has been to run a 'film club', a fun additional weekly session where International Students get together to watch classic films dealing with education and schools in the widest sense. This has proven fascinating for the students who have been enthusiastic about this parallel activity over a 12-week semester. The outcomes have been tangible and students have been able to draw from these films to deepen their understanding of the North American education system. Showing such films as *Dead Poets Society*, *Mr. Holland's Opus* and *Most Likely to Succeed* has in turn metamorphosed the quality and depth of the students' writing on the course themes. There may be other diverse ways to reach such objectives and UDL will support instructors' reflection around the strategies that may provide multiple means of engagement for International Students in such a manner. While many might argue that such activities are not related to the instruction, they in fact need to be seen as intimately connected to the course objectives in the sense that they allow innovative and stimulating ways for International Students to become 'expert learners' in a context that is otherwise foreign to them.

Use and exploration of e-portfolios

E-portfolios are often mentioned within UDL literature, particularly when it comes to offering 'multiple means of engagement' to students (Basham, Meyer, & Perry, 2010). E-portfolios are important for all learners within a UDL lens as they allow students the freedom to become autonomous in their exploration and encourage them to reflect on their learning preferences. They have particular impact for International Students. Indeed, they compel International Students to take a critical look at their background, journey, and expectations within the host country. They also offer freedom and creative initiative that many International Students may have never experienced before. This leads to reflective growth, a rapid personal grounding within their new context, and the development of a vital awareness of the motivations that have led them to study overseas. Students gain a tangible feel for both their outsider perspective and the means to acquire insider insights.

Embedded co-facilitation of course activities with the International Student Academic Coach

This final example can be discussed briefly but it is relevant nonetheless: the author has developed a close working relationship with the 'International Student Coach' allocated to the MEd in question. This close relationship includes working on course outlines together, co-teaching parts of the course and embedding support activities and workshop designed for International Students directly into the very canvas of the course. This is a rich and eyeopening initiative, which could merit a study in itself. It merits a brief needs mention here, nevertheless, as it possesses a UDL dimension. It allows the International Students multiple means of engagement because it blurs the lines between academic course and support services. It also enables them to respond with more fluidity to the demands made on them and to act more freely using all their networks, instead of getting caught in silos that are institution-centric and not necessarily otherwise readily understandable to them as students.

Reflection

- Has this reflection on the challenges faced by International Students in the Higher Education classroom been relevant to your professional context? How?
- Select two specific challenges you have observed International Students face in the post-secondary classroom within your institution. What UDL principles might you use when attempting to eliminate of these barriers to learning?
- What is the re-design solution that is emerging from your use of this UDL principle in the example you have selected?
- How might you explain the powerful impact of this UDL reflection on pedagogical change to faculty who may have little experience with International Students?

Strategic relevance of UDL use with international students

The relevance for the field of this short insight into the use of UDL with International Students is significant. Of course, first, on the one hand developing awareness of UDL among faculty and staff that support International Students in Higher Education will in all likelihood improve learner outcomes, nurture and perpetuate more genuinely inclusive class conditions for these students, and operate over time a mind shift on campuses.

The relevance of this exploration goes further than that, however, and has a more specific pertinence when it comes to the strategic development of UDL across campuses. Although the interest in UDL in Higher Education has risen sharply over the last decade, implementation remains haphazard and sporadically successful only (Gradel & Edson, 2009). One of the obstacles in the development of UDL within this landscape is undeniably the fact that UDL remains perceived by many as a framework which seeks to address primarily the needs of students with Disabilities. As such, UDL implementation efforts are still being waved off and dismissed on many North American campuses because it is felt their impact is limited to a minority of student – the 10% at most who register with disability service providers.

Acknowledging and demonstrating the relevance of UDL to International students, as well as culturally diverse students, demonstrates that the framework in fact has the potential to transform teaching and learning for a much wider percentage of learners. On the specific campus we examined in the case study, the percentage of International Students was 20%. Together with the 10% of students registered with the Accessibility Office this makes up a remarkable 30% of the campus population. All are directly affected by UDL. This has the potential to shift UDL from a minority discourse to a majority agenda on campuses.

It hence becomes increasingly important for a common discourse to emerge, one shared by Accessibility Offices and International Students support units.

By sharing a common vocabulary and presenting a united front in discussions with faculty on the transformation of teaching and learning practices, these units get increasingly closer to giving UDL the place it deserves as the framework that enables both groups of stakeholders to trigger change and implement genuine inclusion. Developing awareness of UDL with regards to International Students also has the remarkable effect of integrating the UDL discourse into the neo-liberal rhetoric that prevails on most campuses and to brand it as a solution adapted to the current economic trends and priorities in admission and retention, something that has not been achieved thus far when UDL has remained associated solely with the disability discourse. In short, campuses have a vested financial interest in seeing International Student succeed. If UDL can be shown to have a part to play in this success it is likely to be incorporated into strategic planning and administrative ethos, campus wide.

Reflection

- Is UDL being discussed by staff and faculty who are not specifically working with or focused on students with disabilities?
- If one was to total on your campus the percentage of International enrolment and of students with disabilities, what figure would this represent?

- What would be the first immediate steps required, on your campus, for International offices and Accessibility services to start working together in their advocacy for inclusive teaching practices?

Conclusion: and now? Looking to the future

What were the objectives of this chapter? On the one hand, the first immediate need is to develop an emerging trend in literature examining the use of UDL with International Students. In doing so, this chapter hopes to trigger curiosity and interest from scholars, student support services and researchers, as well as HEI policy developers, and to crystallize a specific theme that hopefully will now be more explicitly explored.

The second goal of this chapter was to create a bridging reflection among practitioners in Higher Education involved in disability and International outreach. Hopefully this chapter has highlighted the need for the creation of new, innovative forms of collaboration. By bringing their voice together, these advocates and stakeholders will realize that their position on inclusion no longer represents a minority discourse but instead constitutes a current that touches the lives and learning experiences of a significant percentage of the students that live on our campuses.

Finally, this chapter aims to encourage practitioners on our campuses, in both the disability and International outreach fields, to reflect on the need to adopt a common language. This implies a willingness to break away from the existing silo mentality that too often prevails in Higher Education, and to think beyond traditional theoretical frameworks towards more interdisciplinary processes. It is hoped indeed that it is in this interdisciplinary space that UDL will reveal its true potential for the transformation of Higher Education pedagogy.

Reflection

- In what ways might the use of UDL with International Students be relevant to your practice even if you are not specifically working with these stakeholders?
- How might support staff working with students with Disabilities reach out to units supporting International students and adopt a common discourse on the relevance of UDL?
- In what ways might the current language on UDL used in Higher Education need to be transformed so as to include stakeholders other than those advocating for students with Disabilities, particularly those working with International Students?

References

Alim, S., Baglieri, S., Ladson-Billings, G., Paris, D., Rose, D., & Valente, J. (2017). Responding to "cross-pollinating culturally sustaining pedagogy and universal design for learning: Toward an inclusive pedagogy that accounts for dis/ability". *Harvard Educational Review, 87*(1), 4–25.

Altbach, P., & Knight, J. (2007). Internationalization of higher education: Motivations and realities. *Journal of Studies in International Education, 11*(3/4), 290–305.

Arthur, N., & Flynn, S. (2013). International students' views of transition to employment and immigration. *The Canadian Journal of Career Development/ Revue canadienne de développement de carrière, 12*(1), 28–37.

Baker, J. (2017, July 3). Updating the next generation digital learning environment for better student learning outcomes. *EDUCAUSE Review*. Retrieved from: https://er.educause.edu/articles/2017/7/updating-the-next-generation-digital-learning-environment-for-better-student-learning-outcomes

Basham, J., Meyer, H., & Perry, E. (2010). The design and application of the digital backpack. *Journal of Research on Technology in Education, 42*(4), 339–359.

Bergmark, U. (2016). Co-creating curriculum in higher education: Promoting democratic values and a multidimensional view on learning. *International Journal for Academic Development, 21*(1), 28–40.

Bovill, C., Cook-Sather, A., Felten, P., Millard, L., & Moore-Cherry, N. (2015). Addressing potential challenges in co-creating learning and teaching: Overcoming resistance, navigating institutional norms and ensuring inclusivity in student-staff partnerships. *Higher Education*. http://dx.doi.org/10.1007/s10734-015-9896-4

Brown, L., & Holloway, I. (2008). The initial stage of the international sojourn: Excitement or culture shock? *British Journal of Guidance & Counseling, 36*(1), 33–49.

Carastathis, A. (2013). Identity categories as potential coalitions. *Signs: Journal of Women in Culture and Society, 38*(4), 941–961.

Chita-Tegmark, M., Gravel, J. W., Serpa, M., Del. B., Domings, Y., & Rose, D. H. (2012). Using the universal design for learning framework to support culturally diverse learners. *Journal of Education, 192*(1), 17–22.

Chun, E., & Evans, A. (2016). Rethinking cultural competence in higher education: An ecological framework for student development. *ASHE Higher Education Report, 42*(6).

Clark, D. A., Kleiman, S., Spanierman, L. B., Isaac, P., & Poolokasingham, G. (2014). "Do you live in a teepee?" Aboriginal students' experiences with racial microaggressions in Canada. *Journal of Diversity in Higher Education, 7*(2), 112–125. http://dx.doi.org/10.1037/a0036573

Daley, S. (2014). Universal design for learning: Variability in emotion and learning. *YouTube*. Retrieved from: www.youtube.com/watch?v=LDaP-THd-9c&feature=youtu.be

Ellis, C., Adams, T., & Bochner, A. (2010). Autoethnography: An overview. *Forum Qualitative Sozialforschung/Forum: Qualitative Social Research*, [S.l.], *12*(1). Retrieved from: www.qualitative-research.net/index.php/fqs/article/view/1589/3095

Fovet, F. (2016, March). *Doing what we preach: Examining the contradictions of the UDL discourse in faculties of education.* Paper presented at the 2017 AHEAD Ireland Conference, Dublin.

Hackman, W. (2008). Broadening the pathway to academic success: The critical intersections of social justice education, critical multicultural education and universal instructional design. In J. L. Higbee & E. Goff (Eds.), *Pedagogy and student services for institutional transformation: Implementing universal design in higher education* (pp. 25–49). Center for Research on Developmental Education and Urban Literacy, University of Minnesota, Minneapolis, MN. Retrieved from: http://media.education.umn.edu/passit/docs/PASS-IT-Book.pdf

Gradel, K., & Edson, A. J. (2009). Putting universal design for learning on the higher ed Agenda. *Journal of Educational Technology Systems, 38*(2), 111–121.

Groenewald, T. (2004). A phenomenological research design illustrated. *International Journal of Qualitative Methods, 3*(1). Article 4. Retrieved from: www.ualberta.ca/~iiqm/backissues/3_1/pdf/groenewald.pdf

Grove, J. (2017, April). Using laptops in class harms academic performance, study warns. *Times Higher Education* (4th ed.). Retrieved from: www.timeshighereducation.com/news/using-laptops-in-class-harms-academic-performance-study-warns

Hammond, R. A., & Axelrod, R. (2006). The evolution of ethnocentrism. *Journal of Conflict Resolution, 50,* 926–936.

Hershock, P. (2010). Higher education, globalization and the critical emergence of diversity. *Philosophical Inquiry in Education, 19*(1), 29–42. Retrieved from: https://journals.sfu.ca/pie/index.php/pie/article/view/244

Higbee, J. (2008). Institutional transformation: Some concluding thoughts. In J. L. Higbee & E. Goff. (Eds.), *Pedagogy and student services for institutional transformation: Implementing universal design in higher education* (pp. 481–484). Center for Research on Developmental Education and Urban Literacy, University of Minnesota, Minneapolis, MN. Retrieved from: http://media.education.umn.edu/passit/docs/PASS-IT-Book.pdf

Leask, B., & Carroll, J. (2013). *Learning and teaching across cultures.* Melbourne: International Education Association of Australia (IEAA).

Machin, S., & Murphy, R. (2017). Paying out and crowding out? The globalization of higher education. *Journal of Economic Geography, 17*(5), 1075–1110.

Madyun, N. (2008). Linking universal instructional design and cultural capital: Improving African American college outcomes. In J. L. Higbee & E. Goff (Eds.), *Pedagogy and student services for institutional transformation: Implementing universal design in higher education* (pp. 49–61). Center for Research on Developmental Education and Urban Literacy, University of Minnesota, Minneapolis, MN. Retrieved from: http://media.education.umn.edu/passit/docs/PASS-IT-Book.pdf

Manning, K., & Muñoz, F. M. (2011). Re-visioning the future of multicultural student services. In D. Lazarus Stewart (Ed.), *Multicultural student services on campus* (pp. 282–299). Sterling, VA: Stylus Publishing.

May, V. (2015). *Pursuing intersectionality, unsettling dominant imaginaries.* New York: Routledge.

Moore, S. (2016). Transforming inclusive education. *YouTube.* Retrieved from: www.youtube.com/watch?v=RYtUlU8MjlY

Poling, K., Smit, J., & Higgs, D. (2013). In-class use of laptop computers to enhance engagement within an undergraduate biology curriculum: Findings and lessons learned. *Bioscience Education, 21*(1), 29–41.

Pooran, B. D., & Wilkie, C. (2005). Failing to achieve equality: Disability rights in Australia, Canada, and the United States. *Journal of Law and Social Policy, 20*, 1–34. Retrieved from: http://digitalcommons.osgoode.yorku.ca/jlsp/vol20/iss1/1

Robertson, S. L. (2010). *Challenges facing universities in a globalising world.* Bristol: Centre for Globalisation, Education and Societies. Retrieved from: http://susan leerobertson.com/publications/

Roschelle, J., Courey, S., Patton, C., & Murray, E. (2013). Dynabooks: Supporting teachers to engage all learners in key literacies. In C. Mouza & N. C. Lavigne (Eds.), *Emerging technologies for the classroom: A learning sciences perspective* (pp. 31–46). New York: Springer.

Sadowski, J. (2014). *Promoting diversity in the universal: Rethinking universal design for learning.* College of Arts & Sciences Senior. Honors Theses. Paper 55. http://doi.org/10.18297/honors/55

Shin, R. Q., Welch, J. C., Kaya, A. E., Yeung, J. G., Obana, C., Sharma, R., Vernay, C., & Yee, S. (2017). The intersectionality framework and identity intersections in the journal of counseling psychology and the counseling psychologist: A content analysis. *Journal of Counseling Psychology, 64*(5), 458–474.

Taylor, C. A., & Bovill, C. (2017). Towards an ecology of participation: Process philosophy and co-creation of higher education curricula. *European Educational Research Journal, 17*(1), 112–128.

Trahar, S. (2009). Beyond the story itself: Narrative inquiry and autoethnography in intercultural research in higher education. *Forum Qualitative Sozialforschung/Forum: Qualitative Social Research, 10*(1), Art. 30. Retrieved from: http://nbn-resolving.de/urn:nbn:de:0114-fqs0901308

Waitoller, F., & King Thorius, K. (2016). Cross-pollinating culturally sustaining pedagogy and universal design for learning: Toward an inclusive pedagogy that accounts for dis/ability. *Harvard Educational Review, 86*(3), 366–389.

Yamagishi, T., & Suzuki, N. (2009). An institutional approach to culture. In Evolution, culture, and the human mind. In M. Schaller, A. Norenzayan, S. J. Heine, T. Yamagishi, & T. Kameda (Eds.), *Evolution, culture and the human mind* (pp. 185–203). New York: Psychology Press.

Zhang, Y. (2016). Visitors or stakeholders? Engaging international students in the development of higher education policy. MEd Thesis. Faculty of Education, UPEI.

Zhou, G., & Zhang, Z. (2014). A study of the first year international students at a Canadian University: Challenges and experiences with social integration. *Canadian and International Education/Education canadienne et international, 43*(2), Article 7. Retrieved from: http://ir.lib.uwo.ca/cie-eci/vol43/iss2/7

Transforming learning

Redesigning curriculum, format, content and practice

Chapter 11

Transforming teaching and learning in HEIs

Impacts of UDL on professional development of university lecturers

Marian McCarthy and Brian Butler

Case study

Accredited Professional Development for faculty at UCC is structured through a Postgraduate Certificate in Teaching and Learning in Higher Education (30 European Credit Transfer System ECTS) in the first year, followed by a Postgraduate Diploma in Teaching and Learning in Higher Education (30 ECTS). Both programs are now fully integrated, online offerings, designed to engage all staff who support student learning at UCC or at another third level institution. The courses aim to provide staff with theoretical and practical perspectives on teaching and learning. The model is an investigative and developmental one, where faculty and other staff who teach are encouraged to problematize their teaching and look for the evidence of student learning. A third program, a Master's degree in Teaching and Learning in Higher Education (60 ECTS) is also available for staff who teach and culminates in the writing of a publishable paper about a teaching and learning issue. To date, more than 70% of academic staff at UCC have taken the first year of the program and hold a Postgraduate Certificate in Teaching and Learning in Higher Education (30 ECTS). One of those staff members is Dr. Kevin Murphy who also holds a Postgraduate Diploma in this field.

Dr. Murphy teaches third year pharmacy students and discusses implementing TfU and UDL in a module where students have the opportunity to apply knowledge in a clinical setting for the first time. The module is made up of lectures, tutorials and laboratory sessions.

Lectures introduce students to important terminology and concepts and also facilitate their revision. The lab sessions allow students to work in an environment similar to a real pharmacy and each student is responsible for dispensing prescriptions designed by the teacher. The tutorials are made up of sessions in which the students present data from case studies or perform role plays as pharmacist, patient or observer. Over time, students get to play all three roles. Kevin feels that he is fortuitous in teaching on this module which has been designed by colleagues who are aware of how to Teach for Understanding and are aware of the principles of Universal Design for Learning (UDL). Kevin wants to increase engagement in his course and optimize student understanding so his participation in the Postgraduate Certificate and Diploma in Teaching and Learning in Higher Education provides him with the frameworks to meet the needs of all students.

Introduction

Here we provide a context for how Universal Design for Learning (UDL) emerged organically within our work and how we aligned it with other theoretical models and embedded it in our accredited professional development framework. UDL (Meyer and Rose 2000; Rose, Meyer and Hitchcock, 2005; Novak, 2016; Novak and Thibodeau, 2016) was framed by a series of pedagogical lenses that were already part of the original professional development program in our university and that aligned well with UDL, laying a foundation for it. UCC's work on UDL builds firstly on research in the field of Multiple Intelligences (MI) theory (Gardner, 1983, 1999a, 1999b). UCC was keen to address diverse learning from primary to tertiary level in Ireland and to tease out its implications for curriculum and assessment. Substantial philanthropic funding from 1995 to 2000, allowed us to build the Multiple Intelligences Curriculum and Assessment Project with the Project Zero Classroom at the Harvard Graduate School of Education during this time (Hyland, 2000). From 2000 to 2007, UCC continued to chart its progress in this field across the educational spectrum in Ireland (Hyland and McCarthy, 2009), documenting how MI was used in school and university contexts.

Our work was also strongly influenced by the Teaching for Understanding (TfU) model (Wiske, 1998, 2005) which framed much of the MI work at Harvard and gave it a pedagogical focus. As we will see later, the TfU model provided us with a robust approach to developing active learning and student-centered approaches, since it prioritized a performance view of understanding, which we will explain later. We were conscious too of the need to support staff in documenting their practice and problematizing it and developing a language of practice. With this in mind, the work of Ernest Boyer (1990, 1997) and the Carnegie Foundation on the scholarship of teaching and learning (SoTL) also impacted our approach and the decision to purposefully integrate research, teaching and learning at UCC. In short, we were keen to help staff use the same approach they brought to their research in the context of their teaching, to unpack the evidence of the latter and make it visible. Hence, our focus on developing ways of documenting and researching practice through the portfolio process and its many forms from teaching portfolios, to course and research portfolios. Our focus in this chapter will be on the course portfolio and its emphasis on the Design, Teaching (Enactment) and Learning (Results) of a selected course (Cerbin, 1994, 1996; Hutchings, 1998).

University College Cork had the first Teaching Development Unit in Ireland in the 1980s and early 1990s and thus has a strong tradition of interest and expertise in teaching and learning issues and approaches. The original model was based on a training one, common at the time, with a focus on tips and strategies and on discussing ways to improve practice. The accredited continuing professional development model grew out of this approach but is an investigative model, problematizing teaching and learning in its many guises. The accredited program began officially in 2004, with the official founding of the Centre for the Integration of Research, Teaching and Learning (CIRTL), building on five years of lunch time seminars which provided faculty with the opportunity to peer review their teaching through sharing portfolios of practice. The Postgraduate Certificate and Diploma ran most successfully for a decade as a face-to-face model. The program transitioned to an online format in 2015 to provide more flexibility and opportunity for staff to develop their teaching and advance student learning. To support staff to review curriculum design for inclusive teaching and assessment, a module entitled *Diversity in Student Learning* (15 ECTS) is provided in the second semester of the Diploma in year two. This module addresses the application of Teaching for Understanding (TfU) pedagogy and Universal Design for Learning (UDL). We also created a Course Portfolio Rubric (adapted from the work of Cerbin, 1994, 1996; Hutchings, 1998) which guides the process of documentation and reflection that staff/faculty undergo in order to maximize student learning. This approach is scaffolded by an introductory section on UDL in year 1, which is aligned with a focus on Multiple Intelligences (MI) theory, thereby strengthening the focus on students' diverse ways of learning and their impact on assessment. Hence, embedded throughout the program is the realization that students need to be provided with diverse methods of teaching and diverse ways of assessment so that they are equipped to harness and express their learning. All three approaches (TfU, MI and UDL) are grounded ultimately in the Scholarship of Teaching and Learning (SoTL) philosophy, encouraging staff to integrate research, teaching and learning.

In accordance with sector recognized SoTL principles (Bass, 1999; Boyer, 1990, Hutchings, 1998; Shulman, 1998, 2006), staff who teach (including faculty, administrators and post-doctoral researchers) are asked to research a course or module and to create a portfolio to document their learning under the three headings of Design, Teaching (Enactment) and Learning (Results), (Cerbin, 1996; Hutchings, 1998). Staff as students are also invited to discuss each section of their portfolio in an online discussion group of four to six participants and have an opportunity to share and peer review their work. The course portfolio is a SoTL methodology, which is at once a method of documentation and of investigation of a specific course that teachers choose to review, redesign and share in the light of TfU and UDL principles.

Teaching for Understanding (TfU)

TfU is a pedagogical and disciplinary framework (Wiske, 1998, 2005) which emerged from the *Project Zero Classroom* approach at the Harvard Graduate School of Education in the mid 1990s and was a collaborative project between researchers and K-12 and high school teachers in the Boston and Cambridge areas. It is grounded in the work of Howard Gardner and David Perkins as the then co-directors of Project Zero research projects. TfU is conducive to a SoTL approach in its investigative thrust, enabling staff to design, document and pursue student understanding and its evidence. A TfU approach has the advantage of providing staff with two lenses, pedagogical and disciplinary, thus equipping them with a conceptual framework to make teaching and learning in the discipline visible and to enhance it. It is particularly suited to HEI contexts, given its disciplinary lens, though it is not widely practiced in the university sector to date. The TfU framework complements a UDL perspective, since both focus on naming, maximizing and recognizing student learning and on mapping out its pursuit. Within a SoTL tradition, a reflective, research approach provides the opportunity to make teaching public, to make such findings open to the critique of peers, and to share findings with others (Boyer, 1990; Shulman, 1998; Schön, 1983, 1995).

TfU: a performance view of understanding

Understanding a topic, in the context of TfU, is defined in terms of being able to perform flexibly with the topic and being able to explain, relate and apply the knowledge concerned in a new situation (Perkins, 1998; McCarthy, 2011). Perkins highlighted the lack of real understanding taking place in teaching and learning in both the Humanities and the Sciences (Perkins, 1993). He promoted a performance view of understanding that reflects the general spirit of a constructivist approach to learning, which posits that knowledge is a construct, built by the student, and not a product given to the student. By defining the idea of performance in constructivist terms, Perkins claimed that to understand knowledge fully cannot mean that the learner understands the knowledge in a representational way, implying that s/he has an image or mental model of the knowledge only, but that the learner must also be able to perform or play with the knowledge freely and easily. Perkins describes this active learning process as *'an understanding performance'* or *'a performance of understanding'* (Perkins, 1998, pp. 32–33). Perkins claims that most classroom activities are too routine to be understanding performances and that, though these activities have their own role to play, they are not performances of understanding. They do not enhance understanding in the student and take the learner beyond what s/he already knows. The three principles of UDL, ensuring multiple means of Engagement, of Representation, and of Action and Expression, speak well to this performative view since the focus is equally on the active learning and ownership of the student and on creating a learning environment where the student is empowered to demonstrate learning in ways that play to his/her strengths.

The mainstay of a performance view of learning is active engagement with the topic, in a way that involves reflective thought and feedback. It is important to be able to think in different ways with the knowledge and be able to apply the knowledge to different situations. Perkins highlights that understanding takes careful planning and thought. Engagement with the knowledge must involve guided performances with regular feedback to ensure real understanding can take place. In terms of UDL, it also implies that the teacher must scaffold and facilitate the learning over time, using multiple ways of representing the knowledge, through a variety of entry points, analogies and metaphors, and providing the student with multiple ways of expressing the knowledge, through a variety of formative assessment processes.

Teaching for Understanding can be viewed through pedagogical and disciplinary lenses. The pedagogical lens invites teachers at every level to consider their planning and teaching under four headings to maximize learning: *Generative Topics, Understanding Goals, Performances of Understanding* and *Ongoing Assessment*. The Disciplinary lens posits Four Dimensions of Understanding consisting of *Knowledge, Methods, Purposes and Forms*. The following is a brief outline of these attributes of TFU and highlights some of the synergies that exist between TFU and UDL.

TfU: a pedagogical lens

Generative topics

The criteria for this element of TFU suggest that topics chosen by the teacher should be (i) central to the discipline, (ii) interesting to students and teachers, (iii) accessible to students through a variety of resources and entry points and (iv) provide opportunities for multiple connections with other topics on the course.

Several of these criteria address the Why, What, and How of learning in the UDL context and provide opportunities to engage students in the classroom. The criteria of Generative Topics direct a teacher to work to ensure students are interested and to promote diversity in a variety of entry points to learning and of resources. Such variety also addresses the educational requirements of Gardner's (1999a) Multiple Intelligences theory, thus promoting multiple forms of Representation and multiple methods and media of Action and Expression. Providing opportunities to make connections with other material on the course will also serve to engage students. Generative Topics, therefore, create a pedagogy that supports a UDL environment.

Understanding goals

The second pillar of TFU focuses on the importance of understanding goals. The use of long-term goals or *throughlines* and, within these, *short term goals*, make it possible for a student to map out their learning from the beginning, while also keeping them aware of exactly where they are on their learning journey. It is vital that a student has a strong awareness of where exactly their learning journey is taking them and that the repetition and reviewing of these goals drives them forward. Hence, the intentionality of teaching is there from the start, rather than retrofitted, when goals are publically named and prioritized.

This pedagogical pillar is key to enacting the principle of providing multiple means of Action and Expression, and Guideline 3 of UDL, which addresses the importance of executive functions. This addresses the planning, reviewing and achieving of course and personal goals. Two of the demands of providing multiple means of Engagement, asks a teacher to 'heighten salience of goals and objectives' and to 'increase mastery oriented feedback'. The multiple forms of Engagement demand that we 'promote expectations and beliefs that optimize motivation'. These demands can also be addressed through articulating the Understanding Goals of the TFU model.

Performances of understanding

A performance view of understanding ensures students can perform with, or express their knowledge in multiple ways and by using multiple media. Though performances are important in implementing all the principles and guidelines of UDL, they are particularly relevant to providing multiple means of Action and Expression. This is central to both the development and assessment of learning. Multiple forms of expression and the resulting performances of understanding provide material for both formative and summative assessment. Performances of understanding can also facilitate the guidelines of multiple forms of Engagement, which asks a teacher to provide options for recruiting student interest. The checkpoints of this guideline ask that a teacher optimize individual choice and autonomy, and also optimize relevance, value and authenticity for students.

Hence TfU and UDL speak the same language, one mirroring and reinforcing the other.

Providing multiple means of Engagement reminds teachers to provide options for sustaining effort and persistence. The accompanying checkpoints encourage teachers to foster collaboration and community and increase mastery-oriented feedback. Such checkpoints can be met within a series of performances of understanding that scaffold student learning over the course of the semester, moving from introductory, to guided inquiry, to culminatory performances. One of the Engagement principles, which reminds teachers to "provide options for self-regulation, can also be included within this performance pedagogy". The checkpoints ask that a teacher 'promote expectations and beliefs that optimize motivation, and facilitate personal coping skills and strategies'. By definition, a performance of understanding challenges students to own learning and to choose how to investigate and represent their learning. Thus, performances of understanding provide a pathway to UDL and map out its stepping stones.

Ongoing assessment

This fourth element of TfU impacts multiple means of Engagement and of Action and Expression, thus opening up both the 'why' and 'how' of learning. The three guidelines when providing multiple means of Action and Expression encourage multiple options for physical action, for expression and communication, and for executive functions. All of these are central to continuous assessment in whatever form it takes and whether it be summative or formative. Such assessment relies on naming the criteria that count for students to succeed and it is equally dependent on a variety of sources of feedback, peer and self-assessment being as important as teacher feedback.

The first guideline of multiple forms of Engagement, for example, asks a teacher to provide options for recruiting interest, optimizing individual choice and autonomy; the second focuses on maximizing relevance, value and authenticity, while the third urges a minimizing of threats and distractions. Ongoing assessment approaches encourage a teacher to draw students into the planning of assessment, thus helping to ensure a spectrum of assessment methods that will address the multiple ways that students express themselves. This choice and flexibility provide assessment methods attractive to individual students.

The second Engagement guideline points to options for sustaining effort and persistence. This asks teachers to heighten the salience of goals and objectives, to vary demands and resources in order to optimize challenge, to foster collaboration and community, and increase mastery-oriented feedback. Such feedback is essential in bringing a student to the next level and is a central part of ongoing assessment practices.

From the perspective of the four cornerstones of TfU pedagogy, the synergies between TfU and UDL continue to emerge and are useful for us at UCC in creating a context in which UDL can thrive.

Reflection

Throughout our process, we designed reflective questions used to encourage faculty to think about how they would apply TfU and UDL principles to a course they are reviewing. The reader might like to ponder one of these questions at this point:

- How does a TfU perspective influence your design as you revisit your chosen course/ module? For example, what performances of understanding and the ongoing assessment of these will you introduce to engage students and enhance their learning?
- Discuss how you are responding to the three principles of UDL: (i) multiple ways of representation, (ii) multiple ways of action and expression and (iii) multiple ways of engagement. What challenges do you face in redesigning your course with TfU or UDL perspectives in mind?
- How do I know what my students know and understand in this module? How will I teach the module differently in the future in the light of my students' learning and my own critique?
- How has my reading informed my understanding of teaching and learning? What has changed? How can I research my teaching more effectively?

The four dimensions of disciplinary understanding

The Disciplinary lens, emergent in the Harvard context when teachers and researchers began to think about their subjects and course content, reveals four dimensions of understanding that form the foundational basis for the pedagogy. Within HEI's, we are teaching the disciplines and our pedagogical decisions need to grow out of our disciplinary expertise and need to model good disciplinary practice if we are to engage our students as expert learners. The four dimensions of disciplinary understanding are:

- *Knowledge*: the 'what' of learning which relates to the key questions that the disciplinary expert/teacher is asking. We need to be conscious that students come from differing backgrounds and some knowledge they carry may conflict with the knowledge of the discipline. Knowledge needs to be modelled and provided, therefore, if a student is to perform with the knowledge of the discipline, the teacher using multiple means of representation to support learning;
- *Methods*: the 'how' of learning, relating to how the expert finds out and how this is modelled for the student who needs to be a partner in the learning. The Methods dimension addresses the discussion and testing of knowledge in a systematic way and maps on to the method of the pedagogy, which takes its lead from authentic tasks in the discipline, using multiple means of action and expression;

- *Purposes:* the 'why' of learning relates to the central importance of this aspect of the discipline. Purpose also invokes the ethical dimension of the investigation and the moral imperative that such knowledge is used for the good of all. The Purposes dimension is important to all students as it demonstrates how knowledge can be applied to the world around us. This encourages a student to see how knowledge is created, how to take ownership of knowledge and how to apply it in a practical way to real world issues, using multiple means of engagement;
- *Forms:* the various ways and genres through which knowledge is expressed and presented. UDL principles remind us that we need to use multiple forms of Action and Expression to harness student learning. Thus, an awareness of a variety of Forms strengthens authentic assessment and performance, where students own learning and can express it to take context, audience and register into account.

These dimensions of Disciplinary understanding help address the Why, What and How of learning which are so important to UDL. All are relevant to the engagement of a student within any discipline and to the representation and expression of the knowledge within it.

Knowledge is represented in many forms and the Methods of the discipline can be practiced via multiple forms of Expression. Students are engaged when patterns, critical features, big ideas and relationships in knowledge are identified. When students use methods that discuss, test and analyze the real knowledge of the discipline in question, opportunities are created to provide more student autonomy and interest is also sustained through such meaningful performances of understanding. When this is done in group or team work, such collaboration helps sustain interest. The purposes dimension of understanding, for example, offers practical value to the knowledge of the discipline thus optimizing relevance, value and authenticity (checkpoint 7.2). Every discipline has its forms, which the teacher draws upon to build performances of understanding in the classroom. These forms provide the tools to share the concepts, ideas and skills of a discipline and create a learning environment that promotes multiple forms of Representation. A variety of forms also provides multiple ways to perform with the knowledge of the discipline and helps keep students engaged.

Reflection

- Choose one of the Dimensions and consider how it shapes the What, How or Why of Learning. For example, in relation to the Forms Dimension, how can you move beyond the set exam format of expression to encourage students to engage in a more real and connected way with the discipline in a real world setting? What authentic assessment assignment would you consider to bridge this gap?

The frameworks in action

Let's return to Dr Kevin Murphy, who was introduced in the case study at the beginning of the chapter. Kevin based his course portfolio around a clinical practice module on which he wished to reflect. He presented three portfolio entries on his chosen course, based on its three essential ingredients: its Design, Teaching (Enactment) and Student Learning (Results), as defined by the Hutchings (1998) model, based on the work of William Cerbin (1994, 1996). Each 'entry' charts the iterative process of the teacher in predicating student learning at every level of the course, from its vision and design to its facilitation and assessment. As the term implies, an 'entry' opens up the possibilities of the course and also suggests that there is risk – taking and challenge in the quest for learning.

Portfolio entry 1: course design

Kevin sums up his anchor Generative Topic for his lab sessions as follows: From the student desk to the pharmacy counter: integrating and applying classroom knowledge and skills to realistic situations. Another central lecture topic relates to Patient Welfare. In his design, there are two central performances of under-standing that scaffold the module: one relates to the tutorial and the presen-tation of case studies to other students, while the second centres around the lab sessions and dispensing medication in a model pharmacy. In the former, students present to and teach each other, the case student acting as a catalyst for learning. In the latter, students need to integrate their learning to ultimately produce a filled prescription- a bag of medication. Students get immediate feed-back from lecturers in both cases, hence the central role of formative, diagnostic feedback which speaks to TfU and UDL perspectives.

Kevin's design entry also focuses in depth on how the modules speaks to the three principles of UDL:

- *Multiple means of Representation:* Kevin focuses in on the example of inhal-ers for asthma to show how knowledge is represented in different ways during and beyond lectures. Students would first be exposed to inhalers in lectures where the context for their use is provided. They are told that they can be used to alleviate the symptoms of an asthma attack or to prevent the symptoms occurring. Then students are shown pictures of common inhal-ers on the Irish market. Later in workshops, they are provided with dummy inhalers so that they get a more realistic, tactile experience of inhalers and develop an understanding of patients' perspectives.
- *Multiple means of Action and Expression:* There has been a push to develop this aspect of the module as many of the things that students should learn are skills that are not easily taught in a conventional lecture nor examined in a conventional written examination. The most important of these is patient counselling skills. In the role play workshops students are given the

opportunity to practice their student counselling skills with other students and receive constructive feedback from students and staff. They are given multiple opportunities to display their learning in multiple forms of communication. Students can actively display their learning in the patient counselling workshops. Though they are learning counselling and communication skills, students must correctly answer the patient scenario through use of their clinical knowledge and their ability to choose between similar but different medical problems. They must also self-assess their ability to treat the patient; if they cannot, then they must communicate that the patient should be treated by a physician. Students also have the opportunity to vary their form of expression within the written word. Students have two types of written examinations in PF3106, the traditional long-form essay question, and a written unobserved structured clinical examination (WUSCE). A WUSCE consists of a series of tables/stations with different questions and students must rotate through the tables after a defined period of time. This tests the students' ability to think quickly and write concisely.

- *Multiple means of Engagement:* Student interest is harnessed through the increasing relevance of the course to the work of the qualified pharmacist; the module is the first experience for students of integrating knowledge from different disciplines and applying it in a specific context. Hence, it is in the lab sessions that Engagement is maximized. The role play scenarios invite students to engage on a multiplicity of levels with the role of the pharmacist or the patient, indeed with both, as one must dialogue with the other meaningfully. Equally, the role of observer allows the student to stand back and critique the encounter and appreciate the complexity of the scenario and its possibilities. Kevin explains that students need to be able to contract into the experience and he emphasizes that there is much learning in being able to adapt, to empathize, to imagine and to hypothesize in reviewing and reflecting on video footage of the encounter. Opportunities for engagement are also plentiful in tutorial work when students present real case studies to their group and discuss the emerging issues and their potential solutions.

Portfolio entry 2: teaching/enactment

The performance of understanding that Kevin chooses to explore in this entry is the patient – counselling role play where students get an opportunity to play the three roles of patient, pharmacist and observer. From the perspective of UDL, Kevin suggests that there are multiple forms of *Representation* of knowledge in the role plays: students can check their own written notes, while other students can provide feedback and he himself also provides feedback; hence students have information from multiple sources. Equally, their own performance in role provides many opportunities to represent various issues and dilemmas from the perspectives of the pharmacist, the patient and the observer. Role plays also involve the construction of relationships and characters and knowledge is also represented through body language and gesture. Indeed, the dynamic relationship between the three UDL principles begins to emerge in practice as each begets and reinforces the other, indicative in the following example.

Kevin feels that multiple means of *Action and Expression* are literally center stage in the role play scenarios. Students have multiple opportunities to act as pharmacists and vicariously explore the complex and multi-faceted nature of the role. Also, when acting as patient, they still have to focus on the role of the pharmacist and how s/he deals with the patient. Students can also empathize with patient needs and issues by embracing this role. As well as expressing themselves through acting, students also get a chance to express themselves as themselves in the debriefing session post role play. Kevin points out that the main challenge in developing and facilitating performances of understanding, where students apply their knowledge in the applied situation of the role play, is the class size. Kevin would like to play the role of the patient in all scenarios, to maximize student challenge in this complex encounter, but this is not possible in a class of 60. Hence, groups and other students provide the feedback to each other. However, Kevin also learns the benefits of peer learning that emerges from student group work and collaboration which strengthens student engagement and expression.

In terms of *Engagement*, Kevin describes this module as the one that turns pharmacy students into student pharmacists, the one that helps them think and act like pharmacists, integrating the knowledge and practice of the discipline. Thus, performances of understanding, as described, play a large part in the students' learning experience over time.

Reflection

- The role of the lecturer is to design and define the pedagogical promise of the module in the first place in order to facilitate, rather than dictate, learning. What new ways of Engagement might you consider in revisiting a course of your choice?
- How might you take the students to a new starting point, even a new space, to encourage them to re-engage with the course or one of its central concepts or methods?

Portfolio entry 3: student learning/results

Kevin feels that lectures themselves should be more engaging and less didactic in nature. He is working on this by endeavouring to increase class debate and he is also reflecting on his use of PowerPoint and considering the variety of representation that this pedagogical tool can bring. To improve *student engagement*

Kevin's critical friend has suggested *the use of a reflective diary*, which can also act as a very productive expression of learning in the context of authentic assessment. Such a method is a valuable performance of understanding and helps create self-regulation and critique. Though Kevin is pleased that this module works reasonably well from a TfU and UDL perspective, he is even more pleased that he has identified weak points in the learning environment and he is working to address these in the future. In this, Kevin himself is modelling what it means to be an expert learner.

In relation to the lab sessions, Kevin sums up the benefits and UDL impact as follows:

- Students have to think on their feet during the role play using authentic learning situations;
- Students also learn the value of structured questioning in this context;
- Regarding the Purposes Dimension, a pharmacist's raison d'etre is patient welfare, this is instilled by feedback. The Forms (Dimension) come across in the pharmacist's speech, words, and demeanour, so this is not just theoretical pharmacy because the student voice features prominently
- Students learn from other students and show live examples of good practice to avoid mistaken information.

Course portfolio discussion and conclusion

Kevin speaks of TfU and UDL frameworks as making him more purposeful and confident and more conscious of student learning. Kevin states that TfU and UDL have guided him to better pedagogical decisions and ways of addressing student needs. If a student is in trouble with a concept, for example, Kevin now has 'a variety of means to assess knowledge and understanding', a variety of Classroom Assessment Techniques (CATS) (Angelo and Cross, 1993), for example, which provide a good level of reassurance regarding what has been learned. CATS also highlight what has to be worked on and can be used diagnostically to detect student bottlenecks. The authors would also add that Kevin has developed a variety of pedagogical strategies including role plays, case studies and presentations which he can draw on to engage and motivate students and which beget a variety of types of assessment to harness student learning. Finally, Kevin also underlines the importance of the staff- student relationship in creating a trusting and sustainable learning environment.

Conclusion: TfU and UDL – synergies and impact

In our case study, it is clear that TfU is a gateway for UDL and that it provides a solid foundation on which to build UDL approaches. Both frameworks problematize teaching and learning and question that 'one size fits all'. Both provide an architecture of practice which scaffolds good pedagogical decisions.

Both provide faculty with sound advice and direction. Both TfU and UDL are complementary approaches, the former emerging from the cognitive and constructivist traditions, the latter from the neuroscience stable. Both have theoretical and scientific rigour and are robust and have survived the test of time and of classroom practice and intervention. Both draw from the work of researchers and teachers who collaborate and continue to work together across schools and laboratories and to theorize and practice, hypothesize and investigate, in order to influence and transform classrooms and teachers' and students' lives. What matters in the end is that both invite teachers to include all learners and to create curricula that value a variety of pathways to learning and the celebration by students of that learning.

Ultimately, what matters is that students are given the opportunity to be the best that they can be and that they are ready to make a wholesome contribution to society as active citizens who make a difference. It is no accident that one of the principles of UDL speaks to 'multiple means of action and expression'. Students need to take action and make the world a better place. Students also need to learn to 'express' their learning with confidence, to speak it as they might a poem to which they can give their unique voice. Such learning is not about summative judgement. It is about formative, ongoing, dialogic feedback; it is about thought and reflection, which will invite all to go on learning long after their school and college days are over, in whatever ways speak to their strengths, their spirit, their society and their setting. TfU and UDL are the compass points that can take us there in our setting here at University College Cork.

References

Angelo, T. and Cross, K (1993) *Classroom Assessment Techniques* (2nd ed.). San Francisco: Jossey-Bass.

Bass, R. (1999) The scholarship of teaching: What's the problem? *Inventio: Creative Thinking About Learning and Teaching*, 1 (1), 1–10.

Boyer, E. (1990) *Scholarship Reconsidered: Priorities of the Professoriate, The Carnegie Foundation for the Advancement of Teaching*. San Francisco: Jossey-Bass.

Boyer, E. (1997) Prologue: Scholarship a personal journey. In C. Glassick, M. Huber and G. I. Maeroff (eds.) *Scholarship Assessed: Evaluation of the Professoriate*. San Francisco: Jossey-Bass.

Cerbin, W. (1994) The course portfolio as a tool for continuous improvement of teaching and learning. *Journal on Excellence in College Teaching*, 5 (1), 95–105.

Cerbin, W. (1996) Inventing a new genre: The course portfolio at the University of Wisconsin–La Crosse. In P. Hutchings (ed.) *Making Teaching Community Property: A Menu for Peer Collaboration and Review* (pp. 52–56). Washington, DC: AAHE.

Gardner, H. (1983). *Frames of Mind: The Theory Of Multiple Intelligences*. NY: Basics.

Gardner, H. (1999a). *The Disciplined Mind: What all Students Should Understand*. New York: Basic Books.

Gardner, H. (1999b) *Intelligence Reframed: Multiple Intelligences for the 21st Century*. New York: Basic Books.

Hutchings, P. (1998) Defining features and significant functions of the course portfolio. In P. Hutchings (ed.) *The Course Portfolio. How Faculty Can Examine Their Teaching to Advance Practice and Improve Student Learning*. Washington, DC: The American Association for Higher Education.

Hyland, A. (ed.) (2000) *Multiple Intelligences Curriculum and Assessment Project: Final Report*. University College Cork: Multiple Intelligences Curriculum and Assessment Project. Retrieved from https://archive.org/details/ERIC_ED538017

Hyland, A. and McCarthy, M. (2009) Multiple intelligences in Ireland. In J. Q. Chen, S. Moran and H. Gardner (eds.) *Multiple Intelligences Around the World*. San Francisco: Jossey-Bass.

McCarthy, M. (2011) Mapping the journey: The implications of multiple intelligences and teaching for understanding for the teaching of civic, social and political education. In A. Hyland (ed.) *Multiple Intelligences Curriculum and Assessment Project (Digital Version) Originally published in 2000*. Cork: NAIRTL.

Meyer, A. and Rose D. H. (2000) Universal design for individual differences. *Educational Leadership*, 58 (3), 39–43.

Novak, K. (2016) *UDL Now!: A Teacher's guide to Applying Universal Design for Learning in Today's Classroom*. Wakefield, MA: CAST Professional Publishing.

Novak, K. and Thibodeau, T. (2016) *UDL in the Cloud: How to Design and Deliver Online Education using Universal Design for Learning*. Wakefield, MA: CAST Professional Publishing.

Perkins, D. (1993) Teaching for understanding. *American Educator: The Professional Journal of Teachers*, 17 (3) (Fall), 28–35.

Perkins, D. (1998) What is understanding? In M. S. Wiske (ed.) *Teaching for Understanding: Linking Research with Practice* (pp. 39–58). San Francisco: Jossey-Bass.

Rose, D. H., Meyer, A. and Hitchcock, C. (eds.) (2005) *The Universally Designed Classroom: Accessible Curriculum and Digital Technologies*. Cambridge, MA: Harvard Education Press.

Schön, D. (1983) *The Reflective Practitioner*. New York: Basic Books.

Schön, D. (1995, November/December) The new scholarship requires a new epistemology: Knowing-in-action. *Change*, 27 (6), 27–34.

Shulman, L. (1998) Course anatomy: The dissection and analysis of knowledge through teaching. In P. Hutchings (ed.) *The Course Portfolio: How Faculty Can Examine Their Teaching to Advance Practice and Improve Student Learning* (pp. 5–12). Washington, DC: The American Association for Higher Education.

Shulman, L. S. (2006) *Foreword to T. Hatch, Into the Classroom: Developing the Scholarship of Teaching and Learning*. San Francisco: Jossey-Bass.

Wiske, M. S. (ed.) (1998) *Teaching for Understanding: Linking Research with Practice*. San Francisco: Jossey-Bass.

Wiske, M. S. (2005) *Teaching for Understanding with Technology*. San Francisco: Jossey-Bass.

Chapter 12

Cognitive accessibility

Stretching the boundaries of UDL
in higher education

*Shira Yalon-Chamovitz, Neta Linder-Katz and
Ornit Avidan-Ziv*

Case study

Dana is a woman in her early thirties with an intellectual disability
and significant learning difficulties. She enrolled in a class on Child
Development in the Occupational Therapy Department at the Faculty of Health Professions in an HEI in central Israel. She chose this
course as an elective out of interest and a sense that such a course
would give her vital information, should she become a mother.

Dana has limited reading and writing skills. In addition, she faces
substantial memory and learning difficulties, and is challenged by
abstraction, information processing and language organization. She
works in supported employment and lives in a supported residential facility. She was very lonely and unhappy at work, and comes to
school with a lot of motivation to learn and expand her knowledge,
as well as to be exposed to a different environment. She is highly
motivated to succeed, yet, is insecure and dependent. She's busy with
questions about her future, how she measures up to others, and the
possibility to integrate into academic studies. She places importance
on connecting with others. In fact, she defines success in school by
her ability to connect with the other students.

Dana is a relatively short, thin woman who dresses plainly. She is
a little introverted but there are no external signs that indicate the
difficulties she faces. She usually walks into the classroom early and
sits down quietly. She seems shy and unconfident. And although she
indicates that she is very interested in social networking, she rarely
connects with other students in class. Dana prefers not to expose

her disability to the students in her class, but did inform her teacher that she has learning difficulties.

Tal, the professor teaching the course, is an occupational therapist with over 15 years of experience working in the field of child development. She is teaching a number of courses within the Bachelor of Occupational Therapy program at the Faculty of Health Professions. She participated in a UDL workshop as part of a college-wide teacher excellence initiative. Tal is highly motivated and tries to apply the principles of the model in her courses. When Tal learned Dana will be taking her class, she turned to the college UDL implementation team. Her goal was to explore which UDL principles and measures she should apply to accommodate Dana. Her major concern was whether implementing the UDL principles in this course is sufficient for enabling Dana to experience meaningful learning.

Introduction

Although once unheard of, some post-secondary institutions have made great strides to integrate diverse learners, including those with cognitive or intellectual disabilities, into their environments. Historically, people with cognitive disabilities were considered lacking the "ability to benefit" from post-secondary education, or were disqualified for technical reasons such as a lack of high school diploma (Hart et al., 2004). However, global policy and legislation began moving toward inclusion, ensuring that students with cognitive disabilities qualified for grants, and providing appropriate academic milestones for these individuals to work towards. Although the experience of individuals with cognitive disabilities in post-secondary education may differ in some senses, there are parallels with what might be termed the "typical" transition to adulthood and many individuals with cognitive disabilities may have similar goals to their peers. These include advancing academic skills and knowledge, acquiring work experiences for future career opportunities and growing socially and emotionally while learning to build significant relationships with the self and others (Grigal & Hart, 2010).

The representative population of students with any disability in higher education is much lower than the general population, and those with disabilities often take longer to graduate, if they do at all (Raue & Lewis, 2011). Students with cognitive disabilities comprise a proportion of this population, and face many barriers to attending and graduating post-secondary institutions, although the benefits of this education for those with cognitive disabilities are abundant. For example, a study of 125 graduates of such a program found that 94% lived independently (i.e. alone or with spouse or roommates in an apartment or home that they rented or owned), as opposed to 16% of overall population of people with cognitive disabilities (Ross, 2012). Even though there might be some self-selection bias here, it is still impressive that nearly everyone who participated in the program moved on to live outside a group or family home. Smith et al. (2012) found that 43% of this population were employed when they had some post-secondary education, as opposed to 31% of those who had only completed high school. This finding is especially relevant as those with cognitive disabilities and disabilities in general face unemployment rates that are much higher than the general population (Officer & Posarac, 2011). Interestingly, even among individuals with intellectual disabilities it was found that those who participate in a post-secondary program make higher wages on average than those who do not and participate in more challenging work (Moore, 2015).

The models for incorporating students with cognitive disabilities into post-secondary education can be described broadly as ranging from segregated to inclusive and the type of model utilized will vary on the institution (Grigal & Hart, 2010; Hart et al., 2006). In the substantially separate model students might have the opportunity to participate in non-academic activities such as social programs or work opportunities with students from the general popula-tion. They take classes only with other students with cognitive disabilities which tend to cover life skills more than academics. In the mixed/hybrid model, these students can also take classes alongside students without disabilities for audit or credit in addition to the courses offered by the substantially separate model. The inclusive individual support model is the most progressive of the three and requires the most individualization. Here students identify their career goals and receive a flexible range of services to support these. Services can include technology supports, tutors and an educational coach. Students can take courses for audit or credit and work toward a certificate or degree (Grigal et al., 2006).

Is UDL a more appropriate model for including people with cognitive disabilities in HEI? In its current form, can UDL be stretched enough to accommodate diverse learners with cognitive disabilities in higher educa-tion? Let's think about Dana, our student, and Tal, our teacher; would UDL principles, which are supposed to make education accessible for all students, enough to make it accessible for Dana? We propose that best practice would be to combine UDL principles with cognitive accessibility principles, as detailed next.

Reflection

- Do you meet students like Dana in your practice?
- If so, do you feel that the UDL model provides you with the neces-sary practices to fully include these students in your practice?

Cognitive accessibility

Cognitive accessibility refers to the modification of the physical and human environment so that people with cognitive disabilities (e.g. people with learning disabilities, head injuries, intellectual disability, mental disability, autism spectrum etc.) can fully participate and function in it (Yalon-Chamovitz et al., 2015). Cognitive disabilities present a challenge for public accommodation as they are a) often invisible and b) include a very wide range of abilities, difficulties and challenges that vary significantly between people and within the same person at different times and situations. Challenges and difficulties faced by people with cognitive disabilities in higher education may include for example: Cognitive challenges that can be expressed in difficulty understanding instructions or conditions, difficulties regarding orientation in both the physical and technological environment, reaction time variability (slower response, pauses or impulsivity), difficulties in information processing and decision-making, understanding abstract information or subtext, executive functions, memory and problem solving. In addition, many people with cognitive disabilities have limited literacy skills and do not know how to read and write at a functional level; Social challenges that can be expressed in difficulty understanding social conditions, physical gestures, and social norms. Some might find it difficult to initiate social interactions, ask for help or even simply ask questions in class; communication challenges that may be significant and affect students' ability to use, absorb or disclose information.

The Israeli Institute on Cognitive Accessibility defines cognitive accessibility as a process of simplification and adaptation of the physical and human environment, so as to create clarity and simplicity (Rimon-Greenspan et al., 2018). For certain populations, including people with cognitive disabilities, these accessibility measures can enhance their participation in various life situations in which all can take part. The "cognitive ramps" (Yalon-Chamovitz et al., 2015) required to create cognitive accessibility include several dimensions: a convenient and safe built environment (enabling easy orientation and wayfinding); clear and concise communications, easy to understand information; intuitive and easy to use technology and clear, simple, and readily understood processes and procedures (see Figure 12.1).

We would like to propose that the combination of UDL principles with the accumulating knowledge base of cognitive accessibility may enable students with cognitive disabilities to more fully take part and succeed in post-secondary education. The cognitive ramps were developed using UDL knowledge as a base as these can help students access and navigate the learning environment by reducing physical, cognitive, intellectual and organizational barriers (Rose & Meyer, 2002).

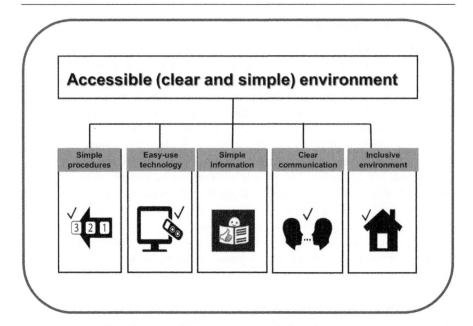

Figure 12.1 A cognitive accessibility model for UDL

Cognitive ramps to UDL

Multiple means of engagement is the first principle of UDL. This principle refers to recruiting interest, sustaining effort and self-regulation, suggesting that providing a variety of options for students' involvement is crucial, as all individuals differ in what they are motivated by and interested in. For example, some individuals prefer spontaneity while others prefer routine. Some individuals work better alone while others like to work together. The important thing is to remember that just as there are many types of learners, there are many ways in which to engage them.

While beneficial for all learners, in order to recruit the interest of students with cognitive disabilities, it is crucial to use simple, clear language and an adjustable speech rate. It is also important to review course objectives in a clear and simple manner, using short sentences and providing examples. Another issue of great importance, not only for those with cognitive disabilities but for all students in HEI, is that of communicating and collaborating with other students. Collaborations between students and creating a sense of belonging are recommended by CAST as best measures to preserve consistency and effort in the learning process. Therefore, it is recommended to create elaborate opportunities for in-class activities in pairs or small groups that will also enable students with social difficulties to get involved with others.

Reflection

- Are you applying any cognitive ramps for engagement in your practice?
- If you do, are they in the form of individual accommodations or can all stakeholders benefit from them?

Tal, the lecturer, usually applies the engagement principle in her courses in several ways. For example, she focuses upon the need to embed early acquaintance, to minimize threats and distractions. In order to reduce potential concerns Tal sends a message to the students through the course website before the beginning of the semester. The message includes her picture, a few words introducing herself to the students, and a PADLET link. She then asks the students to use the PADLET link to upload their picture and introduce themselves. Sending her own picture and introduction serves as an example for students of what is expected and allows them to become familiar with the lecturer upon entering class the first time. However, bearing Dana in mind, Tal realizes that she needs to add a few measures, such as providing clear and simple instructions about installing and using the PADLET application and uploading the files; or allowing students to introduce themselves in various ways not restricted to picture and written introduction. Indeed, she finds that these additional measures were beneficial for other students as well, such as those who were experiencing technological difficulties or were self-conscious and relieved not to be obligated to upload a picture.

Another example relates to the introduction of course objectives (referring to sustaining efforts and persistence). Clearly presenting course objectives and learning outcomes is considered to be a basic step in creating student involvement. Presenting lesson goals at the beginning of each lesson improves students' involvement and focus during class. Tal usually applies this in her courses by including an overall course objective and learning outcomes in syllabi, presenting them verbally at the beginning of each course, and introducing detailed lesson objectives at the beginning of each lesson. Again, as she wants to ensure that Dana is fully included and immersed, she further clarifies and simplifies course and lesson objectives, checks for her own preconceptions regarding previous knowledge, and introduces a flow chart to indicate gradual accumulation of the learning objective throughout the course. (For additional examples of potential cognitive ramps for engagement, see Figure 12.1.)

Multiple means of representation is another major UDL principle. This principle emphasizes the importance of developing and applying a variety of ways to teach and present learning materials. This call for diversity is based on acknowledging the variability between different people in terms of how they perceive, understand information, and learn. While beneficial for all learners, for students with cognitive disabilities it can be crucial to provide cognitively accessible formats of all course material including syllabi, assignments, reading requirements, presentations and course summaries. Beyond language simplification, it is also crucial to clarify and simplify the process of learning. This is especially beneficial, as students can experience difficulties understanding course requirements and the accumulating learning process, even when the language is seemingly clear. For example, using short clear sentences to explain course assignments, or guiding the use of required technologies (such as course website, library website or in-class technologies) might enable students to fully participate. Another important measure is the incorporation of short breaks to check for understanding during class. These breaks may include a short review, a quiz, or allowing for a designated question time. (For additional examples of potential cognitive ramps for presentation see Figure 12.1.)

Additionally, Tal applies the UDL representation principle in her courses in several ways. For example, she incorporates both auditory and visual information in all presentations (refers to perception) by including main bullet points and, at times, graphic representation or illustrative video clips. Such presentations often help students stay focused in class. However, as Dana's reading level is insufficient to follow a textual presentation Tal has to ensure that she incorporates visual non-textual representation (e.g pictures, images, icons etc.), video clips or animation to emphasize all main points. In addition, bearing Dana in mind, Tal allows students to take audio recording of the class. This proves to be an effective measure in supporting Dana's learning process, and other students report that it provides an effective measure in addition or instead of taking notes.

Another example relates to clarifying vocabulary and constructs used throughout the course (referring to language and symbols). Tal applies various measures to ensure students understanding of professional constructs: when first introducing a professional term, she provides a simple explanation and writes the term on the board with a short definition. She also translates such terms into Hebrew (as professional OT jargon is often in English while she teaches in Hebrew); and encourages the students to gradually accumulate and develop their own thesaurus. Again, bearing Dana in mind Tal slightly broadens her vocabulary range, providing explanations also for generally complex non-professional words such as "reasonable" which she explains as the ability of a child to perform an action effectively without having to invest a lot of effort (automatically). She adds some visual representation for complex terms and tries to repeat her explanation of constructs not only the first-time students encounter them but rather throughout the course.

> **Reflection**
>
> * Are you applying any cognitive ramps for representation in your practice?
> * If you do, are they in the form of individual accommodations or can all stakeholders benefit from them?

At the end of the course, Dana reported creating a thesaurus that she can understand and follow.

Providing multiple means of action and expression is the third major UDL principle. The action and expression guideline is based on the understanding that students differ in how they best express their knowledge and the acknowledgment of individual differences in preferred modes of action within learning environments. While beneficial for all learners, for students with cognitive disabilities it might be crucial to allow sufficient thinking, processing and response time. It is especially important as a lack of immediate response often does not represent the lack of knowledge and understanding, and therefore wait time is necessary if we want to allow these students to participate in class and express themselves. Other important measures include providing clear, plain language instructions for class assignments, tests and all other class requirements. Providing alternative instructions or test options, for example via voice or video file, can allow non-fluent readers to maximize performance.

Tal applies the action and expression principle in her courses in several ways. For example, while the child development class is theoretical and usually Socratic in nature, providing multiple means of expression within class (referring to expression and communication) allows students to more fully engage and express their knowledge. Tal encourages the students to express their interests and accumulating knowledge through discussions, interactive questioning and measures such as think-pair-share. She also incorporates interactive exercises such as fine-motor challenges, and short quizzes using Kahoot or Socrative (referring to expression and physical action). However, bearing Dana in mind, Tal makes sure that even with these various activities and measures she keeps a very clear lesson outline, reminding students at the beginning of each lesson and throughout the class about study objectives and their position in the cumulative learning process. In addition, while employing measures such as Kahoot, she instructs the students to work in pairs. This enables Dana to not only participate despite her lack of reading ability, but also provides an opportunity for social interaction, which was one of her goals.

Another example was elaborating on learning strategies (referring to executive functions). From the beginning of the semester Tal involved the students in an ongoing discussion of learning strategies that can improve their learning during the course. This strategy is built on asking questions and is discovery-driven, so that the students themselves think about possible answers and the lecturer only supplements with additional ideas. In addition, about mid semester, Tal leads the students into a discussion about test preparation, and coping with test anxiety. Throughout these discussions, Tal tries to ensure that Dana provides her own insights by allowing ample contemplating time and breaking the discussion into small, clear and manageable sections. Indeed, other, less outspoken students also find their voices given the more relaxed atmosphere.

Reflection

- Are you applying any cognitive ramps for action and expression in your practice?
- If you do, are they in the form of individual accommodations or can all stakeholders benefit from them?

Conclusion

The development of UDL as an inclusive educational model is much further along than other educational models in encompassing people with disabilities. Yet it is far from complete. When it comes to students with cognitive disabilities some questions are still pending, mainly in terms of the differentiation between UDL and individual supports. Indeed, some individual supports and accommodations might always be required but their scope reduces as the implementation of UDL principles becomes more prominent. Moreover, we propose that the incorporation of cognitive ramps into the UDL knowledge base would benefit not only students with cognitive disabilities, but the educational process of all students at large.

Reflection

- Having read the chapter, what would you say are the main cognitive ramps for academic teaching?
- Reflecting on your own educational experience, to what extent would you say that you are currently applying cognitive ramps?
- Can you think of one additional cognitive ramp that might be beneficial to add to your educational practice?

Additional conceptual questions:

- Is cognitive accessibility always beneficial or might it compromise academic standards?
- To what extent are cognitive ramps within a UDL educational context suffice for the inclusion of students with intellectual disabilities in mainstream education? Or would individual supports always be necessary for such inclusion?
- Where do we draw the line between UDL and cognitive accessibility?

References

Grigal, M., Dwyre, A., & Davis, H. (2006). *Transition Services for Students Aged 18–21 with Intellectual Disabilities in College and Community Settings: Models and Implications of Success* (NCSET Information Brief, Vol. 5, 5). Minneapolis, MN: Institute for Community Integration.

Grigal, M., & Hart, D. (2010). *Think College! Postsecondary Education Options for Students with Intellectual Disabilities.* Baltimore, MD: Brookes.

Hart, D., Grigal, M., Sax, C., Martinez, D., & Will, M. (2006). Postsecondary education options for students with intellectual disabilities. *Research to Practice*, 45.

Hart, D., Mele-McCarthy, J., Pasternack, R. H., Zimbrich, K., & Parker, D. R. (2004). Community college: A pathway to success for youth with learning, cognitive, and intellectual disabilities in secondary settings. *Education and Training in Developmental Disabilities*, 54–66.

Moore, E. J. (2015). Postsecondary inclusion for individuals with an intellectual disability and its effects on employment. *Journal of Intellectual Disabilities*, 19, 130–148.

Officer, A., & Posarac, A. (2011). *World Report on Disability.* Malta: World Health Organization & The World Bank.

Raue, K., & Lewis, L. (2011). Students with disabilities at degree-granting postsecondary institutions. National Center for Education Statistics, US Department of Education, *Statistical Analysis Report*, 18. Washington, District of Columbia: Department of Education.

Rimon-Greenspan, H., Tenne-Rinde, M., Avidan-Ziv, O., & Yalon-Chamovitz, S. (2018). Working on it: Cognitive accessibility guidelines for the workplace. *A Matter of Approach*, 22, 25–34.

Rose, D. H., & Meyer, A. (2002). *Teaching Every Student in the Digital Age: Universal Design for Learning.* Alexandria, VA: Association for Supervision and Curriculum Development.

Ross, J. (2012). Postsecondary education and independent living outcomes of persons with autism and intellectual disability. *Journal of Postsecondary Education and Disability*, 26, 337–351.

Smith, F. A., Grigal, M., & Sulewski, J. S. (2012). Postsecondary education and employment outcomes for transition-age youth with and without disabilities: A secondary analysis of American Community Survey data. *Think College Insight Brief*, 15, 1–4.

Yalon-Chamovitz, S., Shach, R., Avidan-Ziv, O., & Tenne-Rinde, M. R. (2015). The call for cognitive ramps. *Work*, 53(2), 455–456.

Chapter 13

From teaching content to teaching students

UDL as a vehicle for improving curriculum and praxis design

Eric Moore

Case study

Professor McElroy is passionate about art history. You can hear it in conversations that often begin as a casual remark and – time allowing – end at the bottom of strong coffee mugs sometimes hours later. Professor McElroy feels fortunate to be able to teach at a high research output institution, where he can dedicate considerable portions of his time to research, exploration, and publication relevant to his field.

Professor McElroy likes working with students (especially those that show budding enthusiasm for art history), but – if he was being honest – he would not say that he particularly enjoys teaching them. In particular, he feels he could do without his annual semester rotation into teaching a general education course. Finding students who share his passion for his subject is challenging in those de-personalized lecture halls.

He is often frustrated by his students' overt expressions of boredom in his lectures, which manifests in frequent early attrition. And, for those who survive past course drop cutoff dates, he sees heavy absenteeism, escapism with technology, and poor feedback on his course evaluations.

His students' work, likewise, is generally mediocre at best. As such, he has had to lower his standards for what to expect of them to prevent giving poor grades to everyone.

This perpetuates a vicious cycle for both Professor McElroy and the students; both parties continue to lower their expectations of the other. With a shortage of graduate assistant support to take over the class, Professor McElroy is looking for some way to change the trajectory of this blighted spot in his otherwise enjoyable and successful career.

Introduction

In the 21st century, higher education institutes (HEIs) have been criticized for emphasizing graduation rates as a primary metric. As these rates have increased, some have suggested that this trend is potentially resulting from lowered standards rather than increased quality (Bok, 2017). The emphasis on graduation rates has been rewarded by governments and ranking systems. For example, the widely used US News "Best College Rankings" (US News, 2017) ranks HEIs based on retention and graduation rates as 30% of the overall score (spread over two categories); a further 30% is calculated based on school resources, which may be an indirect measure of retention (Morse, Brooks, & Mason, 2017). No measure or weighting is given to direct measures of quality.

This has raised the specter that HEIs may be graduating more students than ever before at the expense of quality; that is: higher education graduates may be less prepared for careers than ever before, even as HEIs are being praised for higher graduation rates. Indeed, Bok (2017) reports that "Employers complain that many graduates they hire are deficient in basic skills such as writing, problem solving and critical thinking that college leaders and their faculties consistently rank among the most important goals of an undergraduate education." How can UDL practitioners in higher education seek to address this issue?

As UDL practitioners, we believe that UDL simultaneously increases the rigor of learning experiences and outcomes *and* equips students to do the work of learning more efficiently and effectively. As a result, UDL environments may be experienced as subjectively more accessible and engaging while outcomes are objectively strengthened.

There has already been a global trend toward improving the quality of higher education (Groen, 2017; Hayes, Wynyard, & Mandal, 2017; Tam, 2001). For example, the international Organisation for Economic Co-operation and Development (OECD) submitted a report in 2010 to document quality enhancement initiatives at universities around the globe in the context of increasing societal concern about the quality of higher education programs (Fabrice, 2010). UDL steps into this drive and gives a framework to bring ideas for educational improvement to fruition.

Facilitating quality improvement in higher education

One critical aspect of improving quality in higher education may be to increase the focus placed on students themselves. This notion is somewhat radical in many higher education systems (especially large, research-oriented institutions), wherein faculty are hired, promoted, and tenured based on their focus on research output and grant acquisition rather than a focus on their students (Gallup & Svare, 2015). This is not to say that faculty in such settings cannot, or do not, engage in quality teaching, but that doing so is not always required or significantly supported in the structures of higher education.

Therefore, improvement – if it is to occur systematically – must include top-down re-envisioning of the value structures in higher education. This point is not lost in the larger global discussion around higher education, but as Fabrice (2010) shared with reference to the OECD, this is only one part of the equation. Rather successful approaches to improve quality are complex and iterative. They are at once reflective of both grassroots creativity and administrative policy support, such approaches also utilize quality assurance programming, and often follow a project-style approach (Fabrice, 2010). This provides a comprehensive vision for systemic change.

This chapter will focus on just one aspect of the OECD vision for systemic change: grassroots creativity. This emphasizes the immediate role that individual instructors may have on facilitating change in their own classrooms. As a UDL specialist at a large high research output university in the United States, I recognize that the iterative nature of system change is often slow and the best reach we – as most faculty and staff in higher education have – is localized to individuals and small groups (e.g., departments). Because stories of success within an institution are more likely to affect change than reports in academic literature (Fabrice, 2010), these interventions have both immediate value (for individual classes of students) and longer term strategic value (for changing institutional culture).

Pragmatically, systemic change often begins with a single story. Facilitating a shift toward student-centrism via UDL in the classroom of Professor McElroy may ignite change first in his own practice, then in influence with his immediate colleagues, department, college, university, system and so on (Moore, Smith, Hollingshead, & Wojcik, 2018). Just as student-centrism involves lowering our focus from the content itself to the individual learner (as a means of getting to the curriculum), bringing about this cultural shift begins by lowering our focus from policy and systems to individual faculty and courses (as a means of getting to systemic change).

Reflection

- Have you seen change in your institution come from students or individual faculty?
- How might you draw recognition to practices in your own or a colleagues' classroom to amplify the message of student-centrism through UDL?

Using UDL for student-centrism in curriculum design

Discussion of the construct of student-centered appears as early as the mid-20th century as a juxtaposition to "teacher-centrism" and a means of education reform. For example, "student-centrism" appears in Faw's (1949) report, which presented student-centrism as a "psychotherapeutic method of teaching psychology." Despite its longevity as an education construct (or maybe because of it), "student-centrism" remains a somewhat nebulously defined construct. Broadly, student-centrism (cf. learner centrism, personalized learning) refers to a mindset and a set of approaches to teaching and learning that are tailored to the unique needs, interests and backgrounds of individual learners.

The practice of student-centrism is not always the norm in higher education, especially when juxtaposed with "content-centrism" or "instructor centrism," which are far more normalized. This bears out in the classic structures of university programs (structured around "general education" curriculum and "four-year degrees"), university learning environments (e.g., lecture halls with bolted furniture focusing on an instructor and projection screen), and hiring/promotion practices (which tend to focus on faculty's research and grant winning accomplishments far more than student outcomes). These classic fixtures of higher education form a powerful status quo that cannot be overtaken with nebulous concepts (as "student-centrism" has been), even if they are given theoretical value.

One critical contribution of UDL in relation to student-centrism is that it offers a coherent, research based, practical framework for the design of student-centric experiences. In fact, UDL may present the ideal approach to student-centrism (McClaskey, 2017).

Rather than trying to fully individualize instruction for each student (a challenging and possibly counter-productive feat), UDL calls for the design of learning experiences that center on clear and rigorous learning outcomes, identification of anticipated barriers, and facilitates the development of flexible assessments, methods and materials to support a wide range of students to achieve these objectives (cf. Figure 13.1).

This process often begins with *increasing* the rigor of existing objectives in a course for which UDL is being employed for redesign.

Example case

For example, in a recent course review, an instructor of a 500-level nursing course had as a course objective: "*Compare and contrast* study designs used in epidemiologic investigations."

Compare and contrast is an *analytical* objective, but we decided that it was more valuable for the students to *end* with the ability to evaluate designs, not simply analyze them. Thus, we changed the objective to read: "*Choose* an appropriate study design for epidemiologic investigations and *argue* why, in context, the chosen design is the most appropriate."

This objective is more complex, but also more compelling and more valuable in the context of professional nursing for which the students were preparing. The next steps involved thinking of ways that the learners could argue using flexible tools of communication (i.e., we didn't care how they argued, as this was not the objective. They could write, present, or speak their argument if one of those allowed them to better articulate their perspective).

Then, we devised ways to develop the learners' skills to the point of being able to utilize such high-level cognition. This meant adding more real-life case studies and discussion to the otherwise knowledge-oriented textbook readings. Some of these cases didn't have clear correct answers, and ensuing discussions and debates in class offered rich opportunities for the instructor to have her students explicate their *thinking* and to be pushed toward new resources that they could use going forward both in class and their careers.

All of this wonderful change began by recognizing that her students *could* and *should* achieve more lofty goals, and then using UDL to build options and scaffolds into the curriculum to enable her students to succeed.

In a UDL-designed learning experience, the most effective and scalable experiences are those in which the needs of "students at the margins" are accounted for from the beginning ("students at the margins" refers to those who vary significantly from what is considered "normal" or "average" in terms of why and how they learn and how they express themselves). This reflects the UDL tenet that *what is necessary for some usually benefits everyone* (Meyer, Rose, & Gordon, 2014). More on the intersection of UDL and instructional design may be found in Chapter 7 in this book.

In addition to providing a design frame, UDL also contributes to the construct of student-centrism by emphasizing the role of UDL in the development of "expert learners"; that is, learners who are purposeful and motivated, knowledgeable and resourceful, strategic and goal directed (Meyer, Rose, & Gordon, 2014). Essentially, UDL claims to not only support students in mastering the content at hand, but in mastering learning itself. UDL gives shape to student-centrism and may make it more reasonably attainable. It also provides a way to meet an outspoken need for higher quality education in higher education. Despite this, in my experience UDL remains largely unknown and unused in higher education. There is need for stories change among individual faculty and individual classes.

CAST | Until learning has no limits   Guide to Designing Your UDL Unit/Lesson

GOALS

Standard: _____ _____ _____ Goal/Objective: _____ _____ _____	✓ *Check:* ▫ *Is your goal clear and specific?* ▫ *Are the means flexible?* ▫ *If not, how can you scaffold?* ▫ *Where will the goal be posted?* ▫ *How will students revisit the goal throughout the lesson?*

ASSESSMENT

How will you know if students have achieved the goal? _____ _____ _____ _____ What assessments will you use? _____ _____ _____ _____	✓ *Check:* ▫ *What will "success" look like?* ▫ *Have you offered multiple means for students to demonstrate success?* ▫ *Does the assessment directly measure realization of the goal?* ▫ *Do you have options for both formative and summative assessment?*

BARRIERS

What barriers can you anticipate? _____ _____ _____ _____ _____	✓ *Check:* ▫ *Are there barriers in the context (location, grouping, noise level), presentation (oral, written) or activities (writing, speaking, planning)?*

Figure 13.1a Guide to designing your UDL unit/lesson (CAST, n.d.)

CAST | Until learning has no limits   Guide to Designing Your UDL Unit/Lesson

---

~~ VARIABILITY

What are your options for engagement?
- _____
- _____
- _____
- _____

✓ **Check:**
- Do these options address the anticipated barriers?
- Are there options for choice, relevancy, and minimizing distractions?
- Options for balancing perceived demands and resources?
- Options for mastery-oriented feedback? Collaboration? Self-reflection?

What are your options for representation?
- _____
- _____
- _____
- _____

✓ **Check:**
- Do these options address the anticipated barriers?
- Are there options for audio/visual/display of info?
- Are there options to access language, math, and symbols?
- Are there options to build background knowledge and highlight key patterns?

What are your options for Action and Expression?
- _____
- _____
- _____
- _____
- _____

✓ **Check:**
- Do these options address the anticipated barriers?
- Are there options for physical action?
- Are there options for multiple communication tools?
- Are there options for varying levels of support?
- Are there options for goal setting, strategy development, and self-monitoring?

Figure 13.1b (Continued)

Reflection

- What ways might student-centrism through UDL provide ways to increase content mastery in your discipline?
- Traditionally, designing for students "on the margins" has been deemed impractical. How do you see UDL helping to address this barrier?

Meeting instructors where they are

The first step in a shift toward student-centrism in the context of a higher education classroom or department must – ironically – be to focus on the instructors.

It is true that the goal of UDL is to develop expert learners; that is, learners who are purposeful and motivated, knowledgeable and resourceful, strategic and goal directed (Meyer, Rose, & Gordon, 2014). In this context, instructors are facilitators of the process students follow to achieve academic and learning mastery.

It may be that too much of the burden is placed on instructors who almost surely earned their degrees in settings that do not reflect the environmental qualities promoted by UDL. In other words, it may be unrealistic – if not unfair – to expect colleagues like Professor McElroy to shoulder the responsibility of being a UDL teacher when he has never had the opportunity to be a UDL student. For social cognitivists, teaching most naturally is learned by observations. That is, "teachers teach as they have been taught; not how they have been taught to teach" (Blume, 1971).

In absence of direct experience, it may be too easy for instructors to brush off the claims and opportunities (and efforts) promoted by UDL as "just another edufad," "unreasonably demanding," or even "detrimental to students" by reducing the perception of rigor in higher education (more on the last point follows).

When introducing faculty to UDL intervention as a means of student-centrism, it is critical to practice what we preach. Teaching UDL and its theory and practice is, of course, to teach content. To move into explaining it to faculty or a department with generic material and methods is to undermine the message even as we deliver it.

When working with faculty like Professor McElroy, it is critical to meet them where they are. This often means listening closely as faculty describe their needs and the barriers that they face and/or they perceive their students face. It means carefully reviewing their curriculum to understand their objectives and helping to identify potential mismatches among objectives and assessments as well as spotting opportunities to enhance flexibility in materials and methods.

Barriers are an idea that most people understand very well. When speaking to faculty, it is common to hear them speak of "digital distractions," or "lack of organizational skills" as barriers to effective learning. It is great that faculty are identifying such barriers. The role of a UDL advocate here is to guide the faculty to conceptually transplant barriers as being "student problems" to being "environmental limitations." If one considers one's students to be lazy or unmotivated, then there may be a sense that there is nothing that the instructor can do about that, and that it is, frankly, not the instructor's responsibility. This is a common mindset. But it is also a mindset that allows barriers to remain indefinitely. Instead, it is worth exploring how the barrier can be re-articulated as environmental such that the instructor *does* have ability to affect change. Consider how some common barriers can be re-framed in Table 13.1.

Table 13.1 Reframing barriers from student problems to environmental limitations

Situation	Student Problem Perspective	Environmental Limitation Perspective
Students in a morning class are falling asleep when the instructor dims the lights and begins a PowerPoint lecture.	Students are lazy, unfocused, stay out too late the night before morning class.	Dimming the lights and lecturing is an ineffective way to engage learners in morning classes.
Students frequently use their laptops to engage in off-task behavior (e.g., social media, shopping) during class.	Students don't know how to manage themselves with technology. They are irresponsible and unfocused.	It is important to use (and not use) technology intentionally in class. Students may need routines and strategies for when and how to use technology as a tool for learning.
Essays related to understanding of topics studied in class are of poor quality.	Students lack knowledge from the learning and/ or lack skill in essay composition.	Essay writing is irrelevant to the content and objectives. Students may be provided options to maximize their ability to communicate their understanding.

When speaking of offering flexibility, particularly with regards to assessment, faculty often balk. It is often suggested that "students need to know how to write essays" or "speak in public." That is certainly true in *some* disciplines and fields, but not all. When it *is* important, these skills can be objectives and students can be supported in developing those skills (instead of just being assessed by them). In this way, "flexibility" doesn't necessarily mean providing an alternate form of assessment, but can also mean providing strategies for how to prepare for and deliver a public address.

When instructors feel listened to and their questions and concerns can be aired and addressed, early barriers that would preclude meaningful engagement are reduced. In this way, we use UDL to model UDL and do so explicitly to foster transfer.

Sharing an idea: engaging instructors in professional development

When delivering professional development related to UDL to a department or small group of instructors, it may be valuable to open with an activity to engage them and make a point by way of experience.

One application, when speaking of using UDL for assessment design, has been to tell the room to begin by making sure we are all using shared language. I suggest that the word "assessment" may mean different things to different people, and thus it may be worthwhile to explicitly define what *we* mean when we say "assessment."

I tell them that to do this efficiently, I want them to all use their laptops or smartphones to record themselves defining "assessment" and to then email or link me to their short videos. I give them two minutes to do so.

After they laugh uncomfortably, not sure if I am totally serious, they usually try and struggle through the two minutes, with varying degrees of success usually ranging from completing nothing at all to completing an uncomfortable and poorly made video that they would rather not share.

I follow up with the questions:

- What did we just assess?
- Was the assessment valid?
- How could we make it more valid?

We then discuss how this experience of "wringing" their knowledge or ability through a narrow means of assessment that wasn't something they felt comfortable or strong in is an experience that many students face when presented with multiple choice tests, essays, or presentations. We discussed how assessments of basic knowledge and understanding lend to so many options for expression, but we rarely move past those few methods that some students will invariably find uncomfortable and limiting. And we discuss how they may provide options to facilitate greater achievement for their students and validity of their assessments going forward.

Such an experience takes time. Ten to 15 minutes of my workshop will elapse in this warm-up for a point that I could simply express in 20 seconds as "assessments that provide options are more valid and provide for greater student success." But it is one thing to be told, and a very different thing have an experience. Indeed, this approach provides a powerful introduction to UDL by enabling faculty to *experience* the problems of narrow means of assessment without support and to clearly see how the provision of options could have enabled them to more effectively express themselves; a concept that can be transferred to their own classrooms.

Facing the objection: regarding rigor

One common objection that instructors, such as Professor McElroy, raise when presented with UDL specifically, and student-centrism in general, is that the shift away from content centrism will reduce the rigor of the learning. This objection is common in higher education and it is so closely related to our discussion of student-centrism versus content centrism in this chapter, that it warrants further exploration.

Does focusing learning on the students above-and-beyond focusing on the content reduce the rigor of the course?

This is such an important concern.

Higher education is intended to be a place in which learners come to greatly expand and enhance their knowledge and skills on their way to being professionals. Any intervention that includes more people simply by lowering the standard should absolutely be challenged and most likely dismissed as a poor fit for the context of higher education.

The good news is: UDL absolutely does not reduce the rigor of curriculum. In fact, the implementation of UDL is intended to enable and encourage greater rigor than what is afforded by traditional instruction. Let's explore this claim.

Consider this scenario. A professor of biology, Dr. Xavier, starts a new course on molecular biology with high hopes in terms of the kind of content mastery she expects of her students. She carefully arranges the curriculum, structuring from foundational content to advanced concepts. Then she arranges this content through selecting textbook chapter reading order, and develops associated lectures and PowerPoints. The first semester comes and classes begin.

When she is five weeks into the course and mid-term tests scores are coming in, most students aren't achieving the rigorous goals that Dr. Xavier had so painstakingly prepared.

At this point, we often conclude that the students enrolled in the class are not "strong enough" academically to handle molecular biology to the degree that Dr. Xavier has intended.

This view presents Dr. Xavier with limited options. For example, she can:

1   go on with the course anyway, implicitly or explicitly sending the message that students who cannot keep up don't really belong in this class/field, and/or
2   reduce the expectations placed on students (either by reducing the volume or difficulty of content or by loosening passing.

Dr. Xavier's approach and the situation that she faces are common in higher education. The decision she must make as to how to respond (or not respond) is a frequent frustration.

For many, if we may speak frankly, this is simply the "natural selection" of higher education. Learning microbiology is tough. There may be a perception that some "have what it takes" and some, unfortunately, do not. That's life. But wait!

While it may be the case that not every student taking Dr. Xavier's course is destined for a job in microbiology, I suggest that we often come to the conclusion of who is "in" and who is "out" too quickly. In this scenario, we are not looking at "who can learn microbiology," but "who can learn microbiology the way Dr. Xavier happens to be teaching?" We are not examining "who can practice microbiology," but "who can demonstrate knowledge of microbiology in the form of a scantron multiple choice exam that Dr. Xavier happens to prefer?"

Recognizing that form and content are inseparable is important for our discussion. When we talk about "rigor," what exactly do we mean here? The form or the content or both?

UDL is often understood as a design frame (see Chapter 7: Instructional design with UDL: addressing learning variability in college courses). Through the UDL perspective, instructional design involves looking at each aspect of instructional design and delivery including goals/objectives, assessments, materials, and methods. UDL practitioners believe that rigor is essential in the goals, objectives, and assessments. Methods and materials, in the UDL framework do not necessarily need to be rigorous; they need to be effective in supporting learners as they grow toward mastery of content and skills. This is a key cultural change that UDL brings to higher education.

Indeed, there are different views under the surface of conversations surrounding rigor in higher education, and these implicitly different views may interfere with clear communication. Let's juxtapose rigor of form (methods and materials) and rigor as content (outcomes), for a moment.

- **Rigor as methods and materials.** Some people may – consciously or unconsciously – associate rigor with methods and materials. In this view, maintaining rigor may translate into keeping a challenging textbook as a primary vehicle of content exposition. It may mean insisting that students write essays to demonstrate content mastery. It may mean a desire to maintain the oral-only lecture as the driver of instruction. In this setting, there is an implicit or explicit sense that students who cannot learn via lecture and textbook reading, who cannot write strong essays or perform on multiple choice tests are frankly not college material. While rigor is commonly expressed in these terms, I suggest that this has little to do with rigor and much more to do with inertia.
- **Rigor as outcome.** There is another way to think about rigor in higher education courses: rigor of outcome. In this view, creating or maintaining rigor may translate to setting lofty and professionally relevant student outcomes (what they will know/retain in future employment, be able to do/ transfer to real world applications). Note that this understanding rigor has not yet made statement about how students learn or how they express their knowledge and skill. It is simply a view of outcome. In this setting, there is an implicit or explicit sense that how we teach and assess should support

students in achieving the desired outcomes. There is no need to stick with certain methods or materials if options are available that would enhance students' ability to reach the goal.

Defining what we mean by rigor is an important check. Often, someone will say that they want rigorous outcomes, but in further conversation it becomes clear that this belies a desire to maintain materials and methods, as with Dr. Xavier. UDL is not compatible with the view that one must maintain traditional methods and materials; it is, however, instrumental for enhancing rigor of outcome.

In the case of Dr. Xavier, the confounding of the two types of rigor becomes clear. Explicitly, Dr. Xavier has set high outcome objectives for her students. That's wonderful. Implicitly, and perhaps unconsciously, Dr. Xavier has assumed that college-level courses should be delivered with "rigorous" methods of learning and assessment (i.e., traditional forms). Because of this, she may be prematurely concluding that her students are unable to achieve her rigorous outcomes when they struggled to reach and/or demonstrate those outcomes via traditional channels. The result is that Dr. Xavier is faced with a difficult lose-lose choice. Ironically, in her desire to preserve rigor (of methods), Dr. Xavier must reactively reduce rigor (of outcome) either by excluding who achieves the outcomes or by scaling back the outcomes themselves.

In addition to losses to course rigor, there are also personal and communal loses here. What a tragedy, for example, that there may have been some students in the class that would have made wonderful molecular biologists, but left the program after eeking by with a "D" in the class for reasons that – in fact – had nothing to do with their capacity to be microbiologists.

Re-envisioning with student-centrism via UDL. The same story would play out very differently should Dr. Xavier plan with and implement UDL to shift the focus of her instruction to her students' variability *proactively*.

Rather than reducing the rigor (outcome) of the course, many UDL experts believe that rigorous outcomes are requisite to applying UDL. If UDL doesn't reduce the rigor of the outcome, it increases the ways in which students may achieve the outcome.

The UDL framework involves thoughtful, intentional backwards planning (from objectives to assessments to methods and materials), with a conscious reflection on anticipated variability among learners. The implementation of UDL draws from a collection of well-established best practices, intentionally choosing ways to design flexible methods and materials to address learner variability en route to the stated objective.

When students can spend less time navigating rigid and inhospitable learning environments and assessments, more time and energy remains to focus on meaningful content and skill building.

Reflection

- What barriers to engagement, comprehension, or action-taking do you see or anticipate when it comes to promoting student-centrism through UDL?
- Do you agree that proactively addressing barriers in preparing faculty, staff, and administrators to implement UDL is necessary both pragmatically and as form of modeling?
- Is this approach utilized for other forms of professional development in your context? Why or why not?

Conclusion: the beginning

All the pieces are coming together. There is need for improving the quality of education in IHEs all around the world. That quality must be measured in terms of actual, rigorous student learning from among the diverse body of students now attending higher education. The best way to help students grow in their academic knowledge and skills is to shift focus from content centrism to student-centrism, and UDL provides a powerful framework to actualize this necessary shift.

Because it is instructors like Professor McElroy and Xavier who will be the ones who will (or won't) ultimately facilitate a UDL learning environment, it is essential that we facilitate buy-in from individual faculty prior to attempting any serious interventions, which we hope to set as a model to other faculty and later the department, college, university, and system.

Professor McElroy was passionate about his subject matter and frustrated that he didn't seem able to develop passion among his students, likewise. Dr. Xavier was organized and dedicated as an instructor, but struggled to maintain her rigorous expectations in the face of poor student performance.

Fortunately, Professor McElroy and Xavier's stories end happily.

Both Professor McElroy and Dr. Xavier were passionate about their subjects and had high hopes and expectations for their students. Those are wonderful attributes in a teacher! Learning about UDL gave them the tools to transfer their enthusiasm and good intentions into designing learning environments and experiences that enabled their students to succeed.

After learning about UDL, both Professor McElroy and Xavier began following the same process. Using the UDL framework, they started by articulating rigorous objectives. For Professor McElroy, this meant increasing the rigor of his course. Students wouldn't just *know* and *understand* information through his lectures, they would *explore* and *evaluate* art in historical context. It became quickly clear that lecture and note taking wouldn't allow students to reach these objectives; they would have to be given opportunity to be active learners. With planning, Professor McElroy's role changed from "lecturer" to "facilitator" and his students changed from "listeners" to "participants" as they learned and constructed understanding together. His assessments began shifting from multiple choice inventories of names and dates to creative expressions that enabled students to weave philosophy, history, sociology, and art together as they showcased their discoveries individually or in groups.

Xavier similarly realized that to maintain the rigor of her objectives without losing students, she'd need to provide more flexibility in how they learned and how they expressed their understanding. She began a practice of reflecting on common barriers students faced in her class or in certain topics and began proactively providing scaffolds and supports where needed. For example, she noted that students struggled with the heavy reading loads in her class; she began presenting these readings as both text and audio files so students could play to their strengths and needs when consuming content out of class. She also sought to motivate this reading by converting lecture over the same topic into interactive activities through which students would apply the ideas about which they just read about or listened. She also taught them how to use "shared notes" in Google Docs, so that students in small groups could collectively contribute to notes and benefit from each others' takeaways and their combined intelligence. She was thrilled with the gains she began witnessing in her students and the outcomes they were able to achieve once they were able to learn in ways that worked for them.

Professor McElroy and Xavier learned that UDL provides a vehicle to move past teaching content to teaching students. When students are enabled and equipped as expert learners, content learning becomes much more effective and efficient.

References

Blume, R. (1971). Humanizing teacher education. *The Phi Delta Kappan*, 52(7), 411–415.

Bok, D. (2017). How to improve the quality of higher education. *Inside Higher Ed*. Retrieved from www.insidehighered.com/

CAST (n.d.) *Guide to designing your UDL unit/lesson*. CAST UDL Lesson Builder. Retrieved from http://lessonbuilder.cast.org/ accessed 16th December 2018.

Fabrice, H. (2010). *Learning Our Lesson Review of Quality Teaching in Higher Education: Review of Quality Teaching in Higher Education*. Paris: OECD Publishing.

Faw, V. (1949). A psychotherapeutic method of teaching psychology. *American Psychologist*, 4(4), 104–109. http://dx.doi.org/10.1037/h0060072

Gallup, G., & Svare, B. B. (2015). The undesirable consequences of the growing pressure on faculty to get grants. *Inside Higher Ed*. (n.d.). Retrieved from www.insidehighered.com/

Groen, J. F. (2017). Engaging in enhancement: Implications of participatory approaches in higher education quality assurance. *Collected Essays on Learning and Teaching*, 10(0), 89–100.

Hayes, D., Wynyard, R., & Mandal, L. (2017). The McDonaldization of higher education. Retrieved from https://derby.openrepository.com/derby/handle/10545/621759

McClaskey, K. (2017). *Personalization and UDL: A perfect match. Educational Leadership*. Retrieved from www.ascd.org/

Meyer, A., Rose, D., & Gordon, D. (2014). *Universal Design for Learning: Theory and Practice*. Wakefield, MA: CAST.

Moore, E. J., Smith, F. G., Hollingshead, A., & Wojcik, B. (2018). Voices from the field: Implementing and scaling-up universal design for learning in teacher preparation programs. *Journal of Special Education Technology*, 33(1), 40–53. https://doi.org/10.1177/0162643417732293

Morse, R., Brooks E., & Mason M. (2017). How U.S. news calculated the 2018 best college rankings. *U.S. News & World Report*. Retrieved from www.usnews.com/

Tam, M. (2001). Measuring quality and performance in higher education. *Quality in Higher Education*, 7(1), 47–54. https://doi.org/10.1080/13538320120045076

U.S. News (2017). Best colleges. *U.S. News & World Report*. Retrieved from www.usnews.com/

Chapter 14

Integration through collaboration

Building strategic faculty partnerships to shift minds and practices

Jodie Black and Ruth Fraser

Case study

Jonathan is a first-year student in the Electrical Engineering Technology program at Canada College. He loves learning about electricity, and after he graduates from Canada College with his diploma, he plans to continue studies at a four-year university to complete his degree. In his courses, he excels in lab components and his applied work but struggles in lectures because he finds it difficult to comprehend the content while focusing on taking notes.

Jonathan has tried talking to Sylvia, the faculty member, about having a note taker, but senses her reluctance. To help him navigate the situation, Jonathan contacts Nicole, who is an Accessibility Services advisor. Nicole has been rethinking her approach to faculty conversations, especially in how she discusses Universal Design for Learning, and is excited to try a new approach with Sylvia.

Nicole reaches out to Sylvia to have a conversation about Jonathan's request, and how they can best support his learning success in the course. Sylvia shares that she doesn't want to give Jonathan special treatment. If he has notes taken for him, the other students may want that too; then she is concerned that the students won't attend the lecture and it will impact their success in the course.

Introduction

In many Canadian colleges and universities, Accessibility Services (AS) have led institution-wide efforts to introduce and integrate Universal Design for

Learning (UDL) in order to improve accessibility. At the same time, legislation (such as the Accessibility for Ontarians with Disabilities in Ontario, Canada) and accessibility standards (such as the W3C Web Accessibility Initiative) are also focusing attention on accessible design, requiring efforts beyond those of accommodation in areas such as built environments, digital environments, and customer service. In higher education, AS teams recognize that what works for students with disabilities often works for all students, making them natural leaders of educational frameworks promoting accessible design such as Universal Design for Learning. Their dedication, leadership and partnership have helped make strides in this emerging and important field of practice.

UDL in higher education is in the early process of creating systemic change. And one of the significant evolutions from the early days of awareness building is that UDL is not only about accessibility, it's about developing expert learners. This shift from accessibility to learning expertise means that AS needs to promote UDL leadership in those responsible for teaching and learning. This is supported by the Concord Model for systemic UDL change which identifies eight components for change, including a redefined role for special educators (Rose, Meyer, Strangman, & Rappolt, 2002). AS needs to redefine their role not just as purveyors of accommodations and awareness building, but as campus collaborators with faculty to increase the systemic use of UDL. If we extend this model to the higher education context, AS can be considered to have the special educator's role and, as such, needs to redefine their UDL leadership as one of collaboration with and support of faculty. Since faculty are the primary curriculum authors and teachers, collaborating with them is critical for curriculum planning and problem solving. Collaboration with the Centres for Teaching and Learning (CTL), or equivalent, is another way to redefine the AS role as one of support for faculty-led UDL efforts and integration. Based on Kuh's focus on collaborative dialogue as driver of change, we propose that the AS role in UDL leadership involves leveraging faculty partnerships and conversations to shift minds and practices (Kezar, 2003).

To more effectively scale UDL and move beyond awareness, AS teams must build their practices to increase strategic leadership. A key part of this leadership is clearly articulating and stating the differences and intersections between accommodations, accessibility, and UDL – and why they matter. Conceptual distinctions are critical to UDL integration because how we think about things impacts how we do things (Berquist, Carey, Ralabate, & Sadara, 2017, p. 25). AS needs to lead the shifts in thinking and the clarification of UDL as more than a way to improve accessibility; it is a framework for curriculum development with the ultimate goal of developing expert learners. By making this distinction, it easily follows that creators of curriculum – faculty – lead UDL integration in teaching and learning. Clear language and concrete examples are essential factors in effective change and accurate use of the terms accommodation, accessibility, and UDL plays an important role in shifting faculty thinking and practices that form the foundations for a UDL approach. It is these shifts in thinking that underpin a UDL mindset that will help AS make sustainable change for UDL integration in higher education.

Reflection

- How do you understand and explain the intersection between accessibility and UDL?
- What do you believe are the most impactful ways for AS to partner with faculty to promote UDL integration? What are the least? What are some examples from your experience?
- How has your institution scaled ad hoc or individual UDL integration to a systemic adoption or implementation of UDL?

Intersections of accommodations, accessibility, and UDL

As AS teams redefine their role in systemic UDL integration, they are uniquely positioned to build a common understanding of the differences and intersections between accommodations, accessibility, and UDL. A common understanding is critical when building collaboration and diffusing leadership across teams. In this case, curriculum leadership rests primarily with faculty, accommodation leadership rests primarily with AS, and accessibility bridges both teams. Each team member needs to understand the conceptual and operational differences between these areas. So the journey begins with a shared understanding of these key terms.

This can be challenging, especially if, in the excitement and enthusiasm of UDL, the transformational aspects of the principles and the approach to design has been diluted in an urgency to adopt change. Common, but not fully developed, ways of talking about UDL might promote erroneous thinking – such as defining UDL as a single resource, activity, or method. Myths may also arise – such as the belief that if it's helping a student with a disability, it must be UDL. Critical aspects of UDL, such as the importance of proactive design with multiple options and choices for all students, can get overlooked in favor of finding an innovative solution for one student with a disability and inaccurately labeling it "UDL". This is where technological solutions, for example a Smart Pen used by a student with a disability, can be mistaken for UDL, even though it does not increase options for more than one student. Finally, disconnections from learning goals and curriculum can inadvertently occur – such as adding oral or visual options to a traditional writing assignment, without a clear understanding and match with the skills or knowledge the assessment is meant to measure. These misconceptions often place AS at the center of conversations where a clear and articulated understanding of the differences between accommodations, accessibility, and UDL is required to help guide faculty and other partners.

Table 14.1 highlights the important differences between accommodations, accessibility, and UDL. Despite legislation, organizational requirements, and common usage that may not make the same differentiations, the point here is that these three concepts are linked, but distinct; and that the distinctions are important to both service delivery and teaching and learning in higher education. Being transparent about the differences and clarifying language between partners is a necessary step and one that must be part of AS leadership and its redefined role. It must not be assumed that all the parties on the team share an understanding of these concepts, even if they are familiar with the terms. Here nuances matter greatly; when AS and faculty do not accurately share these nuances, it can impact realization of strategic goals and the student learning experience.

Let's consider Jonathan and his experience in the lecture components of his Electrical Engineering Technology program to further illustrate the differences between accommodations, accessibility, and UDL. If Nicole, his AS advisor, provides him with a note taker based on information about his auditory processing

Table 14.1 Comparing UDL, accessibility, and accommodation

	Universal Design for Learning	Accessibility	Accommodation
Purpose	Designing curricular experiences for the broadest range of learners to support expert learning	Identification and proactive removal or prevention of barriers such as physical, attitudinal, learning, social, technological, to individuals with disabilities	An individualized alteration to respond to or address or retrofit a barrier in the environment
Availability	Options available to all; driven by student choice	Available to all; may or may not increase choice	Available to some upon individual request
Leadership	Primary: Faculty Supporting: Students, AS	Shared: AS, Faculty, Student	Primary: AS Supporting: Students, Faculty
Policy and legislative framework	Guided by the UDL framework; curricular standards	Guided provincially by accessibility standards, such as the Accessibility for Ontarians with Disabilities Act	Guided by Human Rights Code

disorder – this would be an example of an accommodation. It is something only available to Jonathan because he identified a disability-related barrier. If Nicole worked with the faculty member, Sylvia, to set up a rotating or collaborative note taker in the classroom which gave all students in the class access to a set of notes – this would be an example of Accessibility. While access to these notes don't provide students with additional choice, they are made available to the whole class and proactively remove a task that may otherwise create a barrier to learning. If Sylvia were to provide students with choices for accessing course content (such as presentation slides, an audio recording of the lectures, live capture of smartboard diagrams, etc.) and demonstrated to students how they might use these resources to prepare for, participate in, and review classroom lectures – this would be an example of UDL.

While the distinction between accommodations and accessibility can be quite concretely described by which students it benefits (accommodations serve one student and accessibility serves many students) the distinction between accessibility and UDL is more subtle. Accessibility is focused on creating access to existing curriculum, but UDL intentionally focuses on curriculum design with the goal of developing expert learners. One could argue that Sylvia's act of sharing the presentation slides and audio recording of the lecture is an example of accessibility. However, demonstrating how it can be used as a learning tool, assisting students in planning, exploring, and evaluating learning – this moves it beyond the goal of access and into the realm of developing expert learners, the ultimate goal for all students. UDL cannot be achieved without accessibility, but attributes of accessibility can in some instances be realized without a systemic UDL approach. This is a critical point; one of the biggest risks of UDL being promoted as primarily a tool for accessibility is that its power as a framework for excellence in designing learning environments is limited. UDL is not simply a matter of access; it's about equity and experience. As Elliot Eisner wrote, "educational equity is much more than allowing students to cross the threshold of a school. It has to do with what students find after they do" (Eisner, 2013, p. 285) AS must clearly and consistently articulate how accommodation, accessibility and UDL intersect and differ in order to empower UDL leadership among faculty – and continue to lead accommodation and accessibility work.

Reflection

- When, in your experience, has it been important to differentiate between accommodations, accessibility, and UDL?
- What are some of the risks or benefits of having these terms used interchangeably?
- What language, examples, graphics have you found useful in making these differentiations?

Five shifts in thinking

In this redefined role, AS' UDL leadership must work to systemically build capacity in faculty to integrate UDL. In many cases, AS has worked to share teaching and learning practices with faculty in efforts to promote a UDL approach. While this may work in an ad hoc way with keen faculty, there are many faculty that do not adopt UDL at the mere suggestion. As a strategy for building capacity in faculty to integrate UDL, we propose AS contribute to laying the attitudinal foundations for UDL with faculty. By focusing on first shifting minds, practices will shift to align with the developing UDL mindset. Because faculty often cross paths with AS with a disorienting dilemma – like when Sylvia reaches out to Nicole – these dilemmas can often be an opportunity to transform thinking (Glickman, Gordon, & Ross-Gordon, 2014).

Based on our experiences in conversations with faculty, where the goal has been to introduce or develop a UDL mindset, we have identified the following five shifts in thinking. They are concrete yet flexible enough to be useful in identifying, selecting, and maximizing opportunities in both planned and unexpected, formal and informal conversations as summarized in Table 14.2, we work to shift from:.

1   medical to social model of disability,
2   learning labels to learning variability,
3   from response to design,
4   accessibility to expert learning,
5   ad hoc to intentionality.

The first shift in thinking is from the medical to social models of disability. In the medical view, disability exists as a deficit in the individual person; in the social view, disability exists more as a deficit in the environment. By viewing disability in the environment and not in an individual person, the onus to change is on the environment and the designers of that environment. Designers of space, such as architects, do not compel individuals using wheelchairs to be less dependent on a wheelchair; they create barrier-free spaces where an individual using a wheelchair can access the space in the same ways as an individual who is not using a wheelchair. In higher education, this view of disability shifts responsibility for solutions away from individual students with disabilities and special services – to those designing the learning environment. However, as shared by Costa-Renders in Chapter 9, it is important for designers to consult with students who can better inform their design processes. Accessibility Services are challenging themselves to make the changes necessary to ensure that their service delivery promotes this social view of disability, guided by such resources as Project SHIFT's Refocus (Funckes, Kroeger, Loewen, & Thornton, n.d.).

The second shift in thinking is from the idea of learning as a static to a variable ability. When learning is seen as a static ability, labels are seen as critical to providing information about how an individual learner differs from an "average" learner. In reality, learning is highly individual with every learner having a somewhat personal, rather than uni-dimensional, experience and learning profile. Todd Rose calls this the "jaggedness principle" and explains: "Just about any meaningful human characteristic – especially talent – consists of multiple dimensions. The problem is that when we're trying to measure talent, we frequently resort to the average, reducing our jagged talent to a single dimension like the score on a standardized test or grades or a job performance rating" (Rose, 2016, p. 84). Learning cannot be reduced to a specific "style" or "disability" – learning is highly individual and dynamic. Learning is also highly contextual and depends on the unique interaction between traits and the environment (Rose, 2016, p. 106). While a student may be highly participatory in group learning in one class, they may choose to listen and absorb lecture material in another class. Reframing the understanding of learning as dynamic and variable, rather than one dimensional, is a critical shift.

The third shift is from response to design. Even when faculty understand how variable learners are, they need to shift from responding to the needs of individual learners to designing for variable learners. When faculty recognize the individuality and variability of each of their learners, they may quickly become overwhelmed by the conclusion that they should be responding to each student's unique needs. Differentiated Instruction supports this responsive support of individual student needs and interests and remains controversial in higher education (Tulbure, 2012). However, while learning variability is highly individual, it is also highly predictable, so faculty can plan for variable learners without requiring learning labels and individualized responsive planning. UDL demonstrates how faculty can confidently plan in advance to prepare a learning environment that meets a wide variety of learning needs.

The fourth shift in thinking is a shift from the goal of access to one of learning expertise. The ultimate goal of designing with UDL is not just access to learning situations but the development of learning expertise, which is "the lifelong process of becoming ever more motivated, knowledgeable and skillful" (Meyer, Rose, & Gordon, 2014, p. 21). While accessibility is critical to ensure every student can access the learning environment, access alone is not enough to constitute a UDL environment. This does not leave behind the concepts of equity and leveling the playing field, but pushes beyond towards the ambition of maximizing each individual's learning potential. Shifts in thinking to distinguish these two concepts must be clear to articulate the ultimate design goal of UDL; it is not just an accessibility framework, but a learning design framework.

The fifth shift is from ad hoc to intentionality. While some learning moments may appear like a UDL moment, without intentionality they are a happy learning design accident. These accidents can be a powerful experience of engaged learning that can be leveraged into more awareness and intentionality, and that requires a shift in mindset. While the ad hoc moments may achieve some excellent learning moments, only intentionality can sustain change and be adapted to new learning environments. Finding sustainable ways to initiate, implement and evaluate intentional improvements can help systemically transform ad hoc moments to shared change. Approaches such as the Carnegie's Foundation process and resources for Improvement Science in education can help grow these efforts in a sustainable and sharable way that promotes learning not only for individuals, but for the system (Grunow, 2015).

Table 14.2 The five shifts of thinking to build a UDL mindset

Shift from:	Could sound like:	Shift to:	Could sound like:
1 Medical view of disability	What technology will students bring with them?	Social view of disability	How can I design my online module so it's accessible to all technologies, including assistive technologies?
2 Learning labels	What is the diagnosis of the student? How will I know the diagnoses of the students in my class?	Learning variability	All my students are dynamic and are different each year.
3 Responding to individuals	Once I know each student, I can adapt the curriculum or lessons to help them out.	Planning for variability	I know that learning is highly variable but predictable, so I can plan ahead for all students.
4 Accessibility	What I can I do to make sure all students can learn in my class?	Expert learning	What can I do to help all my students become expert learners/lifelong learners?
5 Ad hoc	Why were students so engaged in today's lesson?	Intentionality	What meaningful choices can I provide students in today's lesson to promote engagement?

Reflection

- Which of these five shifts resonates most strongly with you?
- What steps has your AS team taken to make these shifts?
- In your experience, which shifts are the hardest ones to identify? Introduce? Put into practice?

Collaboration with Centres for Teaching and Learning (CTLs)

In addition to building a common understanding of UDL, accessibility and accommodation; and articulating the five shifts, AS needs to build partnerships with CTLs. While they may be named and structured differently across institutions, we are using the term Centers for Teaching and Learning to refer to college and university personnel, teams, and resources dedicated to supporting faculty in curriculum development, professional learning, applying pedagogical approaches, and integrating new technologies. When we refer to this, please think about what that would look like and who would be involved within your setting. Building partnerships with the CTL will help AS exercise their redefined role as collaborative leaders in UDL change, and build systemic change through collaborative curriculum planning and teacher training and development.

CTLs are critical collaborative partners for AS in UDL integration in two key ways. First, CTLs can model and promote use of clear, consistent language, definitions, and examples. Faculty will be looking to both teams to build their understanding of UDL and those teams need to have a shared understanding and response to minimize confusion and build understanding. When faculty ask UDL questions and get different responses from each team, both teams lose credibility and the faculty member may become frustrated or disengaged. While stripping it back down to clear use of terms may seem overly pedantic to some, it really is a critical consideration. This is so because often educators use UDL and mean very different things by the term.

Second, it is critical that CTL and AS have a shared understanding of roles and responsibilities for accommodations, accessibility, and UDL. This gets quickly and dramatically highlighted when there is complex problem solving involving curriculum, teaching responsibilities, students with disabilities, Human Rights, assessment and more. AS and CTL teams are critical partners in scaling and creating systemic UDL change in higher education, and therefore they must have a shared and nuanced understanding of UDL in a postsecondary context. With a clear and shared understanding of language, roles and primary leadership, AS can help CTLs develop their UDL expertise and integrate it with their expertise in teaching and learning.

Finally, collaborating on curriculum and professional learning can be another key area for integration of UDL through collaboration. Curriculum here means the planning, delivery, and evaluation of the "goals, assessments, methods, and materials" that constitute the learning experiences packaged into courses and programs (Meyer, Rose, & Gordon, 2014, p. 15). Professional learning collaborations that focus on strategically integrating UDL is another way that AS can collaborate to help increase the understanding and influence of teams that lead teaching and learning on campus. Through attaching to the existing mechanisms that faculty use for curriculum planning and professional learning, AS can partner "behind the scenes" to build UDL integration through collaboration and strategic partnerships.

Preparing for the conversation: redefining goals

With a clear understanding of the differences between accommodation, accessibility, and UDL, an articulated understanding of the five shifts for mindset, and proactive collaborations with the CTL, AS leaders and teams are better prepared to engage in faculty conversations that will help shift thinking to develop UDL ways of planning and enacting inclusive practices. While there are many types of interactions and conversations that AS would be involved in, the faculty meeting is a relatively transferable example to use to explore these five shifts and that's what we'll focus on here. Please remember that these same approaches and the five shifts can be used in other contexts, for instance meetings, strategic plans, training and development, web content and physical campus design.

Let's return to Nicole, the accessibility advisor, and see how she's preparing differently for her conversation with Sylvia, Jonathan's faculty member in Electrical Engineering Technology. Sylvia requested a private meeting with Nicole to share her concerns for how Jonathan's accommodation request might impact her and the other students in the class. Nicole's new goal is to build a foundational partnership with Sylvia by asking questions about the learning context, the curriculum, and the dynamics of the course and class. She also wants to listen for which of the five shifts might present an opportunity to think differently about the situation and explore different solutions. These two goals guide her preparation.

Usually, Nicole begins such a conversation summarizing the duty to accommodate, the legal responsibilities the college has to provide accommodations, and the rights that Jonathan has as a student with a disability. Because she wants to increase awareness of UDL, Nicole usually also likes to mention UDL and that if the faculty just did more up front to remove barriers, it would be better for all students. She typically would send faculty links to the CAST and UDL on campus websites and tell them how much great information to find there. There is a lot of information to share, so Nicole usually finds herself doing most of the talking, then following up with a written email to share resources she's referenced and ask if there are any other questions.

Nicole has been thinking about the five shifts and has been reflecting on how confusing accommodations, accessibility and UDL might be from a faculty's perspective. Although it's common work in her day to day responsibilities, those terms and the concepts they represent might be confusing, or even intimidating, at first. Sylvia might need some examples to clarify these concepts and help her understand.

In her revised approach, Nicole is going to invite Sylvia to do most of talking in order to identify what shifts might be most relevant to the situation, assess Sylvia's readiness for change, and try to find the most relevant entry point to shift thinking and practice, highlighting the disorienting dilemma. Nicole is determined not to minimize the importance of the accommodations for Jonathan by only advocating for a UDL approach; but she wants to be prepared to introduce accessibility and UDL options.

Based on what she knows about the situation, she's prepared an example to do with note taking and providing some options for Sylvia to consider. Nicole has noted that Sylvia is concerned about attendance for other students if the notes are provided to all students. The goal for the conversation is to clarify the services and resources that Sylvia can use and collaboratively establish some options for her to consider to reduce learning barriers and increase support for Jonathan.

Nicole has also contacted the Centre for Teaching and Learning to learn more about their resources. She has information about faculty consultations ready to share with Sylvia.

Engaging in the conversation: listening for shifts

Each conversation is unique and dynamic. The five shifts may appear in any number of ways, suggesting that change agents may wish to reflect on their principles of coaching, solution focused conversation, and appreciative inquiry, when approaching any growth orientated conversation. Also, having a clear goal, whether stated or co-created, is critical to keeping the conversation focused, productive, and measurable.

In Table 14.3, we share some suggestions of how these shifts may show up in conversation. If it appears, it presents an opportunity to shift the conversation. When a shift arises, this could be an entry point to challenge thinking and offer a new way of looking at the situation. By articulating the thinking and assumptions that lie underneath the behavior or practice, Nicole can better help Sylvia understand the thinking that underlies her practices. Without a shift in thinking, there will be little shift in practices.

Following up: building partnerships

After the conversation, Nicole is excited about the results. Sylvia has agreed to identify another student in the class who can take notes for Jonathan, and is open to discussing other note-sharing options for all students. While Sylvia's

Table 14.3 The Five Shifts: a listening guide

Five Shifts	Listen for	Things Professor Sylvia May Say
Shift 1: medical to social view of disability	• What is the diagnosis of the student?	• Why can't Jonathan take his own notes? • How can we help him fix that situation? • I don't have a policy for laptop usage. It all depends on the student with the disability
Shift 2: learning as a static to a variable ability	• Learning styles guides my teaching • Tony is a visual learner, so I make sure he has lots of images	• If Jonathan's an auditory learner *(here, as authors we recognize the contested nature of "learning styles")*, then he may not need the notes in advance. • I group the students by learning style and it works sometimes
Shift 3: responding to designing	• Once I know what each student needs, I make sure they get it • It takes time to get to know everyone at the start of the semester, but then I can change things up to best suit their needs • I could never predict who will be in my class each year. Just have to wait and see	• Just tell me what to do for Jonathan and I will make it happen • It's hard to keep up with all these accommodation requests. It's like I have to prepare 8 different lessons
Shift 4: access to learning expertise	• Students with disabilities can have their laptops in class, but no one else. They might get distracted. • Some students have a difficult time working in groups, but that's not mine to teach.	• I'll give the notes to Jonathan because he has a disability, but not the other students. They need to learn to take notes. • I'm not sure if collaborative note taking is a good option for everyone.
Shift 5: ad hoc to intentionality	• I had this amazing lesson that just worked out! • Wow – that class/workshop was great. I wonder how I can integrate that into my class.	• One time I was in a workshop and didn't have the notes in advance, and that did make it harder to understand. • I'll try it once, but how will I know it'll work?

not ready yet, her interest is peaked by the idea of sharing notes she has prepared – maybe even in advance for next semester – and to track the impact on attendance and grades. Nicole used a table to illustrate the difference between accommodations, accessibility, and UDL – and was able to add relevant examples for Sylvia to show her how the faculty's role changes a little bit in each. Finally, Nicole was listening with the five shifts in mind, and was able to actively listen and steer the conversation to create those moments of dissonance and learning, not just information sharing. Overall, Nicole felt like approaching Sylvia as a both a colleague and a learner helped her find a way to shift minds and practices.

Nicole contacted the CTL, and is investigating a clearer proactive partnership. She'd like to invite the CTL staff to some learning opportunities to deepen and refine their understanding of UDL. She'd also like to invite them to a lunch and learn or a coffee talk to clarify language and ensure that everyone is consistent with terms such as accommodations, accessibility, and UDL and learn what terms CTL would like to clarify too. Nicole is eager to explore opportunities to collaborate with CTL to support faculty's professional learning. Perhaps faculty can get a direct referral to the CTL, and AS can partner with CTL on providing just in time accessibility and UDL learning opportunities. This could be an important and practical way to start sharing and shifting leadership of UDL to teaching and learning teams.

Reflection

- Think of a time that a UDL conversation did or didn't go well. What happened? What went well? What didn't? What would you have done differently?
- Who are the key partners for systemic UDL change at your college or university?
- Not every conversation goes smoothly or achieves quick results. How do you stay motivated in your UDL work despite perceived setbacks?
- How do you prepare for a UDL conversation with faculty? What works well about it? What could work even better?

Conclusion: collaboratively changing minds and practices

Expertise in learners, teachers and systems is not a destination "but rather a process of becoming more expert on a continuum of development" (Meyer, Rose, & Gordon, 2014, p. 21). AS teams in higher education have an opportunity to develop their own expertise in UDL and also to strengthen understanding of the concept within learners, teachers and systems. To do this, AS needs to be deliberate about supporting leadership of UDL in faculty and teaching and learning teams. AS is uniquely positioned to do so, using everyday conversations with faculty that can bring clarity to the nuances between accommodations, accessibility, and UDL. These conversations are also opportunities to identify and shift the underlying attitudes and ways of thinking that underpin a strategic approach to UDL application within HEIs. These five shifts can become markers and checkpoints for faculty conversations and a way for AS to use their area of expertise to help others deepen their understanding of accessibility and engagement in higher education learning environments.

References

Berquist, E., Carey, L., Ralabate, P.K., & Sadara, W.A. (2017). Changing beliefs: A view inside a coaching experience based on UDL. In Elizabeth Berquist (Ed.), *UDL: Moving from exploration to integration* (19–31). Wakefield, MA: CAST.

Eisner, E.W. (2013). What does it mean to say a school is doing well? In D.J. Flinders and S.J. Thornton (Eds.), *The curriculum studies reader* (279–287). New York: Routledge.

Funckes, C., Kroeger, S. Loewen, G., & Thornton, M. (n.d.). *Refocus*. Retrieved from http://projectshift-refocus.org/

Glickman, C.D., Gordon, S.P., & Ross-Gordon, J.M. (2014). *SuperVision and instructional leadership: A developmental approach* (9th edition). New York: Pearson.

Grunow, A. (2015, July 21). Improvement discipline in practice. *Carnegie Commons Blog*. Retrieved from www.carnegiefoundation.org/blog/improvement-discipline-in-practice/

Kezar, A. (2003). Enhancing innovative partnerships: Creating a change model for academic and student affairs collaboration. *Innovative Higher Education*, 28(2), 137–156.

Meyer, A., Rose, D. H., & Gordon, D. (2014). *Universal design for learning: Theory and practice*. Wakefield, MA: CAST.

Rose, D., Meyer, A., Strangman, N., & Rappolt, G. (2002). *Teaching every student in the digital age*. Alexandria, VA: ASCD.

Rose, T. (2016). *The end of average*. Toronto, ON: Harper Collins.

Chapter 15

Creating synergies between UDL and core principles of the European Higher Education Area in planning for pre-service teacher education

Rebeca Soler Costa and Seán Bracken

Case study

Luciana Rodriguez teaches with a team of professors who are responsible for an undergraduate teacher education course at the Faculty of Education in a large Spanish university. Over the past few years, her Department of Educational Sciences (Pedagogy) has attempted to redesign programs to adapt to the framework set out by the European Higher Education Area (EHEA). This framework seeks greater design alignment within undergraduate programs across the European Union. One of the purposes of the EHEA is to achieve a relatively homogeneous structure of University Degrees; whether at postgraduate and doctoral level, or at undergraduate level so that there will be relatively comparable qualifications across Europe. An additional aim is to encourage the mobility of students, graduates, teaching staff, researchers and administrative staff throughout European HEIs. Whilst aiming to streamline their programs in light of EHEA demands, Luciana and her team have also become increasingly mindful of the need to create a more inclusive approach to teacher education so to underpin a strategic approach to UDL application within HEIs. University staff can model best practices for their trainees when they graduate.

Luciana's students are pre-service teachers in the first year of their university degree. She teachers Didactics and School Organization and she is aware of the students' diversity and how this interfaces with the demands and complexity of the course program. She has recognized that because aspects of the course are somewhat rigid, some of students have failed their summative exams; this has caused her some anxiety. Lately, Luciana has sought to alter aspects of the course and to integrate a greater degree of universal design principles and practices in an attempt to offer all students, regardless of their needs, the necessary tools and resources required to overcome learning difficulties and to acquire the necessary competencies so that they can become fully developed future teachers who are capable of realizing their potential. In response, Luciana has developed several hybrid competency-based programs intended to appeal to the variance of learners on her course. Despite this, at times, Luciana has experienced tensions between the necessity for students to evidence particular professional competencies and the need to provide multiple means of; engagement, action and expression, and representation.

Introduction and background

On May 25, 1998, Ministers of Higher Education in Germany, France, Italy and United Kingdom signed the Sorbonne Declaration, which created The European Higher Education Area (EHEA). As a priority focus, the EHEA proposed that students in HEIs would acquire the necessary skills to meet the economic and social challenges necessary to create a more cohesive social and cultural space. This meeting provided the impetus for the Bologna Declaration of 1999, an agreement that forms the basis for HEI collaboration and mutual recognition throughout 40 European countries. The European Ministers of Education approved a set of measures to achieve the objectives of the Bologna Declaration, especially those concerning student mobility within and between European educational systems, the promotion of lifelong learning, the development of joint academic degrees, the enhancement of joint accreditation processes along with, the collaborative strengthening of shared perspectives regarding the quality of HEI learning.

In the EHEA's view, universities are pivotal agents in the formation, enhancement and dissemination of knowledge for the greater social good. They are inextricably linked with positive changes in the fields of scientific, technological, economic, and socio-cultural well-being and progression. The EHEA assumes that systems of higher education in each Member State, while being cognizant of individual national and cultural differences, will work toward the development of curricular convergence in order to enable mutual recognition of awards and qualifications throughout the EHEA. Because the EHEA promotes the convergence of European University Degrees, it has had a profound effect upon the formation and development of teacher education programs throughout Europe. Accordingly, all new forms of teacher education are required to realize the aims of ensuring mutual professional recognition across the system, whilst also ensuring that citizens are educated drawing on a fundamental respect for social, political and cultural practices that promote the democratic principles of justice, equity, inclusiveness, diversity and solidarity (Alonso et al., 2009; Gewerc, 2014).

Considering the EHEA requirements for universities and their programs to promote wider societal and student engagement and well-being, there is a solid basis for exploring the potential for the UDL framework to ensure that learning requirements of marginalized students are considered to the fore as new programs are developed (Gradel & Edson, 2009; Rao & Meo, 2016). In this chapter, we suggest that UDL offers a coherent conceptual framework and requisite strategies to enhance a competency-based learning approach while, at the same time, strengthening what Doyle (1978) refers to as, the 'mediating paradigm' drawing together frameworks with potential to enhance learning of students and teachers alike.

I The competencies framework in teacher training

The EHEA competencies framework for all disciplines incorporates three key features, namely; the nature of the individual disciplines (what one knows), methodological competencies (how that knowledge is applied), and social competencies (the ways that knowledge contributes positively to wider society) and the personal competencies (values and ethics) that are combined to be adapted within unique contexts and situations. As defined in the 'Delors Report' (Delors et al., 1996), the concept of 'competence' thus integrates the concepts of 'knowledge', 'knowledge application' and 'knowledge to be' because, when individuals engage with a diversity of situations and proposed tasks in the world of work, and within wider society, they do so according to their capacities in terms of knowledge, skills, personal qualities and social attitudes.

Hence, the competence framework encapsulates a set of participatory, social, methodological and technical knowledge(s) that an individual brings into play to meet the obligations and demands posed by professional practice. These competencies are observable and accessible through the ways of being and doing that individuals enact when faced with different problems and social contexts. According to Tejada (2005, p. 27) a competency framework encapsulates: "A set of combined, coordinated, and integrated knowledge, procedures and attitudes into the professional practice, definable in action, where experience shows itself as inescapable and the context is a key element". Critically, particular attention is provided to the dynamic and creative potential inherent in the framework, so that it does not become formulaic, but rather is responsive to the socio-cultural contexts within which it is applied. When interpreted effectively by professionals, a competencies-based framework has potential to bring together multiple forms of knowledge to respond to particular educational challenges. Thus, when enacted in a meaningful way, such a framework calls for the ability to organize, select and integrate knowledge, skills and attitudes that may be effective in meeting requirements of professional activity and problem solving.

Critical interpretations of how the competencies framework has informed the development of teacher education programs in Spain are well researched (see for example; Garagorri, 2007; Perrenoud, 2004; Tejada, 2009). Further, because skills are transferable and subject to personal and contextual interpretation, they can also be transferred and are subject to innovation. In teacher training in Spain and Spanish Universities the most relevant general competencies necessary to be included and followed in any syllabus design are those proposed by Aneca (2005a, 2005b) and the Ministerio de Educación y Ciencia (2007). Further, during the process of syllabus design for each discipline there are also agreed specific competencies. For example, in pre-service teacher development there is a subject entitled 'The school as an organizational space', it has a set of specific competencies to be achieved by students related to assessment. The three hierarchies of general competencies refer to instrumental competencies, personal competencies and systemic competencies, and these are further exemplified below:

INSTRUMENTAL COMPETENCIES

GC 1. To analyze and synthesize information

GC 2. To organize and plan work

GC 3. To identify, formulate and investigate problems

GC 4. To examine alternatives and make appropriate decisions

GC 5. To communicate orally and in the written form with suitable order and clarity in the first language or in a second language

GC 6. To search, select, use and present information using advanced technological resources.

PERSONAL COMPETENCIES

GC 7. To acquire and develop interpersonal abilities

GC 8. To work in groups and to communicate in multidisciplinary groups

GC 9. To express and to accept critic

GC 10. To appreciate social and cultural diversity in a wider context of respect for human rights and international cooperation

GC 11. To promote and guarantee the principles of universal design, equity, non-discrimination and democratic values and to promote a culture of the peace.

GC 12. To develop work with an ethical perspective towards oneself and others.

SYSTEMIC COMPETENCIES

GC 13. To research and continue learning autonomously

GC 14. To innovate with creativity

GC 15. To work autonomously and to participate in/and lead group projects

GC 16. To design and manage projects and initiatives

GC 17. To assume personal and professional challenges with responsibility, security, and critical self-reflection

GC 18. To show ethical engagement with environmental themes.

A model for how a competency-based approach might be applied to a discipline such as medicine has been designed by Miller (1990), whose Pyramid of Practice provides (Figure 15.1) a well-established overview of how critical competency-based learning outcomes, or the learning goals as identified in a UDL context (Meyer et al., 2014), could be formulated and assessed.

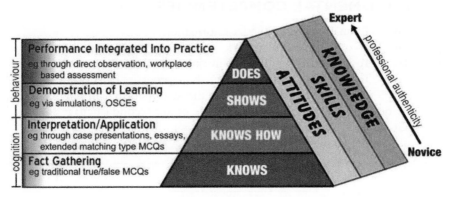

Figure 15.1 A competency-based approach for designing discipline-specific curricula

Source: Miller 1990

Reflection

- Are there other transnational efforts to create synergies among HEI curriculum developments? How might these be incorporated in a meaningful way while professional programs are being developed?
- What are some external competency framework factors that influence the nature of curriculum design in your own discipline or setting?
- To what extent is there scope for interface between such external frameworks and a UDL approach?

2 Creating synergies between the EHEA competency framework and UDL

A key attribute of the European convergence process encourages a systematic review of teaching and learning outcomes so that these are expressed explicitly in terms of skills which, in turn, will allow the student to engage with, and ultimately transform, their professional praxis (De Miguel, 2006; Alonso et al., 2009). It is noteworthy that, according to the EHEA, a fundamental purpose of the teaching process is to consider and involve students' cognitive, affective and social experiences. Once again this reflects the potentials for coherence making between the EHEA and the UDL principles upon which curriculum development are progressed. For instance, this may be promoted by becoming cognizant of students' learning goals, the best pedagogical methods that will assist them to realize their learning, the materials required to facilitate that learning as well as considering the most appropriate types of assessment enabling students to evidence attainment of learning outcomes (Meyer et al., 2014).

One of the fundamental objectives of the drive towards convergence of professional enhancement processes within HEIs across Europe is the desire to arrive at a core understanding of the general, disciplinary-professional and specific skills that practitioners will require across the continent (Mateos & Montanero, 2008; Alonso et al., 2009). Ultimately, a joint negotiation between students and teachers is required to determine how learners will achieve these competencies or goals (Meyer et al., 2014, pp. 134–136).

The UDL framework is intimately concerned with the processes to be used to facilitate learning and it is thus complimentary to competency-based frameworks by providing a clear consideration as to how students might be expected to attain specific learning outcomes. In returning to the case study to the fore, while Luciana and her colleagues are designing their teacher education program they can keep to the fore 'the what of learning' as stipulated in the EHEA competencies, while also considering the 'why' (promoting multiple means of engagement) of learning and the 'how' (multiple means of action and representation) of learning.

Thanks to UDL being introduced into HEI syllabus design, learning has become feasible for all students. Of course design ought to retain its intellectual rigor and challenge, however through multiple means of representation and achievement, students are provided with more options for evidencing their learning (Rao et al., 2015). A focus on formative student knowledge enhancement through continuous self and peer assessment, as encouraged by Boud and Soler (2016), also makes it possible for students to access immediate feedback required for them to prepare for teaching in a professional context. This ensures that learning is simultaneously challenging and sustainable. By focusing on how learning occurs as an informed interaction between teachers and students, and by creating communities of practice among students (Meyer et al., 2014) – as enacted in the formative learning domain of the university, and as practiced within school classrooms – the traditional hegemonic input-output design paradigm gives way to more collaborative and mediated forms of teacher education which are significantly more focused on professional reflection and research.

To some extent, in traditional teacher education curriculum design there has been an over-emphasis upon what teachers should know, especially regarding content knowledge, to the detriment of focusing on how they ought to support students in realizing learning outcomes. The latter reorients learning away from theoretical abstractions and more toward the acquisition of professional skills through praxis. This means guiding the teaching-learning processes toward acquiring professional skills. The term 'competence' or 'skill' has been chosen by a European Community funded project entitled 'Tuning Educational Structures in Europe' (González & Wagenaar, 2003) to synthesize the concepts shared across initiatives within the European Higher Education Areas. Competencies are primarily concerned with identifying specific desired learner capacities, which could then be shared as learning objectives within disciplines but across many European nations. The competencies have emphasized the importance of student-centeredness, and highlight the particular requirement to reflect on what students are able to do. To a large extent then, there are strong synergies between the competencies and the goal oriented nature of UDL, however the design of such goals requires sufficient flexibility to reflect the unique learning requirements of differing groups of learners, as encapsulated in the concept of 'learner variability' (Mayer et al., 2014, p. 9).

Likewise, a concern for supports students may need 'and on' the procedures that will enable them to keep learning autonomously throughout their lives, are at once core attributes of the European concern for lifelong learning processes while also encapsulating the core features of a UDL curriculum design being mindful of goals, methods, materials and assessments (CAST, 2014b). Gimeno (2008) identifies that the European 'competency-based teaching' model creates a new multifaceted knowledge and professional practice framework for action. It integrates disparate attributes of learning including the cognitive, affective and axiological components, among others, within an epistemological arrangement that also allows for a cycle of critical reflection by the practitioner, followed by action with learners, and subsequently involving an informed critical reflection on practice and then a reengagement with the frameworks.

As with the application of the UDL framework (see Novak & Rodriguez, 2018), there are questions as to how the ideas embodied within the structural makeup of such frameworks are operationalized by teachers and their learners. In this context, it is interesting to note Chun and Evans' (2016) conceptualization as to how this process is enacted. They share that a competence framework approach to pedagogical practice necessarily implies: 'teachers trying to solve well-structured problems derived from the systematic knowledge, through the selection of appropriate technical means, often designed by someone else' (p. 10). So, for Luciana and her challenges, as featured in the case study to the fore, essentially, she would like to overcome some of the more 'technicist' attributes of a competency-based UDL curriculum in order to get to the 'beating heart' lived experiences of her students.

However, there does not have to be a polar oppositional tension between a technical professional approach and one that is ethically sound and mindful of learners' variable learning requirements. This is particularly important because the need to support students from 'non-traditional backgrounds' forms a key attribute of current policy initiatives within the EHEA (2017, p. 8) where ministers of education have stated:

> We encourage HEIs to provide flexible learning paths in terms of study pace, study aim and learning methods, using also the opportunities that digitalisation offers and agree to review and adapt higher education support systems.

In practical terms then, Luciana and her colleagues have begun to reflect on the ways in which multiple pathways for learning are created to cater for learner variability. The new curriculum is being crafted collaboratively with peers who are envisioning and anticipating, by using vignettes for example, multiple forms of student variability. In considering student variability they consider for example attributes of learners' socio economic, linguistic, and ethnic backgrounds and/or based on (dis)abilities, or indeed whether the intersectional aspects of learner identities interplay among these attributes of difference and they creatively envision how potential learner variances may impact on learning (Annamma et al., 2018; López et al., 2018; Museus, & Griffin 2011; Tefera et al., 2018). Luciana and her colleagues are professionally 'playing', in a research informed way, and by anticipating how multiple forms of student identity will impact on student engagement and resilience, they are better preparing themselves for greater student diversity on their teacher education program.

Reflection

- A competency-based framework approach is frequently associated with specific professional programs such as medicine or nursing. What are the barriers and opportunities for adopting a UDL approach along with such frameworks?
- Who are the key players involved in the development of national, regional and/or local competency frameworks? In your opinion have they adequately considered aspects of learner variability? How might you convince such persons to come together to adopt a UDL approach?
- How might intersectionality theory inform your consideration of learner variability both in HEIs and in terms of schools and classrooms?

3 Incorporating a social justice perspective to EHEA and UDL frameworks

According to Spencer and Spencer (1993), the constituent attributes of a competency framework may vary considerably according to their capacity to be evidenced. For example, while aspects of knowledge and skill may be somewhat straightforward in terms of practice-based observation and evidence, aspects of self-concept, attitudes, values and motivations are much more challenging to uncover and evidence. So, it may be easier to develop, evaluate and assess some aspects of a competency framework rather than others.

In this context, a supporting conceptualization as to how such complexity might be evidenced would greatly enhance the curriculum development process. In this way, when Luciana and her team are looking to develop strategies for assessing the ways in which students might evidence their values and 'ways of being', they can draw on the UDL framework. While co-constructing expected learning outcomes with their students they could for instance delineate how to, 'build fluencies with graduated levels of support for practice and performance' (CAST, Guidelines 2.0, 2011) within the consideration of providing multiple means of action and expression.

In order to respond to the new demands that arise within the professions, such as teaching, which are dynamic, ever changing and entail a commitment to lifelong learning, recent developments have extended the initial focus upon discipline knowledge, knowledge application and knowledge of being. According to Soler Santaliestra (2013), the UNESCO Institute for Lifelong Learning has suggested that the principles set out in the groundbreaking Delors Report (Delors et al., 1996) be supplemented to consider the following attributes:

a) 'Learning to Learn' as a foundation for achieving lifelong learning, this approach enables learners to assume much greater responsibility and autonomy for their subsequent learning journeys;
b) 'Learning to Transform' as a critically informed strategy enabling learners to develop a critical interpretation of their own realities to introduce changes to improve personal and community well-being and progression;
c) 'Learning to Become' encompasses all the professional outcomes to enable individuals to develop both individually and as members of a more inclusive society (p. 35).

Such principles have the capacity at once to complement and extend the underpinning principles of the EHEA competencies framework and to add a social justice dimension to the UDL framework. It is interesting to note that the concept of 'Learning to Learn' is already incorporated both within the European system of basic competencies (Soler Santaliestra, 2013) as well as featuring in the UDL framework under the guise of 'promoting expert learning'. A comprehensive overview of what such learning entails is clearly articulated within an overarching conceptualization that expert learners are resourceful and knowledgeable, they are strategic and goal directed and they are also purposeful and motivated. Clear exemplification of what this looks like in practice is featured on the CAST website and is also discussed by Meyer et al. (2014).

The other two educational principles, as discussed by Ouane (2011), move beyond the notion of the learner as a cognitive actor within their own domain and suggest that knowledge is employed to effect societal change that is context specific. Thus, through experience of working with students and with fellow teachers, teachers as learners accrue a series of competencies to solve new tasks, apply competencies to new situations, analyze and organize acquired knowledge, address the general and the particular, relate knowledge to action, take risks, direct and redirect change, adapt quickly to changes, and they should be empowered to contribute to, as well as anticipate, transformations required by new challenges, whether these be technological or social (Ouane, 2011).

Further, according to Ouane's interpretation of these additional competencies, professional development reorients curriculum and assessment design away from purely neoliberal market policy models towards constructivist and critical perspectives. Curriculum design not only responds to the economic criteria for social control but also seeks to address 'the question of social transformation through education' (Rizvi & Lingard, 2013, p. 118). There are emerging models as to how such a coming together of UDL and critical pedagogies might be realized. For example, as articulated by David Rose in the Alim et al. (2017):

> UDL has stopped short by not joining with other movements to say; 'How can we make a universal school a school for everybody'? We have to look at all the ways in which people are different from one another and make an education that is both supportive and also challenging. UDL does need to grow, and I think it will only grow in partnership with other key movements about disenfranchised learners.
>
> (p. 10)

In the article, Rose and the contributors to this debate have suggested that a coming together of UDL along with Culturally Sustaining Pedagogies will facilitate a more holistic approach to addressing aspects of ableism or racism within educational systems. As identified by Hanesworth et al. (2018) consideration of a Culturally Sustainability Pedagogies (CSP) approach provides; 'an additional aspect of critical reflectivity on the nature of cultures (*which,*) intends to facilitate a better understanding of, and engagement with, diverse societies as well as active engagement with their developments' (p. 6). As these authors have shared, a cross pollination between UDL and CSP offers an avenue for teacher educators to nurture understanding and agency that will support the active development of justice in society.

For Luciana and her colleagues, considering the nature of curriculum development will necessitate a reflective consideration of wider societal issues that challenge the learning progression of students. For example, in the event that some of the trainee teachers have come from refugee backgrounds, or in the event that the trainee teachers will be working with refugees into the future, it will be necessary to consider how this will impact on desired competencies, whether such competencies may be values-based or based at the level of 'knowledge' of how best to include the cultural and linguistic heritages of all students.

Reflection

- Given the need to extend learning beyond perhaps more observable evidence to consider wider social factors, such as personal or community transformation, what might this look like in your professional context?
- How might the concept of 'learning to become' impact on one's professional identity as a teacher-trainer in Higher Education and how might this concept influence student learning?

---

4 Applying the EHEA and UDL frameworks to practice

Core attributes of curriculum formation and development have been addressed thus far, however, as identified by CAST (2014a) two remaining but highly significant aspects of the process involve materials and assessment. In this section, we briefly discuss these two pivotal attributes of curriculum enactment for teacher education in the realization that these two areas have been comprehensively addressed in other chapters of this publication. These will also be brought together with curriculum goals and methods to provide an illustrative template that captures the potential for synergies between the EHEA and UDL frameworks to enhance teacher education programs in Europe and beyond.

A key common feature of both UDL and the EHEA frameworks looks to the potential for information technologies as a means to enhance accessibility and inclusion for learners. As identified in the research (Benton-Borghi, 2013; Kumar & Wideman, 2014) when HEIs purposefully integrate information technologies into curriculum design and learning processes endless possibilities are provided for enhancing teachers' lifelong learning (Daniel, 2011; Ning, 2011). Having been exposed to technological affordances during their as professional development, teachers can then integrate digital learning into their classrooms more professionally. Modalities such as blended learning, within HEIs and within classrooms, form a central consideration when it comes to reflecting upon the methods and resources to be considered during program planning and implementation (see for example, the chapter by Jackson and Lapinski in this book). Thus, the environmental spaces, whether real or virtual impact on learning capacities and may also play a role in relation to the nature and types of assessment.

As discussed earlier, a more socially aware conceptualization of competencies, and of the UDL framework itself, is key for the further enhancement and application of competency-based learning because it posits the trainee teacher in an agentive role. The teacher-learner also becomes an active participant in fashioning her own learning in a more empowered and autonomous way. Moreover, when the professional pedagogical process posits teacher-learners and their social worlds at the heart of 'becoming a teacher', then there are significant implications for how assessment is to be realized as a central attribute of a formative and professionally developmental praxis. Assessment thus becomes an active and participatory engagement that leads to a more sustainable form of learning impacting on individual capacity as well as positively affecting wider communities (Boud & Soler, 2016). This is best achieved through strong relationship building and through authenticity of assessment practices (Carless & Boud, 2018; Boud & Molloy, 2013).

Unlike the traditional process-product paradigm that focuses on teaching-learning solely from the HEI lecturer's perspective, both the EHEA and UDL frameworks facilitate methodological innovation based on the premise that effective learning can only be attained when students acquire responsibility and autonomy in organizing and undertaking their academic work. To accept this principle, it is necessary to refocus the teaching process from positing the teacher-lecturer as sole determiner of content and rather to positioning learners and their contexts at the heart of the learning dynamics. Consequently, HEIs need to consider a paradigm shift from the teachers' perspective to the students' perspective. As shared by Hanesworth et al. (2018) a UDL approach that 'encourages true representative partnership working has the potential to redress systemic inequities in assessment outcomes'. Such a consideration of power dynamics in the formation of curriculum also enables attainment of specific competency goals such as GC 11; *the promotion of equity and democratic values.* The potential for creative synergies between selective attributes of both the EHEA and UDL frameworks, along with the centrality of learner agency, lie at the heart of following brief exemplification in Table 15.1.

Because Luciana and her team are critically reflecting on the efficacy of the UDL and EHEA frameworks, they are becoming increasingly alert to the need to have authentic assessments that emphasize formative professional enhancement as a basis for learning. As a result, they have revisited their own approaches to curriculum and assessment design. They are moving away from the formalized, summative essays which were initially so problematic – as shared in the case study to the fore – and they now favor more authentic, project-based learning and assessments. As a cohort of teacher educators they have also become increasingly conscious of the fact that the methods, resources and strategies they use in their own learning should provide a model for the

Table 15.1 Creating synergies: UDL and EHEA application in HE teacher training

EHEA/Spanish teacher education competencies (Aneca 2005a, 2005b; Ministerio de Educación y Ciencia, 2007a)	Based on the UDL Framework 2.2 (CAST, 2018)	Select examples of application in curriculum, methods and assessment
Instrumental competencies: GC 1. To analyze and synthetize information GC 2. To organize and plan work GC 6. To search, select, use and present information using advanced technological resources **Personal competencies:** GC 8. To work in groups and to communicate in multidisciplinary groups GC 11. To promote and to guarantee the principles of universal design, equity, non-discrimination and the democratic values and the culture of the peace **Systemic competencies:** GC 15. To work autonomously and to participate in/ and lead group projects GC 16. To design and manage projects and initiatives.	Focus on the development of learners who are purposeful and motivated (Engagement): • Recruiting interest through optimizing relevance value and authenticity. Build capacity for learners to become resourceful and knowledgeable by providing differing options to convey perception (Representation): • Offer ways of customizing the display of information. Strengthen capacity for student success through strategic and goal directed learning. Provide options for executive function. Sustain effort and persistence (Engagement): • Foster collaboration and community. Provide options for executive functions (Action and Expression): • Support planning and strategy development	Trainee teachers identify a cohort of primary, middle or high (secondary) school students and develop appropriate learning strategies and methods to meet their individual requirements Creating intuitive steps to guide learning using online platforms (LMS and/or VLEs), to facilitate work as a group to evidence and expand knowledge and make information accessible to everyone, with consistency of format Jointly, create follow-up tasks to promote the acquisition of knowledge, capacity and professional skills through peer and teacher-based tutorials (virtual or real) time and space to monitor formative learning

INSTRUMENTAL COMPETENCIES

GC 1. To analyze and synthetize information

GC 2. To organize and plan work

GC 3. To identify, formulate and investigate problems

GC 5. To communicate orally and in the written form with suitable order and clarity in the first language or in a second language

PERSONAL COMPETENCIES

GC 7. To acquire and develop interpersonal abilities

GC 10. To appreciate social and cultural diversity in a wider context of respect for human rights and international cooperation

GC 11. To promote and guarantee the principles of universal design, equity, non-discrimination and democratic values and to promote a culture of the peace

GC 12. To develop work with an ethical perspective towards oneself and others

SYSTEMIC COMPETENCIES

GC 13. To research and continue learning autonomously

GC 17. To assume personal and professional challenges with responsibility, security, and critical self-reflection

Providing opportunities for learners to be purposeful and motivated through sustained effort and persistence (Engagement):

• Heighten the salience of goals and objectives

Ensuring that learners become resourceful and knowledgeable (Representation)

• Clarify vocabulary and symbols

• Clarify syntax and structure

• Promote understanding across languages

Provide options for expression and communication (Action and expression)

• Build fluencies with graduated levels of support for practice and performance

Provide options for self-regulation (Engagement)

• Develop self-assessment and reflection

In a context of teaching aspects of a new language, or if teaching Spanish/ English as an additional language (L2) through a content area (for example in a geography class)

1 Use a vignette or real-life story to identify your learners

2 Develop a planning template to overtly identify aspects of cultural considerations, lexis and grammar to be taught and learned according to learners' age & learning requirements

3 Design an effective formative assessment process to monitor learning

4 Provide insights into your own learning as a teacher regarding acquisition of language or literacy

(Continued)

Table 15.1 (Continued)

EHEA/Spanish teacher education competencies (Aneca 2005a, 2005b; Ministerio de Educación y Ciencia, 2007a)	Based on the UDL Framework 2.2 (CAST, 2018)	Select examples of application in curriculum, methods and assessment
Instrumental competencies: GC 1. To analyze and synthetize information GC 3. To identify, formulate and investigate problems GC 6. To search, select, use and present information using advanced technological resources **Personal competencies:** GC 7. To acquire and develop interpersonal abilities GC 8. To work in groups and to communicate in multidisciplinary groups GC 9. To express and to accept critic GC 12. To develop work with an ethical perspective towards oneself and others **Systemic competencies:** GC 14. To innovate with creativity GC 15. To work autonomously and to participate in/ and lead group projects GC 16. To design and manage projects and initiatives GC 17. To assume personal and professional challenges with responsibility, security, and critical self-reflection	Assist learners to become strategic and goal oriented by facilitating options for physical action (Action and expression): • Optimize access to tools and assistive technologies Enhance capacities for learners to become resourceful and knowledgeable by providing, for example, options to enhance perception and comprehension (Representation): • Offer ways of customizing the display of information • Highlight patterns, critical features, big ideas and relationships. The goal is to create expert learners who are purposeful and motivated who are able to sustain effort and persistence and self-regulate (Engagement): • Increase mastery-oriented feedback • Facilitate personal coping skills and strategies	Working individually or in groups trainee teachers conduct desk-based research on processes of video enhanced learning as a pedagogical tool They use this knowledge to assist primary, middle/high school students to use video recording sessions within a pertinent discipline to capture their learning in action As a formative assessment, have peer groups create criteria for assessing the work produced Reflect on the peer critique and use feedback to enhance proposed individual and group based future learning or actions

professional sphere of the school in terms of interpersonal change leadership, curriculum design assessment processes and, importantly, the necessity to consider the potential for the classroom and school space to transform communities through learning.

Conclusion

In this chapter we have discussed the relevance of the Bologna Declaration (1999) which forms the basis for much of the coordinated developments throughout Europe regarding the nature, form and purpose of a Higher Education experience. A critical feature of this has been the development nationally of competency frameworks that adhere to the EHEA, especially as these pertain to the realm of teacher education. Because the EHEA has increasingly identified the need for interpretations of such framework to pay close attention to the learning requirements of learners who may be identified as marginalized or disenfranchised, we argue that the application of EHEA will be significantly enhanced by a consideration of UDL principles and practices and what they have to offer to support all learners overcome challenges.

Further, we suggest in this chapter that a dynamic synergy between these frameworks will also benefit from awareness of wider research in the fields of disability and critical race studies (see for example, Annamma et al., 2018) as well as considering attributes of cultural sustaining pedagogies (Paris, 2012). Such approaches seek to complement the neuroscience of learning typified within the UDL framework and aim to posit such learning in relevant; individual, community, national or transnational socio-cultural contexts. The flexibility inherent within these frameworks, and their capacity for interpretation according to discipline, resources and student identities, ensures they provide a turnkey for relevance and innovation when it comes to considering the design and implementation of truly inclusive teacher education programs in Spain, Europe and beyond.

References

Alim, H. S., Baglieri, S., Ladson-Billings, G., Paris, D., Rose, D. H., & Valente, J. M. (2017). Responding to 'cross-pollinating culturally sustaining pedagogy and universal design for learning: Toward an inclusive pedagogy that accounts for dis/ability'. *Harvard Educational Review* 87 (1): 4–25. doi:10.17763/1943-5045-86.3.366.

Alonso, L. E., Fernández Rodríguez, C. J., & Nyssen, J. M. (2009). *El debate sobre las competencias: una investigación cualitativa en torno a la educación superior y el mercado de trabajo en España.* Madrid: ANECA.

ANECA. (2005a). Libro blanco. *Título de Grado en Magisterio* (volumen 1). Accessed online 1st September 2018, from: www.aneca.es/activin/docs/libro blanco_ jun05_magisterio1.pdf/

ANECA. (2005b). Libro blanco. *Título de Grado en Magisterio* (volumen 2). Accessed online 1st September 2018, from: www.aneca.es/activin/docs/libro blanco_jun05_ magisterio2.pdf/

Annamma, S. A., Ferri, B. A., & Connor, D. J. (2018). Disability critical race theory: Exploring the intersectional lineage, emergence, and potential futures of DisCrit in education. *Review of Research in Education, 42*(1), 46–71. doi:10.3102/0091732X18759041

Benton-Borghi, B. H. (2013). A universally designed for learning (UDL) infused technological pedagogical content knowledge (TPACK) practitioners' model essential for teacher preparation in the 21st century. *Journal of Educational Computing Research, 48*(2), 245–265. doi:10.2190/EC.48.2.g

Bolognia Ministerial Conference. (1999). *Joint declaration of the European ministers of education – the Bologna declaration of 19 June 1999.* Accessed online 4th September 2018, from: www.ehea.info/cid100210/ministerial-conference-bolo gna-1999.html

Boud, D., & Molloy, E. (2013). Rethinking models of feedback for learning: The challenge of design. *Assessment & Evaluation in Higher Education, 38*(6), 698–712.

Boud, D., & Soler, R. (2016). Sustainable assessment revisited. *Assessment & Evaluation in Higher Education.* doi:10.1080/02602938.2015.1018133

Carless, D., & Boud, D. (2018). The development of student feedback literacy: enabling uptake of feedback. *Assessment & Evaluation in Higher Education,* 1315–1325.

CAST. (2014a). *UDL and expert learners.* Accessed online 3rd September 2018, from: www.udlcenter.org/aboutudl/expertlearners

CAST. (2014b). *What is meant by the term curriculum?* Accessed online 20th August 2018, from: www.udlcenter.org/aboutudl/udlcurriculum

CAST. (2018). *Universal design for learning guidelines version 2.2* [graphic organizer]. Wakefield, MA: Author.

Chun, E., & Evans, A. (2016). Rethinking cultural competence in higher education: An ecological framework for student development. *Association for the Study of Higher Education* Report *42,* 7–162. doi:10.1002/aehe.20102

Daniel, J. (2011). Distance education: Ends, means, opportunities and threats. In J. Yang & R. Valdés-Cotera (Eds.), *Conceptual evolution and policy developments in lifelong learning* (pp. 183–191). Hamburg: UNESCO Institute for Lifelong Learning.

Delors, J. et al. (1996). L'Éducation. Un trésor est caché dedans. Rapport à l'UNESCO de la Commission internationale sur l'éducation pour le vingt et unième siècle. Paris: Éditions UNESCO-Odile Jacob.

De Miguel, M. (Coord.) (2006). *Metodologías de enseñanza y aprendizaje para el desarrollo de competencias.* Madrid: Alianza.

Doyle, W. (1978). Paradigms for research on teacher effectiveness. In L. S. Shulman (Ed.), *Review of research in education* (Vol. 5, pp. 163–198). Itaca, IL: F. E. Peacock.

EHEA. (2017). *Policy development for new EHEA goals.* Accessed online 20th August 2017, from: www.ehea.info/media.ehea.info/file/2018_Paris/72/7/ MEN_conf-EHEA_WG3_03_950727.pdf

Garagorri, X. (2007). Currículo basado en competencias: Aproximación al estado de la cuestión. *Aula de Innovación Educativa, 161*, 47–55.

Gewerc, A. (Coord.) (2014). *Conocimiento, tecnologías y enseñanza: políticas y prácticas universitarias*. Barcelona: Graó.

Gimeno, J. (2008). *Diez tesis sobre la aparente utilidad de las competencias en educación*. Madrid: Morata.

González, J., & Wagenaar, R. (Eds.). (2003). *Tuning educational structures in Europe*. Final report. Phase one. Bilbao: University of Deusto.

Gradel, K., & Edson, A. (2009). Putting universal design for learning on the higher ed agenda. *Journal of Educational Technology Systems, 38*(2), 111–121.

Hanesworth, P., Bracken, S., & Elkington, S. (2018). A typology for a social justice approach to assessment: Learning from universal design and culturally sustaining pedagogy. *Teaching in Higher Education*. doi:10.1080/13562517.2018.1465405

Kumar, K. L., & Wideman, M. (2014). Accessible by design: Applying UDL principles in a first year undergraduate course. *The Canadian Journal of Higher Education, 44*(1), 125.

López, N., Erwin, C., Binder, M., & Chavez, M. J. (2018). Making the invisible visible: Advancing quantitative methods in higher education using critical race theory and intersectionality. *Race Ethnicity and Education, 21*(2), 180–207. doi:1 0.1080/13613324.2017.1375185

Mateos, V., & Montanero, M. (2008). *Diseño e implantación de Títulos de Grado en el Espacio Europeo de Educación Superior*. Madrid: Narcea.

Meyer, A., Rose, D., & Gordon, D. (2014). *Universal design for learning: Theory and practice*, Wakefield, MA: CAST.

Miller, G. E. (1990). The assessment of clinical skills /competence /performance. *Academic Medicine, 65*(9), S63–S67.

Ministerio de Educación y Ciencia. (2007). *Real Decreto 1393/2007, de 29 de octubre*, Por el que se establece la ordenación de las enseñanzas universitarias oficiales. *BOE, 260*, 44037–44048.

Museus, S. D., & Griffin, K. A. (2011). Mapping the margins in higher education: On the promise of intersectionality frameworks in research and discourse. *New Directions for Institutional Research, 2011*(151), 5–13. doi:10.1002/ir.395

Ning, K. (2011). The new paradigm of lifelong learning and the construction of a new learning media market – informal and non-standard learning platform for all. In J. Yang & R. Valdés-Cotera (Eds.), *Conceptual evolution and policy developments in lifelong learning* (pp. 192–198). Hamburg: UNESCO Institute for Lifelong Learning.

Novak, K., & Rodriguez, K. (2018). *UDL progression rubric* Available from the CAST Website. Accessed online 1st September 2018, from: http://castpublish ing.org/novak-rodriguez-udl-progression-rubric/

Ouane, A. (2011). Evolution of and perspectives on lifelong learning. In J. Yang & R. Valdés-Cotera (Eds.), *Conceptual evolution and policy developments in lifelong learning* (pp. 24–39). Hamburg: UNESCO Institute for Lifelong Learning.

Paris, D. (2012). Culturally sustaining pedagogy: A needed change in stance, terminology, and practice. *Educational Researcher, 41*(3), 93–97. doi:10.3102/0013189X12441244

Perrenoud, P. (2004). *Diez nuevas competencias para enseñar*. Barcelona: Graó.

Rao, K., Edelen-Smith, P., & Wailehua, C. (2015). Universal design for online courses: Applying principles to pedagogy. *Open Learning: The Journal of Open, Distance and e-Learning, 30*(1), 35–52. doi:10.1080/02680513.2014.991300

Rao, K., & Meo, G. (2016). Using universal design for learning to access academic standards. *Sage Open, 6*(4), 1–18. https://doi.org/10.1177/2158244016680688

Rizvi, F., & Lingard, B. (2013). *Políticas educativas en un mundo globalizado.* Madrid: Morata.

Soler Santaliestra, J. (2013). Estado actual y estrategias para futuribles de la formación a lo largo de la vida. In C. Ruiz Bueno, A. Gámez Navío, M. Fandos Garrido, & P. Olmos Rueda (Coords.) (Eds.), *Formación para el trabajo en tiempo de crisis. Balance y prospectiva. VI Congreso Internacional de Formación para el Trabajo.* Universitat de Barcelona (pp. 369–379).

Spencer, L. M., & Spencer, S. M. (1993). *Competence at work.* New York: John Wiley & Sons.

Tefera, A. A., Powers, J. M., & Fischman, G. E. (2018). Intersectionality in education: A conceptual aspiration and research imperative. *Review of Research in Education, 42*(1), vii–xvii. doi:10.3102/0091732X18768504

Tejada, J. (2005). El trabajo por competencias en el práctícum: cómo organizarlo y cómo evaluarlo. *VIII Symposium Internacional sobre Practicum y Prácticas en empresas en la formación universitaria.* Universidade de Santiago de Compostela, 2007. ISBN 9788469068625

Tejada, J. (2009). Competencias docentes. *Revista de currículum y formación del profesorado*, 1–16.

Chapter 16

Developing assessment and feedback approaches to empower and engage students

A sectoral approach in Ireland

Geraldine O'Neill and Terry Maguire

Case study: 'too much group work assessment and it's not my natural preference'

A student described her assessment experience. She was on a full-time master's program in business studies, within a class of approximately 100 students from a range of business and non-business backgrounds. In one six-week semester she had four modules, all with the same credit value and each with a group project weighted at 100%. In three of the modules, a small part of this weighting was for individual effort. However, the overall grade was dependant on working in a team and the teams were different for each subject. In addition, the group projects she had to complete had many components along with the final project output. This resulted in her having to complete a total of 13 significant pieces of assessment within the 6-week period working with four different teams prior to a compulsory internship. The student, who characterized herself as a hard worker who wanted to achieve good grades, felt strongly that she was over-assessed. She acknowledged that there were some good modules with passionate and supportive lecturers but explained that such over-assessment had a detrimental effect: *'One of my lecturers ... was a really interesting guy and so obviously passionate about what he did and he put so much work into his lectures ... by the last month no-one was coming because we had so much work ...'*

The student expressed frustration that the semester was made up primarily of group work, that there was limited content for which she was personally responsible and that because there were so many assessments to complete there was not enough time to give the projects the level of attention projects at master's level deserve. She described the effect all of this had on her grades and her experience of learning: '*In first term I didn't like the group work because of my personal preference but it was fine. I was able to deal with it to the extent that it was getting done and the grades were good. It was in the second term where I had a serious problem with it and actually the entire class did because it got to the stage where nothing we did was actually any of our own work. It ended up with a number of students, one of whom was me, who just did all of the work. There was a good 40% of the class who were just following along and that reflected in the grades, which was really unfair in the end because they were big projects that should have had a few people working on them. We had such a tight timeline. I think we only had six weeks for a couple of them. It got very frustrating and it wasn't just me . . . just my natural preference*' (Extract from National Forum, 2017c, with permission).

Introduction

Assessment approaches have a powerful impact on both students and staff in higher education. Over 20 years ago, Brown noted that '*if you want to change student learning then change the methods of assessment*' (Brown, 1997, p. 7). Other authors describe, for example, how assessment drives students' behavior (Carless, 2015; Boud & Molloy, 2013) and can have an impact on engagement and attendance (Harland et al., 2015). The student case study here highlights that assessment can impact on students' workload, their grades and engagement/attendance in classes. In addition, it describes that where one assessment approach is dominant there is a risk that it will not accommodate individual learning preferences.

To address some of these assessment dilemmas we need to engage staff in conversations around assessment design and we need to empower and engage students in the assessment process. The universal design for learning (UDL) approach (CAST, 2011) provides a useful lens through which to look at engaging and empowering students in assessment, it supports the idea that assessments should provide 1) multiple means of representation; 2) multiple means of action and expression; 3) multiple means of engagement (see pg iii for more details). Universal design for learning supports the idea that in designing for a diverse cohort all students rather than specific cohorts of students are supported (learner variability) (Rao & Meo, 2016).

These key principles of UDL align strongly with some of the work of the recent enhancement theme of Ireland's National Forum for the Enhancement of Teaching and Learning (The National Forum). The National Forum is a government funded organization whose remit is to support the enhancement of teaching and learning across the Irish higher education sector. *'Engaging with leaders, managers, teachers and students, the Forum mobilises expertise from across the sector to extend and shape good practice across all Irish higher education institutions'* (National Forum, 2019). The work of the National Forum is guided by negotiated enhancement themes that mobilize sectoral energy and promotes strategic convergence around a particular topic. From 2016–2018, the enhancement theme was on *Assessment OF, FOR and AS Learning* (National Forum, 2016a).

This chapter sets out how the National Forum, through this *Assessment OF, FOR and AS Learning* enhancement theme, supported staff and student conversations on assessment and feedback across the sector. In particular it focused on how to empower and engage students through a focus on five key areas through the lens of UDL (CAST, 2011):

- developing a national understanding of assessment
- developing students as partners in assessment
- understanding the diversity and volume of assessment nationally
- supporting program approaches to assessment
- enabling policies and professional development.

Developing a national understanding of assessment

The starting point to the enhancement theme was to explore whether as a nation we had a similar understanding of the language and purposes around assessment, including feedback. The importance of clarity around the purpose of assessment is echoed in the UDL principles.

Within the UDL framework, the overarching goal is to ensure assessments can guide instruction by being comprehensive and articulate (CAST, 2011). It *'is important that students understand the purposes and usefulness of the learning, knowledge and skills that are expected to be acquired in each course'* (UDLL, 2016, p. 69).

Equally, staff need to take time to reflect on and understand the purpose of the assessments they are providing for students. This is a useful starting point for all those exploring inclusive or universal design approaches to assessment. We sought, in particular, to explore the extent to which students engage in and have some power in these different purposes of assessment. The National Forum, working with staff and students across the Irish higher education sector, developed a shared understanding of the purposes and language of assessment (National Forum, 2017a) (see Figure 16.1).

This conceptual understanding of assessment and feedback highlights the importance of developing students' responsibility in the assessment process and how they can be supported to develop their skills of self-monitoring to become more independent in their critical evaluation skills (Sadler, 2010). The most familiar purpose of assessment is often described as *summative assessment* (or Assessment OF Learning). This is the assessment that is graded and is captured in institutional records. It is high stakes because the consequence of not achieving it has a high impact on students, for example, lack of progression, repeat assessments. The other common purpose of assessment is *formative assessment.* This form of assessment, which is encouraged in the *UDLL Best Practice Guidelines* (UDLL, 2016, p. 69), involves giving feedback to students and emphasizes the learning aspect of assessment. The power relationship varies between these two forms of assessment. As a general rule, the power in summative assessment lies with the teacher (or lecturer), whereas the learner begins to have more responsibility in formative assessment (see Figure 16.1).

Formative assessment can be further divided into Assessment FOR and Assessment AS Learning (Earl & Katz, 2006; National Forum, 2017a, see Figure 16.1). From a UDL perspective, this is a useful distinction because Assessment FOR Learning emphasizes the feedback that is <u>given to</u> students, or to staff. Feedback <u>to</u> students is one of the eight UDL performance indicators highlighted by Burgstahler (2015). However, Assessment AS Learning emphasizes students' ability to self-regulate and critically evaluate their own work. This is a more empowering approach to assessment as this supports the idea of students having options for self-regulation (CAST, 2011, Guideline 9). The focus placed on Assessment AS Learning in the enhancement theme was key to the design of the theme's logo (see Figure 16.2). The logo, developed at the start of the project, gave greater visual emphasis to the Assessment FOR and in particular Assessment AS Learning and served as a visual reminder of a clear focus on increasing the use of Assessment As Learning.

Reflection

- How does this section compare with your understanding of the purposes of assessment?
- How would you develop students' ability to self-regulate, so they can become more independent assessors of their own work?
- How do you shift your own emphasis from Assessment OF Learning to Assessment AS Learning?

Developing students as partners in assessment

A key focus in the National Forum's enhancement theme was the development of student as partners in the assessment process. The conceptual overview of assessment and feedback in Figure 16.1, and the logo in Figure 16.2, articulated the shift in power in the process of assessment from the 'teacher' as being fully responsible to the student having more decision-making power and taking

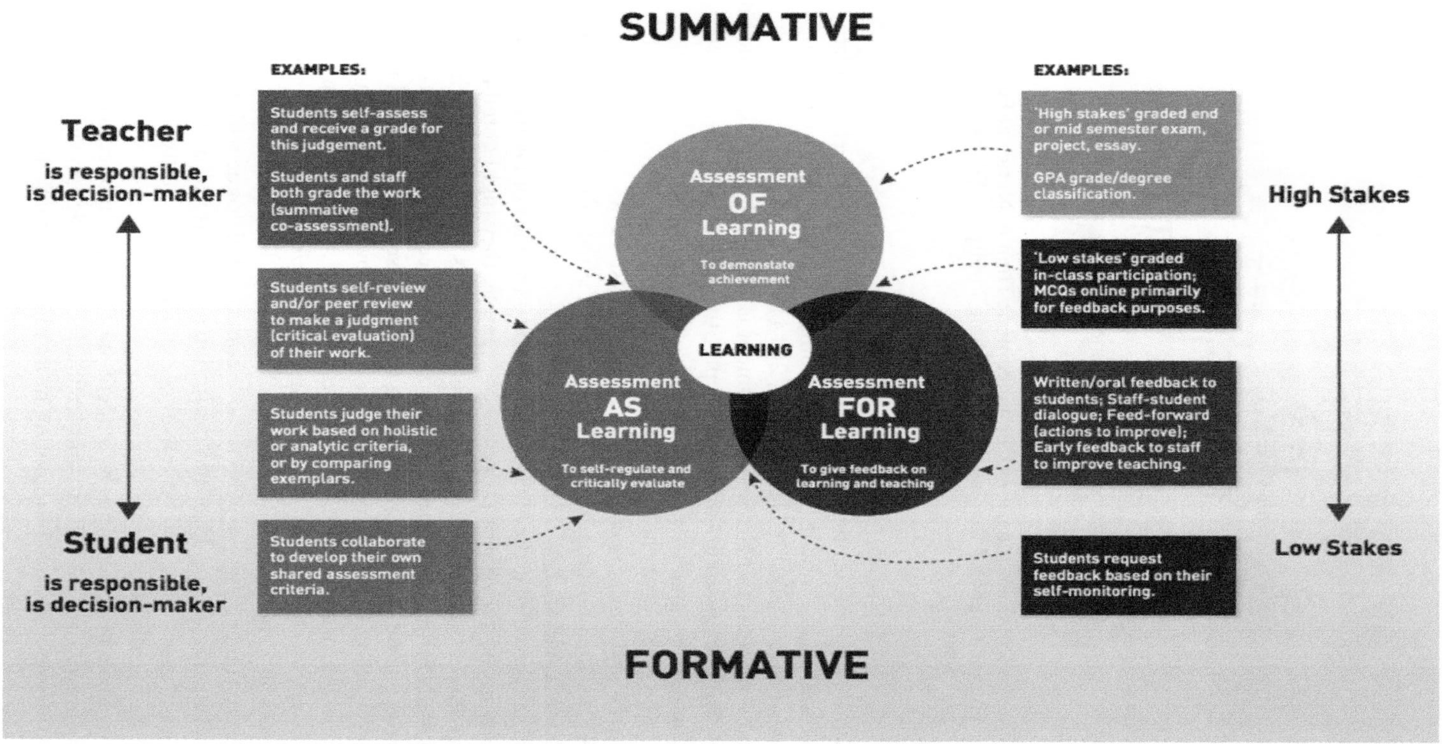

Figure 16.1 A sectoral understanding of assessment: Increasing students' responsibility and engagement

Source: National Forum, 2017a: with permission

Figure 16.2 Logo for the Assessment Enhancement Theme, National Forum for Enhancement of Teaching and Learning in Higher Education (with permission)

more responsibility. This is often described as the principle of developing 'student as partners' in assessment (National Forum, 2017d; Cook-Sather et al., 2014; Deeley & Bovill, 2017; Healey et al., 2014).

Developing students as partners in assessment is challenging because students themselves can find this an unfamiliar concept. Students need to be supported to enable them to become true partners in the assessment process. Working with the Union of Students in Ireland (USI), the National Forum explored what both staff and students could do to develop as 'students as partners' in assessment (National Forum, 2016b). An extract of some of the ideas discussed are outlined in Table 16.1.

Students suggested that they need to be open to the idea of taking on more responsibility in the assessment process. For example, they highlighted that they need to stay informed of their assessment requirements and to plan their assessment workload (National Forum, 2016b). Staff also need to be open to involving student as partners, including engaging them in discussions around the wider understanding of the purposes of assessment. Boville noted that underpinning these approaches which try '*to democratize the assessment process . . . is a belief that students have valuable knowledge and experience to bring to discussions of assessment design . . .*' (Boville, 2017; National Forum, 2017b). The implications of this are that we need to have continued dialogue with students in class and out-of-class (on local and institutional committees) on the different purposes of assessment and on how they can take more control of different assessment and feedback process.

Staff have a role in developing the student-staff partnership because they often have control over assessment and feedback policies, design and methods. One assessment approach becoming more internationally and nationally

Table 16.1 Students as partners in assessment: what do staff and students need to do (National Forum, 2016b)

What can staff do?	What can students do?
• Facilitate students' involvement in assessment-related institutional committees • Give students some choice of the methods used to assess them, from a prescribed range • Give students opportunities to self- and/or peer-assess their work in a module • Allow some choice in the method of feedback (online/written/oral)	• Input into institutional assessment protocols, when possible • Stay informed on your role, and the role of staff, in assessment and feedback regulations • Take responsibility for your learning and assessment activities • Propose methods of assessment that you have found useful to you or other students • Plan your assessment workload

established, in keeping with the inclusive approach to assessment, is staff embedding a choice of assessment for all students into their modules/courses (SPACE, 2011; O'Neill, 2011; O'Connor, 2017). Choice of assessment within a module (course) should be incrementally developed throughout the program, and although more senior students have been found to be most open to this approach, it should be encouraged in all years. For some discipline-specific examples see O'Neill (2011). To become more widespread, this approach needs to be fair to all students and additional staff development needs to be provided to enable staff to explore the design and evaluation of this approach (O'Neill, 2017). One suggested support for staff attempting to implement and evaluate fairness between choice of assessments for all students in their modules (courses) was developed was O'Neill (2017). *Student Information and Equity Template* was used that both assisted staff in designing fairness in the choice and also articulated to the students the details on the assessments to facilitate a more informed student choice. In addition, this study validated a tool for evaluating the students' perception of the fairness of the assessment choices.

Although traditionally grading of an assessment (summative assessment) is seen as the remit of the teacher, a staff-student partnership approach could involve a student and teacher each grading the same piece of work (Example from Figure 16.1). In practice, this is often followed by a process whereby the grades are negotiated between the two assessors. See, for example, Deeley's description of how she used summative co-assessment was used in Scotland (2014).

Other examples of the partnership approach during the feedback process with students, identified during the project (National Forum, 2017a), include:

• *Students are given the opportunity to request specific feedback.* This gives them some ownership of what areas they wish to receive feedback on. From a staff perspective feedback is then more likely to be read by students, making their efforts more impactful.

- *Students collaborate with staff to develop their own shared assessment criteria.* This approach is a useful exercise to clarify expectations around assessment in language that students understand (Carless, 2015; Cook-Sather et al., 2014). This reflects the UDLL recommendation to *'state the purpose and criteria for goal achievement'* (UDLL, 2016, p. 69).
- *Feed-forward process of feedback is used.* This feedback includes some actions on how to improve work. This is more beneficial to students in guiding their future actions, as opposed to past performance (some useful strategies on this type of feedback are discussed in Hine and Northeast (2016)).

Reflection

- How could the student in the case study have been given more ownership of her assessment work?

For staff:

- What are your thoughts on how to incrementally build students as partners in the assessment and feedback process?
- Do you agree with the 'student as partners' approach and, if so, what support would you need to build these skills?

The diversity and volume of assessment in Ireland

Universal design supports the concept of a diversity of assessment approaches, or multiple means of action and expression, to suit the needs of the growing diversity of student cohorts in higher education (Burgstahler, 2015; CAST, 2011). For assessment to support learning it also needs to be manageable in terms of workload for students. Therefore, in order to plan assessment appropriately, there is a need to gain an understanding of the existing diversity and volume of assessment experienced by your students.

In the early phase of the enhancement theme the National Forum identified a dearth of research that captured the diversity and volume of assessment methods in different disciplines used across Ireland. The National Forum addressed this by profiling assessment practices in Irish higher education (National Forum, 2016c). Information on assessment methods and loads was extracted from module descriptors of 30 randomly selected undergraduate degree programs in Ireland, three from each field of study as identified in the International Standard Classification of Education (ISCED) (For more information see National Forum 2016c). Across the 487 profiled modules, there was a range of assessment methods, with some assessment methods more common in specific fields of study (see Figure 16.3). For example, the project/dissertation had a high weighting in the *'Health & Welfare'* field.

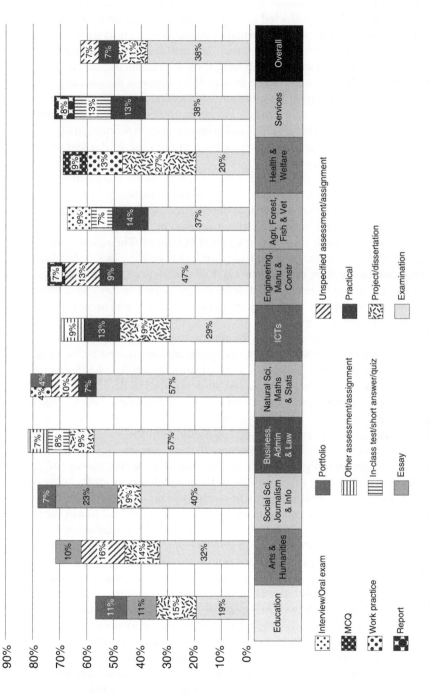

Figure 16.3 The diversity of assessment in Irish higher education

Source: (National Forum (2016c) image with permission from the National Forum)

Despite a range of assessment methods, the examination was very dominant across all fields (fully shaded light gray areas in the figures). Of the 487 modules, 61% used one or more formal examinations, with some fields, such as '*Business, Administration & Law*' and '*Natural Sciences, Mathematics & Statistics*', having a particularly high weighting for examinations. The average relative weighting for examination was 38% (National Forum, 2016c). This was unsurprising given the tradition and familiarity attached to the examination as an assessment format. However, the examination does not suit all students and many emerging 'special accommodation/contingency' and 'alternative assessment' approaches have been in response to this assessment format (SPACE, 2011).

Replacing one dominate assessment method, such as the examination, with another dominant assessment method, such as group work, could equally disadvantage a different set of students, as highlighted by the student in the earlier case study. When staff rely on one form of assessment, they may not be aligning to a broad set of module or program learning outcomes. The reliance on one particular type of assessment by individual staff may reflect a lack of familiarity with different assessment methods or a lack of confidence or time to change their practice. Access to professional development opportunities and learning communities can support staff to adopt and evaluate new approaches to the assessment of their students.

Diversity of assessment methods, for example a poster presentation in a program with multiple essays, need to be systematically planned by the program team across the program. This helps to avoid students having a limited range of assessment tasks, i.e. all exam and essays. Students need to have, where possible, more choice or range in assessment across a program to allow them to engage in assessments that play to their strengths.

In addition to being diverse, assessment should be manageable for students (Hornby & Laing, 2003; National Forum, 2017d). The practice of regular low-stakes assessment, highlighted in the overlap between Assessment OF and FOR Learning in Figure 16.1, can lead to the possibility of students being over-assessed. Regular low-stakes assessment can be beneficial for students (Taylor, 2008) but if not carefully managed across a program it can lead to assessment overload. For some student cohorts, who may already be struggling with the demands of higher education, this can lead to being overwhelmed by assessments. The student experience in the case study exemplified this as a dilemma for both the student, who felt she was over-assessed, and the staff member, who had poor attendance at his lectures.

The way in which credit weightings are distributed across modules within a program can also impact the level of assessment that students experience. The profile of assessment practices in Irish higher education highlighted that modules with lower credit weighting did not necessarily have fewer assessments (National Forum, 2016c). Therefore, a curriculum that has multiple small modules can result in an increased number of assessments for students.

These findings have implications for institutional policy which should guide program developers on the appropriate module size, module length, assessment load and level of assessment diversity.

Reflection

- Do you know what methods of assessments are most common in your field of study or sub-field?
- Is there a form of assessment that you feel could be problematic for some students?
- Are there alternative assessments methods that you could use?
- Are you aware of assessment overload for your students? If so, what are the signs that a student is experiencing assessment overload?

Supporting program approaches to assessment

The development of students as partners, the need to consider the diversity and volume of assessment must be integrated into program design to enable their development over the duration of a program to maximize the role of both students and staff (PASS, 2011). As part of the enhancement theme, a series of structured conversations around program assessment approaches took place (Maguire et al., 2017). This resulted in a comprehensive resource that includes in-depth case studies, commentaries and tools to support program approaches to assessment and feedback (National Forum, 2017b).

These conversations highlighted the need to consider the context which surrounds efforts to lead and enact change in assessment and feedback. Boyd, in his commentary, highlighted that *'both academic staff and students need a safe learning environment within our age of accountability'* (in National Forum, 2017b). Bovill challenged us to think about *'how we might open up assessment to make it a more transparent and democratic process in our own program contexts'* (in National Forum, 2017b). One implication of this safe learning environment that is highlighted by Cook-Sather et al. (2014), is that students need to be incrementally introduced to some of these ideas across a program. You may find their *'Ladder of Active Student Participation in Curriculum Design'* a useful way of describing this to both staff and students.

We mentioned earlier in this chapter the dilemma of trying to interrogate the extent to which there is an appropriate level of assessment diversity and load across a program. The program assessment resources address this by providing examples (case studies) of a range of program assessment mappings tools (see Table 16.2). These tools and processes can help staff to gather evidence of what is going on in their program and can support the use of dialogue to decide on some actions for change.

Table 16.2 Elements considered when using each program assessment mapping tool

Tool & Processes Used	Institution-wide online tool	Institution-wide online tool and follow-up with excel	PASS, using excel sheets	Google doc, Google forms, Google calendar	Discussion based	Excel
Alignment to program outcomes	✓	✓		✓	✓	✓
Summative	✓	✓	✓	✓		✓
Formative	✓	✓				✓
Assessment method	✓	✓	✓	✓	✓	✓
Group/Individual			✓			
Assessment weighting		✓	✓			✓
Volume	✓		✓			✓
Timing in module		✓	✓	✓	✓	

Source: National Forum, 2017b, with permission

But, of course, the main driver for change to our programs must be listening to our students. The student in the opening case study provided some useful guidance on what she would do to improve her program:

> I would have a long talk with the lecturers about speaking to each other when they do assessments. Instead of everyone just assessing and just thinking of their own module, perhaps some actual communication so the students don't end up with what happened to us.
> (Student Commentary, in National Forum, 2017b)

Harland, in his commentary, described the student experience in the case study as representing an 'assessment arms race' between staff (in National Forum, 2017b). He suggested that some 'slow time' for both students and staff needs to be built into the curriculum, including more large, integrative assessment opportunities (see also, Harland et al., 2015).

There is much to be learnt from sharing and considering your approaches to program assessment that have already been tried and tested, for example:

- Integrating program assessments horizontally (across modules at the same time) or vertically (modules that build sequentially on each other over the years of a program) (National Forum, 2017b).
- Allowing some time at the end of a program for capstone modules to integrate learning.

- Using student ePortfolios across a program in such a way that allows students to gather evidence of work that is unique to them (McDermott & Mac Giolla Ri, in National Forum, 2017b). This is an excellent example of 'multiple means of expression' (CAST, 2011), as student select their own evidence that suits their individual learning experience and have different ways of demonstrating this.
- Allowing students to draw on learning from parallel modules using a themed assessment approach has been endorsed by students (see Roche, in National Forum, 2017b)
- Introducing the idea of inclusive teaching and learning into staff development programs and, in addition, role modeling inclusive assessment. For example, Egan and Costelloe used a checklist entitled 'Statement of Inclusion' (see National Forum (2017b) for this checklist).
- Recognizing that involvement of a team of stakeholders is key to the success of a program approach to assessment and to developing students' ability to self-monitor (CAST, 2011, Guideline 9). These should include, for example, students, employers academic staff, libraries, education developers/learning technologists, etc. (National Forum, 2017b).

Reflection

- Do you feel staff are working on assessment in isolation in your program or is there evidence that assessment and feedback are planned at program level?
- Students: Do you get a chance to develop particular skills incrementally in your program? For example, the skills needed for the assessment of group work? Research? Critical thinking?
- Is there systematic use of a diversity of assessment methods across the program?

Enabling policies and professional development

It is more likely that institutions and their staff will support assessment approaches that engage and empower students if this is aligned with local, national and international policies. As outlined earlier in the chapter staff also require the time and opportunity for professional development in order to confidently implement a range of assessment approaches for their students.

At European level, the European Commission (2013) supported the idea that 'curriculum should be developed through dialogue and partnerships with students, graduates and other stakeholders' (p 41). In addition, the ESG European QA standards (2015) highlight that assessment should be consistent and fair, that students should be given feedback and that the criteria for and the methods of assessment are published in advance (p. 12). At national level in Ireland, there is a growing recognition in policies of the idea of students as partners in the curriculum process and support for students under the principles of universal design for learning (HEA, 2015). Further, a guide for institutions, available from the National Forum, provides assistance to those wishing to develop enabling policies in the area of assessment (National Forum, 2018).

In addition to an enabling policy framework, a framework for the professional development of staff who teach is a crucial structure in supporting enhanced approaches to assessment and feedback. The National Forum recently developed a National Professional Development Framework for All Staff who Teach in Higher Education (PD Framework) and many of the elements in this Framework align with empowering and engaging students in ways which support the UDL principles (National Forum, 2016d). For example, staff are encouraged to be:

- Supportive of **active student-centered approaches** to learning that engage students and build towards **students as partners** in their learning (Element 4.2)
- Application of appropriately aligned assessment and **learner-oriented feedback** approaches from one's own discipline and, where relevant, from other disciplines (Element 4.5)
- Knowledge of and application of the theories of how students learn within and across disciplines, and a **responsiveness to the needs of diverse cohorts of students** (Element 4.6).

This professional development framework provides a structure for staff to reflect on their teaching and assessment practices and to identify and address gaps. The framework is designed to be used throughout an individual's career enabling staff to continually develop their practice in an increasingly changing teaching and assessment environment.

Conclusion

The National Forum's Assessment Enhancement Theme had a strong focus on engaging and empowering students. This two-year project gave particular attention to having in-depth national conversations around assessment and feedback with both staff and students. Based on some key areas of focus, resources and research outputs were developed in partnership with the Irish higher education sector. However, from the outset of the enhancement theme our aim was that a set of nationally agreed principles around assessment and feedback would emerge to guide future approaches to assessment in Ireland. The eight principles identified can be readily mapped with UDL principles (Figure 16.4)

When engaging in issues around assessment and feedback it is important to start, as we did, with exploring whether you have a common understanding of

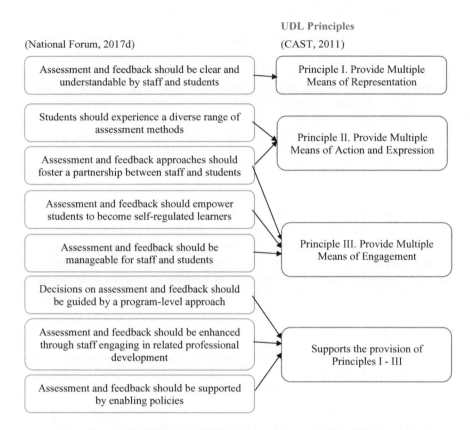

Figure 16.4 Alignment of National Forum assessment and feedback principles with universal design principles

the language and purpose of these terms. As a result of our conversations we developed a working definition, that is now available nationally for staff and students to use (National Forum, 2017a), and a principle to align with this (Figure 16.4). This definition emphasized the importance of students' empowerment in assessment and feedback but this is only the start, work needs to be done to have further discussions with students to get some practical ideas on how they can become partners in these assessment and feedback processes. Students choice of assessment was one approach that emerged from the discussion and research in the project. A related aspect to the idea of student as partners was the shift in feedback approaches to developing student abilities to self-regulate their learning (Assessment AS Learning). Assessment and feedback also need to be manageable to allow space for more integrative learning and to slow down what can be a conveyor belt of assessment submissions for students.

Supporting a diversity of approaches to assessment and feedback, a key principle in UDL, was also central to our work (see Figure 16.4).

These five areas of focus (also developed into five principles, Figure 16.4), supporting students' engagement and empowerment in assessment and feedback, are more likely to be enabled, if they are supported by a program approach to the monitoring and implementation of these approaches. In addition, it is essential that we support staff by providing opportunities for relevant and accessible professional development. Finally policies, local, national and international should be supportive of change: they should be enabling and implementable in practice (see National Forum, 2018).

This chapter set out to describe a national-level approach to assessment in Irish higher education that supports some of the underlying values and principles of universal design. We hope that those embarking on such an approach in their institutional or discipline practices will find the National Forum principles and resources, alongside the UDL principles, a useful guide. In particular, we believe a conceptual shift in emphasis of assessment towards more Assessment AS Learning may go some way to supporting international higher and further education sectors as they attempt to support students to become engaged and empowered citizens in today's society.

References

Boud, D., & Molloy, E. (Eds.). (2013). *Feedback in Higher and Professional Education*. London: Routledge, pp. 202–217.

Brown, G. (1997). *Assessing Student Learning in Higher Education*. London: Routledge.

Burgstahler, S. (2015). *Universal Design of Instruction (UDI): Definition, Principles, Guidelines, and Examples*. Washington: University of Washington.

Carless, D. (2015). *Excellence in University Assessment*. Oxon: Routledge.

CAST. (2011). *Universal Design for Learning Guidelines version 2.0*. Wakefield, MA: Author.

Cook-Sather, A., Bovill, C., & Felten, P. (2014). *Engaging Students as Partners in Learning and Teaching: A Guide for Faculty*. San Francisco, CA: John Wiley & Sons.

Deeley, S. J. (2014). Summative co-assessment: A deep learning approach to enhancing employability skills and attributes. *Active Learning in Higher Education*, 15:1, 39–51.

Deeley, S. J., & Bovill, C. (2017). Staff student partnership in assessment: Enhancing assessment literacy through democratic practices. *Assessment & Evaluation in Higher Education*, 42:3, 463–477.

Earl, L. M., & Katz, S. (2006). *Rethinking Classroom Assessment with Purpose in Mind: Assessment FOR, as and of Learning*. Manitoba Education, ISBN 0-7711-3499-1. www.edu.gov.mb.ca/k12/assess/wncp/full_doc.pdf

ESG European QA standards. (2015). *Standards and Guidelines for Quality Assurance in the European Higher Education Area* ESG: Brussels.

European Commission. (2013). *High Level Group on the Modernisation of Higher Education: Improving the Quality of Teaching and Learning in Europe's Higher Education Institutions.* Strasbourg: European Commission.

Harland, T, McLean, A., Wass, R., Miller, E., & Nui Sim, K. (2015). An assessment arms race and its fallout: High-stakes grading and the case for slow scholarship. *Assessment & Evaluation in Higher Education,* 40:4, 528–541. doi:10.1080/026 02938.2014.931927

HEA. (2015). *National Plan for Equity of Access to Higher Education, 2015–2019.* Higher Education Authority. Dublin. http://hea.ie/assets/uploads/2017/06/National-Plan-for-Equity-of-Access-to-Higher-Education-2015-2019.pdf

Healey, M., Flint, A., & Harrington, K. (2014). *Engagement Through Partnership: Students as Partners in Learning and Teaching in Higher Education.* York: Higher Education Academy.

Hine, B., & Northeast, T. (2016). Using feed-forward strategies in higher education. *New Vista,* 2:1, 1–33. University of West London. http://repository.uwl.ac.uk/id/eprint/2012/1/Hine_Northeast%202016%20New_Vistas_V2I1.pdf accessed 29th November 2017.

Hornby, W., & Laing, D. (2003). *Assessment survey report no 1: Efficiency and effectiveness in assessment QAA Scotland.* https://www.enhancementthemes.ac.uk/docs/ethemes/assessment/reflections-on-assessment-volume-i.pdf?sfvrsn=c449f681_12

Maguire, T., O'Neill, G., & McEvoy, E. (2017). 'Cultivating the Sector's Assessment Literacy through a Conversational Approach'. Assessment in Higher Education (AHE) Conference in Manchester, 28/29th June 2017.

National Forum. (2016a). Enhancement Theme 2016/18 Assessment OF/FOR/AS Learning webpage. https://www.teachingandlearning.ie/resource-hub/student-success/assessment-of-for-as-learning/

National Forum. (2016b). *Assessment OF, FOR and AS Learning: Students as Partners in Assessment,* National Forum Insight. Dublin: Author. https://www.teachingandlearning.ie/publications/

National Forum. (2016c). Profile of assessment practices Irish higher education. *National Forum for the Enhancement of Teaching and Learning.* Dublin: Author. https://www.teachingandlearning.ie/publications/

National Forum. (2016d). *National Professional Development Framework for All Staff Who Teach in Higher Education.* Dublin: Author. https://www.teachingandlearning.ie/publications/

National Forum. (2017a). *Expanding our Understanding of Assessment and Feedback in Irish Higher Education.* National Forum Insight. Dublin: Author. https://www.teachingandlearning.ie/publications/

National Forum. (2017b). *Programme Approaches to Assessment and Feedback.* Dublin: Author. https://www.teachingandlearning.ie/publications/

National Forum. (2017c). *Student Experiences. In Programme Approaches to Assessment and Feedback.* Dublin: Author. https://www.teachingandlearning.ie/publications/

National Forum. (2017d). *Principles of Assessment OF/FOR/AS Learning: National Forum Enhancement Theme.* Dublin: Author. https://www.teachingandlearning.ie/publications/

National Forum. (2018). *Enabling Policies for Digital Teaching and Learning*. Dublin: Author.

National Forum. (2019). *About: The National Forum for the Enhancement of Teaching and Learning*. Dublin: Author. https://www.teachingandlearning.ie/about/

O'Connor, J. (2017). 'It is really difficult to read scientific papers'- Teach me how. In L. Padden, J. O'Connor, T. Barrett (Eds.), *Universal Design for Curriculum Design: Case Studies from University College Dublin* (pp. 115–123). Dublin: Access and Lifelong Learning, University College Dublin.

O'Neill, G. (Ed.). (2011). *A Practitioner's Guide to Choice of Assessment Methods within a Module*. Dublin: UCD Teaching and Learning.

O'Neill, G. (2017). It's not fair! Students and staff views on the equity of the procedures and outcomes of students' choice of assessment methods. *Irish Educational Studies*, 36:2, 221–236. doi:10.1080/03323315.2017.1324805

PASS. (2011). *Programme Assessment Strategies* webpage. www.pass.brad.ac.uk/ accessed 21st February 2011.

Rao, K., & Meo, G. (2016). Using universal design for learning to design standards-based lessons. *SAGE Open*, Special Issue – Student Diversity. 1–12. doi:10.1177/2158244016680688

Sadler, D. R. (2010). Beyond feedback: Developing student capability in complex appraisal, *Assessment & Evaluation in Higher Education*, 35:5, 535–550.

SPACE. (2011). SPACE Project: Inclusive Assessment (Staff-Student Partnership for Assessment Change and Evaluation) (2003–2006).

Taylor, J. A. (2008). Assessment in first year university: A model to manage transition. *Journal of University Teaching and Learning Practice*, 5:1, 20–33.

UDLL. (2016). *A Universal Design for Learning: A Best Practice Guideline*. UDLL Partnership, HOWEST (SIHO), AHEAD and NTNU (Universell). Dublin: AHEAD Educational Press.

Section 5

Providing access to learning for all

Enabling inclusive learning through digital literacy and technologies

Restructuring the blended learning environment on campus for equity and opportunity through UDL

Richard M. Jackson and Scott D. Lapinski

Case study: where we started and our purpose

Two years ago, after much reflection and introspection, we realized that our classes were not as effective as they could be. Our classes were fairly traditional in structure. Each week, students came into the physical space of the classroom, at the designated time, and sat in rows of tablet arm chairs. While seats were not assigned, students all sat in the same places each week, and talked with the same student colleagues. At the beginning of each class, we lectured for part of the time to present new information on the topic of the week and to clarify misunderstandings from reading assignments or previously covered topics. At the close of our lectures, we held collaborative discussions for students to further process their learning. When not in class, students completed a series of readings and discussion posts related to the topic of the week. There were also mid-term and final assignments that covered course content in summative ways.

After careful consideration of course reviews, student perfor-mance, and our own informal data, we decided that our traditional approach to teaching was not sufficient. While there were aspects of our initial design and delivery that we wanted to retain, there were some troublesome areas that we sought to redress. We committed to bringing our course designs into alignment with our espoused beliefs about teaching and learning to create learning environments that would be effective for a broader range of students. After lengthy dis-cussions, we formulated an iterative approach that would accomplish the following goals:

• Authentically reflect our beliefs about effective instructional design and delivery

- Put inclusion, Universal Design for Learning, accessibility, and technology at the forefront of our planning and design thinking
- Transform our traditional classroom/lecture hall experiences into highly engaging, interactive and participatory learning environments
- Provide an exposition of a fully accessible course delivery system for our broader university community
- Model the application of effective and inclusive practices for course participants preparing to be educational practitioners

Introduction: UDL, accessibility, and technology

As instructors and co-designers, we continually reflect on: teaching and learning, course content and structure, the student experience, and our responsibilities as instructors. In our classes, we were talking with students about inclusion, Universal Design for Learning (UDL), accessibility, technology, and learning theories, but we were not always "walking the walk". We needed to change the way we both designed and delivered our courses. We needed to evolve. Our redesign process ultimately resulted in creating a "flipped approach" to our course planning. A flipped approach is one that utilizes digital spaces to deliver content and physical spaces to process learning through activities and discussion (Horn & Staker, 2015). This type of approach allowed us greater flexibility in our practices, but also required us to think critically about the interplay among accessibility, technology, and UDL, three concepts we considered to be core elements of any redesign, within both physical and digital spaces. Before examining the roles that these three elements played in our approach, it is important to establish why we felt this shift in approach was necessary.

Before proceeding, it should be noted that while we made many pedagogical decisions in our design thinking, in preparing this chapter we have elected to emphasize the intersections among UDL, accessibility, and the use of technology, and how our understanding of each of these concepts has contributed to our design of both undergraduate and graduate level courses. In taking a deep dive into these core areas, our intent is to inspire productive thinking about inclusive and effective course design and delivery.

Why take a new approach? Key assumptions

As we mentioned earlier, we had extensive conversations about what our redesign of course work might entail. We thought about a number of existing models and practices, and ultimately, decided to take an eclectic approach that reflected not only our conceptualization of effective teaching and course design, but also one that represented our views on the changing learning landscape in higher education. Why we place UDL, accessibility, and technology at the fore-front of our design thinking is made evident in the following assumptions:

- Assumption 1. A Diverse Student Population Necessitates Inclusive Practices
- Assumption 2. Traditional Practices Have Limited Our Ability to Help All Students Meet High Expectations and Professional Standards
- Assumption 3. Access to Technology Can Expand Possibility
- Assumption 4. Creating Accessible Classrooms Requires More than Accessibility Compliance

It is important to spend a bit more time on each of these assumptions in order to understand the rationale and purpose of our approach.

Assumption 1: a diverse student population necessitates inclusive practices

Students with disabilities in HEI. The student population in higher education is undoubtedly diverse in a number of ways (Snyder, de Brey, & Dillow, 2016). This includes a range of students from both high- and low-incidence disability categories. With advances in college readiness and transition programs, increasing numbers of students with disabilities are successfully transitioning into HEIs (Sanford et al., 2011). We saw these shifts within our classrooms. For instance, we noticed that while the number of students who were specifically requesting accommodations did not dramatically increase, there were an increasingly high number of students in our classes revealing that they had disabilities (why these students chose not to reveal their disability diagnosis in an official capacity is another chapter unto itself) and could benefit from inclusive practices. In order to effectively meet their needs, we realized it was not enough to simply plan for students after the fact through an accommodations-only type approach. Proactive approaches, such as UDL, that address the potential functional barriers for these students, would be essential to ensuring that our courses were inclusive from the start.

International students in HEI. Additionally, there has been an increasing number of international students within many US colleges and universities in recent years (Institute of International Education, 2017). These students come to our universities with a range of knowledge, beliefs, and skills, as well as language and cultural experiences that can differ widely from "traditional" students. Within our classes, we saw a number of potential barriers for these students both within face-to-face classes and within assessment participation. Most importantly, we saw that some of the functional barriers these students encountered were similar to the barriers encountered by students with disabilities. For instance, restricting access to content comprised of text-heavy chapters and academic articles alone unnecessarily restricted learning for each of these groups. Such functional similarities only further pushed our thinking toward inclusive approaches.

Student experiences with technology. Germane to this assumption, it is important to note that students are entering institutions of higher education from immersive, technology rich environments. While in some ways, students do have more knowledge and experience than previous generations and tend to be more comfortable and open to using technology, it does not follow that they can use all tools in flexible and creative ways conducive to learning. There is a common misconception that the current generation of students are all technology experts (Selwyn, 2009). We found that students in our courses had a broad range of expertise and familiarity with technology. For instance, in one of our courses we had students video record themselves implementing a brief lesson. While there were some students who were entirely capable of recording and editing high quality videos, most were only comfortable recording video on their phones. Thus, there was familiarity, but not necessarily expertise. As instructors, we quickly learned that proficiency could not be presumed. Rather, we had to either teach students how to use these tools or somehow ensure there were multiple tools and pathways available for students to express their learning.

Additionally, when it comes to technology accessibility, we have found that many of our students had little to no knowledge of what accessibility means and how they can implement accessible practices, such as captioning. They are familiar with the necessity and purpose of such features, but they were often unfamiliar with how to effectively caption videos. One particular example highlighting this problem was that there had been multiple students in our classes who said they did not need to worry about captioning anymore because YouTube has an auto-captioning feature. While it is true that this service has increased in quality over time and will likely continue to improve, these captions often contain mistakes and are only a good start. Students were not aware of what appropriate captioning entailed. Again, there was awareness, but not expertise.

As instructors, we could not ignore these changes in the student population. The increasing number of students with disabilities and international students necessitated the use of inclusive and flexible practices, and their varying degrees of technological expertise required us to rethink the tools we used and how we used them. Retrofitting was no longer a viable option, and we could no longer rely on disability services offices and accommodations to ensure all students had access to instruction. Likewise, we could assume that students were more familiar with technology, but we could not assume that familiarity meant expertise in technology. We could take advantage of the changes in terms of student familiarity with different tools, but we still needed to change our own practices to ensure students had access to these tools and could use them appropriately. Student preference and use of assistive and universally designed technology defies standardization, thus demanding exhaustive and high quality accessible course design.

> **Reflection**
>
> - What assumptions do you make about your students and their learning?
> - In what ways are students in your classroom diverse?
> - How do you currently account for learner diversity in your goals, methods, materials, and assessments?
> - How proficient are you students in using technology for learning?

Assumption 2: traditional practices have limited our ability to help all students meet high expectations and professional standards

Another key assumption we made is that it is, in part, traditional practices that have limited our ability to help our students meet our high expectations and professional standards. As instructors, we must hold high expectations for our students. We want them to learn the content, build expertise through practice, and demonstrate their increasing expertise through assessments. Traditionally this means lecturing to students so that they hear our expertise, assigning reading from the field so they have the benefit of others' expertise, and requiring them to write papers demonstrating a capacity to perform tasks as an academic expert might. The basic idea is that there will be a transference of expertise through repeated exposure to expert knowledge and practices. Given our previous assumption regarding the increasingly diverse student population and the contextual constraints of the postsecondary environment, these types of methods are increasingly troublesome if we are to hold all students to our high expectations. Students have a variety of goals, only some of which are academic, and learn in a variety of ways that are not conducive to simple transference of information.

In addition to high expectations, professional standards are a vital consideration when thinking about courses like the ones we teach. We teach current and future educators, and in so doing, we want to ensure that our teacher candidates are prepared for the rigors of designing and implementing inclusive education themselves. We also want to ensure that our students can meet professional requirements for both entry into and continued development within the field of education. This requires a certain degree of meta-awareness on our part as instructors. Professional standards and the demands of diverse classrooms require teachers to be innovative and inclusive, yet we were not being innovative or inclusive ourselves. To help students become inclusive educators, we had to meet those standards first. A traditional approach of lecture, discuss, read, write, and repeat would not suffice. Necessary was the consideration of frameworks that would allow us to not only teach about inclusion, but also be inclusive ourselves. UDL was one such practice that allowed us to do just that: teach inclusively.

Reflection

- What assumptions do you make about your personal practices and how they impact students?
- How do your current practices align with what you believe about learning and effective instruction?
- Are there any ways that you are encouraging and limiting students' abilities to meet professional standards?

Assumption 3: access to technology can expand possibility

Our next assumption was that access to technology can expand possibilities within the classroom (Hunter, 2015). Note that the word can is underlined in this assumption, and for good reason. Technology itself is neutral outside of a specific context (the learning environment and material itself) and a specific practitioner (the learner). For instance, a student could be provided with access to text through tools that support text-to-speech (TTS), but if that student does not know how to vary the speed at which the text is read aloud (an important option available in high quality TTS software), then the learner is likely to find TTS tools of limited value due to the lack of customization. Likewise, TTS would be useless if the text were just an image (an important consideration when creating accessible documents and webpages) and therefore not readable by a screen reader. An easy example of how to conceptualize this issue is to think about PDFs. Some PDFs are just images or pictures of text captured for visual display only. When this is the case, individual elements of text cannot be located and identified without additional software conversion (optical character recognition). When text is rendered as more than just an image, the text itself can be highlighted and read aloud because it is available as unique elements. Without careful consideration of the technology itself, TTS software, though vital for non-visual access, would not be used to its full potential.

Still, we find that technology does have tremendous potential to expand what is possible in the classroom. Take the previous example of TTS. If students are taught to use the tool and the text itself is readable (remember, it cannot just be an image), then traditional readings are no longer restricted to a single modality. Students could read and access text through visual or auditory means. Students could then read the text at the library or listen to the text on their ride home (Jackson & Karger, 2015). This seemingly simple tool expands what is possible for all learners within the classroom by expanding access. When we began to think more about online and blended learning environments, the possibilities only further expand due to the availability and variety of possible tools as well as the potential portability across multiple platforms.

Reflection

- What assumptions do you make about technology and how both you and your students use it?
- What technology do you use personally and instructionally? What do your students use?
- What technology is available to you as an instructor?
- What technology is available for students?

Assumption 4: creating accessible classrooms requires more than accessibility compliance

Our last assumption regarding why we needed to take a new approach is related to the notion that mere accessibility compliance is not enough to create fully accessible classrooms. There is a range of important standards, such as WCAG (Web Content Accessibility Guidelines) 2.0; a set of standards focused on ensuring website accessibility. These types of standards allow for publishers and content providers to create content that is accessible from the start (Henry, 2017). This is an important step because it decreases the reliance on retrofitting (making adaptations to an already created material), which can be costly and time consuming and could potentially lead to unequal opportunities for student participation. There are, however, serious questions that need to be asked as an instructor or curriculum developer around whether or not compliance with these accessibility standards is sufficient to create fully accessible classrooms.

For instance, as an instructor you might include a video that has captions, but this does not account for cognitive accessibility or how the video is being used by individual users within the context of your classroom. Likewise, captions do not address the quality of the content itself. There are a range of captioned videos available that have misinformation or do not adequately review the intended content. In our experience, we found that these standards are necessary but not sufficient when considering learning environments in higher education. What we needed to do, at least for this aspect of our broader approach, was to also think critically about how accessibility, technology, and UDL come together.

Reflection

- What assumptions do you make about accessibility?
- How do you ensure your classrooms are accessible to all learners?
- How have you considered accessibility in both face-to-face and digital environments?
- How have you considered accessibility across learning environments?

Recapping our assumptions

As stated earlier, our goal in this chapter is to illuminate one core aspect (the intersections of technology, accessibility, and UDL) of a broader approach. To better illustrate how we came to an understanding of why our practices needed to evolve, we reviewed some of our key assumptions that led us to thinking differently. Specifically, we chose to change our practices because our students had changed. Also, the traditional practices we had been using limited what we were able to do with our students. The technologies available to us could now expand our design possibilities. Moreover, our vision of inclusiveness went far beyond mere accessibility. We will now turn our attention to how we actually began to consider UDL, accessibility, and technology within the broader flipped approach that we took on in our design thinking.

Linking accessibility, technology, and UDL

To start, we need to address what each of these three elements are and how they intersect. Conceptually, accessibility, technology and UDL are related, but they are certainly not interchangeable. For instance, there is a common misconception that the descriptor "digital" means or somehow implies "accessible". This could not be further from the truth. While digital technologies certainly have the potential for greater flexibility, a digital representation can be just as inaccessible as any other analog representation. Another example is around captions. Images or animations presented without closed captions and audio descriptions cannot be interpreted by individuals who are visually or hearing impaired. Similarly, one could plan flexibility into lessons using UDL principles, but the intent of flexibility alone does not mean accessibility has been fully considered. Options for expression and engagement may still contain unintended barriers to access. With this in mind, we need to talk more about how we approached technology and accessibility in order to address how they intersect.

Technology in higher education

Technology seems ubiquitous in higher education. What has come to be known as the "digital shift" in the world of education has created new challenges as well as new opportunities for accessible course delivery. But in one form or another, technology has always been a part of the teaching and learning experience. Go back 40 years and note some of the same tools in wide use today: blackboards, chalk, pens and pencils, paper, books, projectors, calculators, rulers, headphones, videos, audio recordings, and even some forms of assistive technologies (AT). What is noticeably different in today's learning environments is the proliferation of digital technologies such as computers, smartphones, and the internet.

It is digital technology that people tend to associate with the term "technology", but it is important to consider technologies more broadly given the diverse range of learning environments in which students find themselves. If we only think about digital spaces, then we run the risk of ignoring physical spaces, and inclusion requires consideration of all environments. In short, a broad conceptualization of technology that includes both digital and physical spaces is necessary for understanding how we can improve our own practices through UDL, accessibility, and technology.

Reflection

- What technologies are currently available to you as an instructor?
- What role does technology play in your classroom?
- Do you provide students with training for how to use the technologies?

What is accessibility?

Accessibility is not easily defined. Just about any material could be considered accessible in the right context and to the right person. Yet accessibility requires everyone to have equal access to learning, and this is easier said than done. Understanding accessibility requires consideration of the person, the environment, and the dynamic relationship (interaction) between the two, as well as the outcome of said interaction. Because of this complicated nature of accessibility, it is important to include two definitions, one of which focuses on broad goals and the other on the functional nature of accessibility. In other words, what is accessibility and what does it look like?

When thinking about what accessibility is, an appropriate definition can be found in a resolution agreement between the Office for Civil Rights and the South Carolina Technical College System. Within this resolution agreement, accessibility was defined as:

> "Accessible" means a person with a disability is afforded the opportunity to acquire the same information, engage in the same interactions, and enjoy the same services as a person without a disability in an equally effective and equally integrated manner, with substantially equivalent ease of use. The person with a disability must be able to obtain the information as fully, equally and independently as a person without a disability. Although this might not result in identical ease of use compared to that of persons without disabilities, it still must ensure equal opportunity to the educational benefits and opportunities afforded by the technology and equal treatment in the use of such technology.
> (Office of Civil Rights Compliance Review No. 11-11-6002)

It is important to note that this definition focuses on the opportunities afforded to students. For materials to be accessible in this sense, the student needs to be afforded the same access and opportunities. This is a necessarily rights-based focus, and helpful in establishing the overall purpose and scope of what accessibility means. What is also necessary is a more functional definition of what this might look like in context.

A functional approach to accessibility can be found within the Web Content Accessibility Guidelines (WCAG). These are web accessibility standards, but their four principles of accessibility are applicable to far more than just the web and are helpful in articulating what such a rights-based definition might look like in practice. These principles are summarized with the WCAG 2.0 standards by the acronym POUR:

- Perceivable – Information and user interface components must be presentable to users in ways they can perceive. This means that users must be able to perceive the information being presented (it can't be invisible to all of their senses)
- Operable – User interface components and navigation must be operable. This means that users must be able to operate the interface (the interface cannot require interaction that a user cannot perform)
- Understandable – Information and the operation of user interface must be understandable. This means that users must be able to understand the information as well as the operation of the user interface (the content or operation cannot be beyond their understanding)
- Robust – Content must be robust enough that it can be interpreted reliably by a wide variety of user agents, including assistive technologies. This means that users must be able to access the content as technologies advance (as technologies and user agents evolve, the content should remain accessible) (Cooper, Kirkpatrick, & O'Connor, 2016)

Notably, these four key principles act as a guide for developing and structuring content. Whereas the initial rights definition focused on ensuring the same opportunities, the same services, and the same ease of use, this definition describes how such an environment should be structured to be accessible. Designing accessible materials does become further complicated when considering individual materials such as websites (as the WCAG guidelines apply to) and individual standards, but these two definitions help develop a more robust understanding of what accessibility actually is, and how it can be achieved.

Reflection

- Which standards and best practices have you used to ensure accessibility?
- How familiar are you with the accessibility policies of your school?
- How would you know if your course was accessible or not?

Accessibility, technology, and UDL: connecting the dots

Accessibility, technology and UDL are necessary components of effective and inclusive course design and delivery but, importantly, they are more effective when considered together. While we incorporated several other pedagogical considerations in our course design, these three elements were essential to our approach.

Accessibility and technology. As has already been discussed, there are connections between accessibility and technology that should be mentioned. Rather than repeating that information here, it is important to highlight and reiterate a few key points. First, one can talk about accessibility in a generic sense, but in practice accessibility must always be tied to a particular type of material and environment. One can look at generic definitions of accessibility, but to put those definitions into practice one must understand the technology, the audience, the demands of the task, and the context. This is why specific accessibility standards exist for website and building designs, but not for technology in all instances. This inextricable link has important implications for course planning and delivery because, though there are some transferable ideas and practices, understanding accessibility requires understanding of the technology as well. Let us reconsider the previous example of ensuring digital text is presented in a means that is more than an image. One can point towards generic practices such as ensuring the text is readable by a screen reader. However, to actually create accessible documents and to ensure accessibility, one has to know the file format of the document and the software that was used to design it. Designing accessible PDFs is not the same as designing accessible Word documents.

Second, technologies have the potential to increase accessibility. Potential is an important word to consider here, as not all technologies increase accessibility. For instance, while animated graphical presentation software, such as Prezi, may reduce the demand for working memory resources and be quite visually engaging, the presentations may not be screen readable by assistive technologies. In this instance, use of the technology only increases the relative inaccessibility of the technology for some users. In general, however, technology has the potential to increase accessibility by allowing for flexibility in presentation and use as well as increased portability.

Another important connection between accessibility and technology is Assistive Technology (AT). AT was discussed in the POUR principles discussed here and it needs to be considered further because it is a specific type of technology that is essential for some learners. AT picks up where conventional, and even universally designed technology, leaves off. Assistive technology takes into consideration the inherent relationship among the individual, the setting, the task demands, and the available technology. The Assistive Technology Industry Association (ATIA) provides a concise definition. They wrote, "Assistive technology (AT) is any item, piece of equipment, software program, or product system that is used to increase, maintain, or improve the functional capabilities of persons with disabilities" (Assistive Technology Industry Association (ATIA), 2018). AT are necessarily individualized supports that are specifically designed to meet an individual need. In terms of accessibility, for an environment to be accessible, an individual who uses AT must be able to interact in the same way as others. For example, if someone uses a wheelchair, they need to be able to enter and navigate the room as any other individual might. This requires designing and organizing the physical space to ensure the doorways are wide enough and there is sufficient space between tables or desks. In other words, the space needs to be designed to be flexible enough that people with AT will still have equal access.

Accessibility and UDL

Accessibility is an important, though sometimes only implied, aspect of UDL. The reauthorization of the Individuals with Disabilities Education Act (IDEA) in 1997 stipulated that students with disabilities must have access to the general education curriculum. In particular, students must have access to content, be able to participate in instructional routines, and have the opportunity to make progress with the general education curriculum. As a result of this mandate, UDL was proposed as the framework for meeting the important goals of access, participation, and progress for all learners (Hitchcock, Meyer, Rose, & Jackson, 2002). As such, accessibility is imbued throughout the UDL framework as an integral step to ensure all students are included. For example, if students do not have access to alternatives for visual information (Checkpoint 1.3), then it goes without saying that they will not have a chance to participate or make progress. In this sense, accessibility provides a critical baseline within UDL.

Accessibility relates to all three principles of UDL but is particularly relevant to the top level of the UDL Guidelines. The new graphic organizer developed by CAST highlights that point by labeling Guidelines 1 (Perception), 4 (Physical Action), and 7 (Recruiting Interest) as "Access" (CAST, 2018). These are the guidelines that speak most directly to some of the key ways in which students can be provided with initial access to learning. For instance, checkpoint 1.2: offer alternatives for auditory information helps remind instructors and designers that providing only audio information will necessarily limit access to students who are deaf or hearing impaired. Instead options should be provided such as captions or other similar visual supports to ensure accessibility. These Guidelines provide an initial way to begin considering accessibility and potential barriers to student learning. Of course, implementing the UDL Guidelines alone will not necessarily result in full accessibility. Accessibility standards must also be implemented in light of the specific design constraints of technologies.

Technology and UDL

In addition to a range of connections between UDL and AT (Rose, Hasselbring, Stahl, & Zabala, 2005), there are also connections between UDL and technology more generally. An advantageous characteristic of technology is the potential flexibility it offers to both learners and instructors. Consider the simple example of accessible digital text (the modifier "accessible" is important here because as was pointed out earlier, not all digital text is fully accessible). When text is accessible, students can read the text visually or read the text aurally. While this flexibility might be useful for a student who is up late studying with eye strain, driving to and from school, or exercising on a treadmill, it is absolutely essential for a student who relies on text-to-speech to access text. In this instance, the increased flexibility of the technology itself allows for greater access for all learners. UDL is a framework that helps educators and curriculum designers think about ways flexibility can be built into learning environments as well as the technologies that support learning within those environments.

Connecting all three concepts

Now that we have discussed connections between accessibility, technology and UDL, we need to consider how all three come together in reciprocal ways. The key relationship among all three of these elements is that considering all three together allows for an increased capacity to create more effective, inclusive learning environments. Each element can be considered independently, but often, as we pointed out previously, it would be insufficient in fostering inclusion for all students. For instance, technology can be considered as an element of inclusion, but if the technology is not designed proactively to account for a wide range of learner variability, then it is unlikely that all students will benefit from the use of the technology. Accessibility could be considered, but if it does not address the technology within the learning environment, then it is likely that access will still be limited due to contextual idiosyncrasies. UDL can be considered, but if environments are not accessible, then we have to ask if students can participate in the first place.

Learning environments must account for learner variability and effective pedagogy (UDL), accessible physical and digital spaces (accessibility), and a range of tools for both students and instructors to utilize (technology). By taking into account flexible technologies, accessibility requirements, and UDL principles, we are able to support inclusive course delivery and ultimately teach all learners more effectively, and ultimately put the learner and learning first. All three elements can contribute to creating more effective learning environments independently, but there is a particularly powerful impact when they are considered together.

Reflection

1   What are the key factors you have already considered in creating more inclusive classrooms?
2   How do you ensure students can access learning, participate in learning, and make significant progress?
3   How does UDL, accessibility, and technology overlap in your planning?

Conclusion

The challenges and opportunities facing institutions of higher education today are numerous and fast changing. Whether our mission in higher education is to ensure equal learning opportunities for students we admit or to extend learning opportunities to those we have yet to admit, the UDL framework can shift our thinking from living with unintended barriers imposed by tradition to eliminating barriers by intentional design. UDL thinking can transform the traditional course experience by enabling access to content, involvement with instruction and participation with peers. In this chapter, we described a process we employed to redesign our own traditional course structures into flexible modularized learning experiences deliverable in flipped, blended or fully online offerings. At Boston College we have put into practice a flipped blended learning approach informed by UDL thinking, accessibility considerations and applications of technology.

For those who can agree with our assumptions and identify with our design goals, this chapter offers a rationale and beginning steps for creating effective and inclusive course level learning experiences. In particular, our approach centers accessibility, technology and UDL as key elements in course redesign. Accessibility is context dependent and thus resists standardization; technology is ever changing and thus defies prescription; and UDL is a truly transformative yet nascent framework under continuous development and refinement. To those who would apply our approach to course design and delivery, we encourage thoughtful planning in the ways that the areas of accessibility, technology and UDL intersect at your own institutions. What one does with this line of thinking will hopefully raise expectations for successful implementation and serve as a model for emulation.

References

Assistive Technology Industry Association (ATIA). (2018). What is AT? Retrieved February 27, 2018, from www.atia.org/at-resources/what-is-at/#what-is-assistive-technology

CAST. (2018). *Universal design for learning guidelines version 2.2*. Wakefield, MA: CAST. Retrieved from http://udlguidelines.cast.org

Cooper, M., Kirkpatrick, A., & O'Connor, J. (Eds.). (2016). *Understanding the four principles of accessibility*. Retrieved February 27, 2018, from www.w3.org/TR/UNDERSTANDING-WCAG20/intro.html#introduction-fourprincs-head

Henry, S. L. (Ed.). (2017). *Web Content Accessibility Guidelines (WCAG) overview*. Retrieved February 27, 2018, from www.w3.org/WAI/intro/wcag

Hitchcock, C.G., Meyer, A., Rose, D. & Jackson, R. (2002). Providing new access to the general curriculum: Universal design for learning. *Teaching Exceptional Children*, 35(2), 8–17.

Horn, M. B., & Staker, H. (2015). *Blended: Using disruptive innovation to improve schools*. San Francisco, CA: Jossey-Bass.

Hunter, J. (2015). *Technology integration and high possibility classrooms: Building from TPACK*. New York: Routledge.

Institute of International Education. (2017). *International student enrollment trends, 1948/49-2016/17*. Retrieved February 27, 2018, from www.iie.org/opendoors

Jackson, R. M., & Karger, J. (2015). *Audio-supported reading and students with learning disabilities*. Wakefield, MA: National Center on Accessible Educational Materials. Retrieved from http://aem.cast.org/about/publications/2015/audio-supported-reading-learning-disabilities-asr-ld.html

Resolution Agreement South Carolina Technical College System OCR Compliance Review No. 11-11-6002

Rose, D., Hasselbring, T. S., Stahl, S., & Zabala, J. (2005). Assistive technology and universal design for learning: Two sides of the same coin. In D. Edyburn, K. Higgins, & R. Boone (Eds.), *Handbook of special education technology research and practice* (pp. 507–518). Whitefish Bay, WI: Knowledge by Design.

Sanford, C., Newman, L., Wagner, M., Cameto, R., Knokey, A. M., & Shaver, D. (2011). *The post-high school outcomes of young adults with disabilities up to 6 years after high school: Key findings from the National Longitudinal Transition Study-2* (NLTS2) (No. NCSER 2011-3004) (Vol. 2). Menlo Park, CA: SRI International.

Selwyn, N. (2009). The digital native – myth and reality. *Aslib Proceedings*, 61(4), 364–379. https://doi.org/10.1108/00012530910973776

Snyder, T. D., de Brey, C., & Dillow, S. A. (2016). *Digest of education statistics 2015* (No. NCES 2016-014). Washington, DC: National Center for Education Statistics, Institute of Education Sciences, U.S. Department of Education.

Chapter 18

Promoting digital access and inclusivity in open and distance learning in South Africa

A UDL approach

Ashiya Abdool Satar

Case study: increasing access to higher education post-1994

The fall of the apartheid regime in 1994 brought with it hope for democracy and inclusion in all aspects of social, political, cultural and educational realms, which initiated a complete overhaul in legislation and policies (DHET, 2012). The overall policy framework, thus, encapsulated the vision for the new democratic South Africa, emphasizing the formation of an equal, equitable, and inclusive society, underscoring the development of a correspondingly inclusive system of post-school education that will aid in overcoming the developmental challenges the country faces (DoE, 1997; DoE, 2001; CHE, 2007; Soudien, 2010; DHET, 2013; DSD, 2015).

The guidelines for the transformation of the higher education sector in South African was foregrounded in 1997 in the "Education White Paper 3: A Programme for The Transformation of Higher Education" (DoE, 1997), wherein emphasis has been placed on, inter alia, improving equity of access and participation for students with disabilities, and on improving access to information and communication technologies (ICT) in this sector (DoE, 1997; DoE, 2001; DHET, 2013; Nyahodza & Higgs, 2017). Following from the Education White Paper 3 (DoE, 1997), the "National Plan for Higher Education" (DoE, 2001) provided an implementation framework for the restructuring of the higher education system and its alignment to the knowledge and information society (DoE, 2001; CHE, 2007; Matshedisho, 2010). Subsequent policy documents that emphasize the importance of the higher education sector in bringing South Africa on par with the digitized global marketplace are the "Green Paper on Post-School

Education and Training" (DHET, 2012), and the "White Paper on Post-School Education and Training" (DHET, 2013). This overall policy framework particularly underscores the pivotal role of distance education, and specifically, the University of South Africa (Unisa) in increasing access to higher education for previously marginalized groups, thereby placing this institution at the forefront of meeting the development goals in the region. Unisa is a dedicated Open Distance and e-Learning (ODeL) institute in South Africa that caters to close to 400,000 students from diverse backgrounds not just in Africa, but globally as well (DoE, 1997; DoE, 2001; Ngubane-Mokiwa & Letseka, 2015). What do we mean by ODeL then?

Although the concepts of 'distance education' and 'open learning' are interrelated, they are dissimilar. Distance education arises when students and instructors are separated by time and space and instruction occurs via some sort of media, whether digital or print (or both), while open learning refers to an education environment that abates varying access barriers to learning environments (Holmberg, 2005; Braimoh & Osiki 2008; Kanwar, 2017). When the objectives of distance learning and open education fuse, the formation of open distance learning (ODL) institutions come about, eventually leading to the establishment of open distance and e-learning (ODeL) institutes when the assimilation of e-learning technologies and pedagogies occur in ODL environments (Ngubane-Mokiwa & Letseka, 2015; Kanwar, 2017).

ODL is gaining traction in Africa due to the flexibility, affordability, and accessibility it provides to students from diverse backgrounds with equally diverse needs (Braimoh & Osiki, 2008). Kanwar (2017) also draws attention to the fact that ODL institutions appeal to students with disabilities due to the affordability, convenience, flexibility, and confidentiality (from revealing their disability) that these structures provide. Hence, it can be stated that the goal of ODL courses is to reach out to a diverse range of students, irrespective of geographical boundaries, especially the unreached segments of the population (Dell, C. A., Dell, T. F., & Blackwell, 2015; Kanwar, 2017; Ngubane-Mokiwa, 2017).

While ODeL environments promote better access to higher education in various ways and provide immense opportunities for flexible learning, they are not exempt from the trials related to inclusion. In dealing with the challenges of enhancing meaningful inclusion and access, Unisa employs mechanisms of Universal Design of Learning

(UDL) to meet the needs of diverse student populations, including those with disabilities and those without digital access, in making learning environments accessible for students in an ODeL context. UDL encourages flexible learning environments, whether digital or physical, so that students can interact with, and access course requisites in numerous ways (deMaine, 2014; Unisa, 2015; Ehlinger, 2017). The subsequent sections of this chapter put forth theoretical discussions and lived examples of how UDL principles are used in bridging the digital divide in distance education, finally paying particular emphasis on the practical applications of UDL values imbued within Unisa.

Higher education and the digital divide in South Africa: understanding digital exclusion in distance-learning environments

Data on persons with tertiary qualifications in South Africa, derived from the 2011 and 2016 censuses, depicted in Table 18.1, indicates an upward trend in the participation of people, with and without disabilities, in higher education (Lehohla, 2014; DSD, 2015; Maluleke, 2018).

Table 18.1 Distribution of population aged 20 years and older with tertiary education by sex and disability status – census 2011 vs 2016

Year	2011			
Sex	Male		Female	
Disability status	**With disabilities**	**Without disabilities**	**With disabilities**	**Without disabilities**
Numbers	50,250	1,326,124	59,311	1,531,759
Year	2016			
Sex	Male		Female	
Disability status	**With disabilities**	**Without disabilities**	**With disabilities**	**Without disabilities**
Numbers	84,272	1,630,269	104,322	1,790,829
Year	2011		2016	
Sex	Total		Total	
Disability status	**With disabilities**	**Without disabilities**	**With disabilities**	**Without disabilities**
Numbers	109,561	2,857,883	188,594	3,421,098

However, despite this positive trend highlighting increased access to higher education, what is often overlooked in the discussions on inclusive education is the question of digital divides, particularly in a developing country such as South Africa (Kajee, 2010; DHET, 2013; Ngubane-Mokiwa & Letseka, 2015; Philip et al., 2017; Goggin, 2017). Kajee (2010) and Roulstone (2016) add that while technology has the power to create meaningful engagement and participation in higher education and training, it can equally cause alienation when access to digital technologies is uneven (Khalid & Pedersen, 2016; Neves & Mead, 2017). Additionally, although it can be argued that online learning has indisputably reduced many access barriers to higher education, it also overlooks the issues of digital inclusion and disability to some extent (Dell, C. A., Dell, T. F., & Balckwell, 2015; Rao, Edelen-Smith, & Wailehua, 2015; Goggin, 2017).

Engaging with the issue of disability in the discussions on digital inequality in higher education contexts is a critical concern in the establishment of an equitable society, particularly as embedded in the Constitution of South Africa (Kajee, 2010; Dell, C. A., Dell, T. F., & Blackwell, 2015; DSD, 2015; Rao, Edelen-Smith, & Wailehua, 2015; Goggin, 2017; Nyahodza & Higgs, 2017). Hence, the issue of unequal digital access already creates a barrier to realizing the full potential of information and communication technologies (ICT) in higher education, particularly in distance-learning contexts, which exacerbates the challenges that students with disabilities already contend with (Ngubane-Mokiwa & Letseka, 2015; Kanwar, 2017; Ossiannilsson, 2017).

Higher education institutions can address the issues related to meaningful digital inclusion, by providing greater support structures based on the principles of UDL that underpin equity and enhanced accessibility that extends beyond enrolment in higher education (Kelland, 2005; Kajee, 2010; Nyahodza & Higgs, 2017). Although universal design is essentially premised on the notion of creating accessible physical environments for persons with disabilities, "when applied to higher education, universal design brings a framework for making learning more accessible and instruction more responsive and inclusive to all students" (Zeff, 2007, p. 27). UDL makes provision for inclusive learning spaces for all learners by mediating barriers to learning and enhancing student success by creating, inter alia, accommodating physical spaces, fixtures and furniture, information resources, technology and inclusive course designs (Meyer & Rose, 2005; Rose & Meyer, 2006; Burgstahler, 2013; Dalton, 2017; Kanwar, 2017; Ngubane-Mokiwa, 2017). Nevertheless, before delving into the practical application of UDL in a South African ODeL context, a summary on what is meant by the digital divide is firstly presented to contextualize the ensuing discussions and applications of the UDL approach within this setting.

The digital divide deals with various forms of inequities in ICT. The concept not only covers a range of differences in access to and use of digital technologies, equipment, infrastructure, and services, but also encompasses facets of digital (il)literacy and related technological skills (Pórras-Hernández &

Salinas-Amescua, 2015; Khalid & Pedersen, 2016; Nyahodza & Higgs, 2017; Philip et al., 2017). Thus, discussions on the digital divide encapsulate the issues of 'digital access' and 'digital literacy', which generally vary in developed and developing environments (Liebenberg, Chetty, & Prinsloo, 2012; Ossiannilsson, 2017).

Access not only refers to the provision of adequate ICT infrastructure, but also encapsulates, inter alia, issues of costs and ownership of computerized technologies. Furthermore, issues of accessibility extend to acceptable Internet connectivity and bandwidth as well (Liebenberg, Chetty, & Prinsloo, 2012; Thompson et al., 2014; Khalid & Pedersen, 2016). While digital access refers to the tangible properties of the provision of ICT and related apparatuses, digital literacy refers to the cognitive capabilities associated with the use of ICT (Liebenberg et al. 2012). In other words, the proclivity to adapt to, and adopt digital technologies in everyday activities, as well as the capacity to learn to use its functions effectually captures the essence of digital literacy (Neves & Mead, 2017; Ossiannilsson, 2017).

There are genuine, concerning disparities in the uneven access to digital technologies in developed and developing nations, which needs to be considered in the use and implementation of ICT in higher education contexts as they exacerbate the challenge of digital (il)literacy and adoption (Braimoh & Osiki 2008; Kajee, 2010; Khalid & Pedersen, 2016). In this light, although South Africa exhibits better digital connectivity in comparison to its counterparts in the region, it is not immune to the challenges related to disproportionate access, characteristic of countries in developing countries in the Global South, which complicates the implementation of digital teaching and learning in higher education settings (CHE, 2007; Kajee, 2010; Nyahodza & Higgs, 2017).

Naturally, access to digital technologies supersedes the challenge of digital literacy, more so in the higher education context where the use of digital technologies has become paramount in the development of youth with competency and skills for the globalized networked society (Journell, 2007; Khalid & Pedersen, 2016). This means that students on the negative end of the digital divide continuum would be experiencing digital exclusion (Journell, 2007; Liebenberg, Chetty, & Prinsloo, 2012; Khalid & Pedersen, 2016). Many South African students entering the higher education system do so at a disadvantage due to the poor development of technological skills and literacy, firstly due to the digital divide in the country, and subsequently due to the inadequate transfer of digital literacy skills in the basic schooling environment (Badat, 2005; Kajee, 2010; Thompson et al., 2014; Ngubane-Mokiwa & Letseka, 2015; Khalid & Pedersen, 2016). In addition, due to the disparities of the apartheid regime, South African students from disadvantaged backgrounds gain access to computer equipment and Internet connections through external service providers, exacerbating the ensuing question of digital literacy (CHE, 2007; Brown & Czerniewicz, 2010; Nya-hodza & Higgs, 2017).

Although the overall policy framework for higher education accentuates the pressing need for immediate ICT infrastructure development, accessibility, and affordability for students in the tertiary education environment, the current challenges associated with reaching this goal are apparent and institutions of higher education need to implement personalized strategies for ensuring digital inclusion in the interim (DHET, 2013). Likewise, the issue of disability in the digital divide debate in distance education institutions has to be taken into account in a more meaningful way, as persons with disabilities are already mar-ginalized, and the digital divide tends to heighten the problem of exclusion in the knowledge and information society (Kajee, 2010; Roulstone, 2016; Oswal, 2017). This is where the Universal Design of Learning (UDL) framework comes into play.

UDL embraces a wide range of accessibility options for students from vari-ous backgrounds, abilities and disabilities, thereby encouraging greater access and inclusivity in the educational setting (Zeff, 2007). UDL principles also address the pedagogical and accessibility issues related to the use of vari-ous digital technologies in the classroom (whether digital or traditional) to promote the optimum use and usability of these applications "in the provision of equitable education for the full diversity of students" (Treviranus, 2018, p. 1). The subsequent discussion highlights the practical application of UDL at Unisa in promoting digital inclusivity amidst the apparent digital divide in the country.

Reflection

- What do you understand by the digital divide, and its implication, particularly in the context of higher education in South Africa?
- What influence does the digital divide have in distance-learning situations?
- Do you think the digital divide extends to different contexts, coun-tries and institutions? How are the experiences of countries in the Global South likely to be different from other settings?
- The two confounding variables in the digital divide debate are 'digital access' and 'digital literacy'. What do each of these terms mean and how are they related?
- Does your country or institution face any challenges related to digital access?

- To what extent is there a supporting policy framework for promoting digital literacy in your setting and jurisdiction?
- Reflect on equitable and meaningful access to digital instructional materials in your context. How would the principles of UDL promote meaningful access to these materials? Do you think that these practices differ in different contexts? Why do you think so?

Universal Design of Learning (UDL) in practice: rethinking digital inclusion in distance education courses: a case of Unisa

The University of South Africa (Unisa) is the largest ODL University in Africa (Braimoh & Osiki 2008). South African census data captured in 2011 reveals that 62% of the 900,000 students in higher education attend residential universities, while 48% were enrolled at distance education institutions, 83% of whom are registered at Unisa (DHET, 2012). Furthermore, at Unisa, there has been a steady increase in enrolments of students with disabilities over the last few years, with a corresponding increase in support systems for these students (Kanwar, 2017). Table 18.2 reflects Unisa's enrolment statistics of students with disabilities from 2005 to 2018 that indicates a steady rise in the numbers of students with disabilities studying at Unisa.

Table 18.2 Enrolment of students with disabilities status at Unisa from 2005 to 2018

Year	2005	2006	2007	2008	2009	2010	2011	2012	2013	2014	2015	2016	2017	2018
Numbers	1,714	2,314	2,778	3,070	2,902	3,751	4,309	4,333	5,153	4,638	4,553	3,698	4,962	5,004

Source: Used with permission from the Unisa Research Permission Sub-Committee (RPSC)

This data underscores the important role of Unisa in widening access to higher education opportunities for the region as a whole against the backdrop of the challenges of the digital divide that overshadow the region's development goals. When aligned to the scientifically validated guidelines of UDL, distance and e-learning courses can create improved studentship possibilities for scholars with varying abilities and disabilities, without unfairly advantaging or disadvantaging anyone in the process of adapting learning environments (Burgstahler, 2002; Kanwar, 2017; Lawrie et al., 2017). The following section covers how these aspects of UDL are applied at Unisa.

Creating avenues for digital access and inclusion for students without digital access and students with disabilities through UDL

While infrastructure development is still a challenge that needs to be addressed more aggressively at national and regional level, students in rural areas still have to find ways to access online resources to ensure participation in tertiary education activities (Cross & Adam, 2007). Data costs and poor bandwidth speeds are still an issue in South Africa, due to socio-economic factors that also need to be considered when developing strategies for digital inclusion. Moreover, while technology can ease many daily functions for persons with disabilities and opens up environments, access to education and inclusion in society, technology can also "embody the very symbol of alienation for disabled people" (Roulstone, 2016, p. 4). How does Unisa address these challenges, considering its large and diverse student pool?

At Unisa, some of the challenges created by the digital divide are addressed by instituting an inclusive university support system, imbued with UDL foundations, that focuses on online communication approaches to improve access to information and learning resources (Braimoh & Osiki, 2008; Dell, C. A., Dell, T. F., & Blackwell, 2015; Thomson et al., 2015; Roulstone, 2016; Kanwar, 2017; Ngubane-Mokiwa, 2017; Oswal, 2017). UDL guidelines emphasize that the primary element that enables a reduction in the transactional distance caused by the physical separation between instructors and students in ODL environments is the student support system (Zeff, 2007). This support structure would extend to digital and technological platforms in ODeL environments. (Ngubane-Mokiwa & Letseka, 2015; Rogers-Shaw, Carr-Chellman, & Choi, 2018). In this respect, at Unisa many regional centres, regional hubs, telecentres, computer access facilities and support structures for students without digital access across the country have been established to increase access to digital and information technologies, with a few centres across the Southern African region, and one in Ethiopia as well. The regional centres for digital access are additional facilities that the university funds, and equips to ensure widening access. While regional hubs and regional centres are set up and run by the university, the Directorate of Instructional Support and Services (DISS) is responsible for establishing collaborative agreements with telecentres and computer access facilities throughout the country, particularly in rural areas, aiming to reduce the digital divide, based on the UDL foundation of "increasing access" (Heelan, 2015). Parallel digital laboratories equipped with special fixtures, fittings and assistive technologies to accommodate students with various disabilities have also been set up for students with disabilities across the country. These centres are additional facilities for the sole use of students with disabilities, to ensure that these students receive optimum support structures and is coordinated by the Advocacy Resource Centre for Students with

Disabilities (ARCSWiD). Due to the phased roll-out of access centres for students with disabilities, some regional centres and hubs are for "blended" use in the interim, indicating that both students with and without disabilities can utilize these centres until exclusive parallel disability centres can be established in these areas. At times, the regional centres and hubs for students with disabilities could be utilized for specialized examination arrangements, made in liaison with the examination department and ARCSWiD.

There are 23 regional centres across South Africa: 7 in KwaZulu Natal, 5 in Gauteng, 3 in Limpopo, 2 in Mpumalanga, 3 in the Eastern Cape, and 4 in the Midlands Region. 8 of these regional centres are blended facilities while the rest of these centres have parallel digital laboratories with dedicated equipment and staff for students with disabilities. In terms of telecentres, there are 14 telecentres in Gauteng, 4 in Mpumalanga, 9 in Limpopo, 18 in KwaZulu Natal, 3 in the Eastern Cape, 4 in the Free State, 2 in the Northern Cape and 26 in the Western Cape. These practices point out that "more than simple indicators of best practices or lists of possible accommodations, UDL offers an epistemological shift that facilitates design for all learners within a holistic framework" (Rogers-Shaw, Carr-Chellman, & Choi, 2018, p. 20).

My recent visit to the regional centre at the Florida campus in Gauteng provides a glimpse into a "blended-use digital laboratory". The regional centre has 5 dedicated computer access laboratories with 20 computers in each laboratory. Computer laboratory 2 provides access to students with disabilities and features 3 computers: 1 for partially blind students with an extra-large keyboard and widescreen, 1 computer for blind students that features specialized software such as Jaws, and 1 computer for students with no limbs that has additional assistive technologies. Dedicated staff are available from 7h30 to 19h00 every day to assist all students (with and without disabilities) in the digital laboratories. In the second phase of the roll-out of the laboratories, printers will be installed for all students, including a printer for partially blind students as well as additional technologies for deaf-blind and deaf students in the Florida centre. Some of these technologies have already been installed at laboratories in other regions and centres.

Registered students receive free access to computer labs and the Internet at regional hubs, regional centres, and community telecentres that are equipped with all the required digital, information, and Internet facilities required for successful participation in the ODeL environment. Accurate and verified data on the actual frequency of use of these centres is not yet available, as the formal roll-out of this programme was only initiated in 2013 with the primary focus being on establishing the centres. As from 2018, dedicated staff at these centres have been commissioned to collect data on the frequency of access and use of these facilities, particularly with the use of a digital login system for students. This data will be used to roll-out the second phase of establishing and improving the facilities and accessibility of the digital laboratories for students with disabilities and students without digital access.

Seeing that accessing telecentres and regional hubs could involve additional costs of travelling as they could be situated a distance from areas of residences, Unisa has employed additional innovative strategies to try to overcome this barrier as well, based on the UDL principle of providing the student with multiple means of accessing digital courses (Rao, Edelen-Smith, & Wailehua, 2015). Digital media allow flexibility and diversity in the variety of formats that content is presented in online curriculum development in higher education, and present the opportunity to enhance digital and media literacy competencies amongst students (Dalton, 2017). In this respect, some signature courses have introduced the 'digiband', a device similar to a flash drive, in an effort to alleviate the challenges associated with digital exclusion of students with limited or no digital access. All students who register at Unisa for the first time from 2013 have to do a fully online "signature course" at some point during their undergraduate studies, specific to each college within the university. The digiband is a device that allows students to store an offline, yet updatable, copy of their learning management system, myUnisa, group site on a flash drive and enables students to work offline, should they not have ready access to the Internet. It also allows students to access their study material in electronic format at any time even without permanent access to the internet or a computer. The offline copy can be updated, at regular intervals when an Internet connection is available, with the latest information and activities from the online myUnisa site through the synchronization option. Furthermore, Unisa has negotiated deals for reduced prices on tablets and laptops, as well as 3G mobile data connectivity access for registered students that includes everything needed to connect students to their studies at an affordable rate. To further ease access and inclusion that underpin the principle of "flexibility in use" outlined in the UDL framework (Burgstahler, 2013), Unisa provides access to study material and library resources using mobile phones, where submission of multiple-choice assignments (MCQ) assignments, interaction on the myUnisa learning management system and access to course materials can be established via mobile phone.

Creating accessible learning environments using UDL in online instructional design denotes improved pedagogical and learning practices that should benefit all staff and students with a wide range of abilities and disabilities (Burgstahler, 2002; Burgstahler, 2013; Dell, C. A., Dell, T. A., & Blackwell, 2015; Rao, Edelen-Smith, & Wailehua, 2015; Lawrie et al., 2017; Kanwar, 2017). In this respect, while technology can ease many daily functions for persons with disabilities and opens up environments, access to, and inclusion in society, technology can also "embody the very symbol of alienation for disabled people", if accommodations have not been thought of prior to instruction (Roulstone, 2016, p. 4). At Unisa, additional approaches to accommodation and inclusion comprise of access to instructional materials in various alternative formats, providing extra time for exams, and alternative examination arrangements and venues. The university provides various additional distinctive examination arrangements for students with disabilities such as specialized examination centres for students with visual, mobility, and learning difficulties. These arrangements could range from individual invigilation; provision and recording of examination answers in various formats, the arrangement of an amanuensis, examination papers in appropriate and accessible formats; special arrangements depending on the needs of the student and the nature of the disability, or computerized examinations.

Therefore, effective inclusive course designs should ideally begin at the course design phase, integrating the use of assistive technologies and other inclusive apparatuses in instructional blueprints from the onset, instead of creating adaptive approaches later on in the courses (Burgstahler, 2002; Dell, C. A., Dell, T. A., & Blackwell, 2015; Rao et al., 2015; Lawrie et al., 2017; Kanwar, 2017). The UDL framework presupposes that many barriers to learning can be abridged simply through the presentation of content in various audio, visual, textual and a combination of graphic outputs (Meyer & Rose, 2005; Dell, C. A., Dell, T. A., & Blackwell, 2015; Dalton, 2017; Kanwar, 2017; Ngubane-Mokiwa, 2017). This approach entails the convergence between digital technologies, ODL pedagogies, and assistive technologies and devices that permit students with varying disabilities, such as vision, hearing, mobility, and learning difficulties, to access instructional materials in various formats, without adapting course content (Thomson et al., 2015; Ehlinger, 2017; Kanwar, 2017). At Unisa, this is done through ARCSWiD, which is located within the portfolio of Student Affairs. ARCSWiD was set up in 2003 to provide institutional and academic support for students with disabilities within this ODL environment.

ARCSWiD, that also employs staff with various disabilities, mostly deals with student needs 'behind the scenes'; many times, lecturers do not even know that they have these students in the virtual classroom. Interaction between students with disabilities and lecturers is initiated where required or necessary, but mostly, this process begins at the registration phase where student advisors identify the student's specific needs. At this initial point, study materials formats are identified and chosen, special examination and tuition arrangements are made for each individual student, and contact between the advocacy centre and the individual learner is initiated. Services such as conversion of assessments and study material from text to Braille and from Braille to text are carried out by ARCSWiD.

Additionally, sign-language interpretation, speech to-text and text-to-speech conversions are some of the ways in which the university inculcates UDL principles of widening access and participation to learning environments within the distance-learning environment (Matshedisho, 2010; Online, 2013). In this way, the University showcases the principles of UDL by building in accommodation structures in course designs and overall university structures from the outset.

Recognizing the importance of identifying and accommodating the needs of students with disabilities, and in responding to the principle of access for success (Burgstahler, 2015), ARCSWiD strives to provide a range of services for students with disabilities, such as, inter alia, producing study material in alternative formats, including Braille, large print, electronic and audiotapes. They facilitate needs-based support in terms of registration, assessments, examinations (special exam centres, sign-language interpretation, etcetera), and the curriculum. They provide services for including open captions for video and audio files. Moreover, staff across the country are trained on accommodating the needs of students with disabilities and initiating, developing, and implementing campus-wide advocacy and awareness-raising programmes.

In line with Unisa's move towards an ODeL environment, the advocacy centre, along with the campus library, provides digital and technological support with the aid of various forms of assistive technologies and devices, such as: Dolphin Pens, Non-Visual Desktop Access (NVDA), enPathia devices, widescreen computer monitors, ZoomText large-print readers, desktop video magnifiers, as well as audio book readers such as Blaze EZ, BookSense, ClassMate Reader and VictorReader Stratus.

In line with the creative approach in UDL guidelines, assessment structures do not differ in content, but in format and mode of delivery, thereby ensuring equal assessment of content for all students, irrespective of their personal learning requirements. These strategies employ UDL principles of widening access to learning materials, without creating an unfair advantage for any student or group of students, by simply creating more avenues of access and participation in learning activities (Roulstone, 2016; Ehlinger, 2017). The focus is on assessing students on the same content using variable mediums and formats, assimilating greater flexibility and adaptability into course structures that enable greater usability by people with disabilities as well (Roulstone, 2016; Ehlinger, 2017). However, greater variability in assessment, course content and instructional materials needs to be addressed at Unisa to enhance inclusive practices.

Reflection

- To what extent can UDL strategies mitigate against socio-economic inequities?
- How can the UDL framework be applied to promoting meaningful access to educational resources to students with disabilities and students with limited or no digital access in online learning environments? How would the application of UDL principles in this respect vary in different countries? Think of your own country and your own institution. How can UDL principles be used to enhance the online learning experiences of students with disabilities?
- Reflect on the establishment of digital laboratories. What do you think of the different uses and applications of these laboratories used at Unisa? Is there a similar structure used at other universities and how would you compare them?

Conclusion and recommendations

Unisa has adopted many innovative approaches to deal with the issues of digital inclusion of students with disabilities and students without digital access using the basic principles of UDL. Not only is the advocacy centre, ARC-SWiD, a tremendous facility for integrating inclusion, access, and diversity, the additional facilities, such as regional centres and hubs, as well as telecentres and community centres that provide parallel support for students with different abilities and disabilities are also a phenomenal feature of a tertiary education environment striving for inclusion. Nonetheless, more research needs to be done to assess students' perceptions and experiences of the innovative strategies employed to encourage and foster greater inclusion and enhance the inculcation of the principles of UDL, not only in learning environments and content structures, but also in pedagogical approaches and awareness in instructional designs. Hence, more institution wide awareness and training with regard to the needs of students with disabilities and students with limited or no digital access is required. In the same vein, more research needs to be carried out to capture more concrete data on the extent of digital exclusion in the ODeL context and its impact on learners. Finally, greater student-lecturer interactions need to be initiated, as lecturers are mostly unaware of the effects of the digital divide in higher education, more so for students with disabilities, in the ODeL context in South Africa. This would initiate greater awareness of, and implementation of UDL guidelines in distance and online learning courses.

Future Projects

- More research needs to be conducted in the areas of digital inclusion for students with disabilities and students in poorer communities, specifically in an ODeL context.
- More emphasis on benchmarking should be considered when developing strategies for digital inclusion – this way the most suitable approaches for a specific context can be piloted /adopted / adapted.
- Digital literacy and online skills development is another challenge that needs to be considered – more courses and initiatives are needed to address this issue
- Study material, recommended, and prescribed course materials need to be available in Epub 3 formats. Although ARCSWiD is already in liaison with approximately 30 publishers to provide course materials in this accessible format that can easily be converted to more

accessible mediums for students with varying visual, hearing, and learning disabilities, there is a long road ahead before this goal can be realized.

• The university is piloting a project that would provide greater inclusion for the linguistic needs of all 11 official language speakers in South Africa in all university courses. The project is still in its inception phase with great liaison between university structures and academics in this regard. At present, only English and Afrikaans have been considered in the university courses.

References

Badat, S. (2005). South Africa: Distance higher education policies for access, social equity, quality, and social and economic responsiveness in a context of the diversity of provision. *Distance Education* 26(2), pp. 183–204. doi:10.1080/01587910500168843

Braimoh, D., & Osiki, O. J. (2008). The impact of technology on accessibility and pedagogy: The right to education in Sub-Saharan Africa. *The Asian Society of Open and Distance Education* 6(1), pp. 53–62. Retrieved from www.asianjde.org/2008v6.1.Braimoh.pdf

Brown, C., & Czerniewicz, L. (2010). Debunking the "digital native": Beyond digital apartheid, towards digital democracy. *Journal of Computer Assisted Learning* 26(5), pp. 357–369. doi:10.1111/j.1365-2729.2010.00369.x

Burgstahler, S. (2002). *Universal design of distance learning*. Retrieved from www.uvm.edu/~cdci/employees/files/UDLofdistancelearning.pdf

Burgstahler, S. (2013). Introduction to universal design in higher education. In S. Burgstahler (Ed.), *Universal design in higher education: Promising practices*. Seattle: DO-IT, University of Washington. Retrieved from www.uw.edu/doit/UDHE-promising-practices/part1.html

Burgstahler, S. (2015). *Universal Design of Instruction (UDI): Definition, Principles, Guidelines, and Examples*. Washington: University of Washington.

Council on Higher Education. (2007). *Review of higher education in South Africa*. Pretoria: The Council on Higher Education.

Cross, M., & Adam, F. (2007). ICT policies and strategies in higher education in South Africa: National and institutional pathways. *Higher Education Policy* 20, pp. 73–95. Retrieved from www.learntechlib.org/p/69507/

Dalton, E. M. (2017). Beyond universal design for learning: Guiding principles to reduce barriers to digital & media literacy competence. *Journal of Media Literacy Education* 9(2), pp. 17–29. https://doi.org/10.23860/JMLE-2019-09-02-02

Dell, C. A., Dell, T. F., & Blackwell, T. L. (2015). Applying universal design for learning in online courses: Pedagogical and practical considerations. *The Journal of Educators Online* 13(2), pp. 166–192. Retrieved from https://files.eric.ed.gov/fulltext/EJ1068401.pdf

deMaine, S. D. (2014). From disability to usability in online instruction. *Law Library Journal* 106(4), 531–561. Retrieved from http://0-eds.b.ebscohost.com. oasis.unisa.ac.za/eds/pdfviewer/pdfviewer?vid=2&sid=8a3bfc91-764f-4401-bcec-4572b3845916%40sessionmgr102

Department of Education. (1997). *Education White Paper 3: A programme for the transformation of higher education* (Notice 1196 of 1997) Republic of South Africa: Government Printer. Retrieved January 18, 2017, from www.che.ac.za/sites/default/files/publications/White_Paper3.pdf

Department of Education. (2001). *National plan for higher education*. Pretoria: Department of Education. Retrieved January 27, 2017, from www.justice.gov.za/commissions/FeesHET/docs/2001-NationalPlanForHigherEducation.pdf

Department of Higher Education and Training. (2012). *Green paper for post-school education and training*. Retrieved January 2, 2017, from www.che.ac.za/sites/default/files/publications/DHET_green_paper_post_school_education_training.pdf

Department of Higher Education and Training. (2013). *White paper on post-school education and training*. Retrieved February 17, 2017, from www.dhet.gov.za/SiteAssets/Latest%20News/White%20paper%20for%20post-school%20educa tion%20and%20training.pdf

Department of Social Development. (2015). *White paper on the rights of persons with disabilities*. Republic of South Africa: Government Printer.

DHET *see* Department of Higher Education and Training.

DoE see Department of Education.

DSD *see* Department of Social Development.

Ehlinger, E. (2017). Expanding notions of access: Opportunities and future directions for universal design. In H. Alphin, Jr., J. Lavine, & R. Chan (Eds.), *Disability and equity in higher education accessibility* (pp. 204–221). Hershey, PA: IGI Global. doi:10.4018/978-1-5225-2665-0.ch009

Goggin, G. (2017). Disability and digital inequalities: Rethinking digital divides with disability theory. In M. Ragnedda & G. W. Muschert (Eds.), *Theorizing digital divides*. New York: Routledge.

Heelan, A. (2015, November 12–13). *Universal Design for Learning (UDL): Implications for education*. Dublin, Ireland: Universal Design in Education.

Holmberg, B. (2005). Concepts and terminology – Student bodies. In B. Holmberg (Ed.), *The evolution, principles, and practice of distance education* (pp. 9–11). Oldenburg, Germany: BIS-Verlag der Carl von Ossietzky Universität Oldenburg.

Journell, W. (2007). The inequities of the digital divide: Is e-learning a solution? *E-Learning* 4(2), pp. 138–149. doi:10.2304/elea.2007.4.2.138

Kajee, L. (2010). Disability, social inclusion and technological positioning in a South African higher education institution: Carmen's story. *The Language learning Journal* 38(3), pp. 379–392. doi:10.1080/09571736.2010.511783

Kanwar, A. (2017, December 20). *Making open and distance learning inclusive: The role of technology*. Keynote address presented at the 6th International Conference on Information and Communication Technology and Accessibility, Muscat, Sultanate of Oman.

Kelland, J. H. (2005). Distance learning: Access and inclusion issues. In *Adult education research conference*. Athens, GA: New Prairie Press: Kansas State University Libraries. Retrieved from http://newprairiepress.org/aerc/2005/papers/22

Khalid, S. M., & Pedersen, M. J. L. (2016). Digital exclusion in higher education contexts: A systematic literature review. *Procedia – Social and Behavioral Sciences* 228, pp. 614–621. doi:10.1016/j.sbspro.2016.07.094

Lawrie, G., Marquis, E., Fuller, E., Newman, T., Qui, M., Nomikoudis, M., Roelofs, F., & van Dam, L. (2017). Moving towards inclusive learning and teaching: A synthesis of recent literature. *Teaching & Learning Inquiry* 5(1). http://dx.doi.org/10.20343/teachlearninqu.5.1.3

Liebenberg, H., Chetty, Y., & Prinsloo, P. (2012). Student access to and skills in using technology in an open and distance learning context. *International Review of Research in Open and Distance Learning* 13(4), pp. 250–268.

Lehohla, P. (2014). *Census 2011: Profile of persons with disabilities in South Africa.* Pretoria: Statistics South Africa (StatsSA).

Maluleke, R. (2018). *Community Survey 2016: Profiling socio economic status and living arrangements of persons with disabilities in South Africa.* Pretoria: Statistics South Africa (StatsSA).

Matshedisho, K. R. (2010). Experiences of disabled students in South Africa: Extending the thinking behind disability support. *South African Journal of Higher Education* 24(5), pp. 730–744. Retrieved from http://0-eds.b.ebscohost.com.oasis.unisa.ac.za/eds/pdfviewer/pdfviewer?vid=2&sid=f594b733-42e8-4c49-b090-27b1475ff1dc%40sessionmgr120

Meyer, A., & Rose, D. H. (2005). The future is in the margins: The role of technology and disability in educational reform. In D. H. Rose, A. Meyer, & C. Hitchcock (Eds.), *The universally designed classroom: Accessible curriculum and digital technologies* (pp. 13–35). Cambridge, MA: Harvard Education Press.

Neves, B. B., & Mead, G. (2017). The interpretive and ideal-type approach: Rethinking digital non-use(s) in a Weberian perspective. In M. Ragnedda & G. W. Muschert (Eds.), *Theorizing digital divides.* New York: Routledge.

Ngubane-Mokiwa, S. A. (2017). Implications of the University of South Africa's (UNISA) shift to open distance e-learning on teacher education. *Australian Journal of Teacher Education* 42(9), pp. 111–124. http://dx.doi.org/10.14221/ajte.2017v42n9.7

Ngubane-Mokiwa, S. A., & Letseka, M. (2015). Shift from open distance learning to open distance e-learning. In Moeketsi Letseka (Ed.), *Open Distance Learning (ODL) in South Africa.* New York: Nova Publishers.

Nyahodza, L., & Higgs, R. (2017). Towards bridging the digital divide in post-apartheid South Africa: A case of a historically disadvantaged university in Cape Town. *SA Jnl Libs & Info Sci* 83(1), pp. 39–48. doi:10.7553/83-1-1645

Online, A. (2013, May 2). UNISA partner with NCPPDSA to lead the way in creating a culture of inclusiveness for persons with disability in education. *National Council for Persons with Physical Disabilities in South Africa.* Retrieved from www.casualday.co.za/unisa-partner-with-ncppdsa-to-lead-the-way-in-creating-a-culture-of-inclusiveness-for-persons-with-disability-in-education/

Ossiannilsson, E. (2017). Leadership in global open, online, and distance learning. In J. Keengwe & P. Bull (Eds.), *Handbook of research on transformative digital content and learning technologies* (pp. 345–373). Hershey, PA: IGI Global. doi:10.4018/978-1-5225-2000-9.ch019

Oswal, S. K. (2017). Institutional, legal, and attitudinal barriers to the accessibility of university digital libraries: Implications for retention of disabled students. In H.

Alphin, Jr., J. Lavine, & R. Chan (Eds.), *Disability and equity in higher education accessibility* (pp. 223–241). Hershey, PA: IGI Global. doi:10.4018/978-1-5225-2665-0.ch010

Philip, L., Cottrill, C., Farrington, J., Williams, F., & Ashmore, F. (2017). The digital divide: Patterns, policy and scenarios for connecting the 'final few' in rural communities across Great Britain. *Journal of Rural Studies* 54, pp. 386–398. Contents lists Retrieved from ScienceDirect Journal of Rural Studies journal homepage: www.elsevier.com/locate/jrurstud http://dx.doi.org/10.1016/j.jrurstud.2016.12.002

Porras-Hernández, L. H., & Salinas-Amescua, B. (2015). A reconstruction of rural teachers' technology integration experiences: searching for equity. In H. Gillow-Wiles & M. Niess (Eds.), *Handbook of research on teacher education in the digital age* (pp. 281–306). Hershey, PA: Information Science Reference.

Rao, K., Edelen-Smith, P., & Wailehua, C. U. (2015). Universal design for online courses: Applying principles to pedagogy. *Open Learning: The Journal of Open, Distance and e-Learning* 30(1), pp. 35–52. doi:10.1080/02680513.2014.991300

Rogers-Shaw, C., Carr-Chellman, D. J., & Choi, J. (2018). Universal design for learning guidelines for accessible online instruction. *Adult Learning* 29(91), pp. 20–31. doi:10.1177/1045159517735530

Rose, D., & Meyer, A. (2006). *A practical reader in universal design for learning.* Cambridge, MA: Harvard Univesity Press.

Roulstone, A. (2016). *Disability and technology: An interdisciplinary approach.* London: Palgrave Macmillan.

Soudien, C. (2010). *Transformation in higher education: A briefing paper. Republic of South Africa: Development Bank of South Africa.* Retrieved from www.dhet.gov.za/summit/Docs/2010Docs/Transformation%20in%20higher%20education-%20A%20briefing%20paper%20by%20Crain%20Soudien.pdf

Thompson, K. M., Subramaniam, M. M., Bertot, J. C., Jaeger, P. T., & Taylor, N. G. (2014). *Digital literacy and digital inclusion: Information policy and the public library.* Lanham: Rowman & Littlefield.

Thomson, R., Fichten, C. S., Havel, A., Budd, J., & Asuncion, J. (2015). Blending universal design, e-learning, and information and communication technologies. In S. E. Burgstahler (Ed.), *Universal design in higher education: From principles to practice* (2nd ed., pp. 275–284). Boston: Harvard Education Press. Retrieved from www.adaptech.org/sites/default/files/abBlendingUniversalDesign.pdf

Treviranus, J. (2018). Learning differences & digital equity in the classroom. In J. Voogt, G. Christensen, & K. W. Lai (Eds.), *International Handbook of information technology in primary and secondary education* (2nd ed.). Springer. (Submitted) Retrieved from http://openresearch.ocadu.ca/id/eprint/2152/

Unisa *see* University of South Africa.

University of South Africa. (2015). *Unisa 2015 revisited outline of the Unisa 2015 strategic plan.* Pretoria: Unisa. Retrieved from www.unglobalcompact.org/system/attachments/21882/original/Appendix_1.pdf?1368172567

Zeff, R. (2007). Universal design across the curriculum. *New Directions for Higher Education* 137, pp. 27–44. doi:10.1002/he

Chapter 19

UDL, online accessibility, and virtual reality

Designing accessible and engaging online courses

Tom Thibodeau

Case study

Jacob teaches courses in a Bachelor's Degree program in biology at a medium-sized private college in the United States. The degree is offered in a hybrid-online setting and is intended to appeal to diverse students who are seeking a bachelor's degree. The typical demographic of Jacob's courses includes a wide variability of students including recent high school graduates, first generation learners, students with disabilities, and adult learners who enroll in school part time while working. Jacob is aware of the diversity of his students and tries to be a responsive and supportive instructor.

Jacob's courses rely heavily on the use of video. He frequently shows videos in his course and posts lengthy lectures in the LMS (learning management system) so he can "flip" learning and spend more time having discussions with students when they are class. Students also have the option to express what they know with self-made video files.

Unfortunately, LMS reports and student evaluations have shown that student engagement has been minimal and that the videos have not been effective in supporting student learning. Jacob would like to try to use video in a different way to engage his students, but he doesn't know where to start.

Introduction

It's February 2018 and the Winter Olympics are on TV every night and every day for 16 days. The coverage is amazing. Alpine skiing, curling, speed skating, and hockey are on multiple channels, many with options to watch in virtual reality with the NBC Virtual Reality (VR) app. After downloading the app and choosing an event, I put on my VR headset and headphones and give it a try. Suddenly I have a front row seat. I can hear the crowd and can turn my head to see fans sitting next to me. The video quality is not as sharp as the broadcast event but I'm in a single location and I'm there just as if I bought a ticket and made the trip. Imagine the barriers we could remove if we could create similar opportunities for students in higher education. In fact, we can.

Background

Video has grown to become an integral part of higher education. For one, video is incredibly useful in online courses because it "has the potential to transform your online course from words on a page into a multi-sensory experience" while face-to-face courses often use video as means to represent and express information and increase engagement for students (Lay, 2014). Knowing how to effectively use video to scale Universal Design for Learning (UDL) practices is equally applicable to teachers in face-to-face courses.

Video, or more specifically, television, was created and first demonstrated in 1927 by Philo Taylor Farnsworth, a 21-year-old inventor who didn't even have electricity until he was 14 (Fisher & Fisher, 1999, p. 127). TV grew quickly and was first used as an educational tool in 1932, although it wasn't the video that we experience today (Dunham, Lowdermilk & Broderick, 1956, p. vii). The earliest use of educational television required the simultaneous use of radio to provide the audio component of the program while the television provided the visuals. These first educational programs were live lectures broadcast to the area around universities (Novak, 2012). It was predicted, "We will undoubtedly have lectures of every conceivable kind present to us right in our homes, when practical television arrives, possibly a year or two off" (Novak, 2012). Prophetically, educators were skeptical about the value of merely being a recipient of knowledge, as opposed to engaging in dialectical, two-way, instruction. They noted, "Educational Television is a two-way street. The success of a program actually rests upon the ingenuity and capability of the viewer as much as it does upon the producer" (Dunhan et al., 1956, p. 1). Today, we face the same barrier in our courses when we don't build video into meaningful opportunities for students to interact with and express their understanding of content under study. Fortunately, video has further evolved and provided faculty with the opportunities to make video more interactive. The use of video has grown progressively into Augmented Reality (AR) and Virtual Reality (VR) that has not only changed our perception of what television is but also what we can do with it to engage all students.

Universal Design for Learning (UDL) focuses on student engagement through Guidelines that prompt educators to recruit interest and provide options for effort, persistence, and self-regulation. All of this is possible when we consider digital technology, and video, as a cornerstone in the theory and practice of UDL. As shared by the founders of CAST, the organization who developed the UDL framework, "Without the development of digital media, it would have been impossible to conceive of flexible learning environments that could be tuned and adjusted to varied learners" (Meyers, Rose, & Gordon, 2014, p. 18).

Video is an important component in the delivery of a universally designed course, either face-to-face or online. Video can be found, created, purchased and posted by both students and educators and access to video is easier than ever. The equipment needed to create and edit video has gotten less expensive, easier to use, and is integrated throughout elementary and secondary education so many students in Higher Education Institutes (HEIs) have familiarity with the medium and how to use it as a mean to express knowledge.

Most classrooms in HEIs have computers and projectors as well as internet access via cable or WiFi while online courses have multiple ways to add and use video through integrated apps within most learning management systems (LMS). Video is also an accessible medium. In its newest digital form, video not only has sight and sound but it can be easily enhanced with closed captioning, paused and replayed, slowed down, indexed, expanded with zoom capabilities, and individual frames of video can be printed. Extra audio tracks can also be added to videos to provide translations into different languages. Table 19.1 delineates how video aligns to the UDL Guidelines.

Reflection

- In your education experience, how has video played a role in your learning?
- After examining the alignment between the UDL Guidelines and video accessibility, consider the value of thoughtfully using videos in your courses.
- Where is one aspect of a course that could be made more accessible or engaging with the use of video?
- If you're an instructor, how often do you use video in your courses? Do you often use it to represent information, allow students to express knowledge or skills, or both?

Multiple modes of video

Video has multiple modes of creation, recording and delivery, and it's important that HEI students and instructors understand the differences between each and how some of them build together to create the virtual reality that we know today.

Table 19.1 Video accessibility alignment to UDL Guidelines

Provide Multiple Means of Engagement

7: Provide options for recruiting interest

7.1 Optimize individual choice and autonomy	Best created as a technical but artistic endeavor that express an individual (or group) point of view or perception.
7.2 Optimize relevance, value, and authenticity	Can be quickly selected from the internet or created to optimize relevance (today's news), value (documentaries) and authenticity (first person presentations).
7.3 Minimize threats and distractions	Can be watched individually, with headphones, or replayed if necessary.

8: Provide options for sustaining effort and persistence

8.1 Heighten salience of goals and objectives	Can be provided as an ongoing resource that highlights the goals and objectives in each online module in an accessible way. Video can be readily available with a learning management system or Google classroom web page.
8.2 Vary demands and resources to optimize challenge	There is no ceiling on technology, and so both the design and delivery of videos can increase the level of challenge in both content and creation. Video projects can be scaled as necessary.
8.3 Foster collaboration and community	Projects are best "produced" by teams that allow for specialization or individuality and come together using community and communication.
8.4 Increase mastery-oriented feedback	Since videos are reviewable and re-editable, errors and improvements can be added to mastery of not only the production but the content captured.

9: Provide options for self-regulation

9.1 Promote expectations and beliefs that optimize motivation	Proper video selection and viewing can be fun and rewarding, even inspiring. Video creation, with proper support, can help learners experience the power of sharing information using creative, innovative and visual ways.
9.2 Facilitate personal coping skills and strategies	With new cable box interfaces, live or recorded video playback can be paused or stopped as needed. Video creation can be saved in progress and returned to at another time. Additionally volume can be adjusted, closed captioning can be utilized, etc. . . .
9.3 Develop self-assessment and reflection	Personal reviews of self-created videos provide an opportunity for self-reflection. Reviews of videos provided for course content also provide an opportunity for discussion and reflection of one's understanding of the concepts and ideas presented.

1: Provide Multiple Means of Representation

1: Provide options for perception

1.1 Offer ways of customizing the display of information — Can be paused and rewound, offer closed captioning.

1.2 Offer alternatives for auditory information — Alternative visuals can be added with produced videos and augmented reality delivery modes and closed captioning can be incorporated.

1.3 Offer alternatives for visual information — Can provide alternate audio tracks with different languages or simplified language.

2: Provide options for language, mathematical expressions, and symbols

2.1 Clarify vocabulary and symbols — Vocabulary and symbol definitions can be added with produced videos and augmented reality delivery modes.

2.2 Clarify syntax and structure — Additional explanations can be added with produced videos and augmented reality delivery modes.

2.3 Support decoding of text, mathematical notation, and symbols — Specific videos can be created and made available to all students that explain concepts that need additional consideration.

2.4 Promote understanding across languages — Can provide alternate audio tracks with different languages or simplified language.

2.5 Illustrate through multiple media — Can be composed of visual, aural, graphic, animated and additional multimedia.

3: Provide options for comprehension

3.1 Activate or supply background knowledge — Can be edited into individual segments or indexed to provide for quick access to background knowledge.

3.2. Highlight patterns, critical features, big ideas, and relationships — Scripted videos can present information on any specific information that can be organized for quick access and repetition.

3.3 Guide information processing, visualization, and manipulation — Can demonstrate thought process, present any images with additional annotation, and proper scaffolding for any activity.

3.4 Maximize transfer and generalization — Can be edited by teachers and students to create "highlight" videos that can be used for review and presentation.

(Continued)

Table 19.1 (Continued)

Provide Multiple Means of Engagement

II. **Provide Multiple Means of Action and Expression**

4: Provide options for physical action

4.1 Vary the methods for response and navigation	Best used to record student or teacher action to replay and analyze such as when the student is performing a task.
4.2 Optimize access to tools and assistive technologies	Creation tools are becoming more ubiquitous, less expensive and easier to use.

5: **Provide options for expression and communication**

5.1 Use multiple media for communication	Embodies and exemplifies the guideline exactly.
5.2 Use multiple tools for construction and composition	Can include videos of any other real, digital or virtual artifact.
5.3 Build fluencies with graduated levels of support for practice and performance	Enables and empowers students to "tell their own story" and with additional practice and support can build talent and increased communication.

6: **Provide options for executive functions**

6.1 Guide appropriate goal-setting	Selection, creation and review of video is easily scaffolded and used for all levels.
6.2 Support planning and strategy development	Proper development of a video project requires planning and strategy that can be taught and experimented with at all levels as well as provides evidence of the successful use of the tools and process.
6.3 Facilitate managing information and resources	Proper development of a video project requires information and resource management at all levels as well as provides evidence of the successful use of the tools and process.
6.4 Enhance capacity for monitoring progress	Projects can be copied and edited to present the development of draft versions.

Live video: Live video is the most basic type of video possible. It is video of a current event, newscast, or concert, for example, that can only be recorded during the event and is made available to an audience via a television channel, or live streaming in a social media app like Facebook. Live video is used in video conferences, demonstrations and webinars. It is a process made simple by smartphones, video cameras built into laptop computers and simple, inexpensive web cameras as well as video conferencing applications such as Zoom, Skype, Hangout, WebEx, GoToMeeting and others. Social media applications such as Facebook, Twitter, Snapchat and Instagram can also be used. The cost of using video to self-produce a live video event is minimal and the technology needed is relatively inexpensive, available, and easy to use. Live video resources that are created, managed or produced by others are available for teachers and students to use if scheduling can be arranged. Broadcast and Cable TV, including educational channels would be the largest resource. Kaltura (2017), a video storage and streaming service, reports that "99% of institutions report they have teachers regularly incorporating video in their curriculum." In order to understand what this statistic meant at New England Tech (NEIT), a survey of seven questions was developed and emailed to all 399 adjunct and full-time faculty after the questions were approved by the Human Review Board. Forty-five percent of the faculty responded. The survey showed that 93.4% of all faculty use video in their courses regardless of age, years teaching, or discipline.

Examples of how live video is used at the NEIT, the institution where I work, is the broadcasting of a live event in our media presentation theater to additional rooms at the college for audience overflow situations or better viewing of presentation such as when a small object needs to be magnified. For example, in our biology labs, our microscopes have video cameras to display an enlarged sample on an 8-foot diagonal projection screen. This shows students exactly what they are looking at and the sample can be explained with much better visual support. Video conferences are also used to allow students unable to attend a class at the college to participate from home. Live video does provide visual and aural content but it is not universally accessible without closed captioning or transcripts which can be expensive and hard to manage.

In our case study, Jacob could increase accessibility and engagement in his course by using more live video to create more instructor presence in his course. Instructor presence is consistently a strong predictor of student course satisfaction (Novak & Thibodeau, 2016). An effective live video in his course could be a weekly "virtual office hour" where he "sees" students face to face, answers student questions, and reviews content that students find confusing. The time of this video conference should move from week to week to make it more accessible to a variety of students. Jacob may also consider requiring at least one virtual meeting per month or semester to ensure he can build meaningful connections at times that work best for students.

As an instructor, if you are using Live video, ensure that transcription or other means of support is available to meet the needs of all students. This support may have to be delivered after the live presentation date due to the cost of live transcription. Otherwise, such a mode can present significant barriers to learning.

Real-time recorded video: Real-time recorded video is the recording of a live event, presentation, or conversation, in real time, with one camera or more for review at a later time by an audience without further production or editing. Real-time recorded video is often used to "flip the classroom" by recording a lecture either at the board in front of the class or at the desktop simultaneously recording a PowerPoint or other presentation so that students can view the "lecture" before coming to class and using class time for more active learning strategies (Novak & Thibodeau, 2016). While the concept of the flipped classroom has been in the literature for over a decade, the popularity and recent growth in real-time video and on-demand video has added a new tool to engage students in higher education (Mattei & Ennis, 2014).

Screen Capture applications are used to record computer screens and routines along with the video and audio of the presenter. Applications such as Camtasia (Windows), Screenflow (MAC) and Adobe Captivate (Win and MAC) as well as many online applications such as Screencast-o-matic, Jing and others provide a fast and easy way to create video of computer applications as well as any other on-screen activity for demonstration or communication. As an example, as an instructor, you may wish to provide students with an option to create their own real-time video as a means to submit a reflection. You could actually guide students through this process by recording your own video on your laptop, and recording your actual screen as you open the application, record the video, save the video and upload it to the Learning Management system. In this scenario, students have a real-time video that scaffolds the process to create their own video. This can be done with countless aspects of a course.

Recorded video is typically posted to a server for easy access and improved streaming capabilities. YouTube is the largest free service for posting recorded video. YouTube also provides free access to millions of videos. YouTube currently has over 30 million viewers per day and over 300 hours of video uploaded every minute and on average, there are 1,000,000,000 mobile video views per day (Smith, 2018). There are multiple alternatives to YouTube: Daily Motion, Vimeo, flickr, Veoh, Meta Cafe and blip.tv are just a few. Many Learning Management Systems (LMS) allow some storage and hosting of smaller video files and there are multiple options for adding video hosting solutions to an LMS with applications like Kaltura, Media Space and Viddler. These applications can greatly increase the storage and streaming capabilities of the LMS. Once a video is posted to an online system, it can be shared.

The cost of using basic real-time recorded video is minimal and the technology needed is relatively inexpensive, available and easy to use. However, the cost can escalate quickly if the quality needs grow. The added costs will be for additional crew members, higher end cameras and additional production technology. The biggest problem with using this type of video is access to local digital storage (computer hard drives, flash drives, etc.) as the video files can be very large, however, there are multiple options for storing these files in the cloud with services such as Google Drive, Dropbox, pCloud, iCloud, sync.com and Mega. Most of these services offer a free plan with limited options and storage along with various paid plans that offer more storage and options. At NEIT, both faculty and students view and create real-time video for multiple courses. Nursing students record their demonstration of fundamental patient practice in a simulation lab that is reviewed by the student and the nurse educator to make sure that the student nurse is performing the procedure correctly before inter-acting with a human patient. Video, graphics and gaming students create videos as part of their curriculum and all students are encouraged to do the same in their classes.

Real-time recorded video can be universally accessible by using closed cap-tioning systems that are fairly easy to use and inexpensive. Youtube automati-cally closed-captions all videos for free but requires manual correction of format and grammar. Multiple vendors will add closed captioning as a service starting at $1.00 per minute. To ensure increased accessibility for all students, this is a critical consideration.

If we return to our case study, Jacob may consider using real-time recorded video of a demonstration in his bio lab to prepare students for an upcoming lab experiment during one of the face-to-face classrooms. In the video, he could introduce students to different areas in the lab and demonstrate the proper techniques or processes involved in setting up the lab so students know what to expect when completing their lab in the classroom.

Produced video: Produced videos are videos that are planned and produced in such a way as to enhance the message and quality of the video. Produced videos, like real-time recorded videos, can be used to record presentations, lectures, demonstrations and literally anything that needs to be viewed in any situation. However, the process of recording these events is done with much more care, quality and personnel. Most produced video cost more to create and finish, because they use more refined graphics, editing and distribution systems. Most start with the development of a script and are produced with professional talent. At their best, produced videos begin to approach Augmented Reality where the potential for teaching and learning is greatly increased. Produced videos can be self-produced, purchased, or shared. Produced videos can also be animations created in applications such as Powtoons, GoAnimate and Voki which provide for multiple means of action and expression. At NEIT, we have been using produced videos for faculty development purposes and academic student support. For faculty, we created a series called "App of the Week" which highlights a new app each week that instructors can integrate into their courses. The programs are about 5 minutes in length but discuss why the app will increase engagement or accessibility, what the app does, and how it is used to encourage faculty to try the app out in their courses. For academic support, we have been working with our Academic Skills Center to produce videos that explain the APA format and our expectations for use in all research projects. We have also produced videos for students who are unable to make it to campus to attend seminars on time management and study skills. Produced videos must be created in a video editing application such as Avid Media Composer, Adobe Premiere, Apple Final Cut, or iMovie. Produced videos can be made accessible with the same tools as real-time recorded videos.

Jacob should consider using Produced videos whenever he needs to add intensity and quality into his course. A Produced video, if selected or created appropriately, will bring an added message of importance. The produced video should not be too long and can be cut down to just use the portions of the video that are most relevant to the course.

Augmented reality: Augmented reality (AR) is video that is similar to produced video with real-time or edited video but has added virtual elements such as 3D animations that increase the depth and engagement of the video for the audience. Some embedded elements can even be added by the viewers (Schaffhauser, 2017, p. 3).

Billinghurst described AR as, "The ability to overlay computer graphics onto the real world. . . . AR interfaces allow users to see the real world at the same time as virtual imagery attached to real locations and objects" (Billinghurst, 2002, p. 1). AR videos are usually experienced through an AR app on a computer or mobile device. A good example of an AR app is Starview. Starview Lite is a free app that lets the viewer point their iPad to the sky to reveal the stars and constellations. As the viewer moves the iPad across the sky, the stars change synchronously, are named, and constellations are highlighted. The paid version of the app reveals beautifully illustrated images of the constellations. AR is also used for anatomy instruction and provides the user the ability to investigate all the parts of the body with full 3D manipulation and added information. Imagine seeing a heart beating inside of a living human subject! We can offer that to our students today.

Augmented Reality is a 21st-century capability that enables the development of 21st Century thinking skills (Schrier, 2006, p. 1). The mode also gives the viewer/student the possibility of learning by themselves (Karagozlu & Ozdamli, 2017, p. 663). The cost of AR is currently expensive and depends upon the goals of the lesson and the depth of the interaction between the reality and the added animations but new technology is making it easier and faster to create. Now, most projects take a team of creative individuals and time to produce. Creating 3D animations requires the technical capability of a computer programmer and the artistic ability of an illustrator. Because of the complexity of the production process, most AR videos are purchased from vendors. However, apps are available for little or no money and can provide a wide variety of content, and I believe we're only scratching the surface of its use in education. As Billinghurst (2002) stated, "Although Augmented Reality technology is not new, it's potential in education is just beginning to be explored. Unlike other computing technologies, AR interfaces offer seamless interaction between the real and virtual worlds" (p. 4)

On one level, AR videos present barriers to accessibility. Some AR videos require the use of headsets and require additional viewer actions with a controller or mouse to fully experience the augmented components. The manual dexterity required could be a barrier to some users. However, many AR programs can be controlled with eye movements that trigger events in the video. In these instances, the eye movements act as the "mouse" to interact with the video and can improve accessibility options. AT NEIT, AR is used in multiple departments. It is used in the health sciences for anatomy and physiology instructions and students in our nursing department are required to purchase an Apple iPad that is loaded with a 3D A&P application that provides students with a self-driven inspection and review of body parts and systems. The application allows for individual selection of a body part or system that the student can inspect from any angle; can zoom into the inside of that body part; click on additional information on that part and then add other systems to it to see how it relates.

AR would offer Jacob, the instructor in our case study, an exceptional opportunity for raising the engagement of his online students by allowing them to investigate biology in a way that many have never done before. However, before he experiments with AR in his classroom, he should consider possible barriers and eliminate them by using a variety of video experiences as opposed to relying on a single domain.

Virtual reality: Virtual reality (VR) is a produced video that has a 360-degree view of its environment that allows the viewer to look and move around the environment. I was able to experience the Olympics using VR, but it's not just for sporting events. HEIs courses are evolving to feature more and more VR. These produced videos can be created with special 360-degree cameras and/or created with 3D animation. VR can be viewed on a traditional computer monitor with a mouse interface but it is best viewed or experienced with a VR headset. The VR headset provides a closed environment for the viewer that allows the viewer to physically turn their head to view additional areas of the virtual space. This gives the viewer the ability to control the video beyond just being able to start, pause or stop as well as the ability to control the direction and depth of view. As Osberg (1992) states:

> The break [with reality] occurs because of the ability of the participant to interact in real time with a multi-perceptual, multi-dimensional, inclusive, potentially multi-participant environment; to change perspective at will, to make and implement decisions, to experience a "paradigm shift" in a wholly created system that exists only in the computer and the minds of the world designer and participants.
>
> (p. 4)

Virtual reality can be used in courses to provide an experience to students that cannot be provided in any other way. The cost of creating VR is potentially the most expensive option for the use of video in education as it can require the use of all of the varied technology used in video production plus the technology and skill of creating 3D animation and gaming. VR headsets range in price for as little as $7.00 for a Google Cardboard to hundreds of dollars for a high-end system.

Examples of VR includes virtual tour of museums and historic sites as well as complex simulations of flying an airplane. In the NEIT gaming department, students both use and create VR applications as part of their development as a VR game creator. These students use computer programming, applications and art to create unique "games" that can be both entertaining or educational. Finally, in our electronics engineering department, our students are using VR flight simulators to learn how to fly drones before using the drones outside. All of these are options in online courses as well, and there is no doubt, as technology continues to become more and more innovative, there will be an expectation that it is used more frequently in courses. Our admissions department also offers VR tours of our campus, so your university may consider creating similar opportunities for prospective students to tour the campus to learn more about your institution without having to leave their homes.

One important accessibility consideration for VR is that the mode is largely visual. Ensuring that there is a clear auditory component is important for students who may have visual impairment or who may struggle with visual comprehension. However, used with audio, VR can provide students experience to stimulations and be immersed in experiences that are simply impossible with other forms of video (Kavanagh et al., 2017, p. 92).

Written words, and the previous descriptions of the modes, may not do AR and VR justice. If you'd like an option for visual representation, a great presentation exploring AR and VR can be viewed in a TED Talk hosted by TEDx Jackson Hole (2016) by Zenka, a Los Angeles based artist who creates AR and VR art. The talk is titled, "Will virtual and augmented reality move us into the knowledge age?"

If Jacob is committed to engaging his students in a hybrid-online course, he would benefit from learning about the different modes of video and work to incorporate a VR element to his course to provide his students with a student driven exploration of the specific topics. A properly structured exercise that allows students to answer the "big questions" of the course by searching a virtual world would be far more interesting to many of his students than watching a lecture, regardless of how good a lecturer Jacob is. As an example, Jacob could take them on a tour of a cryogenics institute so students can learn about suspension at cryogenic temperatures and learn about storage and security from experts in the field before they discuss the importance of evaluating facilities through laboratory safety inspections.

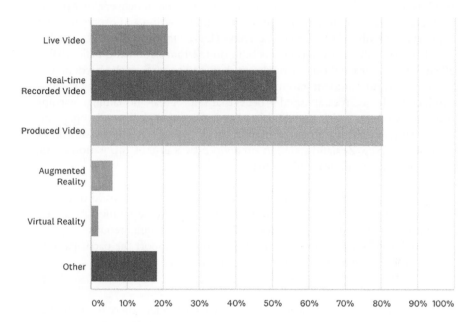

Figure 19.1 Modes of video at NEIT

The survey of NEIT faculty, referenced previously helped to unpack the more popular forms of video used in higher education courses. Figure 19.1 shows that produced videos are the most popular videos to be used in NEIT courses although all the different modes of video are used.

Reflection

- What types of videos are most common in courses you have taken or have designed and delivered?
- After learning about the multiple modes of videos and the benefits and barriers of each, why is it important for instructors to use multiple modes in a single course to increase accessibility and engagement?
- In your course, how could you use VR to maximize the outcomes of your students?

Video as an integral tool

All of the variations of video, regardless how they are produced, can combine to create a formidable set of tools for teaching and learning in any situation. Video in all its forms is important because it provides a mode of delivery that provides multiple means of representation, engagement and action and expression and supports the Universal Design of Learning (UDL) framework. UDL, as all of the chapters in this book support, is built on the foundation and belief that all students can learn if our curricula are designed to remove the barriers that prevent individual students from learning. Using live video, real-time video and produced video is an established process that is a regular and familiar learning mode for students which can eliminate barriers to accessibility and engagement. As one system administrator at a medium-sized higher education institution in Australia/New Zealand stated in survey run by Kaltura Corporation on the "State of Video in Education" in 2017:

> Within five years a radical shift will begin to occur in the world of education. Multimedia [video, AR and VR] is one of the best educational techniques because it addresses more than one sense simultaneously . . . so as to provide effective education, which in turn will support the participation of the different senses of the learners in diverse syllabi.
>
> (p. 3)

Video is certainly not a panacea. When viewing a video, there is a potential lack of intimacy, a potential boredom factor (especially if the video is not well done or too long) and an increased need to support the student in the use of the video, but from an accessibility perspective, video is a digital tool that is far more flexible for all students. First, in its recorded forms, it is instantly repeatable, sections of the video can be played multiple times to review which allows students to take learning at their own pace. Secondly, videos can also be closed captioned thereby increasing its accessibility. We also have tools to make video more interactive. New tools such as EdPuzzle allow the instructor to add questions into the video that stops the video and requires the student to answer before continuing. The addition of AR and VR to the mix of video options gives an immersive layer that cannot be offered in other video modes.

In terms of student engagement, the length of a video is critically important. The average length of the 10 most popular videos on YouTube in January 2014 was 4 minutes and 20 seconds. Gao's (2015) research for EdX recommends a maximum video length for educational videos as 6 minutes and shows that student engagement decreases as the video length gets longer. Ted Talks have found a way to increase viewership time by making sure that they inspire people so if you plan to produce or show a video in your course, be sure it's inspiring.

The length of view time for AR and VR video is very different. Research on the Video Completion Rate (VCR) difference between standard 2D video and 360-degree video done by Omnivert, a VR company, found that:

> On average, we saw an 85% VCR (Video Completion Rate) for 360° video creative. This was a 46% improvement over the 2D videos which had an average VCR of 58.2%. The specific performance varied by creative and

length, but the results were clear. This new 360° video ad experience engages audiences better than standard 2D creative.

Sullivan (2018) states that:

We see virtual reality, as well as 360 video, AR . . . as part of the same spectrum, which is immersive platforms. We see that as part of the future of how people consume media, including journalism.

(p. 3)

And, that future is coming. According to the April, 2018 *eCurrent*, the quarterly newsletter of OSHEAN, the internet service provider to all of the schools, colleges, libraries, hospitals, and municipalities in the state of Rhode Island, in the United States, and surrounding communities, the Warwick Public Library is the first in Rhode Island to open a Virtual Reality service. It will only be a matter of time before our HEI libraries do the same.

Reflection

- Why do you think that VR is able to increase student engagement and persistence in a video learning task?
- Think about the videos you assign in your courses, or the videos that students create to express knowledge. Consider the length and the research on how engagement is affected by the length. What would you do differently the next time you provide students with an opportunity to watch a video?

Conclusion

If we want to increase accessibility and engagement in our courses, we must embrace video as a tool for teaching and learning, knowing that our current efforts will likely evolve into leveraging virtual reality in our classrooms. Multiple research articles can be found on how VR can be used for science and health education (Ferrer-Garcia et al., 2017; Hoogenes J. et al., 2018; Gutiérrez-Maldonado, José et al.), chemical engineering (Tunnicliffe, Helen, 2014), adventure athletic training (Yong-Shun Wang) and poultry science (Kloepper, Marcia Owens et al., 2010) and others. Pantelidis (2009) has researched VR extensively and states:

At every level of education, virtual reality has the potential to make a difference, to lead learners to new discoveries, to motivate and encourage and excite. The learner can participate in the learning environment with a sense of presence, of being part of the environment.

(p. 3)

As stated in the introductory case study, our instructor, Jacob was struggling with student engagement because he wasn't using video purposefully to increase engagement and accessibility. Jacob would be wise to research ways to improve his use of video by leveraging the multiple ways to engage his students with more immersive videos including AR and VR. As Javidi (1999) reports, "By making VR tools and environments available to educators, we may discover more about the very process of learning. By participating in the development of VR, educators can guide the growth of this technology, and perhaps influence the course of educational change."

While Jacob is exploring VR, he should also review how he is using the video resources he already has. Are they the appropriate length? Are they well produced? Are they relevant, authentic, and meaningful to his students? Do they align with UDL principles as suggested in Table 19.1? It looks like Jacob has some work to do, and he shouldn't waste any time getting this started as technology is not standing still waiting for teachers to catch up. Microsoft is developing the next thing: holographic images! If you're interested, start your research on Mixed Reality because soon, that will likely be integrated into your courses as well.

References

Billinghurst, M. (2002). Augmented Reality in Education. *New Horizons for Learning*. 12(5).

Dunham, F., Lowdermilk, R., & Broderick, G. (1956). Television in Education. *Bulletin*, 1957(21). Office of Education, US Department of Health, Education, and Welfare, Office of Education, US Department of Health, Education, and Welfare., eric.ed.gov/?id=ED543828.

eCurrent. (2018, May 1). Warwick Library. *First in State to Offer a Virtual Reality Experience*. Retrieved from www.oshean.org/?page=2018SpringeCurrent

Fisher, D., & Fisher, M. (1999). *Tube: The Invention of Television Hardcover*. Darby, PA: Diane Publishing Company.

Gao, Philip. (2015). *Optimal Video Length for Student Engagement*. Retrieved from EdX Blog, EdX, 11 Aug. 2015, blog.edx.org/optimal-video-length-student-engagement.

Hoogenes, J., Wong, N., Al-Harbi, B., Kim, K., Vij, S., Bolognone, E., . . . Matsumoto, E. (2018). A Randomized Comparison of 2 Robotic Virtual Reality Simulators and Evaluation of Trainees' Skills Transfer to a Simulated Robotic Urethrovesical Anastomosis Task. *Urology*, 110–115.

Javidi, G. (1999). *Virtual Reality and Education*. University of Southern Florida: Florida.

Kaltura (2017). *The state of video in education 2017: A Kaltura Report*. Retrieved from https://corp.kaltura.com/education-solutions/education

Karagözlü, D., & Ozdamli, F. (2017). *Student Opinions on Mobile Augmented Reality*.

Kavanagh, S., Luxton-Reilly, A., Wuensche, B., & Plimmer, B. (2017). A Systematic Review of Virtual Reality in Education. *Themes in Science and Technology Education*, 10(2), 85–119.

Kloepper, M. O., Zweiacher, E., Curtis, P., & Evert, A. (2010). Where's the Chicken? Virtual Reality Brings Poultry Science to the Community College. *Techniques: Connecting Education and Careers*, 85(6), 44–47.

Lay, R. (2014). *Why video is the future of online learning.* Retrieved from http://summitevergreen.com/why-video-is-the-future-of-online-learning/

Mattei, M. D., & Ennis, E. (2014). Continuous, Real-Time Assessment of Every Student's Progress in the Flipped Higher Education Classroom Using Nearpod. *Journal of Learning in Higher Education*, 10(1), 1–7.

Meyer, A., Rose, D., & Gordon, D. (2014). *Universal Design for Learning: Theory and Practice.* Wakefield, MA: CAST Professional Publications.

Novak, K., & Thibodeau, T. (2016). *How to Design and Deliver Online Education Using Universal Design for Learning.* Wakefield, MA: CAST Professional Publications.

Novak, M. (2012). Predictions for Educational TV in the 1930s. *Smithsonian.com*, Smithsonian Institution. Retrieved from www.smithsonianmag.com/history/predictions-for-educational-tv-in-the-1930s-107574983/

Osberg, Kimberly. (1992). *Virtual reality and education: A look at both sides of the sword.* Retrieved from citeseerx.ist.psu.edu

Pantelidis, V. (2009). Reason to Use Virtual Reality in Education and Training Courses and a Model to Determine When to Use Virtual Reality. *Themes in Science and Technology Education Special Issue*, 59–77.

Schaffhauser, D. (2017, April/May). AR and VR Come of Age. *The Journal Digital Edition*.

Smith, Kit. (2018). *39 Fascinating and incredible YouTube statistics.* Brandwatch. Retrieved January 18, 2018, from www.brandwatch.com/blog/39-youtube-stats/

Sullivan, T. (2018) VR Gives Journalism a New Dimension. *PCMAG.* Retrieved from https://uk.pcmag.com/features/93199/vr-gives-journalism-a-new-dimension

TEDxJacksonHole. (2016). *Will virtual and augmented reality move us into the knowledge age?* Retrieved from www.youtube.com/watch?v=2FA-IuDTMjE

Tunnicliffe, H. (2014). Gazing into a Virtual Reality Future. *TCE: The Chemical Engineer*, (880), 24–25.

Schrier, Karen (2006, July). Using Augmented Reality Games to Teach 21st Century Skills. *ACM SIGGRAPH.*

Conclusion

Universal Design for Learning: a global framework for realising inclusive practice in higher education

Seán Bracken and Katie Novak

In the introduction to this book we noted that for centuries traditional education was focused largely on creating environments that catered to privileged populations who acquired knowledge in elite settings. This acquisition of knowledge, through a one-size-fits-all system, tended to perpetuate inequities in HEIs and in wider societies. Archain systems replicated practices that had ensured an elite class of scholars could afford to access and engage in a higher education designed specifically for them. Increasingly, social and economic requirements for a more just and sustainable society have ushered in an era where widening educational participation, enabling accessibility, and an increased focus on educational outcomes for those from more diverse backgrounds has led to systemic shifts in the nature of HEI practices internationally.

Over the past fifty years or so, national and transnational educational systems have shifted more toward valuing human diversity and, as a result, there is much greater scope within HEIs for students from more diverse backgrounds. Increasingly, HEIs have begun to cater for the learning requirements of student cohorts that have been referred to as 'non-traditional'. These students may identify as having single or multiple attributes of 'variability'. Whilst, from a UDL perspective, the notion of variability has most frequently been associated with neuro-cognitive or physical (dis)abilities, more and more frequently UDL principles and practices associated with universal educational planning for variability have resonance and application to differing identify features such as; coming from a minority ethnic or 'racial' background (though of course, we recognise that the concept of 'race' is socially constructed); or being a student with a diverse linguistic heritage, or coming from outside the home country (Stoessel et al., 2015). The term might also to apply to students from historically underrepresented social/cultural groups who may be the first from within generations of their families to attend university (these students are increasingly referred to as 'first gens' within the UK). Additionally, the concept of variability, while understood to encompass the multiple forms of 'everyday' differences among learners, could be applied to students from a higher age or those who are attending university on a part-time basis.

It is evident then that the conceptual basis for variability underpinning much of the UDL framework is broad-based, multifaceted and somewhat context specific. This is why it is so important to learn from the application of UDL as experienced in a variety of geographical, cultural and transnational perspectives. As educators in HEIs, we can all learn from the similarities and differences in the ways that the core attributes of UDL are interpreted according to need. The endeavour responds to a call for additional research in the field shared by Burgstahler (2013). As the UDL framework is tested, (re)interpreted and enriched by the additional research provided in this text, so our depth of understanding regarding the framework is made more insightful – especially because UDL has not, until relatively recently – been applied to contexts of higher and further education. A comprehensive engagement with each of the differing chapters in this book reveals that while there are, of necessity, differing ways in which the UDL framework is applied, what strongly rings through is the shared conviction amongst all of the authors as to how an asset-based approach to variability enriches the educational landscape for all learners and, perhaps more importantly, it has the potential to transform the lives of individuals or groups of students who may have otherwise been marginalised within HEIs. UDL then posits learners at the centre of the educational experience. It offers policy makers and practitioners alike a sound, research-informed basis for future planning and actions that will continue to strengthen the capacity for all learners to realise their full potentials. We do not pretend that UDL, of itself, is a full panacea for all of the challenges faced by 'non-traditional' learners, to do so would be to grossly over simplify the very complex nature of teaching, learning and assessment in HEI contexts. However, when carefully and judiciously enacted, the UDL framework provides both a compass and a roadmap for navigating some of the more challenging terrain when creating learning avenues for those who have traditionally been marginalised in HEIs.

It is clear from synthesising the main learning emanating from the chapters in this book, that when HEIs (or even individual learning programs) commit to the implementation of Universal Design for Learning (UDL), they consciously set about attaining the ethical imperative for HEIs to make a significant contribution to wider society. In doing so, and while they maintain a challenging and rigorous approach to curriculum planning and enactment, they are successfully preparing a much wider cohort of students for a richer life of empowered social and economic learning, engagement and reward. What is truly promising about this journey is that it is founded on a growing body of research that has revealed how students learn and how we as educators must respond accordingly. Taken together the previous chapters contribute to our desire to know more about how this journey can be mapped out, by setting out a rich tapestry of case studies, research and opportunities to prompt reflection as to how our institutions can transform teaching and learning from the institutional level, to the faculty level, to the student level, and at the curriculum and assessment levels. The authors provide us with a multifaceted response that deepens our understanding and grasp of the complexity underpinning the change agenda. The book also responds to the observation made by Testa and Egan (2014) that HEIs must make significant systematic transformations to meet the needs of diverse learners in a more interconnected world.

In the first section of the book, *UDL and strategic leadership: a whole university approach to inclusive practice*, multiple authors examine how the UDL framework lends itself to an institutional approach to meeting the learning requirements of students who are increasingly diverse. This section draws in experience of educational leaders across Europe who have not only had an impact within their own settings, but they have gone on to advocate for large-scale policy or legislative changes by fostering collaboration with other critical stakeholders.

In the first instance, a truly transnational research perspective is adopted. Olauseen et al., reveal how colleagues working across territorial borders can extend our understanding of institutional inclusive change processes through UDL. In their chapter "Universal Design for Learning – license to learn: *A process for mapping a Universal Design for Learning process on to campus learning*", they turn an investigative eye on the different stakeholder groups who impact the adoption of UDL at an institutional level. A fundamental part of their work was the description and analysis of the different stakeholder groups when it comes to ideas, views, assumptions, contributions and behaviours' they have identified within their institutions that either inhibit or encourage a culture of inclusion. Ultimately, they contend that in order for successful change to occur there is a necessity to overcome misconceptions about prior learning (Uzunöz, 2018). This conceptual change is further discussed in terms to immunity to change, which describes how individuals and organisation fail to change because of unconscious agendas that may inhibit progress. These have to be addressed through open dialogue, proactive and thoughtful planning in order to facilitate deeper organisational learning (Kegan & Lahey, 2009). Because this chapter has provided insights from key stakeholders including students, organisational leaders, academic staff and student support staff, it enables an insightful triangulation of data. It also exemplifies an important framework for facilitating progressive change at large-scale multi organisational level.

A historical analytic investigation of HEI change processes informs the work of Geoff Layer who, in *"From whole university to national practice: using UDL to frame a national perspective in HEIs"*, explores how national policies impact, and are informed by, the learning and teaching experiences of a diverse student body, specifically those with disabilities. Using educational experiences in the UK as a lens, Layer reveals the symbiotic relationship between policy and a strengthening student capacity to shape the nature of the educational experience overall and how this has bolstered potential for student self-actualisation. He provides critical insights into the evolutionary development of universities as somewhat isolated centres acting as seats of learning for scholars, to spaces that are becoming more attuned to the learning requirements of their students. Thus, he argues that UDL provides the intellectual and research rigour necessary to transform institutions from a "community of scholars" to student-centered teaching and learning organisations focused on realising the learning requirements of more marginalised students. This work builds on the previous chapter (Olauseen, et al.) as it problematises the experiences of some students who lack a sense of belonging at university and it seeks to address this conundrum through dialogue between student voice and future policy orientations. Ultimately, this chapter suggests that an overarching UDL framework provides the architectural design for embedding a culture of inclusion throughout HEIs.

The themes visited in the first two chapters; namely the interplay between policy formation and its enactment and impact upon multiple stakeholders is studied in the rich microcosm of one university, which decided to adopt a 'Big Bang' strategy for implementing UDL across a whole organisation. The contribution scripted by Moriarty and Scarffe, "Universal Design for Learning and strategic leadership: *a whole university approach to inclusive practice*", illustrates the centrality of empowering critical change agents at middle leadership level through a dynamic and purposeful strategy of "middle-out" innovation and collegiate adoption of inclusive planning and action (Cummings et al., 2005). Though the authors stress that this change process came about as a result of external policy drivers, there is a strong sense of moral purpose, local leadership and collaborative authorship as senior colleagues in student services and in the teaching development domain worked closely to set a longer-term strategic vision for how a truly inclusive university might be realised. This chapter provides a powerful insight into how this approach has impacted positively on learning outcomes of all students. The workings of UDL are revealed, for example, in the ways that technologies are employed for all learners so that they have access to learning when it suits them, as opposed to when it may suit the lecturer. The complex synergies and generative interplay between multiple strands of activity involving for example; student services, estates, learning technologies, library and information services, the students and their teachers appears to have created the essential ingredients required for a comprehensive and convincing adoption of UDL across the whole organisation. This model provides an important template for other senior leaders within HEIs who may be interested in leading and managing inclusive change across the university.

While Section 1 provides an institutional focus on UDL, each subsequent section examines differing institutional facets of implementing a UDL approach. For example, aspects of UDL adoption can occur when students and teachers collaboratively address aspects of one or more of the following; curriculum and assessment, or faculty professional enhancement, student engagement and autonomy, or ensuring that resource materials – such as technological affordances – contribute to anticipatory universal design. A key shared theme in all of these approaches is the centrality of planning and collaboration in contributing to transformation of HEIs. Taken together the chapters in

Section 2: *Working in partnership with key stakeholders to engage all students*, investigate specific organisational capacity drivers and discuss how HEIs can use stakeholder beliefs and feedback to inform professional development on to facilitate capacity for implementation of UDL within the sector.

As identified in the introduction, the diversification agenda has brought to light some challenges for the HEI sector, including the necessity to ensure that all faculty have access to requisite resources and professional learning to enable them to understand what UDL is and how it may be effectively implemented. The concept of professional enhancement is addressed in Coy's chapter, "*Transforming the professor: motivating university students in every discipline through design*". The case study provides an opportunity for reflection on the affective dimensions to learning as articulated in the UDL core feature of 'engagement'. Through a process of purposeful interrogation of the UDL guidelines, the professor concerned in the chapter case study becomes more self-aware of her actions and this in turn enables her to strengthen her professional practice. Thus, the promise of the UDL framework is exemplified as having a twofold impact; positively informing pedagogy of students whilst simultaneously providing a conceptual framework for professional enhancement.

Increasingly in the research, it is recognised that supporting more disadvantaged students through times of transition is pivotal to success in further and Higher Education (for example see the seminal article by Thomas, 2013), Hitch and her colleagues explore and extend this body of research by examining the importance of making UDL explicit to students in their chapter "*The transition to higher education: applying university design for learning to support student success*". From their research, it is clear that students entering the 'novice' phase of their HEI experience require well taught through, and highly personalised, scaffolded social and educational interactions that assist them to map their way through what is termed as being a 'foreign land'. Just as travellers attempt to learn the language and culture of new spaces where they may find themselves, so students need to acquire what Hitch et al. refer to as 'pedagogical literacy'. In doing so, the authors suggest that care is required so students are not overloaded with choice. They also illustrate that a fusion of UDL with other learning frameworks is likely to lead to best social and learning outcomes for students.

Following this, Berquist and Neopolitan's chapter, "*Using professional learning communities to redesign learning environments in HEIs*" illustrates how the processes of inclusive change are enhanced when leadership and vision is shared among key stakeholders. The chapter identifies that the variability of student cohorts has prompted a new way of addressing students' engagement so that their learning takes centre stage and a major way of addressing their learning requirements comes from focused capacity building among the academic staff. What is noteworthy in this chapter is how staff are empowered, through UDL methodologies, to form sustainable self-supporting networks of peer advisors. This initiative draws on earlier research, for example that of Knowles (1984), to energise colleagues so that they are better enabled to address the changing nature of the student experience in diverse HEIs.

The collaborative relationships between faculty and students is examined more closely in Section 3: *Facilitating multiple identities and student engagement*. The chapters in this section explore the implications of emergent variance in the nature of student identities, especially where enrolment changes may be perceived as altering a prior 'norm' of relative monoculturalism. To enhance student engagement and learning outcomes, faculty are encouraged to proactively anticipate the diverse range of student learning requirements while considering course design. Additionally, all of the authors in this section acknowledge the necessity to consider the dynamic and process-oriented nature of learning, so that a co-construction of knowledge with students throughout the learning experience is optimised as are the conditions for engagement, representation and expression.

By enacting a structured approach known as 'instructional design', Rao argues in her chapter, "*Instructional design with UDL: addressing learner variability in college courses*", that colleagues can avoid ambiguity about the learning process and ensure that learning methods are appropriate for desired learning outcomes. Clarity of goals and purpose enable both learners and professors to realise what is required to attain good learning outcomes for all students. The focus on proactive course design while being mindful of accessibility and engagement is critical to maintain high levels of quality and inclusion in global contexts (Pounder et al., 2016). Rao emphasises the importance of increased flexibility and choice to personalise learning for students, thereby increasing both accessibility and student engagement, while also ensuring that courses are adequately challenging, culturally responsive and linguistically appropriate.

Johnston and Castine first provide a global overview of a cohort of learners aged 16–24 who are exceptionally marginalised, being at once out of formal education and out of work. In their chapter "*UDL in apprenticeships and career training programs that serve youth with untapped talent*", they then explore in greater depth how one career training program based on UDL principles in the United States, is addressing this heretofore chronically underserved cohort of learners. They illustrate, for example, that a significant minority of this group of people are those who have some form of disability. Providing learning pathways through career training programs, such as industry recognised certificate programs and pre-apprenticeship and apprenticeship programs, enables these learners to define future goals and transform their lives through personal growth and self-actualisation by learning authentic workplace-based skills that assist them to find meaningful work. The authors argue that in order to attain their goals, due care must to be paid to the core attributes of the UDL framework, especially when considering the concept of assessment, which for this group of learners, may have previously been fraught with negative feelings and experiences that have hindered subsequent learning. Drawing on the work of Aceves and Orosco (2014), they make a cogent point for the necessity to employ culturally responsive teaching that takes into consideration the identities and prior experiences of marginalised groups and individuals so that challenges to learning can be overcome in a meaningful way.

Considering the cultural, spatial and temporal identities of students, especially those with disabilities, lies at the heart of Costa-Renders' chapter "*Pedagogy of Seasons and UDL: the multiple temporalities of learning involving the university as a whole*". A touchstone concept informing the interpretation of UDL within the author's context of São Paulo in Brazil, is how by their presence and actions within the university space, persons who are physically disabled prompt reflection and change to occur. This impacts on the nature of learning and teaching, especially where conscious efforts are made for inclusion and incorporation. According to Costa-Renders, an innovative reimagining of the 'university for all' provokes, through ethical research, constructive design anticipations that closely align with the UDL framework. Through mutual and dynamic interaction with difference, students and teachers creatively reinterpret curriculum, physical spaces, learning time and new ways of being emerge. This chapter posits learners at the heart of a more caring and responsive educational experience where the affective and physical needs of individuals provide a meaningful context within which the framework can be interpreted as a means to challenge linear, or 'monocultural' one size fits all epistemologies and thereby learning spaces become truly accessible, thus transforming how learning takes place in the cognitive and physical domains.

The following chapter expands the application of UDL to consider the implications of dynamically changing student populations in one Canadian university. Focusing on the learning requirements of a growing body of international students, in his chapter, "*Not Just Disability: Getting Traction for UDL Implementation with International Students*", Fovet argues there is an urgent need to re envision how curriculum is designed and enacted so that flexibility and choice create the required conditions to foster inclusion and belonging – no matter what the nature of student variability might be. Using reflexive strategies, and applying a phenomenological research methodology, this chapter provides an impassioned insight into the author's personal experiences of UDL application to a wider cohort of students. Ultimately, this chapter illustrates how effective inclusive strategies work for all learners, incorporating consideration of intersectionality for example, rather than being adopted only for those with disabilities as has historically been the case with the UDL framework. Such strategies challenge ethnocentrism, and monoculturalism and they promote an asset-based approach to learning and teaching.

Section 4: *Transforming learning: redesigning curriculum, format, content and practice* provides an opportunity to interrogate the nature of curriculum enactment and the praxis of how the UDL guidelines are brought to life through engagement, representation and action and expression. When considering curriculum here the chapters are concerned with the nature of goals, methods, materials and assessment. In the first instance, McCarthy and Butler argue in their chapter, "*Transforming Teaching and learning in HEIs: impacts of UDL on professional development of university lecturers*" that in order to empower professors to make changes, there is a necessity for them to have a sound grasp of the conceptual frameworks informing such changes. This is realised when there is a shared language that facilitates change and the resulting dialogue is underpinned by shared professional perspectives within the HEI community. A strong case is made for the adoption of a socio-cultural perspectives to support learning. According to McCarthy and Butler, this is most clearly articulated in the ways that disciplinary practices are constructed and learned in the joint student teacher development of knowledge, methods, purposes and genres or forms of expression.

Considering the requirements of learners with cognitive disabilities Yalon-Chamovitz and her colleagues discuss the development of 'cognitive ramps' and how they can be constructed to act as learning scaffolds in their chapter entitled, "*Cognitive accessibility: stretching the boundaries of UDL in higher ed*". by highlighting the importance of universally designing supports for students who may not access HEI using traditional pathways. The chapter identifies how practical, foresightful adaptations to a 'traditional' curriculum enables accessibility. This theme is one that is shared in all of the chapters in this section.

Moore proposes a pivotal reorientation from a sole focus on discipline content to a multi-varied focus on learner requirements as a means of enhancing accessibility in his chapter "*From teaching content to teaching students: UDL as a vehicle for improving curriculum and praxis design*". This chapter also addresses a topical consideration in HEIs, the maintenance of a challenging high quality educational experience whilst also ensuring that students are enabled to engage with the curriculum goals and materials. The author argues that a sound balance between access and quality is attainable when the basic ingredients for learning include flexibility, innovation and challenge. In the following chapter, Black and Fraser further enhance understandings of how to position learners at the centre of a changed dynamic that provides a quality educational experience for all. In their chapter, "*Integration through collaboration: building strategic faculty partnerships to shift minds and practices*", they illustrate how the UDL guidelines provide the conceptual rigour that grounds meaning making for multiple partners to regenerate learning from an inclusive perspective. A strong argument is made for the development of shared partnerships between Accessibility Services (AS) teams and Centres for Teaching and Learning (CTLs) so they can provide common understandings about how best to scaffold learning for all students.

The concern for discipline-based expectations and their dynamic interrelationships with UDL, a concept initially explored by McCarthy and Butler, is revisited when Soler Costa and Bracken discuss how a professional competency-based framework for teacher education in Spain could be enhanced by re-envisioning its development through the lens of inclusive design. In HEIs, the argument is frequently made that particular courses cannot be inclusively reimagined due to the specific constraints of professional bodies and their particular framework expectations. However, in the chapter "*Creating synergies between UDL and core principles of the European Higher Education Area in planning for pre-service teacher education*", Solar Costa and Bracken contest this notion and highlight the potential to strengthen professional practices by appealing to the ethical and values base upon which such professional frameworks were initially developed. Rather than seeing professional frameworks as straitjackets of conformity, the chapter illustrates how guidance, offered in the form of creative synergies between the EHAE competency-based framework and UDL, can actually enhance creativity and inclusion. Towards the end of this chapter, the concept of authentic, sustainable and meaningful assessment is touched upon; these notions are further explored in the subsequent chapter.

Drawing on a significant body of research, O'Neill and Maguire make the point in their chapter "*Developing assessment and feedback approaches to empower and engage students: a sectoral approach in Ireland*", that the multifarious attributes of assessment are posited right at the heart of the learning and teaching. They argue that affective, cognitive and academic impacts of assessment approaches are nothing short of 'powerful' in their capacity to affect the experiences of students and academic faculty alike. As such, assessment practices have contributed significantly to the ways in which marginalised communities have either been further excluded or enabled in terms of educational engagement. With this in mind, the authors focus on the necessity to target assessment design if students are to be empowered and if they are to remain motivated and involved right throughout the duration of their courses in HEIs. Traditionally marginalised learners have tended to leave their courses before completion as a result of poor assessment results, so the challenge for the sector is to raise learning capacity and to ensure that assessment processes are socially just while being simultaneously robust in terms of intellectual and cognitive challenge. O'Neill and Maguire illustrate how a strong research-informed strategy has enabled the HEI sector in Ireland to come to a shared agreement that the differing attributes of assessment; including assessment; 'of, for and as' learning, underpin a combined UDL approach that is complemented and further informed by eight key assessment principles. What is potentially transformative about this approach is that there is whole sector support for the concept that by increasing assessment literacy and accessibility all students will be provided with the requisite learning to realise their academic potentials.

Whilst academic literacy and praxis were the key concerns of the chapters discussed, the notions of digital literacy and maximising use of accessible information technologies are the preserve of the final section; Section 5: *Providing access to learning for all – enabling inclusive learning through digital literacy and technologies*. Many of the constituent aspects of the UDL Guidelines make reference to tools and resources, for example the need for educators to 'optimize access to tools and assistive technologies' (CAST, 2018). The concluding three chapters carefully tease out the implications of this guidance for individual learners, their settings and the jurisdictions within which learners may be studying. The authors in this section explore the barriers and affordances of open, distance, or virtual education and they provide concrete strategies for enabling all students to optimise optimise learning through the use of facilitative technologies. These chapters underscore the cutting-edge nature of UDL, illustrating how it is providing innovative sector-based, research-informed responses to the challenges students encounter while striving to succeed in differing socio-cultural and national contexts.

By providing a critically reflective analysis of a three-year journey of pedagogical transformation, Jackson and Lapinski have clearly stepped out how a significant change management process for one program was realised at Boston College. Their chapter, *"Restructuring the blended learning environment on campus for equity and opportunity through UDL"* further elucidates how this shift in design has been constructed on three strategic pillars of strength, namely; the UDL framework, the concept of accessibility, and a conscious focus on the uses of technology. The authors revealed how presumptions regarding the supposed high levels of digital literacy among undergraduate student cohorts had to be revised and, as Johnson and Lapinski share, 'there was familiarity, but not expertise'. So, it was necessary to set aside assumptions and to 'think critically about how accessibility, technology, and UDL come together'. Student teachers taking their redesigned course learned about, and through, the practical application of inclusive technologies, thereby providing the vital knowledge, skills and capacities these students would require within their professional lives as teachers. Significantly, this initiative has proven so successful within the College, that it has provided a template for enabling whole institutional change thereby providing a well-researched approach to closing opportunity gaps within the learning organisation. The chapter contribution thus strengthens understanding within the sector about how best to build inclusive and highly sustainable change management processes within HEIs.

The pivotal role played by technologies in reaching out to heretofore educationally underserved populations is explored by Abdool Satar in her chapter entitled *"Promoting digital access and inclusivity in open and distance learning in South Africa: a UDL approach"*. Drawing on an informed and in-depth discussion of the policy context within South Africa, the author explores the concept of digital exclusion especially as this pertains to persons with disabilities. She argues that HEIs in Africa can assist in bridging digital inequities by specifically addressing the learning requirements of people in the community who are disabled. Abdool Satar believes that issues related to meaningful digital inclusion can be addressed by providing designing support structures based on UDL principles. Clear examples are provided regarding the nature of anticipatory design including investment in digital hub centres that cater for all learners. It is clear from this chapter that purposeful strives have been taken to overcome barriers to learning and that full use of technological innovations are being incorporated to ensure that national policies are addressed inclusively.

In the final chapter "*UDL, online accessibility, and virtual reality: design-ing accessible and engaging online courses*", Thibodeau provides a glimpse of the products and practices that have the potential to revolutionise the ways in which learning is made accessible through video and virtual reality tools. Clear exemplification is provided linking particular strategies to each of the UDL guidelines. This is followed through with suggested strategies for making the most out of current functionalities available in the use of video to strengthen access to learning. A particular strength of this chapter is the clarity with which educators are informed about current and future applications of technologies to ensure greater access to learning for all.

Taken together, all of the chapters in this book provide an exciting and energising overview of the dynamic ways in which UDL is informing theory, policy and practice in HEIs across the globe. There is significant breadth and depth in terms of the themes addressed, from reflecting on individual profes-sor and student experiences, to exploring the implications for adopting UDL strategies within institutions, or beyond to particular jurisdictions and ultimately to impact on transnational policies and practices. The chapters share what is possible when educators are provided with clarity of purpose and enabled to enact change because they have insight and guidance provided. As the chap-ters testify, the application of UDL in higher education has come a long way, but there is no room for complacency. The challenges for enabling access and outcomes success for all students, from all backgrounds is a perennial one. The nature of barriers to learning shift and change with the changing policies and practices within the higher education sector. What is important to recognise is that educators, acting as committed agents of cognitive and social change for good, and drawing on the inspiration that UDL provides, can make a significant difference in transforming the lives of learners. What is clear from this text is that only when UDL is optimised at all levels will all students have access to the same opportunities for success as their peers and for all of us who are commit-ted to this work, that can't come soon enough. The inspired work of colleagues who have contributed to this text is testimony to that vision.

References

Aceves, T. C., & Orosco, M. J. (2014). Culturally responsive teaching (Document No. IC-2). Retrieved from University of Florida, Collaboration for Effective Edu-cator, Development, Accountability, and Reform Center website: http://ceedar. education.ufl.edu/tools/innovation-configurations/

Burgstahler, S. (2013). Introduction to universal design in higher education. In S. Burgstahler (Ed.), *Universal design in higher education: Promising practices.* Seattle: DO-IT, University of Washington. Retrieved from www.uw.edu/doit/ UDHE-promising-practices/part1.html

CAST. (2018). *Universal design for learning guidelines version 2.2* [graphic organ-izer]. Wakefield, MA: Author.

Cummings, R., Philips, R., Tilbrook, R., & Lowe, R. (2005). Middle-out approaches to reform of University teaching and learning: Champions striding between the "top-down" and "bottom-up" approaches International. *Review of Research in Open and Distance* Learning, 6(1). ISSN: 1492–3831.

Kegan, R., & Lahey, L. L. (2009). *Immunity to change: How to overcome it and unlock potential in yourself and your organization.* Boston, MA: Harvard Business Press.

Knowles, M. (1984). *Andragogy in action: Applying modern principles of adult learning.* San Francisco, CA: Jossey-Bass.

Pounder, J. S., Ho Hung-lam, E., & Groves, J. M. (2016). Faculty-student engagement in teaching observation and assessment: A Hong Kong initiative. *Assessment & Evaluation in Higher Education*, 41(8), 1193–1205. doi:10.1080/0260 2938.2015.1071779

Stoessel, K., Ihme, T. A., Barbarino, M. L., Fisseler, B., & Stürmer, S. (2015). Sociodemographic diversity and distance education: Who drops out from academic programs and why? *Research in Higher Education*, 56(3), 228–246.

Testa, D., & Egan, R. (2014). Finding voice: The higher education experiences of students from diverse backgrounds. *Teaching in Higher Education*, 19(3), 229–241. doi:10.1080/13562517.2013.860102

Thomas, L. (2013). What works? Facilitating an effective transition into higher education. *Widening Participation and Lifelong Learning*, 14(1), 4–24.

Uzunöz, A. (2018). Conceptual teaching based on scientific storyline method and conceptual change texts: Latitude-parallel concepts. *International Journal of Higher Education*, 7(1), 32–50.

Index

Note: Page numbers in *italics* indicate figures and page numbers in **bold** indicate tables.

53–54, 64; inclusive educational practices in 3; massification in 35–36; strategies for widening participation **45**; student feedback 38; students with disabilities in 38, *38*, 39, *39*, 40, *40*, 41–43, 46–48, 50, 53–54; *see also* De Montfort University (DMU)

United States: accessibility settlements and 144–145; career training in 134; disabilities legislation 3; government support for UDL 136–137; international students in 299–300; out-of-school youth 131–132; youth with disabilities in 133; *see also* Fresno State University; Towson University

Universal Design for Learning (UDL): accessibility and 161–162, 248, 304, 307–309; assessment and 58–59, 109, 147–151, 278–280, 284; barriers to 20, 23, 27, 29; as best practice 3; common language for 196–197; contributions of people with disabilities to 160–162, 166–169; course components 122, **122**, 123; culture of inclusion and 47–48; curricular change and 43, 47, 55, 93; defining 73, 102, 117, **247**, 248; engagement in 77, 86; expert learners and 6, 139–140, 194, 232, 235, 248, 250; in faculty support initiatives 74–82; implementation of 5, 7, 12, 14–15; institutional change for 54, **54**, 55, 348; instructional design and 116–124, 126; leadership and 25; maturity model for 64, *65*; middle-out approach to 50–51, 55, *56*, 58, 66, 349; mindsets for 249–250, **251**, 254, **255**; organizational change and 3; positive outcomes of 88–89, 94–95; principles of 4–5, 86, 138, 174–176, 186, 207, 222; proactive planning with 39, 102; professional development for 107; rigor and 237–242; social justice and 266–268; staff development and support for 61–64; student-centrism and 231–232, 241, 349; student experience with 90–95; support for all students through 55, 66, 74; technologies and 304, 307, 309; transition and 88, 96–97; U.S. investment in 136–137; variability

and 170, 346–347; *see also* multiple means of action & expression; multiple means of engagement; multiple means of representation

Universal Design for Learning: A License to Learn (UDLL) 12–14

Universal Design for Learning Professional Development Network (UDL PDN): adult learning theory and 105; goals of 104; implementation phases of 105–110, **110**; online component of 107; UDL framework and 103–104

Universall 12

Universidade Methodista de Sao Paulo (UMESP) 168

universities *see* higher education institutions (HEIs)

University College Cork (UCC) 203–206, 216

University of Al-Karueein 1

University of Arkansas 117

University of South Africa (Unisa): accessible learning environment at 321–322; assessment and 323; assistive technology and 323; digital access and 319–321; digital inclusion at 314–324; digital media and 321, 323; enrolment in 318; inclusive support system at 319–324; open distance and e-learning in 313, 318–323; students with disabilities in 318, **318**, 319–323; UDL framework and 313–314, 319–324

U.S. Department of Education 73, 102, 117

U.S. Department of Justice 144–145

U.S. Department of Labor 134, 136–138

Valente, J. M. 267

variability 170, 346–347

video: accessibility and 342; augmented reality (AR) 338–339, 342, 344; in higher education 329–331, 335–344; length of 342; live 335–336; multiple modes of 331–341, *341*; online courses and 330; produced 337–338, 341; real-time recorded 336–337; screen capture applications 336; student engagement and 342–344; teaching and learning